Dress

in Eighteenth-Century Europe
1715–1789

Aileen Ribeiro

Dress
in Eighteenth-Century
Europe 1715–1789

Yale University Press
New Haven & London

Designed by Gillian Malpass

Printed in Singapore

Library of Congress Cataloging-in-Publication Data

Ribeiro, Aileen, 1944–
    Dress in eighteenth-century Europe / Aileen Ribeiro.–2nd ed.
        p.   cm.
Includes bibliographical references and index.
    ISBN 0-300-09151-6 (hardback : alk paper)
    1. Costume–Europe–History–18th century.   2. Europe–Social life and
customs–18th century.   I. Title.
    GT720   .R53   2001
    391'.0094'09033 – dc21   2001006305

A catalogue record for this book is available from
The British Library

Page i and endpapers   D. Chodowiecki, *Two Dressing Rooms* (detail), n.d., pen and pencil,
whereabouts unknown

Frontispiece   L.-J. Le Lorrain, *Before the Masked Ball* (detail of pl. 180)

Page iv   A. R. Mengs, *Isabel Parreno, Marquesa de Llano* (detail of pl. 178)

Page vii   F.-H. Drouais, *The Marquise d'Aigurandes* (detail of pl. 93)

Preface to the Revised Edition

'La dernière chose qu'on trouve en faisant un ouvrage, est de savoir celle qu'il faut mettre la première'

Pascal, *Penseés*

PASCAL'S WORDS ARE PARTICULARLY TRUE when it comes to introducing a revised edition of a book that was originally published in 1984. How far should the author incorporate recent research to the extent that the book is virtually re-written? How far should the book under consideration, if worth re-issuing at all, be worthy to stand (with factual errors corrected), largely unaltered, on its own merits? In this case, I have chosen the latter option.

I have no illusions that this book is perfect. Like many youthful enterprises, it suffers from green judgements, and were I to write this book now, I might be more tentative about some of my generalizations and perhaps curtail the descriptive and anecdotal in favour of more stringent analysis.

In recent years there have been new approaches to the history of dress, some more welcome than others. Theoretical approaches, for example, are worth taking only if they enlighten the past and do not prove inimical to historical understanding. While acknowledging the contributions made over the last decade or so in particular by French and English historians in the field of consumption (their work features briefly in the revised footnotes and the bibliography), this is not a book about the economics of clothing, although some elements of consumption, of necessity, play a part in the narratives of elite fashion as well as of non-elite dress. In a similar way, although this is not a cultural history of dress, *per se*, it is about the different cultures in eighteenth-century Europe that contextualized costume as custom and fashion.

The book is, quite simply, a survey of dress in eighteenth-century Europe, and as such I believe it continues to be of value, for there is still no other work that deals with the period in such a wide-ranging way, geographically, chronologically and thematically.

Contents

facing page   Detail of pl. 9

Acknowledgements to the Revised Edition

ALL WHO HELPED WITH THE FIRST EDITION of this book have been thanked in the Acknowledgements to that work, and I should like to reiterate my gratitude for their assistance. The list of people who have helped with this new edition, therefore, is mercifully brief. With regard to the new illustrations included in this book, I should like to thank all institutions and individuals for permission to reproduce works of art in their collections.

I owe my customary debt of gratitude to the libraries of the Courtauld Institute for their help and efficiency. Thanks are due also to the Courtauld for financial help which enabled me to employ Cally Blackman as research assistant, and I am particularly grateful for her persistence in tracking down recalcitrant images.

At Yale University Press I should like to thank Sandy Chapman for her hard work in coping with the text and illustrations. And – yet again – my thanks to Gillian Malpass for being an exemplary designer/editor, and for being such fun to work with.

Acknowledgements to the First Edition

I SHOULD LIKE TO THANK THE MANY PEOPLE in art galleries and museums both in the United Kingdom and abroad who helped me during the research for this book, and who, along with many private owners, provided me with photographs, which they kindly allowed me to reproduce.

The Leverhulme Trust Fund was most generous in giving me a Research Grant for travel with which I was able to visit the following museums and art galleries: in the United States, the Metropolitan Museum of Art, the Costume Institute, the Museum of the City of New York and the Brooklyn Museum, all in New York; the Museum of Fine Arts, Boston; the Yale Center for British Art, New Haven; the Smithsonian Institution, the National Gallery of Art and the National Portrait Gallery, all in Washington, D.C.; the J. Paul Getty Museum and the Los Angeles County Museum of Art, both in Los Angeles. In Belgium: the Musées d'Art et de Costume, Brussels. In the Netherlands: the Rijksmuseum, Amsterdam; the Nederlands Kostuummuseum, the Hague. In Germany: the Bayerisches Nationalmuseum, Munich. In France: the Musée de la Mode and the Musée des Arts Décoratifs, both in Paris. In Sweden: the Nationalmuseum, the Livrustkammeren, the Nordiska Museet and the Drottningholms Teatermuseum, all in Stockholm. In Austria: the Modesammlungen des Historisches Museums at Schloss Hetzendorf and the Museum für Angewandte Kunst, both in Vienna.

Space precludes a list of individual members of staff from the institutions listed above; I hope they will take my thanks as read, not only for their professional help, but also for their hospitality. Other acknowledgements include the staff of the Witt Library at the Courtauld Institute for their customary help and efficiency, and Caroline Pilkington who typed the final draft of the book. Last, but certainly not least, I owe a debt of gratitude to Tim Auger at Batsford for his help and encouragement.

Introduction

C'est le siècle des lumières, de la maturité, et de la raison.

J. F. Sobry, 1786

THE EIGHTEENTH CENTURY IS A CENTURY OF CONTRASTS. To most of us, thinking idly about the period, the essence of eighteenth-century costume is the sophisticated urban dress – embroidered velvet coat and knee breeches, rustling silk taffeta dress over paniers, powdered hairstyles – that was France's great contribution to the world of fashion and civilized living, part of the 'douceur de vivre' recalled by Charles Maurice de Talleyrand, Prince of Benevento, as he was witnessing the break-up of a society that relied on layers of privilege and servitude to survive. In my study of this society, based as it was on obvious differences in wealth and status, I shall be concentrating on the fashions set and worn by the upper classes in most of Europe, internationally recognized symbols of caste. This kind of dress, and the more modest versions of it worn by the middle classes, involved only a small percentage of the population. The dress worn by the common people was in many cases a mixture of received fashions long since vanished from the wardrobe of the *haut monde*, allied to a basic, functional costume which had not changed much for the past hundred years. Indeed, in certain parts of Europe the peasants wore regional costume with striking local characteristics that went back to the late Middle Ages. Most people in Europe were locked into an agrarian system, earning their living from the land; although the Industrial Revolution began in England in the second half of the eighteenth century, its impact on society was not profound until after the French Revolution.[1]

To cast a brief look at Europe in the beginning of the eighteenth century is to see how far France had established itself as the leader of fashion. Blessed with a wealth of natural resources and a diversity of climate and produce, including well-established textile industries, France had, at the beginning of the century, a large population of between eighteen and nineteen million people. This was exceeded only by the population of the Holy Roman Empire, although Russia (with a population of about fourteen million at the beginning of the century) had caught up with the French by the time of the French Revolution with approximately twenty-five million people. In comparison, countries such as Spain and England, for example, had at the beginning of the century very small populations, around five million. By the end of the century England had about nine million, roughly twice as many as the United States of America where the first census taken in 1790 showed a still small population of about four million.

1 Detail of pl. 87

This detail from Boucher's *Marquise de Pompadour* highlights the frothy sleeve ruffles, perfect examples of curving rococo forms in dress. Good breeding – and pretty arms and hands – are shown by the elegant way the fan is held.

French pre-eminence in wealth and culture had been achieved under the firm rule of Louis XIV. Although the last years of his reign were clouded by war, the basic strength of the economy ensured a relatively quick recovery when, in 1715, titular power was transferred to his five-year-old great-grandson, Louis XV. French power was visible, also, in Spain: since 1700 Spain had been ruled by the grandson of Louis XIV, Philip V, who remained a Frenchman at heart. Much of his foreign policy revolved around attempts to have himself considered heir to the French throne (although this was forbidden by the Treaty of Utrecht of 1713), until the birth of the Dauphin (1729) put an end to such hopes. Although the King of Spain was himself uninterested in clothes (except to urge Spaniards to replace the traditional and old-fashioned seventeenth-century collar, the *golilla*, with the French-style cravat[2]), his court was quick to take advantage of the opening up of this hitherto remote country which had been cut off (as the Iberian peninsula always had been, owing to its geographical position) from events in the rest of Europe. A new court dress based on the French model was introduced, and French dominance of the arts generally was a feature of Spanish cultural life in the first half of the eighteenth century. Portugal, too, which in the eighteenth century was enjoying a kind of sleepy golden age outside the mainstream of European politics, was closely allied to Spain through royal marriages and followed the Spanish trend towards the adoption of French styles in dress.

Perhaps the most striking effect of French fashions in all the arts was on the German states. Nothing is more confusing than trying to define 'Germany' in the eighteenth century. As the recent biographer of Goethe has noted, '"Germany" in the eighteenth century was not even a geographical, at most it was a linguistic expression'.[3] An English visitor in 1778 talked of 'a large country of Europe divided into several states and principalities';[4] in fact, Germany consisted of more than three hundred sovereign states, some, like Brandenburg-Prussia, being large enough to have a viable government and economy, and others having as their only source of revenue the hiring out of mercenary troops – in return for subsidies – to England, France and Holland who were involved in the European territorial struggles of the period. Some small states were made even smaller by the practice of subdivision within different lines of the same family; when James Boswell visited Germany in 1764 he found, for example, two Brunswicks and two Anhalts, and five duchies of Saxony as well as the Electorate. The main aim of many of the German rulers was to keep a brilliant court on the French model: all social life was concentrated at court, to the exclusion of any other section of society, such as the professional or middle classes. In many cases, the minor German princelings and their aristocracy were obsessed by rank and precedence, although their style of living might not have warranted such pride. Voltaire, in *Candide*, was only repeating a well-worn theme when he poked fun at the sister of Baron Thunder-ten-tronck who refused to marry a worthy gentleman 'because he could claim only seventy-one quarterings, the rest of his family tree having suffered from the ravages of time' and because 'the Baron was one of the most influential noblemen in Westphalia, for his house had a door and several windows and his hall was actually draped with tapestry.'

It was in Germany also that relics of the past could be seen in the continuing of sumptuary legislation long after it had been phased out by the more forward-looking countries of western Europe. In addition, many of the old medieval trading towns kept to regional styles of dress, worn by the merchant oligarchies. Some of the larger German courts, such as those of the Wittelsbachs in Munich and the Elector of Saxony in Dresden, were renowned for their ceremony, elegance and lavish entertainments. The Elector of Saxony was also ruler of Poland for most of the first half of the eighteenth century – the country did not, however, see much of its rulers until the late eighteenth century when a native Polish king established a court based on that at Versailles – although Poland had by then become a semi-protectorate of Russia. Warsaw was a long way from Paris but there were traditional links between the two countries, cemented in 1725 by a marriage between the young Louis XV and the daughter of the dispossessed King of Poland, Stanislas Lesczynski.

Perhaps the most significant of the German states was Prussia, which under the rule of the Elector (later King) Frederick I adopted totally the French taste which, according to his grandson Frederick the Great, 'regulated our kitchens, our furniture, our dress and every other kind of trifle which is subject to the tyrannical sway of fashion . . . A young gentleman was taken for a fool if he had not been some time at the court of Versailles'.[5] Even though in 1713 this Francophile king was replaced by a military martinet, Frederick William I, whose aim was to make Prussia self-sufficient in terms of a strong army and who tried to enforce strict regulations regarding civil clothing, travellers noted that 'those of some rank go dress'd after the French Fashion'. Like most cultivated people in the middle of the eighteenth century, Frederick the Great's tastes were French; French was the lingua franca of Europe in this period, replacing Latin, except in learning and law, and it was the language of courts and diplomacy. The German language and culture, which had suffered as a result of the Thirty Years War (1618–48), was not to recover until the very end of the period under discussion in this study.

Much of the political history of Europe in the eighteenth century revolved around the rivalry between Prussia and Austria for ultimate supremacy within the German Empire. This title, in theory, belonged to Austria, for from the fifteenth century there had been a fairly well-established habit of choosing successive heads of the house of Habsburg, the reigning archdukes of Austria, as Holy Roman Emperor. This convention was effectively shattered in 1740 with Frederick the Great's cynical invasion of Austrian territory on the death of the Emperor Charles VI, and not until 1745 was the Empire back in Habsburg hands, where it was to remain until extinguished by the armies of Napoleon in 1806.

In the early part of the eighteenth century much of Habsburg foreign policy was motivated by hostility towards France, through the loss of the Spanish connection. The court at Vienna was noted for its elaborate Spanish ceremonial and hauteur, and the wearing of Spanish court dress was obligatory. With the marriage of Maria Theresa in 1736 to the Archduke Francis of Lorraine (later Emperor), French influence came to the Austrian court, for by this time no court with any pretensions to status or culture could afford to ignore the styles emanating from Paris.

This was equally true of countries with an important past, like Holland, now gently stagnating under the benign rule of a burgher oligarchy, and countries previously on the periphery of Europe, but with an important future, like Russia. From the beginning of the eighteenth century, Russia was pushed violently into the European limelight by Peter the Great, who forced his nobles to adopt the clothes of western Europe. He himself preferred plain cloth suits in the English style, but the Russian court with its love of flamboyance and an almost oriental splendour soon adopted French clothes, under a succession of empresses noted for lavish spending and discerning patronage of all the arts of France. In Sweden, the most powerful of the Scandinavian countries, there had long been an alliance with France, which manifested itself in a brilliant display of French culture around the throne, reaching a peak in the last quarter of the century with the last great Swedish king, Gustavus III. It is important to stress, however, that by the time we reach these outer fringes of Europe, the gulf between a tiny élite at court and the mass of the rural peasantry would be emphasized by striking differences in dress.

Like Germany, Italy was hardly even a geographical expression. In the Middle Ages and in the Renaissance it had been a fashion leader and had produced the best silks in Europe, but for the whole of the eighteenth century, with no great fashion impulse, Italy fell into a kind of retirement, with conflicting influences at work owing to the vagaries of foreign rule – Austrian in the north of the country, and Spanish in the Kingdom of Naples and Sicily. Strong regional influences were dominant in Italian dress and sumptuary legislation tried both to limit foreign styles and to regulate the clothing of the patrician classes in the old city states. Such legislation was only partly effective though, and by the second half of the eighteenth century, French fashions were widespread.

Compared with Italy, England gave the impression of being a compact unity that had been more or less untroubled by the accession of a new dynasty in 1714. By defeating the armies of Louis XIV, England had become a first-class power, a success attributed partly to the relative freedom of its laws and institutions. Contemporaries, such as a German visitor, Johann Wilhelm von Archenholz, in 1789, noted that England was 'so different from all other states of Europe in the forms of its government, in its laws, its customs, and in the sentiments and manners of its inhabitants'. The English rather self-consciously cultivated this difference, even viewing their clothes, in their relative simplicity of cut and fabric, as extensions of their hard-won liberties. Yet there was in the eighteenth century, as today, a curious ambivalence with regard to France; coupled with a dislike of French policies at

2   Detail of pl. 127

This detail from Tocqué's portrait of Queen Maria Lesczynska showcases the luxurious fabrics worn in official royal costume: flowered silk brocade for the dress and embroidered velvet, lined with ermine, for the mantle.

home and abroad went the feeling that only the French possessed the secrets of haute couture and high fashion, particularly with regard to women's dress.

That contemporaries were aware of the value of French fashions as cultural propaganda is evidenced by an Italian writer, Louis-Antoine de Caraccioli, whose *Voyage de la Raison en Europe* (1772) put forward the thesis that people in his lifetime had become more civilized and peaceful not just through the virtues of philosophers who ridiculed war, but through the unifying influence of French dress: 'que les modes même avoient contribué à cette heureuse metamorphose; qu'en prenant la frisure & l'habillement des François, on avoit insensiblement pris leur language, & que l'amenité qui leur est propre, sembloit donner le ton' (the fashions themselves had contributed to this happy metamorphosis; in adopting the hairstyles and costume of the French, people imperceptibly adopted the French 'language' of charm and good manners).[6] Not only was dress a unifying factor but it was also a civilizing one in an age in which Reason was the prevailing goddess. When Joseph Baretti, in Exeter in 1760, heard a sermon preached against dress, he wrote indignantly:

> Dressing is one of the many things that increase the difference between the reasonable animal and the unreasonable, and anything, be it ever so small that increases that difference, is never much amiss. Extremes to be sure are extremes; and the variety of dressing may be carried so far as to be ridiculous; yet sinful it can scarcely ever be; therefore if I were a preacher, I would never bear hard upon this point, because I have observed that people well dressed have in general a kind of respect for themselves, and whoever respects himself, does a very good thing.[7]

By 1760, French standards in taste and fashion were universally adopted; France was not only exporting the actual styles of fashion, but the way of life in which this fashion played such an important part. The concept of 'society' as defined by the French had, from the end of the seventeenth century, meant the growth in the civilized relationships between the sexes, characterized by wit, elegance and style, and was seen at its best in the salons in Paris, where groups of cultivated men and women discussed all that was new in matters of politics, society and the intellect. Unlike the court where rank alone counted, the salons admitted a wider range of people whose passport for entry could equally be a brilliant work in the realm of letters or their membership of one of the great noble families. The credo of the salon was expressed by an English visitor to Paris in 1712, where he found that 'Civility is more study'd in France than in the Kingdom of China'.[8] Such civility in the seventeenth century was practised at court almost exclusively, among 'Persons of Quality', but in the eighteenth century the concept spread to a wider section of society: first to Paris and then, later in the century, to provincial towns. Madame de Staël, writing after the French Revolution (although her words could apply equally to the whole of the eighteenth century) defined the difference between the essence of society in Germany and that in France: 'La Bonne Compagnie, en Allemagne, c'est la cour; en France, c'étaient tous ceux qui pouvaient se mettre sur un pied d'égalité avec elle . . .' (well-bred society, in Germany, is the court; in France it was all those who could place themselves on equal footing with the court).[9] The salon was a useful link between the court and the aristocracy; the French nobility, deprived in most cases of the substance of power in return for mere proximity to the sovereign and social advancement, turned to the cultivation of the arts of gracious living.

An integral part of the increased refinement of relationships between the sexes was the improvement in the status of women in France. Although they had no political importance (and no philosopher was prepared to make an improvement to their political status a central plank of his philosophy), they were expected to provide an intelligent and sophisticated visual adornment; as arbiters of taste and judgement they were expected to lay a greater emphasis on the role of dress and displaying the person to best advantage as essential ingredients of society. The impetus towards greater education for women crept forward slowly. More perceptibly, progress was made in marital relationships, and one can see a gradual change from the essentially cynical mercenary compacts of the first half of the century to a growing feeling that the ideal should be mutual affection and respect, however imperfect the reality. At the same time there was increasing recognition that the lot of children should be improved; Jean-Jacques Rousseau's *Emile* (1762) encouraged the public to believe that children's physical and social needs (including clothing based on practicalities rather than on a display of rank and wealth) should be considered independently. The English were, as shall be seen, pioneers in the liberation of children from many of the restrictions imposed on them by adults.

Rousseau based much of his work in this respect on that of the English philosopher John Locke; the writings of English philosophers of the later seventeenth century with regard to the liberty of the subject and individual freedom proved fruitful sources for the French philosophers of the eighteenth century. No truly original or revolutionary modes of thought characterize the eighteenth century until the French Revolution: for most of the period there was a re-statement of ideas that had first been promulgated in the seventeenth century, a time of religious unrest and civil upheaval which had undermined men's faith in the fundamentals of their society, causing them to question prevailing values and to establish a new critical climate which taught people to rely on their own judgement. Alexander Pope's maxim that 'the proper study of mankind is Man', in itself a reworking of the Renaissance ideal, can be seen both in the feeling of enlightenment (that all problems could be solved by reason) and in the growing demands for greater justice in the treatment given to the less privileged sections of society. This can be seen particularly in the second half of the eighteenth century with the growth of 'sentiment' and humanitarianism so characteristic of the English philanthropists and philosophers who took over the intellectual leadership

Walpole's child

from France. Good taste in dress by the time of the French Revolution virtually meant middle-class taste, as simpler styles in plainer stuffs had become the accepted everyday costume.

New discoveries in science, applied to the textile industries, meant that by the end of the century there was greater life expectancy and better hygiene among the lower classes and a wider availability of comfortable, washable clothing. These industrial inventions occurred during the second half of the eighteenth century in England, due not so much to the natural advantages of the country, but more to a new entrepreneurial spirit unhindered by the medieval restrictions that beset most other European countries. Accelerating industrial improvements had been noted from the early eighteenth century (and machines and factory systems from before then); Daniel Defoe in his *Tour thro' the whole Island of Great Britain* (1724–6) was proud of 'new discoveries in metals, mines, and minerals, new undertakings in trade, engines and manufactures, in a nation pushing and improving as we are'.[10] Capitalism and free trade made the Industrial Revolution possible in England; its extension and impact on the rest of Europe, in the early nineteenth century, is beyond the scope of this study.

As in the rest of Europe, there was for a variety of reasons a remarkable increase in the population in the second half of the eighteenth century in England. It was perhaps more noted in England, where a combination of decline in many rural industries and the social effects of the enclosures of land led to a vast increase in the population of the cities. London was the largest city in Europe with a population of a million, and by the time of the French Revolution one-fifth of the population in England lived in the towns, compared with one-tenth of the French population, the nearest rivals to the English with regard to urbanization. Tensions were the inevitable outcome as society tried to cope with such an influx; violence, never far from the surface, erupted on many occasions and threatened to destroy the fabric of a society based on an implicit acceptance of the rights and privileges of the upper classes. Contemporary writings are witness to the part played by dress in enforcing the status quo, with constant complaints about the usurpation of the kinds of dress thought to be the prerogative of one particular class. This was particularly so in relatively open and fluid societies like England (and, to a lesser extent, France), where sumptuary legislation was no longer an aid to the distinguishing of class by means of dress. So, for example, a London newspaper reported in 1744 that 'every illiterate coxcomb who had made a fortune by sharping or shop-keeping will endeavour to mimic the great ones'. Such imitation would, according to an English visitor to Paris early in the century, contribute to 'the End of excessive Luxury, there being nothing that can make Noble Personages so much despise Gold Trimming, than to see it upon the Bodies of the lowest Men in the World'.[11] In fact, even with the finest dress in the world, the lower classes would look awkward, for they would not have the correct manner of wearing their clothes; the correct dress, elegantly worn with a kind of nebulous grace and

3   Detail of pl. 167

The relative simplicity of this dress – a delicate Spitalfields silk, worn with a white apron – is characteristic of girls' costume in the mid-eighteenth century.

9

4   Detail of pl. 10

An example of Lord Chesterfield's claim that young Englishmen were prone to imitating the clothing of their inferiors ('brown frocks') and to carrying 'great oaken cudgels in their hands'.

even a carelessness of deportment was part of the seemingly effortless aristocratic superiority, as taught by the French and admired from St Petersburg to Madrid.

Equally remarked on as a trait of English society from the middle of the century was the habit of some of the younger members of the nobility to adopt the clothes of the working classes. Lord Chesterfield, arbiter of English elegance, wrote to his son in 1748 that 'some of our young fellows affect the tremendous, and wear a great and fiercely cocked hat, an enormous sword, a short waistcoat, and a black cravat; others go in brown frocks, leather breeches, great oaken cudgels in their hands, their hats uncocked and their hair unpowdered, and imitate grooms, stage-coachmen and country bumpkins' (pl. 4).[12] This was a forerunner of the mood for ostensibly 'democratic' clothing, which spread from England in the 1780s on a wave of Anglomania. In the years before the outbreak of civil violence by the Parisian mob, fashionable men had adopted dark, workman-like colours and cloths, boots, unpowdered hair instead of a wig, and even pantaloons, the trousers which had been worn by working men and sailors throughout the eighteenth century. J. A. de Ségur, writing during the upheavals in France after the Revolution, remarked that during the 1780s the aristocracy had begun to dress like their valets, appearing in company in informal sporting clothing – 'en cessant de respecter le public, on oublia toutes nuances en société' (thus, in ceasing to respect the public, all the distinguishing nuances of society were forgotten).[13] Louis-Sébastien Mercier, an avowed Republican himself, lamented the demise of French elegance; even politeness was out of fashion. For women the 1780s were also a decade of novelty. Simple linen or cotton dresses anticipated the neo-classical mood of post-Revolutionary France. In effect, of course, what started life as variations on working clothes were soon changed out of all semblance to the original in quality of cut, fabric and disposition of ornament. Yet even an intelligent man like Charles James Fox believed that 'the neglect of dress in people of fashion had contributed much to remove the barriers between them and the vulgar, and to propagate levelling and equalizing notions'.[14]

Dress has always been one of the most sensitive barometers of the sensibilities and attitudes of a period; not only does it reflect the dominant mood of society, but in some cases it can appear even to anticipate abrupt and revolutionary changes. The French Revolution did not cause the immediate introduction of wholly new garments, but it did accelerate the pace of change already in the pipeline. It is for this reason that this book ends with the French Revolution, which, to people who had lived before and during the momentous events associated with it, seemed like the end of the known world. It appeared to deal a mortal blow to a society based on privilege and the unbridgeable gulfs between classes. In retrospect, however, the upper classes were never in serious danger of losing their place as the dominant force in society; nevertheless, the early events of the Revolution, with its unleashing of long-suppressed violence, gave them a shock which they never quite forgot.

★ ★ ★

This study begins in 1715, a year marking the beginning of a new period in France after the seemingly interminable reign of Louis XIV. There was a new feeling of freedom after the dead hand of tradition was lifted from a society dominated by a rigidly formal court. In 1715 also, one year after the beginning of a new dynasty in England too, came the first test (with the Jacobite rebellion) of the stability of this new regime, a test which was successfully passed.

France and England, old enemies and rivals both in the European and colonial spheres, dominate the history of dress in the eighteenth century, the former through the splendour of formal costume, and the latter, particularly in the second half of the century, through informal, outdoor and sporting costume. For the first half of the century, fashion changes were more noticeable with regard to women's dress. The stately gowns with sweeping trains and bustles, decorated with baroque ornament, which dominated the court at Versailles, gave way at the beginning of the new reign to more informal, negligée gowns worn over the newly fashionable, cone-shaped hoops, which seemed to float as the wearer moved and which can be seen most clearly in the paintings of Watteau and de Troy. A new lightness was also to be seen in textiles; alongside the heavy floral brocades of formal dress went plain light silks and painted silks from the Far East. Throughout the whole of the eighteenth century, the most fashionable silks came from France and from Lyons in particular – the French silk industry was supported by the state and boosted the development of the fashion industry in France. For the heavier silks such as velvet, Italy produced the best examples, which in the first half of the eighteenth century went to make the finest-quality men's suits; by the later period, however, with the trend towards lighter silks, and fine cloth, velvets were more and more limited to use as furnishing fabrics.

By the time that Louis XV achieved his majority, the supremacy of French style in the fashion world was undoubted, and although he was too lazy to regulate on dress like his predecessor, the king liked fashionable women around him. Of all his mistresses, Madame de Pompadour was the most influential in the dissemination of French taste and fashions; she was almost the personification of the playful, three-dimensional elegance of the rococo style in dress, arguably the most seductive clothing ever invented for women. In the second half of the eighteenth century, such frivolity in dress gave way to simpler styles, with an increasing use of linen and cotton, and a growing emphasis on more functional clothing for a more active life.

For most of the eighteenth century there were no profound changes in men's dress, for the basic format of three-piece suit and coat had been well established by the end of the previous century. The changes to be chronicled were, essentially, the progress from the heavy, baroque fullness of material and cut to a slimmer silhouette, with a corresponding movement from heavy, decorated silks to lightweight silk or cloth with delicate ornamentation. Although formal embroidered clothes continued to be worn at court throughout the eighteenth century, by the last quarter of the period the new fashion impulse was towards English sporting clothing; the last pre-Revolutionary decade was dominated by informal and middle class dress. For both men and women, the second half of the eighteenth century was characterized by a growing dichotomy between formal and informal clothing.

The impetus towards change was accelerated by the newly established fashion magazines, which began to appear regularly from the early 1770s, first in England and France and then in Germany. Such magazines emphasize the way in which ceremonial and court dress had frozen into a kind of uniform; for court dress in particular, there is a valedictory feel to the almost icon-like splendour that could never occur again in the vastly different world of post-Revolutionary Europe. It might also be noted here (although the scope of the book precludes its discussion) that it was during the eighteenth century that military and naval uniforms were systematized. They had of course existed before, but in a rather haphazard way linked very often to the personal whim of a commanding officer and it was only owing to the eighteenth-century love of reason and order (and the fact that warfare was endemic throughout the period) that such uniforms were for the first time established.

In the eighteenth century dress was not truly innovatory, but was essentially a refinement of already existing styles. The part played by dress in the regulation and civilizing of behaviour was an crucial part of Louis XIV's grand plan in the seventeenth century, to cope with what was in many ways a nasty, brutish and insolent aristocracy. 'Persons of Quality must now become Persons of Taste' was the guiding rule, and for many nobles a brilliance of style in dress became almost their *raison d'être*. The etiquette of dress that visibly demonstrated one's place in society was a tyranny gladly accepted by the ruling classes, for uniformity of taste could encompass also an individualism of approach. The contribution made by the eighteenth century was to add a freedom of expression and imagination to the aesthetic unity that had already been conceived by 1700, by which time the rules of art, conduct and intellect had been codified. The unity of the arts, politics and sciences can best be seen in the work most typical of the eighteenth century, the *Encyclopédie* of Diderot and d'Alembert. Particularly from the middle of the century, a variety of tastes were allowed to be fashionable in all the arts; these included the exotic, the historical, the picturesque and a taste for classical antiquity, all of which manifested themselves in portraiture, fashionable clothing and the fancy-dress entertainments that were such an important aspect of social life.

The evidence for our knowledge of dress in the eighteenth century is vast, and the pitfalls of approaching a period about which everyone has firm ideas are legion. I have chosen to concentrate not so much on the details of construction (enough clothing survives to make this a study best attempted in detail in a narrower context than the scope of this book), but on the range and variety of dress in Europe as a whole, and by looking through the eyes of contemporaries at what they considered to be the part played by dress in society. Nor have I attempted in any detail to cover the consumption of clothing over such a large area as the whole of Europe; as has recently been noted, '. . . early modern consumption is a relatively new topic of enquiry and mapping its history remains largely preliminary'.[15] In a period in which there are no major changes in costume, contemporary works of art assume a greater importance – they are the words translated into style and movement – for they tell us how people moved and had their being, and how they saw themselves as they really were, or as they wished to be.

The eighteenth century is a feeling as well as a period of time; it is the last time in which taste and individuality in all the arts, including dress, reached a peak never since equalled.

1   *The Dominance of France: 1715–1740*

> They invent every Day new Modes of Dressing, and weary of living
> in their own Country, you may see 'em sometimes gadding into . . . a
> World of different Countries . . .
>
> *The Present State of the Court of France, and City of Paris*, 1712

IN 1715 THERE OCCURRED A DRAMATIC CHANGE in the fortunes of the new ruler of France, Philippe, duc d'Orléans, who came to power on the death of Louis XIV as Regent to the new king, Louis XV, a child of five. In the last few years of the old king's rule there had been a sense of gloom in public life, resulting from the demands made by the War of the Spanish Succession and the personal disasters suffered by Louis XIV in the loss of his heirs. Although inheriting a national debt of 2000 million livres (much of it caused by the wars), the Regent also inherited the professional government system created by Louis XIV which, with slight changes, lasted until the French Revolution. Like his young monarch, the Regent was a man, in Saint-Simon's phrase, 'born bored', a boredom which doubtless led him to the self-indulgences that killed him at an early age, but also led to a highly cultivated court keen to patronize the best of the new in design and art. Women, including his many mistresses, began that female dominance of the court which was to continue under Louis XV and which contributed to the sophisticated development of the arts of fashion. One of the first moves of the new regime was to leave the gloomy old court at Versailles and to establish the new centre of power in Paris, home of society, where the salons were beginning to disseminate new artistic ideas. The Regency style, the forerunner of the rococo, was characterized by a sense of lightness and a playful exoticism seen in art, interior design and textiles, all of which reacted against the measured classicism and conformity of the previous reign. Light colours and floating silks, with a growing vogue for the informality of the négligé, were typical of women's dress in the early eighteenth century; indolence and sensuality were the keynotes of the new dispensation.

Yet fashion changes do not occur overnight and alongside these new fashion influences went a continuity of the old order with regard to formal dress – particularly for men's dress, where a kind of baroque heaviness in style and fabric lasted well into the eighteenth century.

★ ★ ★

5   Detail of pl. 25

The young gentleman paying court to a lady is the epitome of elegance and gentility in both deportment and clothing – the new bag wig with ribbon *en solitaire*, a stylish suit and red-heeled shoes, which imply that he has been presented at court.

6 and 7 Two fashionable men, *c*.1715

The relatively crude technique of these images on tiles, relying on a simplification of outline, nevertheless conveys the exaggeratedly heavy and stylized male dress of the early eighteenth century. The wig is huge, built high on top, the coat is waisted with reinforced side pleats, and the high-heeled shoes with their turn-over tops are cut square across the toes.

Men

Let us first look in detail at a fashionable man's wardrobe in 1715, bearing in mind that the main garments remained essentially the same throughout the eighteenth century. The suit was the basic unit of the male wardrobe throughout the eighteenth century, composed of coat, waistcoat and breeches, usually, but not always, of the same fabric. The idea of the suit had originated in the 1660s, possibly influenced by oriental or theatrical modes but more probably deriving from the idea of the sleeved coat of the earlier seventeenth century worn with sleeveless jerkin and knee-breeches.

The tailoring of the coat in its early stages was still fairly crude: two fronts and two backs were sewn together with straight side seams stitched to just

The passion for stylized contortion in dress can be seen in the knotted wig and the cravat twisted into the buttonhole *à la* Steinkirk.

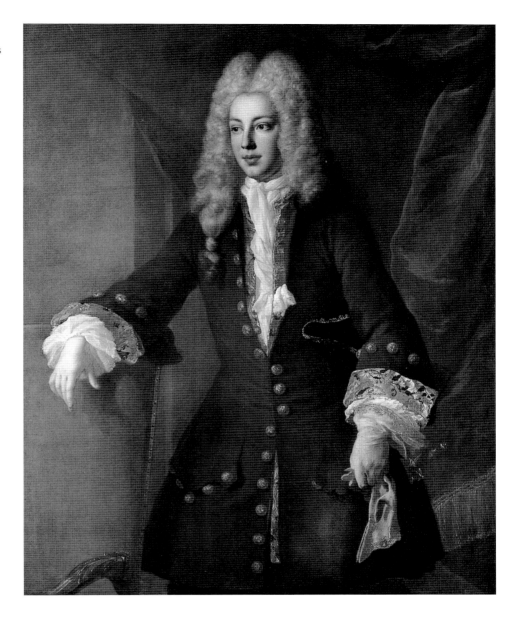

below the waist to leave room for the sword which hung from a sword-belt under the coat, the hilt coming through the side vent and the end point through a centre-back vent. It had no collar and was decorated with braid or metal lace or frogged clasps, and similar trimming outlined the horizontally flapped pockets set half way between the waist and the hem. By the beginning of our period the coat was tailored more tightly to the body; the French name *justaucorps* can be literally translated as 'close to the body', and this tightness was emphasized by heavily stiffened side pleats, five or six in number, which swung as the wearer walked. By the end of the 1720s these side pleats, stiffened with gummed linen (buckram) and interlined with wool or horse-hair, were obviously comparable to the huge hoops being worn by women; the *Mercure de France* for March 1729 noted of the total effect: 'le tout pour donner de la grâce, dit on, & faire le panier' (the whole effect, like the hoop petticoat, is graceful and elegant).[1]

In line with the more complex tailoring, the front edges of the coat swung slightly off the straight, the tendency to curve in this way increasing as the century progressed. Coats were, on the whole, buttoned just at the waist so as to show the waistcoat and the fine lace cravat or stock. Buttons and buttonholes were prominent pieces of jewellery and were often embroidered to match the embroidery on the coat.

Large, stiffened and decorated cuffs formed the focal point for the wide sleeves; the flaring, turned-back cuff which was open behind was part of more formal suits and lasted until the middle of the eighteenth century. In the second quarter of the century the most characteristic cuff was a closed cuff, keeping to the width of the sleeve, but coming almost up to the elbow; in England this type of cuffed sleeve was known as a 'boot-sleeve', and, according to the novelist Henry Fielding, was particularly useful as a receptacle for stolen goods.

The waistcoat was cut on the same lines as the coat, but without the side pleats, and with less width in the skirts. In the early years of our period many waistcoats had long sleeves, the upper sleeves often matching the back of the garment, which, as it did not show, was composed of coarse linen or cotton mixture fabric, but with a cuff matching in splendour the brocade or embroidery of the waistcoat front. In 1715 the waistcoat would be about the same length as the coat, that is knee-length, and with similar horizontal pockets; as the century progressed the waistcoat became shorter, and curved round at the front.

As for the final component of the suit, the breeches or *culotte*, these were in 1715 immensely full and baggy in the seat, sometimes being cut on the bias to stretch and give ease of movement. In an age in which, as the Vicar of Bray put it, 'moderate men looked big', to have 'bottom' had a meaning added to the usual one of solid dependency. These breeches were gathered into a waistband which could be adjusted by laces at the back or the sides; buttons closed the centre front and there were pockets, including a fob pocket in the waistband. Sometimes the breeches ended above the knee, when the stockings (usually of knitted, coloured silk, worsted or cotton) were rolled over the knee-band. This fashion lasted into the early 1730s, when it was replaced by slightly tighter breeches fastening firmly below the knee, but the earlier style lingered on into the 1750s in the dress of the elderly and conservative. Unlike the coat and waistcoat, the breeches were not decorated except for little buttons fastening the small open side seam above the knee-band. The coat and waistcoat were so long in the early eighteenth century that the breeches did not show much beneath them and therefore, in an age in which visible show was important, they could be comfortable rather than elegant. For men it was a period of considerable ease and comfort, a time of well-fed gentlemen with slightly bulging eyes and florid complexions so familiar through the portraits of Kneller and his contemporaries; by the

9   J. Ranc, *Charles, Prince of the Asturias, later King of Naples and Sicily, and then Charles III of Spain*, 1724

Grandeur and luxury are evident in this formal portrait of a young Spanish prince, from the heavily gold-embroidered court coat of blue velvet with stiffened cuffs of pink silk, the knightly orders of chivalry (including the Order of the Golden Fleece on a red ribbon) and red-heeled black shoes with diamond buckles, to the hat with gold lace and pink ostrich feather trimming that lies on a chair behind him.

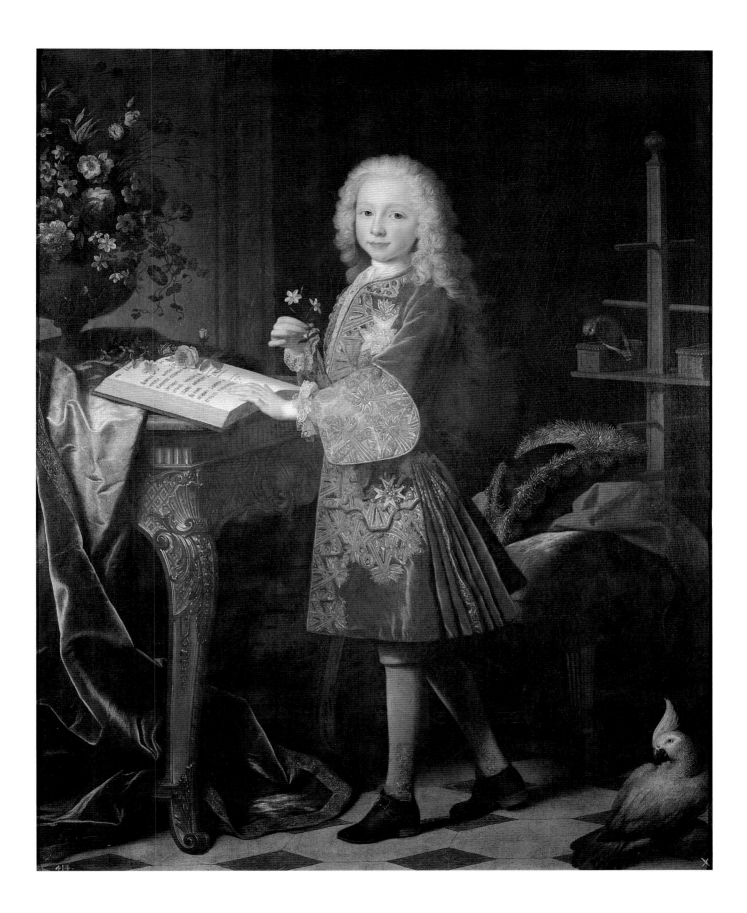

middle of the century a new, slimmer silhouette made embonpoint increasingly unfashionable.

Throughout the eighteenth century, the coat was the focal point of attention, through the luxury and disposition of fabric and trimming. Decoration on the coat, in the form of braid, embroidery or lace, was applied down the centre fronts, the centre backs from the waist downwards, on and around the pockets and on the cuffs. From about 1730, this decoration, usually heavy and three-dimensionally ornate, was woven in position on the coat lengths.

For formal and grand occasions embroidery would be heaped upon suits of brocade. To the modern eye the colours would seem very bright, but they were meant to be worn in the evenings when the candlelight caught the diamond buttons and reflected the glitter of gold and silver tissues, gold and silver lace and embroidery. In many cases, the embroidery constituted the greatest expense; in 1740, for example, Frederick the Great, in the first year of his reign, before his legendary military prowess enabled him to wear a suit spartan in its simplicity, received from the court tailor a bill for a suit of which the fabric cost ten thalers, but the silver embroidery of which cost eighty-five thalers. The embroiderer Jean Pally sent, at the same time, a bill for silver embroidery costing 1000 thalers.[2]

In the early years of our period, large floral silk brocades were worn for coat and breeches, but by the end of the second decade of the century such large floral patterns were increasingly limited to the waistcoat. In the 1720s, woven silks with small stylized floral designs were specially woven for men's suits, and the designs of these did not change much in the first half of the eighteenth century. By the end of the 1720s, it is possible to note the first faint shift in taste from elaborate woven patterns towards plain stuffs, often with subtle and understated colour combinations. At court in 1729, Mrs Delany saw the Prince of Wales 'in mouse-colour velvet turned up with scarlet and very richly trimmed with silver'.[3] In the same year the *Mercure de France* told its readers that the winter colours were shades of tobacco, 'marron foncé', 'feuille morte', agate and grey.[4] By 1739, at the English court Mrs Delany found the men 'chiefly brown with gold or silver embroidery and rich waistcoats'.[5] Woven silk suits were usually lined with the lighter silks such as taffeta; for velvets, satin was used, and sometimes plush or fur in very cold climates.

For winter wear, the heaviness and richness of velvet was admired, the finest examples coming from Genoa. In 1736, the Hofrat (Court Councillor) Freiherr von Seckendorff listed in the *Frankfurter Intelligenzblatt* that the clothes stolen from him in transit from Bonn to Berlin included a black velvet suit, the coat lined with red velvet and the waistcoat lined with white taffeta, and also a coat and breeches of brown cut velvet, the coat lined with blue velvet and the waistcoat made of blue satin decorated with silver.[6] From this, it can be seen that a fashionable wardrobe could comprise a three-piece suit made of the same fabric or a suit consisting of coat and breeches of the same material with a waistcoat of contrasting fabric. This latter taste was to increase as the century wore on, with growing emphasis on the richness of the waistcoat, more of which was revealed by the cutting away of the side of the coat.

Court waistcoats were sometimes decorated with fringes of silk, silver and gold thread and chenille in the first third of the eighteenth century; thereafter decoration on the waistcoat included sequins and metal foils in various colours as well as the ornate serpentine embroidery. In the first years of the century, waistcoats were sometimes made from 'bizarre' silks, silks of French design, with curious and fantastic patterns derived from the Orient, which were fashionable until about 1720.[7] Such designs, beginning at the very end of the seventeenth century, were indicative of the restless and experimental phase in art and design at that period, reacting against the rigidity imposed by the late Baroque style, and were sent whirling into action in the Regency due to a variety of fresh design impulses. The exotic and imaginative effect of such silks also seemed to qualify them for dressing-gowns, which were thought of as an oriental garment, and indeed were sometimes called Indian gowns.

Such silks, with their elaborate and lengthy repeats, were very expensive; a roomful of fashionable gentlemen dressed in such exotic finery and laden with embroidery would serve to impress a visitor from out of town. Against the splendour of the French court, foreign visitors could either choose to vie with their hosts in luxury or be the more noticed, often for political reasons, for the plainness of their attire. One such visitor, the Russian Emperor Peter the Great, impressed the duc de Saint-Simon in 1716 with 'a simple linen collar, a brown and unpowdered wig falling short of his shoulders, a coat of plain material with gold buttons . . . neither gloves nor shirt ruffles. The star of his order was worn outside the coat, and the ribbon beneath. His coat was usually unbuttoned all the way down; his hat was always on a table, never on his head, not even out of doors'.[8] Saint-Simon, an indefatigable recorder of trifles and imagined slights, was quick to pick up the quintessentially Russian combination of richness and slovenliness which characterized their dress; he was amazed at the gold buttons on a plain cloth suit and by the fact that for ease the Emperor did not, as the fashionable did, fasten his coat at the waist. He was impressed by the Russian ruler; less so by the unprepossessing, manic-depressive King of Spain, Philip V, whom he found on a visit to Madrid in 1721 in a poor-quality suit of brown serge.[9]

The plainness of male attire was from the beginning of the eighteenth century a recognized feature of English dress, from the king downwards. Horace Walpole remembered as a small child being taken to kiss the hand of George I who wore 'a dark rye wig, a plain coat, waistcoat and breeches of snuff-coloured cloth with stockings of the same colour, and a blue ribband over all'.[10] A foreign visitor to England commented in 1722 that: 'The dress of the English is like the French but not so gaudy; they generally go plain but in the best cloths and stuffs . . . not but that they wear embroidery and laces on their cloathes on solemn days, but they dont make it their daily wear, as the French do.'[11] The main differences between the French and

English man with regard to dress were thus stated early in our period, and these were to be the two most important influences on masculine clothing.

One of the earliest English influences to be felt was in the adoption of the frock coat, first appearing in the fashionable English wardrobe in the mid-1720s and on the Continent in the middle of the century. Like so many elements of masculine wear, the frock started life as a working-class garment. A loose coat with turned-down collar, sometimes made of fustian or coarse linen, it was a forerunner of the overall designed to protect the clothes beneath. As adopted by gentlemen, it was first worn for hunting and shooting and other rural pursuits; it was cut on similar lines to the formal coat, but with no stiffened side pleats, and was made of woollen cloth. It had a small turned-down collar called a cape and the sleeves either had small closed cuffs or, for even greater ease of movement, decorative slits. Decoration, in fact, was minimal, often consisting of braid on the pockets and cuffs and down the centre fronts, sometimes with frogging or looped buttons. Originating from a garment worn to provide protection from the weather, some of the hunting frocks had fairly elaborate double-breasted fastenings, which fell back to form lapels. As such, the frock or jacket had been worn since the beginning of the century by European gentlemen for sport and the curiosity was to find this humble garment rising in the world. César de Saussure in the mid-1720s was amazed to see Englishmen in 'little coats called "frocks" without facings and without pleats, with a short cape above'.[12] As late as 1733 a German visitor, Charles Lewis Pöllnitz, was ready to link the lazy habits of the Englishman with his informal clothing: 'He rises late, puts on a Frock (which is a close-body'd Coat without Pockets or Plaits, and with strait Sleeves), and leaving his Sword at Home, takes his Cane and goes where he pleases.'[13]

For out-of-doors, the fashionable man had a choice of garments. The overgarment with the oldest tradition was the cloak. Since the earliest recorded times, man wrapped a piece of material (either square or rectangular) round himself; by Roman times this had turned into a cloak made in the shape of a circle or segment of a circle and worn for protection against the weather. This garment, wholly necessary for horse-rider or pedestrian, was worn throughout the eighteenth century by all classes in varying lengths: for the walker, a capacious cloak reached to calf-length, and for the horseman a shorter and more up-to-date version was worn. In the first half of the eighteenth century, in line with the gradual tailoring of clothing, a more fitted cloak called a *roquelaure* was worn; this was a cape cut in three pieces, the side seams shaped to the shoulders.

Yet as the century progressed and public transport improved, so also did the civilized amenities of the city. As the streets became places where it was easier to walk, so did walking become a fashionable pursuit, and the 'surtout' or overcoat, originally a sturdy working garment, became a fashionable item at first in the Englishman's wardrobe, and then adopted by the rest of Europe. This took the form of a loose-fitting coat with a back vent necessary for riding and a large collar which could be turned up in bad weather.

10 Anon., *The Country Squire*, 1740

This pen and ink sketch (from an album of drawings once the property of Horace Walpole) pokes gentle fun at the vogue for men to ape the clothing of their social inferiors. The 'dressed-down' country squire adopts the frock coat from a footman, the frizzed wig with a pig-tail from a soldier and a working-man's cudgel instead of a sword.

According to the poet and playwright Joseph Gay (who had begun his life in London as an apprentice to a silk mercer) in *Trivia; or The Art of Walking the Streets of London*, published in 1716, the surtout was also called a great-coat, joseph or wrap-rascal, the last name indicating that one version was a wrapped gown similar to the dressing-gown. Although the *Mercure de France* of 1729–30 advised velvet surtouts, Gay advocated the wearing of kersey as the hardiest fabric for the English weather, and noted how essential a garment it was for his native climate: 'That Garment best the Winter's Rage defends, Whose shapeless Form in ample Plaits depends.'[14] The shape of the surtout did not change much until the last quarter of the century, when, taken up by the man of fashion, it became a tight-fitting, streamlined overcoat.

It has already been noted that although men's clothes were roomy in fit, they were uncomfortable in weight, both from linings (especially in the side pleats of the coat) and from the heaviness and rigidity of the surface deco-ration. Respite was needed from such cares and it was found in the loose gowns that had been worn since the end of the seventeenth century as a popular form of informal déshabillé. The nightgown was a long loose garment rather like a modern dressing-gown, with a wrap-over front, either held in place by the hand (a consciousness of clothes in the eighteenth century, their weight, texture and disposition is demonstrated in the way sitters are so often portrayed holding out their garments, or grasping them close to the body) or tying with a sash. Sometimes this was called a 'morning-gown', according to Dr Johnson's *Dictionary*, for it could be worn informally in the morning before one was fully dressed for the day. The cut was similar to that of the kimono, which was essentially two widths of material joined up the centre-back and the custom for wearing such gowns, often of expen-sive oriental fabrics, came from the Netherlands at the beginning of the seventeenth century and spread via the East India companies to the rest of Europe. Some came from Japan and many came from India; in fact in England they were known as 'Indian gowns', although by the early eigh-teenth century they were not necessarily made in India or of Indian mate-rial. A popular fabric, in fact, was chintz, originally of Indian origin but imitated by the resourceful European printers. Such printed cottons were so popular in England in the early years of the eighteenth century that accord-ing to Defoe (1724) they were adversely affecting the trade of stuffs in Norwich, for long a home of the light wool and wool-mixture cloths which draped well for gowns.[15] A series of acts in England (1712, 1714 and 1721) prohibited the import and sale of all printed cottons including Indian goods, but the ingenious calico printers evaded the acts by printing on linen or mixed fabrics of linen warp and cotton weft, which was still allowed. Other materials used for these loose-fitting nightgowns were quilted cotton, wool, Scottish plaid and various weights of silk, some being lined for winter use or for protection from the frequent draughts which affected even the best houses. In the inventory of effects left by Frederick the Great (1786) was 'a blue wrapper, like a woman's, of satin, trimmed with rabbitskin, which the King wore when he had the gout'.[16] Even warmer was the blue, woollen

11   J. Smibert, *Colonel George Douglas, later twelfth Earl of Morton*, 1727

Painted when the sitter was sixty-five years old, his costume is both comfortable and stylish, comprising a green damask dressing gown and matching cap.

12   W. Hogarth, *Captain Thomas Coram*, 1740

The honest, unpretentious nature of the founder of the Foundling Hospital is reflected in his sober suit and functional, capacious greatcoat.

13 W. Hogarth, *A Rake's Progress: Surrounded by Artists and Professors* (detail), *c.*1733

Standing next to the dancing master with his exaggeratedly fashionable costume and mincing pose, the Rake wears an elegant frogged *banyan*.

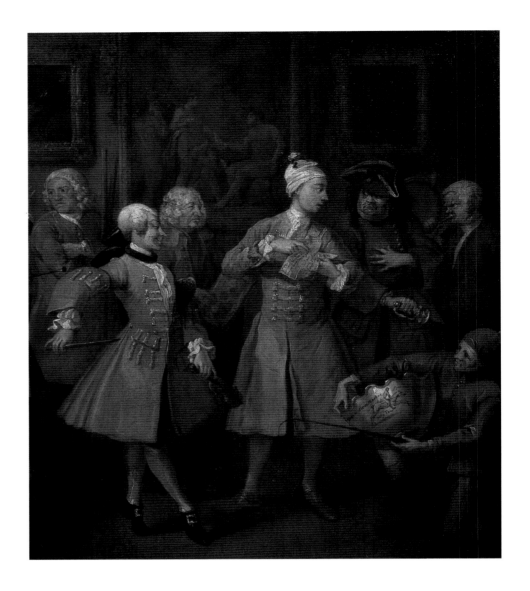

damask gown worn by Jonathan Trumbull, governor of Connecticut, which is preserved in Hartford; a similar gown appears in the portrait of the governor painted by his son and dated 1778.[17] The basic shape of these gowns changed little during the eighteenth century and most were full-length, but a French nightgown, the *Apollon*, of mid-thigh length, was briefly popular in the mid-eighteenth century.

A more formal nightgown was the *banyan*, a tight-fitting and double-breasted gown very often with elaborate cord or frogging fastenings; the length varied, but the most popular was a mid-calf length. The curious name derived from the name for a Hindu trader in the province of Gujerat, which came to be applied to the dress he was (erroneously) thought to wear. Some were, in fact, made to order from the finest silks from India; others, made in Europe, were of local woollen cloths and silks. Very often, for extra warmth and formality when the banyan was left unfastened, matching waistcoat fronts were built into the gown; in 1772, the Duchess of Northumberland, on a pilgrimage to Voltaire at Ferney, saw the famous author in 'a long Banyan & Waistcoat of Brown Sattin with colour'd Flowers'.[18]

An impressive display of wealth and taste could be created by the nightgown. Among Freiherr von Seckendorff's lost clothes in 1736 (as recorded in the *Frankfurter Intelligenzblatt*) was a nightgown of red velvet lined with white fur. Fine examples of damask and brocade which had been used for nightgowns were sometimes made into religious vestments – this was the case with the rich gown worn by the Emperor Franz Stephan of Austria on his deathbed (1765) which was later made into a chasuble and given by his widow to the chapel of the castle in Innsbruck where he died.

Nightgowns figured largely in the male wardrobe. Peter the Great with his love of informality in clothing possessed a considerable number, of which thirteen survive in the Hermitage Museum in St Petersburg; all are made in the kimono style, the summer ones of silk and the winter ones of padded silk or cotton. Regular references occur to the purchase of nightgowns in the accounts of a Scottish gentleman, George Baillie of Mellerstain. Many were bought in London where he spent part of the year as an M.P. and in Naples, as part of his Grand Tour of Europe in the early 1730s, he bought two nightgowns, one of velvet and one of armosin, both trimmed with gold loops and buttons.[19] Such grand gowns would have been worn to receive visitors in the morning. Those that survive sometimes have matching caps or turbans to wear over shaven heads, many believing with Boswell that some kind of head-covering was necessary to keep out the damp and draughts and to preserve the teeth.

The nightgown was a garment useful in a variety of climates. In the cool and unfashionable air of Amsterdam, a German visitor noted in the 1720s that the usual costume of the men was 'a Nightgown lined with Flannel, under which they are swaddled in three or four thick waistcoats', while the students in Leyden also preferred this informality of dress, making them look, he thought, like so many hospital patients.[20] In the 1730s, the French historian Charles de Brosses, travelling in Venice, discovered that the Venetian patricians wore morning gowns and slippers, a costume that he himself adopted. Thirty years later, Baretti visited Spain and found Spanish gentlemen constantly wearing 'cap, night-gown and slippers'.[21] Lightweight silks, cottons and linens made easy and comfortable gowns for hot climates and for colonies where the rules of etiquette could be relaxed. The nightgown's popularity is reflected in the numbers of portraits of sitters wearing such garments; those artists in particular who did not want to be bothered by the minutiae of the suit and its decoration chose a gown for the possibilities of the drapery and for the air of agreeable negligence which the eighteenth century found so attractive.

The shirt was an essential part of male clothing, a garment deriving from the Roman tunic in its basic rectangular form. In the eighteenth century, the shirt still conformed to the basic 'T' shape but with the back slightly longer than the front and with wide sleeves ending in a narrow wristband which fastened with a button. For formal occasions, a sleeve ruffle of fine lace, usually Flemish, was attached; some shirts had a plain front opening, but most had a ruffle of linen or lace, which became larger when the cravat disappeared in the 1720s. Shirts, because of the enormous amounts of material they required (they came almost to the knees and acted as an all-purpose undergarment – even worn in bed by the poor), were quite costly if they were made of the finest linen which came from Holland; in 1740, an English country gentleman, Henry Purefoy, paid seven shillings an ell for what was called Dutch Holland, and only three shillings for a comparable amount of inferior Irish Holland linen.[22]

The body of the shirt was gathered into a neckband closed by linen-covered buttons, and over this vent, in the early years of the eighteenth century, men wore a cravat.[23] No better description of this can be given than by Randle Holme whose *Academy of Armory* (1688) – a typically seventeenth-century mixture of fact and fiction with a superfluity of costume and heraldic detail – describes this kind of neckwear as 'a long Towel put about the Collar, and so tyed before with a Bow knot',[24] a fashion which had been in use from the middle of the century. The two main ways of tying the cravat were to knot it at the front and let it hang straight down, or to twist the linen into a plait at the front and pass one end through a button hole to keep it in place. This latter method, called the 'steinkirk', was popularly supposed to derive from the battle of the same name (1692) when during the campaigns of Louis XIV some French soldiers, attacked unexpectedly, had time only to put their neckcloths on this way, instead of tying them in a formal bow. The steinkirk continued into the 1730s as a fashion kept to by elderly men, but from 1715 to 1725 the more fashionable cravat hung straight down, described by an English visitor to France as 'spread about the Neck from whence they hang like Bologna-Sausages down to the Middle'.[25]

At some point in the 1720s the cravat was replaced in fashionable wear by the stock, a made-up neckcloth fastening at the back. Sometimes this was a piece of muslin or lace gathered onto a stiffened band tying at the back of the neck, or it was simply the band itself fastening with a brooch or pin at the back, allowing the shirt ruffle to be seen.

The most typical, perhaps, of all the elements of male costume at the beginning of the eighteenth century was the wig, its high crown and profusion of curls adding to the gravitas imposed by the dignified heaviness of the clothing. This cumbersome and full-bottomed style of wig was beginning to pass out of common use by the end of the reign of Louis XIV, although it was retained by the learned professions in a less top-heavy form. The military campaigns of the War of the Spanish Succession encouraged more manageable wigs; such was the 'campaign wig', or *perruque à marteaux*, shorter than the huge periwig and with the hair divided into two locks hanging over each shoulder and with a long curl at the nape of the neck, this wig was in use until the middle of the century.

Another form of military wig in use in the early eighteenth century was the Ramillies wig with a single plait at the back of the head; this was par-

14 Detail of pl. 60

In this detail from Mercier's conversation piece, both men wear campaign wigs and plain linen neckcloths and sleeve ruffles.

ticularly popular in the Prussia of Frederick William I, as it was considered economical and neat. It was, in fact, popular among the military of all European nations throughout the whole of the eighteenth century, and passed in a truncated form into the early nineteenth.

By the early 1720s, men were beginning to adopt the lighter tie-wigs, which were tied at the back with a black silk ribbon. In fact, one of the first mentions of this style is in the *Guardian* in 1713, but it was not widely worn until a decade later. Alternatively, the hair could be tied back and enclosed in a small bag, called by the French a *bourse*, or *crapaud*, sometimes with a black silk ribbon coming from the bag to tie at the front in a bow, or with a brooch – this was called a 'solitaire', and was the usual style for formal occasions from about 1730 (see pl. 5), although for court balls a wig (or the natural hair) in long ringlets was *de rigueur*. For informal occasions, undress wigs were worn. These were usually 'bob wigs', made undivided into sections, but with all-over curl or frizz; the short bob came to just below the ears, the long bob to the shoulders. Formality also demanded that the wig be powdered with finely ground starch or wheat flour (sometimes perfumed) which was puffed on after the wig had been dressed with pomatum. For those men lucky enough to have thick and luxuriant hair, it was perfectly possible to be seen in company with the hair dressed and powdered in the style of the currently fashionable wig. A powder room was necessary in a gentleman's establishment so that his valet could retire with him, cover him in a powdering gown and puff the powder on his hair. Not until the 1740s, when hairstyles were more complex, close to the head and tightly curled, were most men of whatever class wearing wigs, even if they were not always of the finest hair.

The finest hair for wigs was, in fact, human hair, Diderot claiming in his *Encyclopédie* that the best came from beer-drinking countries such as Flanders. A rumour was current (as it had been from the middle of the seventeenth century when men had begun to wear wigs) that graves were robbed to provide hair; an anonymous author recording a trip to Paris in 1712 commented that 'the sepulchres and the Women furnish the finest ornament for the Heads of the Men'.[26] When French women (followed by other ladies in Europe) began to cut their hair in the 1720s, this was an obvious source for the wig-makers and added to the regular supplies from girls entering convents. Human hair, however, was expensive and for those who could not afford it horse-hair was a popular cheap alternative with the added advantage that it did not uncurl in the rain.

The wig was usually so imposing in the early years of the eighteenth century that the hat often appeared as an afterthought, not being worn on the high-piled wig because it would destroy the toupet, but being carried under the arm. Even when wigs were reduced in size, men continued to carry their hats (always black) in this way on formal occasions, a fashion which lasted throughout the eighteenth century; in the 1770s a hat, the so-called *chapeau bras*, was made specifically for this purpose and was not meant to be worn. For protection against the weather, for business and for those with no pretentions to elegance, hats were worn firmly on the head.

The most expensive hats were produced from beaverskins, which made a glossy and impermeable fabric; half-beaver, made by sticking beaver hair onto woollen felt, was considerably cheaper. Whatever the fabric, it had to be rigid enough to be shaped into the three-cornered style, which was the form of the formal hat through the eighteenth century. The brim was turned up (the contemporary word was 'cocked') on three sides to form a kind of triangle, with more or less equal sides. Slight inequalities in the length of the sides, the depth of the crown, or the angle at which the hat was cocked, created hats known to contemporaries by a variety of names, though to our eyes the distinctions are relatively small. Those wearing uncocked hats were either travelling in bad weather, were members of the lower classes or were young men-about-town deliberately setting out to shock their elders by adopting such uncouth attire. This latter attitude was more current in England than in the rest of Europe, as was, towards 1740, the vogue for jockey caps, round caps with peaks in front, which reflected the growing interest in racing.

The trimming of the three-cornered hat was more important than the relatively unchanging shape, the brim being usually edged with braid or lace, often with a feather fringe. The *Mercure de France* for October 1730 noted that the most fashionable hats were slightly smaller than of late and edged with *point d'Espagne* (a kind of metal braid), or gold or silver lace. Hats were fastened with a button and loop, which provided an opportunity for a display of precious stones; in 1729, Mary Delany noted that George II's hat was 'buttoned up with prodigious fine diamonds' that matched the buttons on his blue velvet suit.[27]

At the other end of the body, the solidity of the footwear complemented the general heaviness of outline. Shoes were usually of leather with, at the beginning of our period, square blocked toes and high square heels; the uppers covered the foot, ending in square tongues rising high in front of the ankle. The sides were closed, and the shoes fastened by straps from the heel leathers, buckled in front over the tongues. Red heels were widely worn at court and on formal occasions until the middle of the century. At the end of the 1720s, the square toes were gradually being replaced by rounder toes and by 1740 these were almost universal. The square toes, however, remained for some time in official and thus more conservative dress – 'square-toes' becoming slang for an old man, according to Francis Grose's *Dictionary of the Vulgar Tongue* (1785).

Shoe buckles took various shapes with the most popular being small squares or oblongs that, from the middle of the 1720s, they gradually increased in size. For the rich attending court, shoe buckles were made of diamonds or silver; baser forms were of metal such as steel or pinchbeck, an alloy of copper and zinc imitating gold (named after a Fleet Street watch-maker, Christopher Pinchbeck, who died in 1732). For the ballroom a lighter shoe with a lower heel was worn; this was called a pump and was even adopted out-of-doors by some of the more foppish men.

15 Detail of pl. 12

This detail from Hogarth's *Captain Coram* (1740) shows the elderly sitter's preference for the heavy, square-toed shoes of his youth, here fastened with pinchbeck buckles.

16 Detail of pl. 12

There is a deliberate echo here of Renaissance portraiture in the elegant hand holding gloves. Captain Coram's hand, a signet ring on his little finger, has a firm grasp of his leather gauntlet gloves.

The arduous nature of travelling in the early eighteenth century demanded the wearing of boots; heavy jackboots which reached above the knees and with slightly spreading tops were also worn by the military. For hunting (and for the informal Englishman on his walks), jockey boots were worn; these were of softer leather, turned down at the top below the knee in a contrasting colour. Apart from the changeover from square to rounded toes, no real change took place in boots in the early eighteenth century. As it was thought rather eccentric in the early eighteenth century even for an Englishman to wear boots in town, a more usual form of leg-protector was the side-buttoning gaiter or spatter-dash, covering the leg from the knee to the ankle. The *Mercure de France* first noted these in the cold winter of 1729–30, advising that they should be made of the same colour and stuff as the suit, but for the less fashionable, the more functional leather or canvas were worn.

The eighteenth century is not, on the whole, an age for emphasis on male accessories: the hat played a minor role subservient to the wig, and gloves, of plain untrimmed leather in shades of tan or buff throughout the century, set off the fineness and delicacy of lace ruffles at the wrist.

A small number of men carried muffs instead of gloves, these increasing in size in the 1730s, but the most usual accessories carried were swords and canes. The sword was not only a mark of gentility, but also necessary in a violent age. It continued to be worn even when, in the first decade of the eighteenth century, men began to carry canes, and it remained part of formal dress until the end of our period. The English were the first to abandon the sword (except for the most formal occasions) in preference to the cane, and César de Saussure was surprised to see in 1726 that almost all men he met

17 Two fashionable young men, 1725, from F. Octavien, *Figures Françoises Nouvellement Inventées*

The emphasis here is as much on elegance of deportment as on fashionable dress, the balletic pose of the feet, the ability to cope with a sword (a necessary mark of gentility in France) and the newly fashionable cane that is tied to the wrist with ribbon. The hat can be either worn on the head or carried under the arm; in the latter instance it is held in place by the characteristic eighteenth-century gesture of inserting the hand into the waistcoat. The waistcoat is unbuttoned to the waist, revealing the fine linen shirt frilled at the front.

in the streets 'wear small round wigs, plain hats, and carry canes in their hands . . . You will see rich merchants and gentlemen thus dressed and sometimes even noblemen of high rank.'[28] The canes were made with a tasselled loop fixed to the top so that they could be hung from the hand or from a coat button and the cane heads were made of gold, silver, rock crystal, agate or other rare or exotic material. The traveller Aubry de La Motraye bought on the Baltic coast in Courland in 1726 an amber 'Head for a Cane wherein was a Fly with Wings extended'.[29] Some men, careful of their health or adversely affected by the stench of the streets, carried canes with pomander tops; as a preventive against infection these were carried by doctors in the first half of the century.

★　★　★

Women

By the beginning of the eighteenth century, a nearly perfect costume for men had evolved: a suit that did not need to vary in style whatever the occasion, but which could be distinguished through excellence of fabric and taste in decoration. In contrast, women's dress (as in the modern period generally) was at the same time far less international and far more complex. Opportunities for women to travel were limited to a tiny fraction of the upper classes, and while it has been said that French dress was the ideal at which many women aimed (and French court dress was almost universally adopted at all courts) there were enormous differences in the extent of attaining this goal; women showed a far greater diversity of clothing from country to country, from region to region and from class to class, than did men. Elite women were also hampered by the nature of their sexual and social roles in society from developing much in the way of functional clothing; instead, they had the much more enjoyable task of channelling their creative intelligence and energy into 'new Modes of Dressings', which led, with increased rapidity of change as the century progressed, to the fashion industry dominated by France.

The complexity of women's dress and its regional variations, and the semantic difficulties attendant upon interpretation of the many confusing terms for various garments, make a study of female clothing in the eighteenth century infinitely more difficult than an analysis of the relative simplicity of male clothing.

It is, perhaps, best to begin with the basic statement that for most of the eighteenth century women's dress consisted of open and closed robes.

The commonest type of gown was the open robe, which consisted of a bodice and overskirt joined together but with the skirt open in front to reveal an underskirt or 'petticoat' (the contemporary name until the late 1780s when the word 'skirt' took over). When the robe and petticoat were made of the same or complementary fabric as a basic unity, this was known as a 'suit'. The bodice, which was always joined to the open overskirt, was, in the first half of the century, open to reveal a 'stomacher' piece or an underbodice, often with elaborate embroidery or lace decoration. Occasionally, for less show, a closed bodice was worn, pinning or lacing at the front or sides.

The other main type of dress was the closed robe, made all in one piece, with the bodice fastened to the skirt by means of a front-fall opening, like a bib, which tied round the waist with the bodice then laced or pinned over it. This was a popular form of undress for the first half of the eighteenth century; by about 1750 it had vanished from the fashionable wardrobe (although it continued to be worn by the middle and lower classes), until in the 1780s it re-emerged with the vogue for simple all-in-one dresses. Finally, there was a costume composed of a separate bodice or jacket and skirt; for the fashionable woman, this was very much a strictly informal attire, worn either in the privacy of the home or for country pursuits. It was, in fact, the costume worn by working women, and not until the 1780s did it really enter the fashionable wardrobe.

18 Detail of pl. 20

Among the participants of the tea-party at Lord Harrington's, Lady Betty Germain (who commissioned the painting) is the most prominent, in her expensive dress of blue and gold silk, decorated with diamond buckles and bows.

It is the open robe which dominates formal female dress throughout the eighteenth century and particularly in the first half. The bodice was edged with flat sewn-down revers, sometimes double, extended to the waist, and, in the second half of the century, to the hem; in England these were known as 'robings'. The stomacher, which filled in the gap between the sides of the bodice, was a panel of triangular shape, stiffened and sometimes boned down the centre front, and decorated with embroidery or ribbons. One of the most popular types of decoration was a row of ribbon bows decreasing in size from the top to the bottom and known as *échelles*. The stomacher was either pinned, laced discreetly with eyelet holes beneath the robings or had decorative lacings across the front. The sleeves were full and loosely fitting, ending in a wide cuff which was often stiffened; the most fashionable sleeve in the 1720s was the pagoda sleeve, with a wide flat cuff horizontally pleated to fit the bend of the arm.

The petticoat was always cut straight across without any gores, the fullness being pleated into the waist and tied by a drawstring, leaving holes at the sides so that women could reach their pockets, which were tied on a belt round their waist over the under-petticoat. When the petticoat was worn over a very wide hoop, the side fullness was gathered separately onto a tape and horizontal flounces of lace or of the same fabric as the skirt (*falbalas*) were used as decoration.

The most usual word for the formal gown in the early eighteenth century was 'mantua' or 'manteau'. Like so much that was formal, it had originally been an informal, loosely fitting négligé gown, described by Randle Holme as popular in the 1670s, 'a kind of loose Garment' worn with 'Stiffe Bodies' or stays beneath.[30] Like the male nightgown, the early mantua was made in the kimono 'T' shape, and draped to show the repeats of the large-patterned silks then in vogue. Early examples that survive show loosely stitched wide back pleats, with a train lightly pinned up at the sides but still trailing on the ground. The author of *The Present State of France* (1712) noted how 'The Quality trail behind 'em a long Tail of Gold or Silk, with which they sweep the Churches and Gardens'.[31] At about this date the mantua lost its negligent appearance and the train became more elaborately fitted at the back; although never itself boned (but worn over boned stays) it became tight-fitting at the waist. It gradually became a formal dress, being accepted at many European courts except for the grandest occasions. The elderly Madame, widow of Monsieur, the duc d'Orléans, brother of Louis XIV, sighed for the old days when the *grand habit* with its excessive bodice boning and massive train was ordinary court dress, but in spite of her strictures against the mantua, she had one 'so constructed that . . . all my underskirts are tied to the bodice with tabs, and my manteau is sewn onto it'[32] (1721). The English court adopted the mantua with enthusiasm; heavily embroidered, with a curtailed train sewn in place (a detachable train was also sometimes added) and worn over the huge hoops of the early and mid-eighteenth century, it lumbers through the pages of the letters of Mrs Delany, that indefatigable recorder of court and social life in England. So universally was it

19 A. Hérisset, 'Les Manteaux', 1792, from *Recueil des Differentes Modes du Temps à Paris*

The formal manteau or mantua, worn over a wide pyramid hoop, is distinguished by the stylized back drapery.

Les Manteaux

adopted in England as the formal robe *par excellence* even outside court that the term for a dress-maker was 'mantua-maker', remaining so well into the nineteenth century, long after the style had ceased to be fashionable.

Yet the most characteristic dress of the early eighteenth century, and one that caught the eye of the artists with its graceful lines, was the 'sack' or 'sacque' dress. Like the mantua, it started life as an informal négligé, probably a dressing-gown; an early example, in Nuremberg, is a simple kimono shape of white linen with a quilted pattern, but made to put on over the head.[33] The early sack dress was usually called a *contouche*, (although there is an isolated reference in Pepys's *Diary* in 1668 to his wife's 'French gown called a sac'). This name probably came from the Polish *kontusz* (originally from the Turkish *gontos*), a caftan-like garment with split or hanging sleeves and in the shape of a cone, falling from neck to hem and being put on over the head. Its use to conceal increasing girth, for whatever reason, and its ease and grace made it immediately popular. Madame, in a famous letter dated 1721, stated that these *robes battantes* (so called because of their bell shape) were originally invented by the old king's mistress, Madame de Montespan, to conceal her pregnancies.[34] Whether this was in fact true, this early form of the sack, made to hang full at the front, continued to be useful for pregnancies; Mrs Delany advised her pregnant sister in 1747 that they were 'easier and handsomer . . . for a lady in your circumstances'.[35]

Although Madame insisted that ladies visiting her wore the formal *grand habit*, many ladies at court adopted the sack dress; the king was very young and there were few occasions at which the *grand habit* was compulsory. Early

21   A. Watteau, studies of women's dress

No other artist has so successfully captured the refinement and elegance of the graceful floating sack dress.

20   C. Phillips, *A Tea-Party at Lord Harrington's* (detail), 1730

The stiff, doll-like poses of the ladies are accentuated by their rigid bodice boning and tight-fitting formal mantuas.

versions of the sack dress had loose pleats unstitched at the front or back. It was worn either with the front seamed from just below the waist, or it was completely open in front, revealing the petticoat. Gradually in the 1730s the back pleats became more formalized and set in two double box pleats, giving the graceful, controlled fall so often referred to erroneously as a 'Watteau pleat' (the artist died in 1721) even though, as the most fashionable dress of the period, it was painted by a number of artists.

Another contemporary term for the sack was 'robe volante', implying the flowing, lilting movement so noticeable in the early unfitted versions of the sack, which paradoxically attracted censure, for it was felt that the looseness of the shape hid a multitude of sins and at the same time declared its origins in a garment suitable for the intimacy of the bedroom. For the playwright Marivaux, writing in the *Spectateur François* in the 1720s, such gowns (also known as 'negligées') were 'comme un honnête équivalent de la nudité même . . . une abjuration simulée de coquetterie' (like an honest equivalent of nudity . . . a feigned rejection of coquetry).[36] Such a garment made of light floating taffeta or embroidered muslin was mentioned as being 'all the rage' by the *Mercure de France* for March 1729: 'Les Robes volantes sont universellement en règne. On ne voit presque plus d'autre habit; on les a porté l'Été dernier, le plus grand nombre de taffetas blanc ou de couleur rose, surtout pour les jeunes personnes qui portoient aussi des robes de gaze ou de mousseline brodée sur un taffetas, dont la couleur paroît au travers' (the *robes volantes* are all the rage and one hardly sees any other dress. Last summer the most popular were of white or pink taffeta, worn especially by young women who wore also robes of gauze or embroidered muslin over coloured taffeta).[37] The *Mercure de France* noted also that large striped and floral

22 J.-F. de Troy, *La Déclaration d'Amour*, 1725

Dress is a crucial part of such a *scène galante*, particularly this voluminous front-fastening sack with its tantalizing lacing at the bosom, perfect for seduction.

23 Detail of pl. 123

This modiste (from Boucher's *La Toilette*) wears her sack *retroussée dans les poches*, a style that emphasizes the curves and the movement of the shining silk.

patterns could be displayed to advantage on the vast areas of material needed for the sack, especially as worn over the hooped petticoat. Large brocades and damasks increased in popularity in the 1730s as the sack became more a formal gown, fitted into the waist and with the bodice cut separately from the skirt and seamed to it. In the middle of the 1730s it was adopted by fashionable English ladies, happier with the security given by the more tailored cut than with the earlier loose-flowing gown. So typically French was the sack, however, that it was known all over Europe as the *robe à la française*; conversely, the waisted gown deriving from the mantua became known in the second half of the century as the *robe à l'anglaise*.

The sack, whether a formal trained garment or an informal kind of dressing-gown, dominated female dress for the first half of the eighteenth century. By the early 1730s, it had become an open robe, a form it was to keep until its demise in the 1770s, worn with stomacher, robings on the bodice and falbalas or embroidery on the skirt. So comfortable, however, was the early loosely draped model that it continued to be worn, with front bow or button fastening, as a travelling garment until the middle of the century. One of the more popular versions of this was the *andrienne* or *adrienne* (named after a celebrated performance, in 1703, of Terence's popular, classical comedy *Andria* in which the actress Marie Dancourt appeared in this kind of informal gown). Tightened up slightly and worn over stays with a small train and hoop, it entered the fashionable wardrobe of the Italian lady with its introduction in 1721 by the new Duchess of Modena, Charlotte-Agläe of Orléans, daughter of the Regent of France. Another version for the active lady was the *robe retroussée dans les poches*, where the fullness of the back material was caught up into the pocket holes of the skirt (pl. 23); it seems to have been especially popular with women whose pretensions to style were limited by their busier life – the middle classes and fashionable personal maids.

A dress with a similar origin to that of the sack was the 'wrapping gown', sometimes worn with a sash or pinned at the waist. Like the sack, it had fullness at the back (where it was worn loose) and was put on over the stays, but with a modesty piece or tucker made of fine linen showing at the bosom. It was a flexible garment, which could be quite formal when worn as a closed gown over the hoops of the second decade of the century, but could also be worn by middle- and lower-class women over petticoats made of quilted linen or cotton or embroidered wool. In *The Purefoy Letters* there are a number of references in the 1730s to such wrapping gowns: in 1739, Henry Purefoy ordered from London 'fine thick printed cotton enough to make two wrappers for my Mother', which may refer to shortened versions of this gown to be worn over the 'neat white quilted calico petticoat' that he ordered at the same time.[38] Such wrapping gowns were fashionable until the late 1740s and they continued to be worn by less fashionable women for the rest of the century.

The female 'nightgown' also derived from the dressing-gown; the term nightgown is confusing, and in the early years of the century may have referred to a bedroom gown, as Lady Mary Wortley Montagu describes in her *Town Eclogues* (1715) a lady in a 'night-gown fasten'd with a single pin'.[39] As late as 1737, Queen Caroline of England, awakened at Hampton Court by the news that the wife of the Prince of Wales was in childbirth, and thinking that the birth was taking place on the premises, cried out 'My God, my nightgown' but was told that this informal gown would not suffice as in fact the princess was at St James's Palace and the queen would need her coaches too.[40] Yet by the early 1730s, the nightgown appears in a puzzling variety of guises, made of rich and humble fabrics, and sometimes a closed and sometimes an open gown. When closed, it might have taken the form of a wrapping gown securely pinned, or with an open bodice front, laced over a handkerchief; it was frequently worn with an apron of plain silk, calico, linen or embroidered muslin. In the 1720s, Mrs Delany advised that for country mourning a black nightgown was admissible, but at the same time her letters of the period note the purchase of nightgowns of 'gold coloured tabby' (1729) and pink damask (1731). In 1734, the inventory of Margaret Cavendish's wedding clothes listed some nightgowns, including one of 'white lustring, imbroidered all over the faceings and robings with silver and purple',[41] implying that this was an open gown with costly embroidery (a number of petticoats are listed, of calico and quilted satin). By the end of the 1730s, the nightgown was usually worn as an open robe, tight-fitting at the waist; it still kept the feeling of informality deriving from its name, and was often worn in England with a quilted petticoat and fine transparent apron. Whereas on the Continent most fashionable women wore the sack from the beginning of our period in preference to the tight-fitting nightgown, this latter garment was the favourite English wear and was greatly to influence the development of the *robe à l'anglaise* in the last quarter of the century.

The trousseau of Margaret Cavendish Duchess of Portland in 1734, mentioned above, emphasized plain satins richly embroidered; her best suit was of 'white Padusoy richly imbroidered with gold and all coulers'. Rich three-dimensional embroideries in large floral designs, on silk, satin or velvet, decorated the dresses in which ladies in England were presented at court in the early eighteenth century. Mrs Delany in 1739 noted that Lady Huntingdon wore a gown of white satin with vases embroidered on the train, and with it a petticoat of black velvet embroidered with chenille, 'the pattern a large stone vase filled with ramping flowers that spread almost over a breadth of the petticoat from the bottom to the top . . . much properer for a stucco staircase than for the apparel of a lady'.[42]

Mary Granville, later Mrs Pendarves and later Mrs Delany, was born in 1700. Her letters, full of information about the details of costume, are indispensable for the student of eighteenth-century dress and her name occurs many times in these pages. She was typical of her age, a mixture of courage and good nature tempered with a gentle malice and with a sophisticated perception both of good taste and of the absurdities of fashion. Her letters chart the changing of textiles, styles and taste, particularly in the first half of the eighteenth century, and from them we can appreciate how difficult it is to make definitive statements about popular patterns when a variety of fabric and design was acceptable in any one period. Bright, single colours as well as more subtle floral designs were popular in the 1720s and 1730s for the woven silks which made up the most fashionable dresses. Large-patterned damasks were widely worn in the early eighteenth century; in 1729, Mrs Delany bought a 'scarlet damask manteau and petticoat' and in the same year an English lady in Moscow, Mrs Ward, was also buying 'very handsome scarlet damask' to wear as a long-sleeved travelling gown over a fur petticoat.[43] For the wedding in 1734 of the Hon. John Spencer with Lady Georgina Carteret, Mrs Delany detailed the dresses, many of which were damasks, including 'a blue damask night-gown, and a white damask, the robings and facings embroidered with gold and flowers'.[44]

But of the woven silks, the brocades were the most expensive and showed the greatest variety of pattern and colour. From the first years of the eighteenth century, the floral patterns were either the heavy, rather ornate baroque forms with silver or gold thread or the more delicate and naturalistic depiction of flowers and foliage. In the 1720s, small flower patterns of the 'meadow silk' type occur, and it is possibly one of these that Lady Lansdowne, writing from Paris in 1721, had in mind when she noted that 'there are very pretty silks come into fashion without gold or silver'. She might also have meant the newly popular 'lace pattern silks', with a notable asymmetrical movement created by lace motifs mingling with flowers. Mrs Delany paid £17 a yard for a French silk in 1729, 'the ground a dark grass green, brocaded in a running pattern like lace of white intermixt with festoons of flowers in faint colours'.[45] Light-coloured silks brocaded in silver were picked out by Mrs Delany at court in 1724; she particularly admired Lady Sunderland's dress which was 'the finest pale blue and pink, very richly flowered in a running pattern of silver frosted, and tissue with a little white' and Lady Carteret's 'pale straw lutestring . . . flowered with silver'.[46]

The 1730s were dominated by a return to the large, heavy fruit-and-flower designs, but far more naturalistic than before (pls 24 and 25). In Lyons, the centre of the silk industry, designers such as Jean Revel had developed a system by the middle of the 1730s of modelling in dark and light and dovetailing tones of colour, which meant that instead of just a surface pattern on the silk, three-dimensional forms could be represented with greater subtlety and almost overwhelming realism. Flowers in full bloom and gargantuan fruit were woven into huge repeats, as much as twenty-eights inches or longer, suitable for the more structured dress with vast hoops of the later 1730s. Some of the inspiration for the large floral designs was from embroidery; for the wedding of Princess Anne of England to the Prince of Orange in 1734 the newspapers noted that the most fashionable silks 'were white paduasoys with large flowers of tulips, peonies, emmonies, carnations & in their proper colours some wove in the silk and some embroidered'.[47] Mrs Delany herself had chosen for the occasion a 'brocaded lutestring, white ground with great ramping flowers in shades of purples, reds and greens'.[48]

It is easy to forget that striped and plain silks were also popular in the 1720s and 1730s; very few plain silks survive in museum collections (they were not expensive enough to alter and keep and many were given to servants or made into children's clothes), although they were liked by artists for the opportunities they afforded to display virtuosity in the painting of light on the lustrous satins or shining taffetas. Plain silks were informal attire, suitable to be worn for taking tea, or playing cards or just for sitting in a garden or on a terrace — all typical scenes depicted in the newly fashionable conversation piece.

Other stuffs popular for négligé gowns were painted silks from the East, or printed cottons, in spite of prohibitions against such fabrics in various countries to protect native silk industries. César de Saussure in the mid-1720s noted how fond the English ladies were of 'cotton from the Indies', and the *Mercure de France* advised for summer 1729 'robes de toile de coton ou petit bazin des Indes blanc, tout uni ou brodé en soye & en laine de diverses couleurs' (robes of white cotton from the Indies either plain or embroidered in silk or wool in various colours).[49]

Many of the large-patterned silks and the heavy, plain silks were meant to be worn over hoops, that curious and essential component of female dress for a considerable part of the century. The originating country may have been either Germany or England, both countries renowned for extremes in fashion; in any case, the eighteenth-century hoop had as its predecessors the farthingale of the late sixteenth century and the stiffened bustle effect created by the back draping of the late-seventeenth-century mantua. The logical consequence of the weight of petticoats at the end of the seventeenth century was to wear a single-hooped underskirt which would be lighter and more comfortable and would provide a more effective framework for the lightweight silks coming into fashion. The first hooped petticoats or *paniers* (the French name derived from a type of basket under which chickens were kept) appeared at the French court in the last years of Louis XIV, although they had, since about 1710, been around in England. Also, from the earliest years of the century, actresses on the French stage had been wearing (to accentuate their waists and give them an imposing presence) gum-starched petticoats called *criardes*, a name coming from the loud rustling noise which they made in movement.

The first hoops were roughly in the shape of a birdcage or rounded dome;
the anonymous author of *The Art of Dress* (1717) attributed their inspiration
to St Paul's cathedral, and the French term was 'panier à coupole'. They were
made of linen or stiffened canvas with rows of whalebone (wood was a
cheaper alternative); the English hoops had eight tiers, the French usually
five.

By the middle of the 1720s, the hoop had assumed an oval shape, sometimes more than eleven feet in circumference, and by 1730 the front of the
skirt was flattened by a system of cords inside, which made the hoop more
manoeuvrable and more decent when the occupant sat down. As it flattened
in the front, so it dramatically increased in width at the sides during the
1730s and 1740s, causing problems during movement (women had to go sideways through doors) and in a confined space.

Edmond-Jean-François Barbier's *Chronique de la Régence* noted that by the end of the 1720s women sitting in the theatre took up enormous amounts of room. In 1728 he reported that the queen, who herself preferred a modest hoop, was incommoded by the paniers of the princesses of the blood, whose right it was to sit next to her. The chief minister, Cardinal Fleury, took time off from matters of state to advise that there should be a spare armchair on either side of the queen to accommodate her skirt and those of the princesses. Yet this served only to cause a chain reaction; the princesses protested that they too should have chairs free on their side away from the queen, which then caused offence to the duchesses who were next in rank.[50] Barbier does not record how this was resolved. Although the very large hoop disappeared some ten years later, the problem persisted with the hoops that continued to be worn for court until the Revolution.

Although attracting more than its fair share of abuse – the *Mercure de France* of 1730 stated flatly that paniers were 'une mode outrée & hors de toute raison' (an extravagant and totally irrational fashion) – the fashion had by then caught on for all classes. The lilting swing of the hoop when elegantly worn (it was impossible to stride out: the correct way was to take tiny, gliding steps), although distorting the shape of the body, was highly attractive and gave a lightness of movement not possible with layers of heavy skirts. The swinging skirts gave a glimpse, really for the first time, of the ankle and shoe; raising the skirt to show the delicately embroidered stocking clocks or even the embroidered garters tying the hose above or below the knee had an almost sexual innuendo. The stockings were made of knitted cotton, silk or worsted, the clocks either knitted in or embroidered; bright colours ensured their notice. The shoes, made of plain leather or of silk (sometimes brocade or damask, and decorated with gold or silver lace or fringe), had pointed toes and a sturdy heel with a height of two to three inches; in the 1730s, the shoes became more rounded and generally more delicate, with slenderer heels, but retained the fastening of latchets buckled or tied over the instep. Such shoes were not meant for hard use, and many women wore out-of-doors an overshoe of matching material.

The correct shape was the all-important fashionable attribute in the eighteenth century, and more particularly in the first half, when the body was compressed into a somewhat unnatural form. Next to the skin was worn the shift or chemise, the main undergarment; for the fashionable woman this was made of fine Holland (linen) edged with plain linen or lace at the neck and sleeves; the sleeves were quite short and the frills attached to them were visible beneath the gown sleeve, until by the middle of the century they were replaced by sleeve ruffles tacked to the sleeve of the dress itself. Over the shift the stays were laced, either down the front or the back, and boned down the centre and side fronts to give the firm rigid line with raised bosom which was so fashionable in this period. It was impossible to imagine an existence without this reinforced structure, boned more or less according to the activity undertaken – there were stays for riding and even for pregnancy.[51] The English, with their already noted fondness for the support of

26   Detail of pl. 25

Small feet were regarded as desirable, an effect enhanced by delicate silk mules, and in contrast to the large hoop skirt. The pale blue silk stockings match the colour of the ribbons on the dress and cap.

27   F. Boucher, 'Study of a woman fencing' or 'Nicole', from *Le Bourgeois Gentilhomme*, 1734 (Boucher illustrated the complete works of Molière that were published in 1734)

One of the jacket-and-skirt costumes thought suitable for a more active role, delightfully impractical though it appears; the tight-fitting jacket bodice fastens down the back and flares out over the hips, and the skirt is worn over the bell-hoop characteristic of the 1730s.

tight garments, wore stays which were appreciably higher, longer and tighter than those worn on the Continent, and these usually laced behind; the lines were already drawn between the more informal French with their low décolletage, and the strait-laced English, when Pöllnitz in 1733 remarked on the latter:

> Their gowns so close before, with strait Sleeves which don't reach beyond the Elbow, make them look as if they had no Shoulders nor Breasts. And what is worse than all, they have broad flat Rumps to their Gowns, and Hoop-Petticoats, narrow at the Top and monstrously wide at the Bottom. They are always laced, and 'tis as rare to see a Woman here without her Stays on, as it is to see one at Paris in a full Dress.[52]

The Englishwoman made her stay-hook an important accessory, either displayed on a châtelaine or hooked to the front of her bodice and used for suspending her watch chain.

The existence of a jacket-and-skirt style of dress for women has already been noted; such jackets could be fitted to the body and laced or fastened with hooks and eyes at the front – this was the French *casaquin* – or they could be shortened versions of the tight-bodied gown, with robings and separate stomacher. *Casaquins*, furred *à la polonaise*, were worn for sleighing at Versailles in 1729 according to the *Mercure de France*. It was a similarly tight-fitting jacket that Catherine I of Russia wore, made of cloth of silver and with a petticoat trimmed with galloon, when she assisted in 1727 at the ceremony of benediction of the waters of the Neva.[53] Popular in France was the thigh-length jacket made like the sack dress with the fullness coming from the shoulders at the back. In most cases the sleeves followed the fashionable line, being full and with a winged cuff, but occasionally a working woman would wear a cuff slit at the wrist like that of the male frock coat.

Definitely adopted from the male wardrobe, first by English women and then by other European women, was the masculine suit adapted for the female riding costume. It consisted of a coat, waistcoat and petticoat; the coat was usually of camlet, a coarse and closely woven worsted sometimes mixed with silk, and was cut on the lines of a man's coat, with back vent and side pleats and fastening left over right, as did the waistcoat. The waistcoat matched the coat with its gold or silver trimming and was sometimes made with just the panels sewn to the coat lining. It was very often worn with male accessories such as the three-cornered hat or the jockey cap and the lace cravat; in the early years of the eighteenth century women even wore long periwigs. From about 1730, women's riding habits copied details from the frock coat, such as the small turned-down collar and the closed or slit cuffs.[54]

The riding habit, with its long sleeves and the extra warmth given by the waistcoat, proved an ideal travelling garment, though often attracting comment from Europeans unused to it. Lady Mary Wortley Montagu astounded those she met in her journeys across Europe to Turkey in 1716/17 in her 'travelling habit which is a riding dress'. By the end of the 1730s, people were more receptive, and Frances Hawes, eloping to France with Lord Vane in 1737, found Parisians impressed with her 'blue English riding habit trimmed with gold', until she 'metamorphosed' herself into a Frenchwoman, cut her hair, wore powder and a robe.[55]

The more usual wear for out-of-doors was the cloak; a modest woman would not wish to be seen much in the streets in the early eighteenth century, and the loose-fitting cloak, often hooded, was discreet and concealing and was a practical garment to wear over the hoop. In the early years of the century it was the custom to walk masked. In France in 1712, women 'have the Priviledge of going maskt at all times, concealing or showing themselves when they please. With a Black-Velvet-Visor they go sometimes to Church as to a Ball or Play, unknown to God and their Husbands'.[56] This fashion continued for reasons of morality or modesty in Italy and Spain for at least the first half of the century; until about the same time it remained in the rest of Europe as a protection against the weather, and for those ravaged by smallpox. The author of *The Art of Dress* (1717) stated:

> When for the Morning Air abroad you steal, The Cloak of Camlet may your Charms conceal; . . . That, with a Mask, is such a sure Disguise, Twould cheat an Argus, or a Spaniard's Eyes.[57]

For very bad weather, Gay's *Implements proper for female Walkers* in the streets of London in 1716 included umbrellas, which were regarded as effeminate for men but necessary 'to guard from chilly Showr's the walking Maid'; he also mentioned pattens, overshoes made with wooden soles raised on iron rings, which protected the leather or fabric shoe from the mud.[58]

From about 1715 to the early 1730s, the cloak was very often full-length, and usually of camlet. Pöllnitz, whom we have already mentioned for his disparaging comments on the dress of English women, noted that: 'When they go out in a Deshabille, they commonly put on a camblet coat as long as their Petticoats, which is closed before, and on each side there's a Slit thro' which they put their Arms; they have withal a Hood of the same Stuff as the Cloak, which is tied under the Chin with a colour'd Ribband.'[59] By the early 1730s when Pöllnitz was visiting England, the long cloak was gradually being reserved more for citizens' wives and daughters; the more fashionable cloaks were short, sometimes with hoods and known as *capuchins*.

Short cloaks or mantles were necessary also not just for cold weather outdoors, but to cover the décolletage of everyday dress. These cloaks had a number of names and the *Mercure de France* for 1729 mentioned *bagnolettes*, which were hooded short cloaks made of satin in winter and muslin in summer; *mantilles* of velvet, satin and ermine for winter; and *palatines* (wide-shaped stoles or tippets falling in two ends at the front) of marten fur in winter and in summer of blonde lace or fine muslin painted with butterflies and decorated with artificial flowers.[60]

At a humbler level, women kept their modesty and warmth by wearing a lace-edged handkerchief, a diagonally folded square of muslin or linen draped round the neck, with the ends knotted in front or secured under or

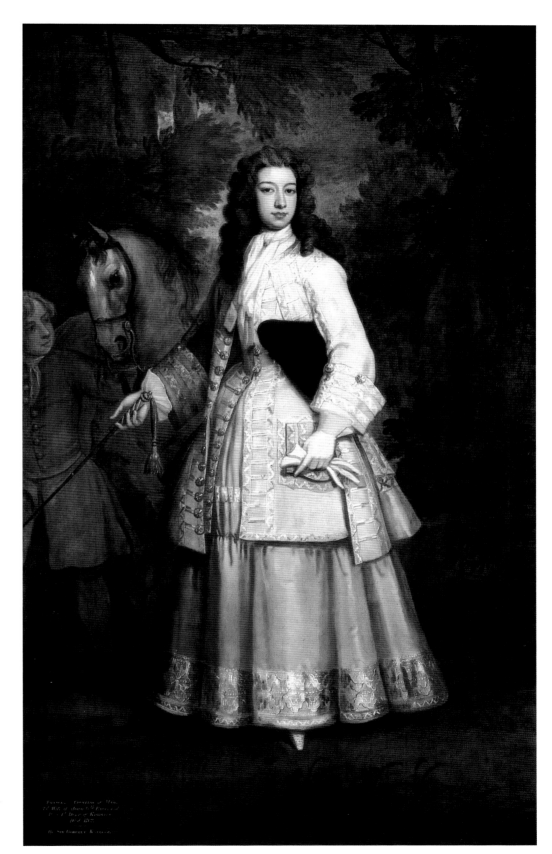

28   Sir G. Kneller, *Frances Pierrepoint, Countess of Mar*, c.1715

Nothing could be more stylish (or so impractical) as this wonderful riding habit of dusky pink and silver worn by Lady Mar. Adapted from the masculine wardrobe, her costume includes a wig, a cravat, a coat and waistcoat and a *chapeau bras*; only the skirt is conventionally feminine.

29 Detail of pl. 117

Hogarth often uses tiny details of costume to underscore the moral context of his work. In his depiction of a rather crude seduction scene, he includes this telling and somewhat pathetic detail of the woman's plain linen, everyday cap pinned to the curtain of the bed.

over the stomacher. The size and shape remained unaltered throughout the first half of the century, but the lace changed with the fashion, from the heavy, three-dimensional, Venetian needlepoint lace, looking like carved ivory, at the very beginning of our period, to the fine, supple, densely patterned bobbin lace, such as Brussels, popular from the 1720s to the 1740s. Very often, the lace on the handkerchief matched that on the sleeve ruffles and on the cap; as hairstyles became simpler, so the various forms of head-wear assumed an increased importance, with women of all social classes wearing some form of head-covering in the first half of the eighteenth century.

With the change in dress that can be seen to have begun just prior to the death of Louis XIV, there is a movement of emphasis from the elaborately trained skirts to the lighter *robe volante*. Similarly, the piled-up towers of hair decorated with wired lace caps, which formed a counterpoint to the heavy baroque costume, had been largely superseded by 1720, with small, neat hair-styles, either combed off the forehead into a knot at the back of the head, or closely curled. The elaborate tower headdresses which had been in vogue since the 1680s remained for some time for court wear and for the elderly. In 1716 Lady Mary Wortley Montagu noted in Vienna that the ladies at court 'build certain fabricks of Gause on their heads about a yard high consisting of 3 or 4 storys fortify'd with numberless yards of heavy riband', which, she said, they placed on a padded roll covered with a mixture of their own and false hair;[61] these were no doubt the 'frizled tours' that Lady Mary poked fun at in her *Town Eclogues* (1715) as being worn only by 'ancient matrons'.[62] Already by 1711 Jonathan Swift remarked that at dinner with the Duchess of Grafton, she wore 'a great high headdress such as was in fashion fifteen years ago and looks like a mad woman in it'.[63] Such headdresses, known as com-modes, were unwieldy structures prone to accidents; Saint-Simon recounted in 1719 that the elderly marquise de Charlus, leaning forward at dinner, caught her towering headdress in the candle flame, and the gallant Arch-bishop of Rheims, thinking to save her by knocking her tower to the ground, received for his pains the lady's egg in his face.[64]

The wife of the English ambassador at Versailles was the first to wear her hair low, in 1713. Although the automatic reaction of the French court was to mock, the king was quite impressed and soon the fashionable ladies fol-lowed suit.[65] By 1720 (although the long ringleted hairstyle remained in England for a few more years), most fashionable French women curled their hair tightly to the head in the style known as *tête de mouton*; the *Mercure de France* for 1730 advocated the use of false hair, *boucles à la Médicis*, for those women unwilling to frizz their own hair. An alternative and more formal hairdressing was a decoration of ribbons, silk lace and gauze flowers, worn with powdered hair; Lady Mary Wortley Montagu noted in 1718 that the French ladies powdered their hair so heavily that it looked like white wool, a startling contrast to the English, who, according to de Saussure (1726) did not curl or powder their hair and 'seldom wear ribbons or flowers, but little headdresses of cambric or of magnificent lace'.[66]

30   Detail of pl. 60

The woman wears the auster, plain linen cap with lappets that was common in the 1720s.

The English were renowned for their advocacy of caps and hats throughout the century and the commode was popular. This was a linen cap, with edgings of lace and layers of lace-edged pleats, supported by a wire frame and with two long streamers called lappets or *barbes* made of lace, which either hung down or were pinned up. These lappets were retained in the simpler caps of the second decade of the eighteenth century, which were of linen with a frill of lace or muslin. In the 1720s, caps became smaller and more delicate and began that complicated language of innuendo and allusion which was to distinguish the millinery trade throughout the century; caps were *en dormeuse, avec désespoir, en négligé, en Papillon, en équivoque, dont les barbes sont retroussées*, and so on.[67] Not until the 1730s did the English belatedly adopt the French taste for curled hair with delicate rococo decorations, and many preferred the loosely waved 'Dutch' style with side curls and ringlets falling to the shoulders. A popular cap in the 1730s was the 'coif' or 'round-eared cap', which was somewhat like a bonnet, curving round the face to the level of the ears or below, with lappets either pinned on top or tied under the chin. The mob cap also hid much of the face, with side pieces which were either left hanging or tied under the chin. These plain caps retained their appeal for middle-class women and the more conservative throughout the century in most countries of Europe, some developing their own regional characteristics. Such caps were usually worn out-of-doors, under either hoods or the flat wide-brimmed hats which, made of silk or straw, were by 1730 a fashionable accessory.

2 Getting and Spending

People, where they are not known, are generally honour'd according to their Cloaths and other Accoutrements they have about them; from the richness of them we judge of their Wealth, and by their ordering of them we guess at their understanding.

B. Mandeville, *The Fable of the Bees*, 1714

No man is ignorant that a Taylor is the Person that makes our Cloaths; to some he not only makes their Dress, but, in some measure, may be said to make themselves. There are Numbers of Beings in and about this Metropolis who have no other identical Existence than what the Taylor, Milliner and Periwig-Maker bestow upon them. Strip them of these Distinctions, and they are quite a different Species of Beings; have no more Relation to their dressed selves, than they have to the Great Mogul, and are as insignificant in Society as Punch, deprived of his moving Wires, and hung up upon a Peg.

R. Campbell, *The London Tradesman*, 1747

THE STATEMENT MADE BY PIERRE-SYLVAIN MARÉCHAL in the 1780s that Paris 'par ses modes, est le maîtresse du monde' was true in fashionable society in the eighteenth century. Not only did Paris establish new modes, but it also had the best fabrics and accessories available in its shops — it was a Mecca for the fashion-conscious.

The clothing trade was still, at the beginning of the century, organized on medieval specialist lines. At the top were the mercers who sold the best silks and also the finest woollen stuffs. They were based in the rue Saint-Honoré and supplied the materials for the fashion industry. It was not surprising that the *marchands de modes*, the ancestors of the couturiers and suppliers of trimmings and accessories, also had their premises in this area. Many of the drapers were situated in the rue de la Vieille-Draperie and supplied the less valuable woollen materials, cottons and linens. Other suppliers to the fashion industry included the shoe-makers in the rue de la Cordonnerie and the goldsmiths and jewellers in the quai des Orfèvres. In all, some twenty guilds specialized in various items of clothing, from fabrics to ribbons.

By the early years of the eighteenth century, visitors were commenting on the large numbers of shops in Paris and their wide range of goods, although standards of display were fairly poor, with tiny windows and dark interiors. It was, in fact, easier to shop at the Lent Fair in Saint-Germain 'in a great Place fill'd with Shops, where an infinite Number of Merchants set out all the finest and richest Goods that are made in this great City'.[1] By

31 Detail of pl. 74

This detail from Paret's *The Shop* shows a wealthy couple contemplating a purchase. The woman is dressed fashionably in the Spanish style, in black silk with a hoop, and a white *mantilla*; she examines a delicate filigree head ornament of the kind worn on gala days. Her seated companion is dressed formally in the French style, in silk suit and sable-trimmed coat, with decorative, frogged fastenings.

32 Detail of pl. 52

In the background of a painting attributed to Nebot can be seen the range of street signs to be found in early eighteenth-century London; these include a glover's, on the left.

the end of the century, the Lent Fair, which lasted for three months in the winter, and the Saint-Laurent Fair, which lasted for the same time in the early summer, were less fashionable and more patronized by provincial French people. To meet an increased demand for luxury goods, including those related to dress, in the second half of the century, many shops were transformed into handsomely decorated mirrored saloons, illuminated at night. The most fashionable shops in the 1780s were in the Palais Royal, built by the duc d'Orléans in 1782 in the grounds of his town palace; the arcades covered shops, coffee houses and promenades, where, according to a Russian visitor, 'all the riches of the world are displayed to the astonished eye . . . all the inventions of luxury to embellish life'.[2]

In every large city in Europe the contrast between poverty and the display of wealth was enormous. In an age in which illiteracy was the norm, a visual shorthand was used to announce shops, services and trades. The proliferation of shop signs and the noise and commotion on the streets were more akin to the sights and sounds found in a modern Arab city than to those of contemporary Paris or London. W. H. Pyne in *Wine and Walnuts* (1823) remembered seventy years beforehand in London 'the thousand monster signs swinging and loudly creaking in a wintry wind, joining in concert with the multifarious wares suspended o'er the open shops'.[3] Shop signs included the universal pair of scissors for the tailor, for the hosier a pair of stockings, hats (in Rome a cardinal's hat) for the hatter, and so on. The London shop signs were taken down or placed against the sides of the shops in the 1760s, at about the same time that the old City gates were removed and the fashionable populace gravitated towards the West End. But throughout the century those involved in the business of adorning the human body were recognizable through their trades:

> Then the tailor was well known . . . whilst a stay-maker was distinct from he. A barber could be descried the full length of Cornhill . . . Each branch of business which a man pursued stood manifest either in his coat, hat or wig – his apron, sleeves, jacket or general gait . . . Never did a country lout newly dubbed a London porter after a month's sojournment midst the bustling scene accost a leather-parer for a perruquier, nor baker for a plaster-manufacturer, though all were, as the miller, white.[4]

Barbers, who spent Sunday mornings covered in powder from carrying wigs to their customers, were known, says Louis-Sébastien Mercier in his *Tableau de Paris* of the 1780s, as 'merlans' or whitings.[5]

In London in the early eighteenth century, the City contained the most fashionable shops. In the mid-1720s, de Saussure admired the shops along Ludgate Hill with 'silken tissue of beautiful and costly kinds being sold there', and at the Royal Exchange, a kind of covered market, he saw 'booths along either side covered with rich merchandise, jewellery and other tempting wares'.[6] Fashionable people had long patronized the mercers' shops in Covent Garden, and this area remained a traditional home of the fine specialist textiles. But it was Oxford Street that in the 1780s became the English equivalent of the Palais Royal. The shops, open until ten in the evenings, dazzled the eye by the novelty of the large expanse of glass window and were built 'with a little projection on to the street so that they can be seen from three sides'. Sophie von la Roche in 1786 admired the silk fabrics and chintzes hanging in the windows, but most of all the linen shops where anything could be bought 'from swaddling cloths to shrouds'.[7]

So much did Paris and London dominate the retail clothing trade in the eighteenth century that one is likely to forget that only a small proportion of fashionable people were able to visit these capitals to order clothes or to buy fabrics. Some provincial cities, such as Bath, were able to provide a good range of metropolitan goods for the local nobility, but many people found

33   D. Chodowiecki, *Ein Friseurlehrling mit Perücken*, 1773

The barber, running through the streets carrying dressed wigs to his customers, was a familiar sight of metropolitan life. Mercier, in Paris in the early 1780s, describes the way in which on Sunday mornings 'the streets are crowded with a swarm of barbers and hairdressers, holding in one hand their curling-irons, in the other a ready-dressed perriwig, their clothes bepowdered from top to bottom' (*Tableau de Paris*).

34 After H. Gravelot, *Exeter Exchange,* 1762

Exeter Exchange in the Strand was a fashionable shopping arcade, particularly noted, according to Strype's *Stow's London,* 1720, for its seamstresses, hosiers and milliners.

distances too great for regular visits to large towns. Some enterprising merchants travelled with their goods to their customers; in the 1760s an English traveller in Prussia found that at a nobleman's house 'were spread all sorts of mercery goods as silks, stuffs, velvets, brocades' that were brought by a mercer from Gustrow twice a year to save the ladies the trouble of visiting his shop.[8] At a lower level of society, pedlars (including many Jews distinguished in some countries by coloured badges[9]) sold cheaper textiles such as cottons, lace and millinery items; travelling sometimes hundreds of miles, they passed on changes in fashion as well as local news.

In this detail of Hogarth's famous painting showing various attempts at bribery during an election, the Tory candidate wishing to impress two girls on the balcony above buys for them items, including a purse, from the tray of a bearded Jewish pedlar. Before him kneels a porter wearing the belted smock and wide shovel hat typical of his profession.

Specialist fairs were also sources of clothing materials. Perhaps the most famous was held three times a year at Leipzig and was known for the quality of its rich silks and gold and silver laces. Goethe tells us that it was called 'klein Paris' for the range of its luxury goods and Lady Mary Wortley Montagu was able in 1716 not only to buy liveries for her servants but also 'gold stuffs for myselfe'.[10] In England, a number of fairs concentrated on the wide variety of woollen goods for which the country had long been famous and which were increasingly to dominate the market for men's wear. In *A Tour Thro' the Whole Island of Great Britain* (1724–6), Daniel Defoe noted that

36 D. Chodowiecki, *A Fair in Berlin*, 1774

Among the wide range of goods sold at this fair can be seen rolls of fabric and second-hand clothes.

the most famous fair was at Stourbridge, which was devoted to the sale of woollen goods, including those from Yorkshire. In Leeds, the Brigg Market attracted buyers from all over Europe, and by 1790 there were two cloth halls established, one for white and one for coloured cloths.

For most of our period, silks ruled the fashionable wardrobe. Although there were other silk centres in France, such as those at Tours and Marseilles, the best silks came from Lyons, a city which had prospered under Louis XIV's great minister, Colbert. With state patronage and mounting prosperity, the silk trade was not unduly depressed by the wars at the end of the seventeenth century and was free to expand with the opening of foreign markets granted by the Treaty of Utrecht in 1713. By 1768 there were 11,000 looms in Lyons and over 100 pattern-drawers for new designs. As early as the beginning of the century there would appear to have been new silk patterns every year, and seasonal silks by the middle of the period. Design, and its importance in the growing fashion industry, was recognized as an art, and artists were, in fact, employed at the first school for silk design opened in Lyons in 1756. French silk-designers and weavers were sent all over Europe, notably to Spain and to Sweden, and the French influenced design through the settlements of Huguenot refugees in the Protestant Netherlands and Germany. Even in England where there was a flourishing silk industry in Spitalfields in London, the most famous designers such as Anna Maria Garthwaite (1690–1763) relied to some extent on French patterns, and snobbery in any case dictated that French silks were the most highly prized. Although many countries in Europe produced their own light silks of varying qualities, the best woven silks came from France; the only other country worth mentioning here is Italy which, apart from making the best velvets in Europe, also made lightweight silks of great quality, and enough figured silks for home consumption.

Clothes made from silk were expensive owing to the cost of the silk and the yardages required. The raw silk needed to be imported (and even within one country there were often regional customs dues), mounting a draw loom to weave a new pattern was a long, expensive business and a weaver could weave only a few inches a day of a very complicated silk. A rich, flowered silk brocaded in gold might cost 70 shillings or more, a figured silk 20 shillings a yard and a plain taffeta about 8 shillings. Although it is difficult to make useful comparisons, Peter Thornton reminds us that 'a prosperous merchant's house might be valued at about £500, while a lady's silk dress could cost anything from about £10 to £60' – and much more for a court dress.[11] Silks were very often ordered by the piece, of anything from 18 to 80 yards. Large amounts were needed for suits and dresses and also for their repairs as it was difficult to get exactly the same quality and colour again, especially if the fabric was imported. Walter Spencer-Stanhope, a member of the Macaroni Club, ordered a suit from Paris in 1775 of plum-coloured silk embroidered in silver, but the English customs seized the breeches. After Stanhope had failed to get them back, an English tailor tried but failed to match the colour. The Parisian tailor sent another pair but even these were not the right shade, and the suit was abandoned.[12]

There was no uniformity of measurement, a fact which caused confusion to the importer and the customer. An English ell was 45 inches, a French ell about 43 French inches or about $46\frac{1}{2}$ English inches. Cotton and silk fabrics were usually half-an-ell wide, though the lighter silks such as taffeta might be wider. Woollen fabrics could range from either a French or an English ell in width to 58 French inches wide. Therefore the amounts of material required depended on the width of the fabric as well as the size of the person. The grander the dress, the greater the amount of stuff needed and this was particularly true for the court dress, the *grand habit*, which required a vast hooped skirt often decorated with swags of material and a train. In 1789, for example, at the presentation of the vicomtesse de Moges, the *marchande de modes* used 22 ells of black taffeta for the gown and 14 ells of striped gauze for the skirt decoration and the train.[13] Rose Bertin, the greatest of all the *marchands de modes*, made for a presentation dress in 1786 a gown of black velvet, taking 19 ells at 380 livres and a garniture of black gauze, spangles, and fringe with crystals at 800 livres; in some cases, the total sum for a court dress could run into many thousands of livres.[14] The huge mantua and skirt worn at court in Vienna in the first half of the eighteenth century took about 30 ells of silk at prices ranging from 32 to 40 florins the ell;[15] in 1737, Mrs Delany found that she needed 16 yards for a court dress. For the sack dress or for any open robe with a matching skirt, the amounts ranged from 15 to 25 ells. The more shaped gowns of the last quarter of the period, worn without hoops, necessitated approximately 15 to 20 ells, depending on the amount of back draping. The invaluable album of Barbara Johnson,[16] who kept an account of all her purchases of dress materials from the end of the 1740s to the end of the century, often attaching swatches of material and fashion plates to her records, illustrates the complexity of widths and the varying amounts of stuff needed as styles changed. In 1767, she needed 22 yards of lilac silk for a negligée (sack dress) at half an ell wide;

ten years later, for an informal nightgown of blue and white striped lustring, $11\frac{1}{4}$ yards of the same width were needed and in the following year a 'Devonshire brown Lutestring negligée' took 19 yards of material at three-quarters-of-an-ell wide. The most expensive dress listed in her album was a negligée of garnet-coloured paduasoy, taking 22 yards at 10 shillings the yard, but a modest sum compared to the amounts spent by others on court dress.

For mens' suits, amounts of material needed were not so large and there were no huge variations in style which demanded widely differing yardages. By the 1780s, when a slimmer line was fashionable, 2 ells of material were needed for the knee breeches, and it was customary to order these in pairs as they wore out more quickly than the coat or waistcoat. About 5 ells was average for the coat, but it is difficult to gauge how much was needed for the waistcoat for this was often ordered from pieces already prepared with the design embroidered on; in the 1780s, white waistcoats were popular and it was the custom to order these by the dozen.

The mercers were the all-powerful middle men between the silk weaver and the customer and there were many complaints about their insolence to those they summed up as infrequent clients. In many cases, they had close business links with the weavers and they were able to indicate likely fashionable lines; they offered samples to the customers to take away for consultation with tailor or dressmaker and they recommended currently modish styles and colours. Much of the economy of France was based on their prosperity and their reputation as arbiters of taste. Many foreign princes and princesses ordered their wedding clothes from Paris; the duchesse d'Orléans in 1706 was commissioned to choose the wedding trousseau for a Hanoverian princess and on showing this to the king, Louis XIV, 'wish'd, for the sake of the Mercers of Paris, that there were more Princesses who could afford to make such Purchases'.

One of the most important silk merchants was Jean-Nicolas Barbier, who supplied silks to the French court; his letters in the Victoria and Albert Museum' show how closely he worked with his customers, discussing the best fabrics for certain garments and marking his sample books for those who were not so confident of their own taste.[17] Although the client chose the main fabric of a dress or suit, the choice of linings was left to the silk merchant. The skill and taste lay, for much of the century, in the choice of the fabric and decoration and not with the tailor, whose status was low. It is possible that some of the more important silk merchants had tailors on the premises to advise on yardages and to cut the required lengths or even roughly to sew up the fabric for a foreign customer so that customs duties could be avoided. A merchant like Barbier, with such a distinguished clientèle, had to be very patient with regard to money (as did most of those dealing with the nobility, some of whom who felt that the settlement of bills was the last priority), and a wide use of credit was the rule for well-connected customers could bring in others. Madame du Barry, for example, was a customer of Rose Bertin for many years and brought her much busi-

37a and b Two pages from Barbara Johnson's *Album*, 1767–8 and 1771

These pages are typical of the useful information to be gained from this scrapbook of fashions and fabrics. Here we see some early fashion plates (probably cut out from almanacs or diaries) depicting a range of costume from court dress to 'undress', and also dress materials such as silks (note the importance of trimmings, such as fly braid, to formal wear) and the newly fashionable printed cottons and linens.

ness, but many of her debts to the *marchande de mode* were still unpaid when she was guillotined in 1793.

The basic fabric was only the beginning of a suit or dress, and the fashionable customer needed accessories and trimmings. By the middle of the century, women's dress was increasingly dominated by decorative trimmings such as ribbons, lace and silk flowers; such trimmings or *agréments* were made and sold in special shops or warehouses in Paris. In 1767 Lady Mary Coke went shopping 'to one of the great Mercers. I wanted to buy all his Shop, but chose only one Gown, a very fine winter silk, which I carried immediately to the famous place where they make all the Trimmings, & bespoke one to sute it. They asked me ten louis d'ors, but I hope to have it for nine'.[18] By 'gown', Lady Mary meant enough fabric for a dress, which she might either have had made up in Paris with the trimming loosely stitched on or brought home for her mantua-maker.

38 (*facing page*) P. Longhi, *The Tailor* (detail), 1742–3

The tailor holds up a fashionable sack dress of brocaded blue silk to his customer.

It was widely accepted that the law could be flouted with regard to the customs dues on imported materials such as lace and silks. The Scottish novelist Tobias Smollett noticed at Boulogne in 1765 that there were large numbers of English smugglers from Kent and Sussex with an impressive trade in 'ribbons, laces, linen and cambrics'.[19] A professional smuggler in his novel *Ferdinand, Count Fathom* (1753) was discovered; having been 'stripped of his upper garments, and even of his shirt, [he] appeared like the mummy of an Ægyptian king most curiously rolled up in bandages of rich figured gold shalloon that covered the skirts of four embroidered red waistcoats . . . a considerable body of the same sort of merchandize was found in his boots, breeches, hat, and between the buckram and the lining of his surtout'.[20]

Towns along the Kent coast were particularly suitable as depots where smuggled goods could be seen. In 1768, Lady Mary Coke visited Deal where she went to 'three of the houses that smuggle Indian goods. I saw several pieces of very pretty silks . . . tea and musline is extremely cheap'.[21] At this period, Indian muslins and painted silks from China were coming into fashion for women's dresses and as they could not be made up in their country of origin they were liable to import duty.

Fabric and trimming, once obtained, had to be made up by the mantua-maker or the tailor. For men this was less of a problem, for styles changed fairly slowly and the relative simplicity and uniformity of men's wear ensured easy access to the fashionable line. For women, with their more restricted lives, it was more difficult to follow the fashions; at the beginning of the eighteenth century there were no regularly produced fashion magazines and one could not rely on returning travellers (especially men) to report accurately on the niceties of cut or trimming.

Many of the fashions, therefore, were transmitted via dolls in the early part of the century, dressed in the latest taste and sent out from Paris to the courts of Europe. Two dolls were usually sent, one in court dress, *la grande Pandora*, and the other in fashionable everyday clothing, *la petite Pandora*. The dolls, dressed in the latest styles, were a popular sight in the rue Saint-Honoré; Mercier in a famous passage in his *Tableau de Paris* described how visitors were taken to see the 'fameuse poupée, le mannequin précieux, affublée des modes les plus nouvelles, enfin le prototype inspirateur passe de Paris à Londres tous les mois, et va de-là répandre ses grâces dans toute l'Europe. Il va au Nord et au Midi: il pénetre à Constantinople et à Pétersbourg; et le pli qu'a donné une main françoise, se répete chez toutes les nations, humble observatrices du goût de la rue Saint-Honoré' (the famous doll, the precious mannequin dressed in the newest fashions, which travels from Paris to London each month, and from there distributes its charms all over Europe. It goes to the North and the South: it reaches Constantinople and St Petersburg; and the pleat created by a French hand is copied by all nations, humble observers of the taste of the rue Saint-Honoré).[22]

The dolls, having been copied by the court dressmakers, were displayed in the windows of fashionable shops for ladies to examine. In Bologna in the 1730s, the French visitor de Brosses noted with some exaggeration that

39   Tailor's doll or shop model, *c*.1790

This elegant standing figure made of beeswax (27 inches high), shows off the clothing of the man of fashion at the end of our period; the look is streamlined, with cutaway silk coat and short waistcoat cut horizontally at the waist.

the ladies there 'wear nothing but what comes from Paris', for 'they have large dolls sent to them daily, robed head to toe in the latest fashion'.[23] In Venice, a doll called the *piavola de Franza* was placed in the window of the *merceria* so that it could be examined in detail. The poet Francesco Algarotti described to his readers how the ladies, with rapt attention, noted all the details from the headdress to the petticoat:

> To le vedresti a lei dinnanzi in frotte
> L'Andrienne, la cuffia, le nastriere
> L'immenso guardinfante a parte a parte
> Notomizzare a sino addento a sotto
> Spinger gli avidi sguardi al gonnellino.[24]

(You will see them flocking before you, scrutinizing piece by piece the andrienne, the cap, the ribbons, the vast hoop, and casting their eager looks even to the inside and underneath of each petticoat.)

Although the most fashionable dolls were sent from France, other dolls were sent from England. The *Gentleman's Magazine* for 1751 reported that dolls dressed in the English style had been sent to the Empress Elizabeth of Russia. Such dolls, known in English as 'babies', were also sent to the American colonies, where England was the dominant cultural influence. The *New England Weekly Journal* for 2 July 1733 stated that at Boston (the main fashion centre in America) was to be seen at a mantua-maker's 'a Baby drest after the Newest Fashion of Mantuas and Night Gowns, & everything belonging to a dress. Lately arrived on Capt. White from London'; it would cost ladies five shillings to borrow the doll, and seven shillings if the mantua-maker attended them in their own homes.[25] The *Lady's Magazine* for 1773 remarked sarcastically on the 'contagion' of fashion transmitted from the court to the city and then to the country 'by means of dolls which are sent thither and in a short time the provincials . . . are dressed like the gaudy doll which is sent from Paris. I imagine I see the women of a village, at least those of the better sort, collected together about the newcomer examining it from head to foot and running in rapture from the sweet idol to their milliners or mantua-makers . . .'[26] This was not just moral indignation on the part of the *Lady's Magazine*, but perhaps irritation at the lingering practice of sending such dressed dolls when fashion plates were available that could not only spread the newest styles to a wider section of the populace but do so far more speedily.

It was, in fact, in the *Lady's Magazine* in the early 1770s that fashion plates first appeared regularly: each month a black-and-white engraving was produced, which could be coloured by the reader and sent to her mantua-maker with instructions for making up. Previous fashion magazines such as the *Mercure de France* (which originally began as the *Mercure Galant* in 1672) issued fashion plates only sporadically (pl. 40), as did the earlier editions of the *Lady's Magazine*. In addition, in the first half of the eighteenth century, a number of well-known artists and engravers produced collections of costume drawings and fashion plates. Some, like those of Watteau, were more prepara-

40 Fashion plate from the *Mercure de France*, October 1730

The accompanying text describes the large hoops in fashion – 'plus grands & plus amples que jamais' – but what is also clear is the taste for the rococo, manifested first in France and indicated by the half-open fan (a perfect scallop-shape), frills and *falbalas* on the dress, the curled hairstyle, the flowers on the bodice – 'les gros & amples Bouquets de fleurs artificielles sont toujours fort à la mode' – and the jewellery springing from a large pin-cushion between the putti.

tory sketches for paintings; others, such as Picart's *Diverses Modes Dessinées d'Aprés Nature* (1728), were engravings of the dress currently worn by all sections of society in Holland and North Germany, and not a fashionable ideal to be followed (the purpose of a fashion plate proper). An early and rare example of a collection of fashion plates and accessories was that published by Antoine Hérisset in 1729 under the title of *Recueil des Differentes Modes du Temps à Paris* (see pl. 19). In 1744, the French artist Hubert Gravelot published a collection of English fashion plates, which were instrumental in the spread of the more informal English styles (see pl. 86).

The innovation introduced by the *Lady's Magazine* in 1770 was not just to have a monthly fashion plate but also a detailed descriptive text. The aim was to provide the most distant readers 'with every innovation that is made in the female dress' but to avoid the 'fleeting whimsies of depraved Elegance'. Like the *Gentleman's Magazine* (which began in 1731), the *Lady's Magazine* also carried society news, theatre reviews and informative articles on the intellectual topics of the day; increasingly, however, towards the end of our period, there was a greater emphasis on moral advice and serialized, sentimental stories.

In France, similar magazines were established in the 1780s, the most important being the *Cabinet des Modes* (later called the *Magazin des Modes Nouvelles Françaises et Anglaises*) which ran from 1785 to 1789. French and English fashion plates were copied all over Europe. The only other country producing fashion plates in the 1780s was Germany; Daniel Chodowiecki illustrated German fashion almanacs in this decade, and from Weimar in 1786 came the first important rival to the French and English magazines, the *Journal des Luxus und der Moden*.

Fashion was taken more seriously in France as an art and a source of economic prosperity. Well-known artists, through their fashion illustrations, helped to ensure French superiority in that refinement of taste and elegance of style which could be imitated but never surpassed. The most famous collection of fashion plates designed to point a moral or adorn a tale, the *Suite d'Estampes pour servir à l'Histoire des Moeurs et du Costume des Francois dans le dix-huitième Siècle*, was issued in three parts in 1775, 1776 and 1783. It was published in 1789 as *Le Monument du Costume Physique et Moral de la fin du dix-huitième siècle ou Tableaux de la Vie*, with a text by Restif de la Bretonne. Augustin de Saint-Aubin and F.-L.-J. Watteau – great nephew of the famous artist – were among a number of illustrators to the superb *Gallerie des Modes et Costumes Français*, a set of 342 coloured fashion plates published from 1778 to 1787 by Jean Esnauts and Michel Rapilly; most of the designs were taken from the *marchands de modes*.[27]

It was not surprising that the names of some of the most important, fashionable tailors occurred in the *Gallerie des Modes*, for France was acknowledged as the centre for the best tailoring. Those with any taste or pretensions to style not only bought their fabrics in Paris, but had them made up by a French tailor. The Richelieu collection in the Bibliothèque Nationale in Paris contains samples of the sumptuous French fabrics (including, for example, chenille velvets brocaded in gold, at 140 and 150 livres the ell) made up for the King of Portugal in 1735. Even for humbler clothes, the quality of tailoring in Paris was supreme: Christian VII of Denmark ordered there in 1768 his hunting suits of blue and red broadcloth trimmed with gold braid. The cachet of French clothes was particularly striking in the first half of the century; in Fielding's novel *Joseph Andrews* (1742), the author poked fun at the ultra-fashionable Englishman Bellarmine whose praise of French tailoring was addressed to Leonora:

> Yes Madam this Coat I assure you was made at Paris, and I defy the best English Taylor even to imitate it. There is not one of them can cut, Madam, they can't cut. If you observe how this Skirt is turned, and this Sleeve, a clumsy English Rascal can do nothing like it . . . I never trust anything more than a Great Coat to an Englishman . . . for myself I would see the dirty Island at the bottom of the Sea rather than wear a single Rag of English Work about me, and I am sure after you have made one Tour to Paris, you will be of the same Opinion with regard to your own Clothes.[28]

A gentleman of fashion, like the eponymous hero of Smollett's *Peregrine Pickle* (1751), had made in Paris 'several suits of cloaths suitable to the French mode'. Some French tailors even sent their servants to the places patronized by foreign gentlemen to get custom; John Russel, a young English painter, was accosted in 1739 in the Café Anglais by a person 'dressed in black velvet with a gold-laced hat, silver-hilted sword . . . ready to equip me à la mode de Paris'.[29]

41   L.-P. Boitard, *The Tailor's Shop, c.*1749

In this drawing of the interior of a tailor's shop, the master tailor, in gown and slippers, measures a customer for a coat. Paper or cloth patterns are pinned to a wall, and in the background, the journeyman tailors assume the traditional cross-legged pose for their sewing.

Travelling on the Grand Tour was a useful way of adding to the wardrobe, particularly as there was a universal belief that clothes were cheaper out of one's native land. When Robert Adam went on the Grand Tour with his brother James in 1754 he bought at Lyons 'a gold Stuff Vest which I verily believe in London would cost 16 or 18 pounds but here does not amount to above $\frac{1}{3}$ of that sum. I am also getting one of the genteelest and richest embroidered Vests that I ever saw which will cost me at least £14 or £15 sterling'; in Genoa, the next stage of his trip, he proposed to buy a suit of black velvet with which he could wear all his waistcoats in turn.[30] If unable to visit Paris, gentlemen should, advised Lord Chesterfield, use the services of French tailors, established in all the major capitals of Europe.

The most important treatise on tailoring in the period 1715–89, *L'Art du Tailleur*, was written by François-Alexandre de Garsault for the *Description des Arts et Métiers* (1769). It detailed the fairly crude systems for measuring the customer (with paper tape measure) and cutting out the fabric using paper patterns as templates. Ideally, according to the *London Tradesman* (1747), the tailor 'must be a perfect Proteus, change Shapes as often as the Moon, and

42   G. D. Tiepolo, *At the Dressmaker's*, 1791

The rather hoydenish customer, wearing chemise, back-lacing stays and short skirt, stands before the mirror while the dressmaker measures her sleeve. On the left sits the girl's mother or her chaperone, wearing the traditional Venetian *zendaletta* over her head.

still find something new; He ought to have a quick Eye to steal the Cut of a Sleeve, the Pattern of a Flap, or the Shape of a good Trimming at a Glance . . .'[31] Much of his skill lay in hiding any deformity, so that the coat hung well, and 'the Cloaths sit easy in spite of a stiff Gait or awkward Air'. The cutting of the coat and waistcoat was much more important than that of the largely hidden breeches; the latter were usually cut by the tailor and then made up by the less-skilled breeches maker. In addition, there were specialist makers of leather breeches, worn by the upper classes for riding and by the lower classes for work; the English philanthropist Francis Place was apprenticed to a leather-breeches maker in 1785 but by then the trade was decaying as working men turned to cheaper and washable cloths such as cotton cord.

Cloth, whether silk or wool, was expensive and cost far more than labour; tailors were very often in the vanguard of any radical movements to increase their standard of living. The journeyman tailors in London published in 1754 a breakdown of the cost of a suit: the twelve yards of velvet cost £1. 4s. a yard, plus the cost of the linings, facings and buttons, but the tailor could only charge 2s. 6d. for each of the seven and a half days it took to complete.[32] Admittedly, in England the quality of tailoring was not high; Henry Purefoy sent a letter to his local tailor in Oxfordshire in 1736 saying: 'The Gold laced wastcoat you made nice last year has done you no credit in the making, it gapes so intolerably before at the bottom when I button it at the wastbone of my breetches & everybody takes notice of it. As to my size I am partly the same bignesse as I was when in Town last, but you made the last cloaths a little too streight.'[33] It was not surprising, in view of the information – or lack of it – regarding size and fit, that complaints were made

43 J.-B. Mallet, *Une Marchande de rubans au Palais Royal*, n.d.

The Palais Royal was famed for its arcade of luxury shops which included those specializing in accessories such as millinery and ribbons.

to the tailors. In the more remote areas of the countryside it was, paradoxically, easier to have more personal service. Travelling tailors with their journeymen would visit their clients once or twice during the year and, carrying news as well as their needles and thread, they would make repairs and alterations as well as make up new. Some households were provided with servants skilled at tailoring; Goethe's father, a well-off citizen of Frankfurt, chose men-servants who could tailor so that clothes could be made for the family at home.

For most of the seventeenth century, tailors had made the clothing of men and women, but in 1675 women were officially empowered to make clothes. The profession was divided into two branches: the *maitresses couturières*, after an apprenticeship of three years, could make various female garments such as the loose *robes de chambre*, the petticoats and jackets, unboned gowns and bodices, underwear and children's clothing, including that of boys up to the age of eight years. In practice, couturières specialized in various branches of clothing. The tailoring of gowns reinforced with whalebone and the stays themselves were made by men in the first half of the century, as it required male strength to work the whalebone. As the stiff-bodied gowns became limited to court wear, the couturières took over the job of making all gowns and the lighter stays that were worn in the second half of the century; in 1776 they were allowed to make stays, corsets and paniers, and after 1789 all restrictions were lifted. Roughly the same pattern occurred in England (although dress-makers seem to have had little training), with men making the boned bodices until the boning became lighter, but with women, from the earliest period, making the court mantuas, because they were not boned; throughout the century, however, tailors kept the privilege of making female riding habits, which was not surprising, based as they were on the masculine suit.

From the second half of the eighteenth century, with the diminution of the size and richness of the fabric design, the trimming came to be all important, which was when the *marchands de modes* (men and women) came into their own.[34] An offshoot of the mercers' guild, they supplied and arranged the ribbons, lace and other forms of trimmings on gowns and hats (the latter becoming highly complicated confections by the 1770s), and supplied also articles of dress that did not require fitting, such as mantles and scarves; everything 'qui sert à la parure et au luxe' (which is at the service of ornament and luxury), according to the *Encyclopédie* (1765), was supplied by the *marchands de modes*, and in some cases they took over the work of the couturière, although in theory the dress was fitted by the dress-maker and then sent to the modiste for the trimmings. Much of the credit for this successful appropriation by the modiste was owing to the greatest *marchand de modes* of all, Rose Bertin, whose flair for publicity and ability to catch the popular mood made her the Ministre de la Mode in Paris.

Born in 1747 in Abbeville, Bertin came to Paris aged sixteen to work for a milliner. Her early achievements in designing toilettes for such leaders of fashion as the duchesse de Chartres encouraged her to open her own establishment in 1770, the Grand Mogul, in the rue Saint-Honoré, from where she furnished some of the dresses offered to the new Dauphine, Marie Antoinette. She was actually introduced to the Dauphine, probably by the royal hairdresser Léonard, in 1772 and soon became the most fashionable modiste in Paris. Much of her success was in devising witty and topical items for her royal and aristocratic clientèle. In 1774, the new king, Louis XVI, was vaccinated and immediately Rose made a headdress, a 'pouf à l'innoculation',[35] incorporating a rising sun and an olive tree laden with fruit round which a serpent, representing Aesculapius, the god of medicine, was entwined. The success of Beaumarchais's play *The Marriage of Figaro* (first performed in 1784) inspired Rose to offer a dress *à la Suzanne*, comprising a tight-fitting bodice with a fichu worn with a white skirt and apron (a fashionable version of the tasteful dress of a lady's maid), and a *toque à la Suzanne* with white feathers and ribbons.

By the 1780s, even royalty felt flattered to be accepted as Bertin customers; travelling to Europe in 1782 under the name of the comtesse du Nord, the Grand Duchess of Russia bought from Rose Bertin a number of dresses including, according to the Baroness d'Oberkirch, one of silk brocaded with velvet flowers with an overskirt of lace interwoven with gold.[36] The baroness herself was given in May of that year a preview of the thirty or so headdresses which Rose had designed for that month; such was the fickleness of public taste that the fashionable modiste had always to be a step ahead of the current whim.

The importance of the *marchands de modes* was recognized in the reform carried through in 1776 by Louis XVI, when the out-of-date guild system was replaced by various corporations of arts and trades, among which was a new corporation called the Marchands de Modes, who were to be allowed to make court dresses (previously a male preserve) and to play a greater part in making ordinary dresses. Rose Bertin was made Master of the Corporation for the first year of its existence and by virtue of this office dressed *la grande Pandora* for its journeys to the courts of Europe.

Rose Bertin's fame and fortune reached their peak in the mid-1780s; from then on the fortunes of the queen, bound up with those of Bertin, were on the decline. Not only were the relative simplicities of the more tailored English styles forcing out some of the more frivolous excesses of the French fashions (the Anglo-French commercial treaty of 1786 allowed great increases in imported English fabrics), but the queen was at last forced to see the financial abyss looming and had to retrench on her expenses: she was allowed only 120,000 livres a year, but in one year, 1786, she had spent 272,000 livres, a considerable proportion of that finding its way to Rose Bertin. Although Bertin continued to supply the queen, even in her imprisonment in the Temple during the revolutionary years, the great days were over. However, like the Vicar of Bray, Bertin was a survivor under changing regimes; she spent the early years of the Revolution supplying both aristocrats and republican sympathizers from her new shop in the rue de Richelieu, but she was prudent enough to have a business in London which she visited during the Terror and from where she sent out her fashion doll.

Rose Bertin was not the only modiste working for the French court and aristocracy; other names included a Mlle Mouillard (who seems to have worked for the royal children), a Mme Pompey and a M. Beaulard, who was known principally for a coiffure of his own invention, called *à ressort* or *à la grand'mère*, a bonnet fitted with springs so that the towering edifices of the 1770s and '80s could be lowered as occasion demanded.[37]

Mme Eloffe was another fashionable modiste working for the queen; her account book, dating from 1787 to 1790, demonstrates the simpler royal tastes for 'des robes de lingerie, de satin ou de taffetas de Florence de diverses couleurs', in contrast to the highly elaborate court presentation gowns. Her clients included the aristocracy as well as artistic and literary ladies such as Vigée-Lebrun and Madame de Staël – she even had the notorious Chevalier d'Eon as a customer. Mme Eloffe was also one of the *couturières lingères* to the queen, although the distinction between the goods supplied by the *marchand de modes* and those made by the *lingère* is not at all clear for both dealt with lace and fine linen. According to de Garsault's *L'Art de la Lingerie* (1771), the *lingère* supplied the fabric and made the garments which were her speciality, such as shifts, shirts, caps and mourning linen for coifs, weepers and so on. Some of the best linen came from Holland, and linen from all over the Netherlands was sent to Haarlem to be bleached. Cotton was supplied by the *lingère*, in particular for men's shirts and children's clothing, and so was the fine muslin from India which was fashionable not only for peignoirs and mantles, but increasingly in the early 1770s for dresses. Linen laces were sold by the *lingère*, but not the gold or silver laces which were sold by weight in specialist shops.

44 F.-A. de Garsault, 'La Boutique d'une Lingère', from *L'Art de la Lingerie*, 1771

The seated customer is shown bolts of linen by smartly dressed assistants, while on the right one of the *couturière lingère's* apprentices cuts out a chemise.

45 Detail of pl. 44

A great proportion of the work of the *couturière lingère* revolved around trousseaus and layettes. Items such as chemises, sleeve ruffles, pockets, peignoirs and caps were supplied by the dozen to the bride; in addition the *lingère* supplied the linen and lace trimmings for the stays and for the *corsets de nuit* (lightly boned stays worn at night) as well as the fine embroidered *manteaux de lit*. Although lace was in the last quarter of the century no longer fashionable for the trimming of caps and sleeve ruffles (except for court dress), it continued to decorate night wear, the shoulder mantles worn by women in their boudoirs and the fine cottons and linens that were used for informal dresses. When in 1787 the marquise de La Tour du Pin was married, her trousseau, costing 45,000 livres,[38] consisted mainly of linen, lace and muslin gowns, and in the same year the bride of the baron de Montmorency spent, according to an English traveller, Henry Swinburne, £25,000 on her trousseau which included a hundred dozen shifts.

The layette had to be prepared as soon as the bride married; again, a fashionable mother-to-be ordered by the dozen her *chemises de couches*, open in front for feeding the baby, and numbers of muslin gowns and *manteaux de lit* for the period of convalescence.

46 After G. Morland, *The Coquette at her Toilet*, 1780s

This engraving shows a fashionable modiste in a printed cotton ensemble and black silk hooded scarf, showing a newly designed muslin cap to an interested customer. Such visits were an essential part of the morning toilette.

The
COQUETTE
at her
TOILET.

Fine linen and lace demonstrated taste and wealth; the best lace came from the Austrian Netherlands and French Flanders, and travellers in those areas were often commissioned to bring back lace for their friends and relatives. Lady Mary Coke in 1767, at Spa, the fashionable watering place in the Austrian Netherlands, bought 'two . . . sutes of lace & a little Cloke of Brusselles lace'; a complete suit of lace comprised a cap (with optional lappets), ruffles and neckwear. Lady Mary also ordered eight guineas' worth of Holland for shifts. These would have been made up probably by her personal maid, for Lady Mary's ideas of grandeur would have precluded herself from this task.[40] It was, however, customary for well-born ladies of the upper classes to make some of their own everyday underwear and men's shirts; the latter were either plain or ruffled, and made by the dozen. Linen was usually bought in large quantities for the needs of the household, one of the tasks of young girls being to sew shirts and shifts.

In England there were less strict demarcation lines between suppliers of services and goods. The English equivalent of the *marchand de modes* was the milliner, who provided linen and lace and also every conceivable kind of made-up accessory, as described by the *London Tradesman* (1747):

> The Milliner is concerned in making and providing the Ladies with Linen of all sorts, fit for Wearing Apparel, from the Holland Smock to the Tippet and Commode . . . the Milliner furnishes them with Holland, Cambrick, Lawn and Lace of all sorts and makes these Materials into Smocks, Aprons, Tippits, Handkerchiefs, Neckaties, Ruffles, Mobs, Caps, Dressed-Heads with as many Etceteras as would reach from Charing-Cross to the Royal Exchange.
>
> They make up Cloaks, Manteels, Mantelets, Cheens and Capucheens, of Silk, Velvet plain or brocaded and trim them with Silver and Gold Lace or Black Lace. They make up and sell Hats, Hoods, and Caps of all Sorts and Materials; they find them in Gloves, Muffs and Ribbons; they sell quilted Petticoats and Hoops of all Sizes . . . The Milliner . . . imports new Whims from Paris every Post . . . The most noted of them keep an Agent at Paris, who have nothing else to do but watch the Motions of the Fashions, and procure Intelligence of their Changes.[41]

Some provincial milliners also provided a making-up service for the fabrics sold in their shops.[42]

In the first half of the eighteenth century in particular, the stay-maker was crucial to the fashionable tightly girt shape; this was usually a man (although 'Girls of Strength' could, according to the *London Tradesman*, be successful at making hooped petticoats) who 'takes the Lady's Shape as nicely as he can; if it is natural, and where it is not, he supplies the Deficiency; then he cuts out the Tabby and Canvas by the Shape in Quarters, which are given out to Women to be stitched'.[43] Usually a woman's measurements would be available at her dressmakers, but where the stay-maker 'is obliged by Art to mend a crooked Shape, to bolster up a fallen Hip or distorted Shoulder', he would usually, with whalebone bought from the haberdasher, visit her in her home. Specialized tradesmen were also needed at every court; they sold the quality 'Gold and Silver Lace, Gold and Silver Buttons, Shapes for Waistcoats, Lace and Network for Robeings and Women's Petticoats, Fringes, Bugles, Spangles, Plates for Embroidery . . . Gold and Silver Wire',[44] which gilded the lily of fashionable formal dress for most of the eighteenth century.

Professional embroiderers were needed at every court. They provided embroidery not only of gold and silver and silk, but coloured spangles, chenille, wool and even fur. For the grandest occasions precious stones were embroidered onto fabrics; in Charles Germain de Saint-Aubin's *L'Art du*

47 N. Dupin after P.-T. Le Clère, '*Tailleur costumier essayant un cor à la mode*', 1778, from the *Gallerie des Modes*

The fitting of such whaleboned corsets, themselves often works of engineering, seems to have required scrupulous attention from the stay-maker.

TAILLEUR COSTUMIER ESSAYANT UN COR A LA MODE.
Il est vêtu d'un habit noisette à collet noir de velours, deux boutonières d'or, les boutons et boutonières de l'habit de même, une veste de tricot cerise avec une trésse d'or, culotte de velours noir, et bas de soie gris. la jeune personne n'a qu'un simple jupon et des bas blancs, et son cor couvert de batiste teinte en jaune.

Brodeur (1770) the coat worn by the Dauphin for his wedding that year was embroidered with diamonds and that of the comte de Provence included opals in the border.[45] For the arrival in 1722 of the Infanta of Spain as his future bride (though the wedding never took place) the young king, Louis XV, held a ball at the Tuileries at which guests dressed in cloth of gold or silver with embroidery to match;[46] the French were famed for the quality of their fine embroidery, their guild going back to the thirteenth century. Saint-Aubin claimed that after the French, the embroidery produced at Vienna was the next best, much of it made in the convents.

On a smaller scale, embroideresses worked for the English court; fine embroidery, *opus anglicanum*, had been an English art since at least the fourteenth century. Some of their work was recorded by Mrs Delany; at court in 1740 she admired the embroidery on the Duchess of Bedford's petticoat: 'the pattern was festoons of shells, coral, corn, cornflowers and sea-weeds, everything in different works of gold and silver except the flowers and coral'.[47]

48 P. Sandby, *A Sailor selling Stockings*, 1760

A sailor stands before a slop-shop where a number of ready-made articles of clothing could be purchased.

Apart from the highly professional work of the court and trade embroiderers, much embroidery was done by ladies of gentle birth. In the first half of the century, embroidery in gold, silver and coloured silks was popular. In the 1740s Frederick the Great's sisters embroidered his waistcoats in silver, and in Richardson's novel *Clarissa* (1748) the heroine had herself embroidered the cuffs and robings of her primrose-coloured gown 'in a running pattern of violets and their leaves; the light in the flowers silver; gold in the leaves' (pls 90 and 91).[48] From the beginning of the century, women had embroidered their silk or linen aprons with white work or coloured silks; in the 1760s, the round tambour frame was introduced from Turkey and eagerly taken up with the vogue for things oriental, the embroidery produced being used to decorate the fine muslin dresses which came to be popular in the late eighteenth century.

It is difficult to assess how many ready-made garments were available to buy in the eighteenth century; they were mainly the more informal items which required less fitting or could more easily be altered. For men, the

49   W. Hogarth (engraved by T. Cook), trade card for Mary and Ann Hogarth

Hogarth's apprenticeship to a silver-plate engraver enabled him to produce the often detailed and intricate shop interiors that were frequently used for trade cards or bill headings in the eighteenth century. This card, dating probably from the late 1720s or early 1730s, indicates the range of ready-made garments that were available to the lower classes of society. Sizing was virtually non-existent and the sewing was fairly crude, but this was a more acceptable alternative, perhaps, and sometimes cheaper than the buying of second-hand clothes.

Mary & Ann Hogarth

from the old Frock-shop the corner of the Long Walk facing the Cloysters, Removed to ȳ Kings Arms joyning to ȳ Little Britain gate, near Long Walk. Sells ȳ best & most Fashionable Ready Made Frocks, suites of Fustian, Ticken & Holland, stript Dimmity & Flanel Wastcoats, blue & canvas Frocks, & bluecoat Boys Dra[...]: Likewise Fustians, Tickens, Hollands, white stript Dimitys, white & stript Flanels in ȳ piece; by Wholefale or Retale, at Reafonable Rates.

most obvious garments to be bought ready-made were nightgowns and banyans; a trade card of 1764 from the Golden Lion in Tavistock Street informed customers that made-up 'Gentlemen's Banyans, Gowns and Caps' were available.[49] For the poorer classes, where fit was not so important but economy of material was, a greater range of ready-made clothes could be bought; the trade card which Hogarth engraved in about 1730 for his sister's shop advertised for sale 'ye best and most Fashionable ready-made Frocks, suites of Fustian, Ticken and Holland, stript Dimmity and Flanel wastcoats, blue and canvas Frocks . . .' (pl. 49). For women, the early unstructured forms of mantua and nightgown were sometimes sold ready-made; the *Spectator* of

9 June 1711 advertised ready-made gowns, several of them 'Japan'd Sattins', possibly mantuas.[50] Lady Mary Wortley Montagu asked her sister in Paris in the 1720s to send her 'a made-up Mantua and petticoat' and 'a nightgown ready-made', but this might have been to avoid the duty on unmade-up materials. As discussed earlier, cloaks and mantles which needed no exact fit were sold at the milliners along with the quilted or hooped petticoats, and, in the second half of the century, loose-fitting sleeved coats, under various names, were advertised for sale in shops known as 'warehouses'.

It is virtually impossible to ascertain the proportion of income spent on clothes, but it is safe to say that clothes were expensive compared with other goods (eighteenth-century newspapers were full of advertisements offering rewards for stolen clothes) and, even at the very top reaches of society, they were meant to last and were often altered.

The amounts spent on clothes by the princes of Europe were astounding. The Empress Elizabeth of Russia seldom wore the same dress twice and, when she died in 1761, had 15,000 dresses in her wardrobe. Marie Antoinette with a yearly allowance of 120,000 livres usually ordered thirty-six formal and semi-formal dresses a year and many more informal gowns. Some indication of the amounts of clothing purchased in the eighteenth century can be gained from trousseaus. The Archduchess Maria Carolina of Austria, who married the King of Naples in 1767, had a trousseau costing 200,000 florins which included ninety-nine dresses made of rich silks with gold and silver lace. According to Henry Swinburne, £5000 was the average spent on a trousseau in France in the 1780s.[51] But many trousseaus were more modest, even those of princes. In 1748, the Countess Palatine, Frederica Sophia of Bayreuth, married Duke Karl Eugène of Württemberg, and her trousseau consisted merely of five rich robes, six informal gowns and two negligées ornamented with Brabant lace.[52] In many cases, the trousseau was the most complete wardrobe any woman possessed, and Mrs Piozzi, in Rome in the 1780s, commented that Italian women had for their weddings 'as many clothes as will last them seven years, for fashions do not change as often here as at London or Paris'.[53] In England a modest trousseau was the rule rather than the exception. When in 1748 Lady Frances Carteret married the Marquis of Tweeddale, Mrs Delany noted that she had six dresses including her wedding dress of flounced white satin with a silver trimming, and in 1756 the very wealthy Mrs Spencer had made 'four negligées, four night-gowns, four mantuas and petticoats'[54] – a very large number of clothes when the average for much of the century was four to six. Four to six also appears to have been the approximate number of suits a gentleman of fashion would order per year, but attendance at court or on occasions of spectacular splendour could double or treble this amount. It is also fair to say that some princes kept a meagre wardrobe; Frederick the Great's 'economy or carelessness or both, induce him to wear his cloaths as long as decency will permit; indeed sometimes rather longer. He is accustomed to order his breeches to be mended and his coat to be pieced under the arms'.[55] When Frederick died in 1786, his wardrobe comprised only some fur-lined cloaks, old uniforms and thirteen shirts and it was sold for 400 thalers to a Jewish clothes dealer. And in the 1760s, an English visitor noted that the Duke Frederick II of Mecklenburg-Schwerin 'has seldom more than one suit in wear throughout the year'.[56]

This attitude may explain why there are relatively few male items of clothing in museums; where suits exist they do so in many cases without the breeches, which wore out more quickly than the coat or waistcoat. Smollett, visiting Paris in the early 1760s, noticed that the man of fashion changed his suit with the seasons: for spring and autumn he wore camlet trimmed with silver, for summer camlet lined with silk and for winter cloth of velvet laced with gold.[57] Changes occurred, as has been pointed out, not so much in cut but in fabric and decoration, changes more perceptible to contemporary commentators than to us. At about the time when Smollett was pouring scorn on what he considered the foppery of Frenchmen, a French visitor to London, Pierre-Jean Grosley, remarked that 'a mode begins to be out of date at Paris just when it has been introduced at London by some English nobleman. The court and first-rate nobility immediately take it up; it is introduced about St James's by those that ape the manners of the court; and by the time it has reached the city, a contrary mode already prevails at Paris, where the English, bringing with them the obsolete mode, appear like the people of another world.'[58]

Pierre-Jean Grosley here implies that it was only a matter of a few months before fashions changed noticeably, but this was (except for the faddish man of mode) an exaggeration. Small-patterned textiles, the usual wear for men's suits throughout the century, did not date as much as women's dress patterns; although the character of the trimming was all-important, especially in the last quarter of the period when plain suits were judged by the quality of their decoration. William Hickey, who had gone out to India in the late 1760s with a wardrobe of rich silk suits covered in lace, found on his return to England in 1780 that taste had changed. Apart from one 'full suit of beautiful velvet of four colours . . . and two others of those least ornamented with lace'[59] he took them all to the second-hand clothes dealers who gave him 47 guineas – he had originally paid seven times that amount for them.

The relative rapidity of changes in silk designs meant that there was a greater turnover of dresses in the eighteenth century. The fashionable Parisienne, said Smollett, 'must have her taffeties for the summer, her flowered silks for the spring and autumn, her sattins and damasks for winter';[60] Casanova remarked that patterned silk stuffs halved in value after a year. Yet silks were expensive, and so, to give a new appearance to a dress, many were in fact altered in style. This refurbishing was easier later in the century, with the popularity of plain silks and trimmings that could be removed. This happened even at the most exalted levels of society: Madame Eloffe's *Livre-Journal* of the late 1780s listed the many alterations and alternative trimmings to some of the French queen's dresses – in August 1787 alone she re-made the sleeve trimming of a blue satin *lévite*, refurbished a 'robe turque' and retrimmed a *lévite* 'vert glacé violet uni en blonde et gaze' (of green and violet watered silk with blonde [silk lace] and gauze).[61]

One reason for the importance of the trimmings of a gown or suit was that they were tangible signs of wealth that had to be renewed. Silk gauze, for example, could not be washed because it lost its crispness and gold and silver lace tarnished and had to be removed to be sold for melting down. The difficulties of keeping clothes clean were legion and included the hazards of street encounters (the mud thrown up by carriage wheels, the powder scattered by the barber racing along, to name but two) and human wear and tear – Casanova claimed that tinder inserted in the coat under the arm would reduce perspiration,[62] but this does not seem to have been widely used. For women in particular, the shift afforded no real protection for the silk dress with tight sleeves that often rotted under the arms. Grosley in London in the late 1760s found terrible weather (and Londoners intolerant of 'our umbrellas of taffeta or waxed silk') and 'swarms' of shops offering services 'scouring, repairing and new furbishing' clothes ruined by the coal smoke.[63] Woollen clothes were scoured or cleaned with teazels and then pressed; fuller's earth was used to absorb grease from wool and turpentine to remove stains. Another primitive form of dry cleaning was smoking with sulphur; in Smollett's last novel, *Humphry Clinker* (1771), the maid Win Jenkins, given a soiled yellow silk dress by her mistress, was advised by 'Mrs Drab, the manty-maker' that it would 'look very well when it is scowred and smoaked with sulfur'.[64] Light silks could sometimes be washed – Win Jenkins used a mixture of vinegar, urine and stale beer – but they often lost their colour. One way of renewing clothes was to dye them, but this was often respon-

50   W. Hogarth, *The Distressed Poet*, c.1735

The poet, wearing ill-fitting wig and striped morning gown, racks his brains for inspiration, while his wife mends his breeches; her hooded cloak hangs by the door. The stylish milkmaid, with flowers in the straw hat, and yoke over her shoulder, demands to be paid.

sible for rotting silks: in 1759, Martha Washington, wife of the future President of the the United States of America, sent her green sack to be dyed back to its original colour or, if it would not take the dye, then the dress was to be altered into a nightgown.[65] The quality of dyeing improved as the century progressed (and it was easier to dye the fashionable cottons and linens of the 1780s), and specialist dyers set up in major cities. Mark Thornhill Wade set up as a dyer in Soho in 1788 and his records indicate the extent to which people of all classes had their clothes dyed, the most popular colour being black for mourning.[66]

Clothes, if not exactly exchanged freely from one wearer to another, were cherished possessions to be handed on to relatives or friends. It was the custom for the aristocracy to give their clothes to their personal attendants, although these had to be worn altered. One of the perquisites of serving the Queen of France was to receive her cast-off clothes: the *dames d'atours*, the noble ladies of the Bedchamber, were given the court and full dresses, and the *femmes de chambre* were given the undress gowns.[67] These latter were usually sold to the second-hand clothes dealers in Paris, the *fripiers*, some of whom were rich enough to have shops in the rue Saint-Honoré.[68]

Before the manufacture of clothing on a large scale for the mass of society, the part played by the dealer in second-hand clothes was very important.[69] Many cities had a central area devoted to such a trade, convenient for the servants of the rich, who provided much of the stock from their masters and mistresses. In Rome, the streets near the Piazza Navona were where second-hand clothes could be bought. In Paris, the place de Grève, according to Mercier in the 1780s, housed the Fair of the Holy Ghost, which specialized in the selling of women's and children's clothes. Second-hand wigs could be bought at the quai des Morfondus; in London there was a wig market in Rosemary Lane which dealt mainly in stolen wigs – one of the dangers of walking the streets of London, according to John Gay, was that 'sly boys', sitting in baskets on the shoulders of their confederates, would snatch the wigs off passers-by.[70]

In London, the second-hand trade was divided into the poorer clothes sold on the east side of the City and the better quality stuff in Covent Garden and Monmouth Street. Some shops sold a mixture of second-hand and ready-made goods, and some were specialists; the 'slop-shop' sold 'all kinds of Shirts, Jackets, Trousers, and other Wearing Apparel belonging to Sailors, ready made',[71] and other shops in the East End of London did a good trade in 'Negro Cloathing', light, cheap, ready-made clothes for the slave-trade. By the end of the period, in the North and Midlands of England, clubs were formed for providing clothes, promoted by the tradesmen supplying the articles in question, and paid for on a weekly basis – an idea which lasted into the twentieth century in some industrial areas.

For the middle and professional classes, depending on their status and resources, their clothing was recognizably imitative of current fashion, and indeed, the plainness that they cultivated particularly with regard to men's dress in the 1770s and 1780s was to influence fashion in its turn at the end

51 Detail of pl. 36

A cloth dealer measures fabric with a wooden rod; on the right is a second-hand clothes stall.

of the century. All those, both men and women, coming into contact with the upper classes and with sufficient financial resources, attempted to copy fashionable clothing with a mixture of native and imported fabrics, although at some remove and after a time-lag which varied from country to country. Some countries, like England, were more flexible with regard to the occasional crossing of class barriers in dress and foreigners found it difficult, for example, to distinguish serving maids from their mistresses. In France, too, the shop girls attracted admiration in their inexpensive versions of fashionable dress and the American Abigail Adams, wife of John Adams, the second President of the United States, visiting Paris in 1784, commented that the mantua-maker would appear in a silk gown and petticoat even if she lived up five flights of stairs and ate only bread and water.[72]

For the majority of the population, reliance had to be placed on locally produced stuffs for clothing, for imported materials were prohibitive in price given the average wage. In the American colonies, for example, during the wars of Independence, Mrs Adams noted that while a labourer earned 9 dollars a day, anything other than the cheapest homespun cloths could not be bought: imported linens cost 20 dollars a yard, ordinary calicoes were at 30 and 40 dollars and the fine English broadcloths could cost as much as £40 a yard.[73]

Sir Frederic Eden, in the first real analysis of poverty in England, *The State of the Poor* (1797), declared that there were considerable differences between the rural and the urban poor, and between north and south. In the north of England he claimed that most articles of dress were made in the home, of locally woven materials; this was a continuation of the custom noted by Defoe in the early eighteenth century when he found nearly every house in some of the Yorkshire villages such as Halifax weaving their own kersey or shalloon. The custom of wearing home-made stuff was not, in fact, limited to the lowest classes: in 1740, Richardson's heroine Pamela (considerably chastened after her attempts at gentility had only encouraged the advances of Mr B.) decided to return home to her parents. She 'bought of Farmer Nichol's wife and daughters a good sad-coloured stuff, of their own spinning, enough to make me a gown and two petticoats',[74] and some years later, Mrs Delany found a poor clergyman using the fleeces given to him by his parishioners to clothe himself and his family. This clergyman's customary dress (when at home) was 'a coarse blue frock trimmed with black horn buttons, a checked shirt, a leather strap about his neck for a stock, a coarse apron, and a pair of great heavy wooden-soled shoes plated with iron to preserve them'.[75] For the poor, colours were usually dark for economy, very often the natural greyish-brown of woollen mixture cloths, and the white linen was replaced by the more practical checked or coloured shirts. Visitors to Spain and Portugal noted the almost universal dark brown linen/woollen cloths worn by the poor; much of this was woven in the houses of correction in the major cities such as Barcelona.

The stuffs woven and worn by the rural poor, either in their homes or by itinerant weavers, were usually of hard-wearing but coarse quality, pro-

52   Attributed to B. Nebot, *The Curds and Whey Seller, c.*1730

This unusual painting shows a seller of curds and whey sitting by the Little Conduit in Cheapside. As a contrast to the blackened and ragged costume of the chimney sweep (notice particularly the functional trousers), the curds and whey seller wears the clean and modestly fashionable dress of the self-respecting working girl. Her skirt is protected by a rough apron and her shoes by pattens; a characteristic of working-class costume is the headscarf tied under the straw hat˙– Boitard's studies of women in Covent Garden in the 1740s shows a similar style (see pl. 55).

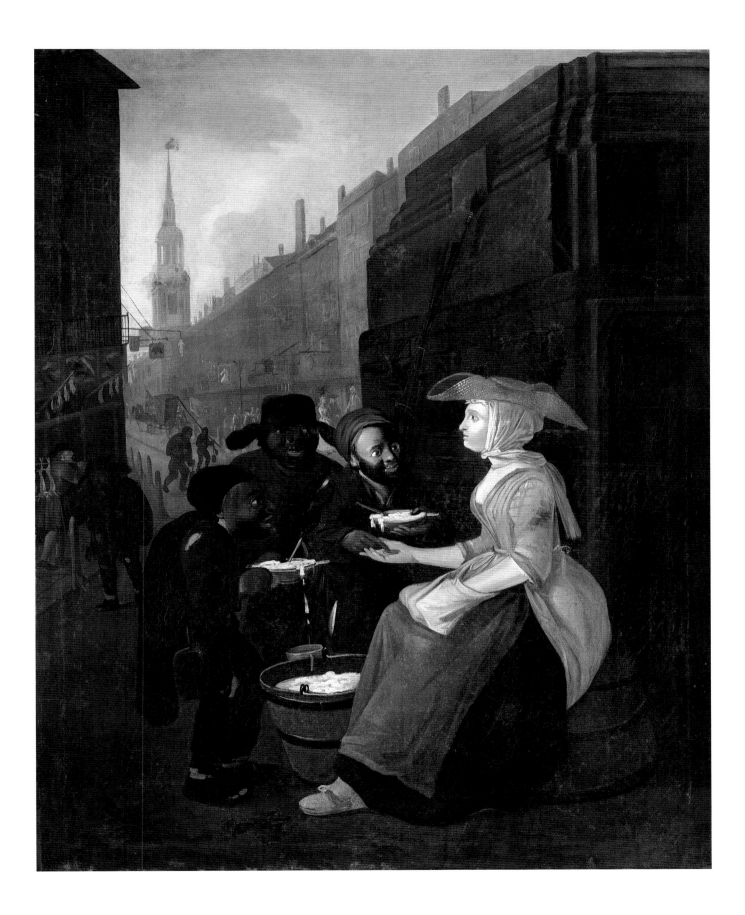

ducing a kind of uniformity of clothing in small communities which was a contrast to the more varied clothing found in towns. Thomas Nugent, in the 1760s at Groningen, found the peasants 'all uniformly clad in dark brown frize coats' and the women in black coarse cloth or linsey-woolsey, a mixture of linen and wool. At about the same time, the Duchess of Northumberland saw poor people near Antwerp, the men in frocks of harden lined with swanskin, striped linsey-woolsey waistcoats and breeches and grey yarn stockings, and the women in jackets made of snuff-coloured frieze and blue petticoats of matching material. While much of the home-made clothing of the rural poor was in shades of buff or brown, some checked and striped fabrics were produced for aprons, handkerchiefs and jackets. In the 1780s, a visitor to Norway found the peasants weaving their own stone-coloured cloth and 'a kind of stuff like a Scotch plaid'.[76] Plaids or checks were widely used for men's morning gowns: they were cheap, did not show wear and tear as would a fashionable silk gown and enabled the suit to be kept for best.[77]

Although, on the whole, men wore clothes that resembled fairly closely fashionable dress, there were some garments such as knee-length tunics, smocks (worn in the country and for heavy work in cities) and trousers that were worn for reasons of practicality. These trousers took various forms according to the climate. In Russia they were sometimes made of fur, usually sheepskin, and worn under 'a short wide Coat without plaits, which wraps over . . . round the waist',[78] or they consisted of bandages of flannel or wool tied round the legs; in the 1780s, an English traveller in Spain saw the Basques in leg-coverings of black wool fastened with tapes. Trousers of linen or cotton were made for hot weather and tropical climates; the inventories of the poor whites living in the southern states of North America, for example, included jackets, waistcoats and trousers of locally produced light cotton and cotton-ade, a heavy coarse twilled cotton fabric widely used for work clothes.[79]

There were immense variations on footwear (or lack of it) for the rural poor across Europe: some wore strips of cloth, others cord sandals and many wore wooden clogs. On the other hand, good-quality footwear, worn even by the poor, was one of the many features noted by visitors to England throughout the eighteenth century. To a Swedish visitor, Pehr Kalm, visiting England in 1748, the country seemed a paradise for women: he was surprised not to see them working in the fields and concluded that they did not work. In fact, England was unique in Europe in that there was no true peasant class, and foreigners who travelled mainly in the south of England found it hard to distinguish between town and country women. According to the writer Marie-Anne Fiquet du Bocage in 1750, 'the poorest country girls drink tea, have bodices of chintz, straw hats upon their heads and scarlet cloaks on their shoulders';[80] this was echoed by Smollett in his novel *Sir Lancelot Greaves* (1762), where similar girls appeared 'in their best apparel, their white hose and clean short dimity petticoats, their gawdy gowns of printed cotton'.[81]

These were probably unmarried girls, possibly domestic servants, with some pretensions to fashionable status. Generally, the range of clothing worn by poor women, particularly in towns, was greater than that worn by men and more subject to regional variations. The basic wardrobe for a working woman comprised a shift, stays, a thick hard-wearing petticoat and a jacket. Francis Place, writing in 1824, recalled the working costume of 'the wives of journeymen tradesmen and shopkeepers' who

> either wore leather stays or what were called full-boned stays . . . These were never washed although worn day by day for years. The wives and grown daughters of tradesmen . . . wore petticoats of camblet lined with dyed linen stuffed with wool and horsehair and quilted. These were also worn day by day till they were rotten . . . Formerly the women young and old were seen emptying their pails or pans at the doors or washing on stools in the street in the summer time without gowns on their backs or handkerchiefs on their necks, their leather stays half-laced and black as the door posts, their black coarse worsted stockings and striped linsey-woolsey petticoats standing alone with dirt.[82]

Since much of the dress was made of non-washable materials, it was important to keep linen − shifts, caps and handkerchiefs − clean, a matter of pride with many working women. A common hazard in the poorer streets of cities was to stumble into ropes of drying linen crossing the streets (this happened to Johann Georg Keysler, a German traveller in Rome in 1729), and it seems to have been a universal practice in hot climates to dry clothes in this way with the sun also acting as a bleach. For many very poor women with only one chemise or handkerchief, cleanliness was a problem; Mercier's *Tableau de Paris* of the 1780s described them rising at 4 a.m. so that the linen could be washed in the river near the Pont Neuf before work.

Over the shift a pair of stays was worn, sometimes of leather and sometimes of canvas boned with reeds (when whalebone could not be afforded). The thick skirt, often quilted or made of flannel, provided warmth and durability; hoops were not usually worn because they wore out the fabric above them. Regional variations showed, particularly in the jackets worn. The fashionable tight-fitting versions, the Italian *carmagnola* and the French *casaquin*, were comfortable and attractive and made of a variety of materials; similar tight-fitting padded jackets were worn in the north of Europe. A very popular working jacket in the second half of the century was the 'caraco' of three-quarter length and made tight-waisted or with a loose sack-back. A version of this mid-thigh jacket called the 'short-gown' had a cross-over front and was perhaps the most usual working jacket, deriving possibly from the informal fur- or fabric-lined Dutch short gowns of the late seventeenth century. With the Dutch and German immigrants it came to North America,[83] the most popular fabrics being linens and cottons in checks and stripes, and the printed calicoes including the blue resist prints called 'indianas' in the Spanish areas, possibly denoting an oriental design origin. With such wrapover gowns women wore aprons, the colour and fabric denoting status: white linen for upper servants, blue or brown sacking or similar coarse material for those involved in hard, physical work. The studies made by

53 After E. Bouchardon, 'La Balayeuse', 1738, from *Les Cris de Paris* (third series)

The caraco with loose sack-back, worn with a striped skirt of mixed stuff, and with a coarse apron pinned over the bodice, forms almost a kind of working-class uniform in France.

54 B. Bellotto, *View of the Castle of Königstein from the South* (detail), *c.*1756–8

As well as the clothes lines familiar to us, it was a well-established practice to lay linen flat on the grass where it could be bleached by the sun.

Louis-Philippe Boitard of the working women in Covent Garden in the 1740s show that for really menial work there could be little pretence at any fashionable style; women wore scarves tied under hats, padded linen rolls to carry head loads, short skirts with patterned aprons and even cast-off male clothing such as coats and heavy leather shoes (pl. 55).

For all wage-earners, clothing took a considerable proportion of their income. At the end of our period in England, the average weekly wage for a labourer was around 10*s.* to 15*s.*; women could earn as little as 3*s.* per week for the poorest domestic work. Eden found that the prices paid for second-hand clothes were high in relation to income – 13s. for a 'good foul weather coat' which would last two years, stout breeches to last one year at 3s. 9d., and a shirt of dowlas (a strong cotton) cost 4s. 6d.; for women, a common stuff gown cost 6s. 6d., a linsey-woolsey petticoat 4s. 6d., the cheapest kind of cloak which would last two years also cost 4s. 6d. and a pair of stays lasting six years were 6s..[84]

Those really poor, described by Defoe as 'the miserable that really pinch and suffer want', often wore several layers of clothing both to keep warm and to keep all their hard-earned wardrobe together. In Richard Cobb's survey of the clothing worn by suicides in Paris as recorded by the Basse-Geôle de la Seine for the late 1790s, he found this particularly applied to men; they wore as many as three pairs of breeches or trousers and several waistcoats. The suit was rarely mentioned, being an item beyond the reach of the really poor, their clothing gathered as it was item by item from the second-hand stalls.[85]

In England, the beginnings of the Industrial Revolution ensured the glimmerings of improvement in the clothing worn by the poor classes at the end of the eighteenth century. A series of inventions in the 1780s, based on earlier experiments, rendered possible the large-scale production of textiles; developments in the production of cotton in particular, fostered by colonial trade, made cheap printed and plain materials available to a wider section of society. According to Francis Place, a life-long advocate of better conditions for working people, writing in the early nineteenth century, the great increase in the use of such washable cloths contributed to greater health and longevity. They were cheaper than the second-hand clothes, most of which 'are now sent abroad to Holland and Germany and some few to North America'. Few were needed in the independent United States, for the new inventions, very often brought over by English entrepreneurs, were enthusiastically taken up to make the country virtually self-sufficient in all but the most expensive fabrics such as high-quality silks and wools.

3 Wider Europe

This is the utility of travelling, when by contracting a familiarity at
any place, you get into the inside of it, and see it in its undress. That
is the only way of knowing the customs, the manners, and all the little
characteristical peculiarities that distinguish one place from another.

Lord Chesterfield

So far, this study has focused largely on fashions in France and
England, where the main factor in their introduction was the working of
a completely free market in which no sumptuary legislation determined the
clothes that people could or could not wear. Such countries, where fashion
was a strong impulse, had long been unified nation states, with growing
urbanization and a central, authoritative fashion centre. In other European
countries, with less cohesive political structures or more recent political and
social unity, a greater variety of taste and culture was to be found. Goethe,
a townsman himself and a product of a century in which uniformity was
something of an ideal, deplored the individualism that he found in the
German states with their lack of what he called a 'general culture' – that is,
uniformity of taste allied to a breadth of outlook which he found admirable
in France and England.

Although Europe was still fundamentally rural, with few cities containing
more than 100,000 inhabitants and all but the greatest and wealthiest living
very parochial lives, a closer analysis reveals a multitude of societies including the tight-knit and still essentially medieval guild-dominated cities of some
areas of Italy and Germany; the expanding capitals like Paris and London;
the huge, feudal estates in eastern Europe; and tiny village communities regulating their lives by the strength of unwritten traditions. Whether in the man-
agement of the agrarian serfdom of much of Russia, the Balkans, southern
Spain and southern Italy, the infant democracy of the English House of
Commons or the rule of patrician merchant oligarchies in German or Italian
city states, all societies were governed by small groups of men (and sometimes women) interlinked by family relationships and personal loyalties.

Even in a relatively advanced industrial society like that of England, town
wear differed to some extent from that worn in the country. This difference
was magnified many times over in the remote areas of, say, central Europe
or any place where comparatively static regional peasant costume existed
alongside cities in which French and English fashions were increasingly the
norm. It is impossible to discuss dress in the eighteenth century without
giving at least a token recognition to the great varieties of dress that lie

56   Detail of pl. 72

This detail from Bayeu's design for a
tapestry cartoon shows Spanish men
dressed mainly in the French style,
although on the right one man wears the
traditional capacious Spanish cloak. The
women wear the *mantilla*, which serves, as
an English visitor said, as a hood, cloak
and veil.

89

57 J. Chapman and P.-J. de Loutherbourg, *The Interior of the Royal Exchange*, London, 1777

This was a meeting place for merchants from all over Europe and the East; those characterized by their costume include, on the right, a Jewish merchant with beard and huge cloak; in the centre, a Pole with knee-length caftan and trousers; and on the left, in the background, a Dutchman with round, baggy breeches and hands in his pockets.

outside the general chronology of high fashion, although it is emphasized that only a small fraction of the range of dress seen at any one time in Europe can be mentioned in a book of this extent.

At the top level of society, people attempted on the whole to wear fashionable clothing derived from France, although this was in many cases in opposition to the desire of princes who wished to protect infant textile industries from foreign competition and their subjects from the supposedly corrupting influences of foreign clothing. In Germany, there were a small number of important states, like Saxony, where rulers followed French tastes, magnificently embellishing their courts. At the other extreme, in Prussia, Frederick William I from the time of his accession in 1713 began to put into practice his views on martial simplicity in clothing. In fact, the needs of the army were put first; the export of wool was prohibited so that the country could clothe its soldiers, and by 1725 Prussia was even exporting the woollen cloth that they made to the Russian army (a monopoly that had once belonged to the English). This could be achieved because regulations were

58 Anon., *Völkertafel: Kurze Beschreibung der In Europe Befintlichen Völckern Und Ihren Aigenschafften*, late eighteenth century

This illustrated table, dating from the end of the eighteenth century, lists the qualities as well as the costume of various countries in Europe. The French, not surprisingly, are the most fashionable, a startling contrast to the archaically dressed Spaniard still in trunk hose, ruff and round feathered hat.

put into effect, as Frederick the Great tells us in his memoirs, limiting the amount of cloth in a coat to three yards. The king himself would have found this no hardship, for he was 'a decided enemy to gaudy dresses and new fashions; and while yet a boy, he had vowed vengeance against French wigs and gold brocade dresses, so they still continue to be objects of his displeasure'. This attitude was derived partly from a reaction against the Francophile tastes of his father, but also from a desire for economy; his wife and daughters commonly wore locally produced serge on all but the grandest occasions. The king himself 'till 1719 . . . dressed sometimes in plain clothes, at others in uniform; in the following years he was scarcely ever seen but in the uniform of Colonel of the regiment of Potsdam grenadiers, blue turned up with red, yellow waistcoat and breeches, white linen gaiters with brass buttons and square toed shoes. Everything was made to fit very tight.'[1] Such

Namen	Spanier.	Frantzoß.	Wälisch.	Teutscher.	Engerländer.	Schwöd.	Poläck.	Unger.	Mußkawith.	Türk oder Griech.
Sitten	Hochmüttig	Leichtsinig	Hinderhaltig	Offenherzig	Wohl Gestalt	Stark und Groß	Bäurisch	Untreÿ	boßhafft	Wie das Abrißweter
Natur Und Eigenschaft	Wunderbarlich	Selbselig Und gesprächig	Eifersichtig	Ganz Gut	Lieb-reich	Graus-sam	Nochwilder	AllerGraussambst	Gut Ungerisch	Ein Lung Teüfel
Verstand	Klug und Weiß	Fürsichtig	scharffsinig	Witzig	Immuthig	Hartnätig	Gering Liechtent	Nochweniger	Gar Nichts	Oben Aluß
Anneigung deren Eigenschaften	Männlich	Kindisch	Wie iederwill	Über Allmit	Weiblich	Unerkendlich	Mittlmässig	Bluthbegirig	Unentlichkrob	Zärt-lich
Wissen-schaft	schrifftgelehrt	In Kriegsachen	Geistlichen Rechte	Weltlichen Rechte	Well Weis	In Freuen Künsten	In Underschidlichen sprachen	In Ladeinischersprach	In Kriechischersprache	Ein solcher Bolliticus
Tracht der Klaidung	Ehrbaar	Unbeständig	Ehrsam	Macht alles Nach	auf französische art	Von Löder	Lang Röckig	Viel Färbig	Mit böltzen	auf Weiber Art
Untugent	Hoffärtig	Betrügerisch	Geissichtig	Verschwenderisch	Unruhig	Über Glauberisch	Braller	Veräther	GarUnrätherisch	noch Veräterischer
Lieben	Ehrlob und Rum	Den Krieg	Das Gold	Den Trunck	Die Wohllust	Köstlichespeisen	Den Adl	Die Aufruhe	Den Brügl	Selbst eigne Lieb
Krankheiten	Verstopfung	An Ligner	An bösser seuch	An bodogrä	Der schwindsucht	Der Wassersucht	Den durchbruch	An der freis	An Reichen	An Schwachheit
Ihr Land	Ist fruchtbar	Wohlgearbeith	Tröstlich Und Wohllistig	Gut	Fruchtbaar	Bergig	Waldich	Und goltReich	Voller Eiß	Ein Liebreiches
Krigs Tugende	Groß Müthig	Arg listig	Fürsichtig	Unüberwindlich	Ein See Held	Unverzagt	In Gestimt	Aufrirerisch	Miesamb	Gar faul
Gottesdienst	Der aller beste	Gut	Etwas besser	Noch Undächtiger	Berenderlich Wie der Mond	Eifrig im Glauben	Glaubt Allerleÿ	Unmüessig	Ein Abtriniger	Zwen einsolchen
Erkennen für Ihren herrn	Einen Monarchen	Eine König	Einen Bäterärch	Einen Käiser	bald den bald jene	Freÿe Herrschaft	Einen Erwelden	Einen Unbeliebigen	Einen Freimiligen	Ein Thiran
Haben Überfluß	An Früchten	An Waren	An Wein	An Geträid	An sich Weid	An Ärtz Kruben	An Böltzwerch	In Allen	An Immen	Undweichensachen
die Zeit Verdreiben	Mit Spillen	Mit betrügen	Mit schwätzen	Mit Trincken	Mit Arbeiten	Mit Essen	Mit zancken	Mit Miessigehen	Mit schlaffen	Mit Kränkeln
Vergleichung Mit denen Thiren	Ein Elöfanthen	Ein Fuchsen	Einen Luchsen	Einen Löben	Einen Pferd	Einen Ochsen	Einen Bern	Einen Wolffen	Ein Esel	Einer Katz
Ihr Leben Ende	In Böth	In Krieg	In Kloster	In Wein	In Wasser	Auf der Erd	Im stall	beÿm sawel	In schnee	In betrug

59 J.-A. Rossmässler, *Habillemens de Leipsic*, early 1780s

Leipzig was a centre of fashion in the eighteenth century so it is not surprising to find French influence in formal dress, and England perhaps being the inspiration for the walking costume at the bottom.

was his hatred of anything French that when in the summer of 1730 the Crown Prince of Prussia made an abortive attempt to flee the country, the king, reported the English ambassador, sent him two suits cut in the French style 'to remind the Prince of his intended absconding to France which had rendered him unworthy to wear the uniform of a Prussian officer'. After a reconciliation the next year the king signalled his forgiveness by ordering his son a coat made in the Prussian style, which was, presumably, the very tight fit with military trimmings notably influenced by army uniform.[2] On state occasions, female members of the royal family were embarrassed at the lack of grandeur at court; when in 1728 the King of Poland and Elector of Saxony came with a magnificent entourage to seek the hand in marriage of the Princess Royal of Prussia, the intended bride was ashamed at the regimental air given by the Prussians' short coats which 'could not have served as fig-leaves to our first parents and so strait that they did not move for fear of rending them'.[3]

Although he had infinitely more cultivated tastes, Frederick the Great continued the Prussian practice of wearing uniform on most occasions. A French visitor found him early in his reign awkward in demeanour, unwilling to carry his hat beneath his arm and so used to wearing boots that he found it difficult to walk in shoes;[4] like his father, out of uniform he dressed in dark blue, Boswell finding him in Berlin in 1764 in 'a suit of plain blue serge with a star' – the star was the Prussian order of the Black Eagle.

The Prussian rulers were in a hurry to impose order and uniformity on a fairly recently united and sprawling country, and distinctive regional fashions were not much remarked on by foreign visitors such as Aubry de La Motraye, who noted in 1726 that 'those of some rank go dress'd after the French but in General after the German fashion, the single women wear white that Long Vail which covers the Body from head to Foot. In Winter they wear a kind of short Cloak, such as that which has been since few years brought to Fashion in England, but Linned with Furs as in Poland'.[5] The long, light cloak, covering the head and body like an Arab mantle and dating back to medieval times, was common to many parts of Germany and Holland; Thomas Nugent in Hamburg in 1766 found women of fashion 'generally veiled with black silk like the ladies in Flanders',[6] the veil being worn over their ordinary clothing.

Throughout the eighteenth century, the German states that prospered were the more flexible ones that were able to impose protectionist policies and rely on the skills of immigrant workers, particularly in the textile trades. The range of home-produced textiles in Germany was wide; they included woollen cloth in Prussia, cotton and linen goods in many south German cities and silk production at Krefeld, Berlin and Hamburg. Nugent noted on a visit to Hamburg that there was a flourishing trade in the weaving of velvets, brocades and damasks and in the manufacture of gold and silver lace. He found that the quality of the goods was high, but in his travels through a number of the German states he found that rich silks were still imported from France (though forbidden in Austria and Prussia)[7] due to 'the passion

60 P. Mercier, *A Hanoverian Party on a Terrace*, 1725

The participants display stiff English-influenced elegance in their dress, tightly boned mantuas for the women, and for the men plain, untrimmed suits and rather square, ponderous periwigs.

the German ladies have for French modes'. To be 'französich gekleidet' was the fashionable ideal for women; for the men, Nugent noted that 'those that live anything tolerably decent, would not go without English stuffs and cali-mancoes',[8] although these, too, were forbidden in Austria and Prussia.

At the beginning of the century, foreign visitors noted the effectiveness of sumptuary legislation in the conservative free towns. Lady Mary Wortley Montagu, travelling through Germany on her way to Constantinople in 1716, felt that laws regulating dress prevented 'that Excesse which ruins so many other Citys, and has a more agreable Effect to the Eye of a Stranger than our Fashions'. In Nuremberg, she found that people knew their place and dressed neatly according to it, whereas 'under the Government of absolute Princes' there was no such ease and people tried to dress above their means;

Ein FrauenZimmer im Winter ausgehend
Demoiselle sortant en hiver.

C.P.S.C.M.   I.G.Merz, exc. A.V.

Eine Jungfer so zur Hochzeit gehet

G.F.L.Debrie Excudit. 1749.   I.Filhema sculpsit.
Strasbourgeoise. Fille de Condition
allant aux Noces.

even 'people of Quality' were sometimes 'tawder'd out & beggarly', attempting to follow French fashions beyond their purse.[9] For the ruling burghers in the towns, the self-imposed costume was sometimes a sober version of fashionable dress some years behind the times: a black suit with a short cloak remained almost a uniform for many conservative men in the religious and moral air of many of the north German towns. In some towns, the officials wore black, sometimes trimmed with lace and with a ruff, in styles reminiscent of early-seventeenth-century Spanish costume. Dark colours, of a mixture of imported and local stuffs, characterized the dress of many middle-class women; Goethe, who was brought up in Frankfurt, described the burgher's wife wearing a black dress of English cloth, a brown cloth skirt, a black camlet bodice, a black cotton cape and a crape cap.[10]

Sumptuary laws were designed to identify the lower classes, and women especially, and to keep them subservient. The clothing they wore was kept far behind current fashion – and some of the headdresses in particular were of considerable antiquity – and created a uniformity of dress that appealed to the authorities and critics of fashionable clothing. In Hamburg, Nugent noted that 'the servant maids all wear the same kind of uniform habit consisting of a petticoat and jacket of serge on week-days; and of cloth or slight silk on Sundays; a linnen cap close to their heads and no farther than their ears, with an edging or border of muslin, a linnen or silk handkerchief and they all wear black aprons'.[11]

In the more conservative towns of southern Germany, serving maids' dress was even more old-fashioned. In Ulm, a travelling Berliner, Friedrich Nikolai, found at the end of the century that they wore long pointed bodices trimmed with silver, and with ruffs, but these were increasingly reserved for special occasions such as church-going or christenings.[12] Even patrician ladies sometimes wore regional costume, particularly in those cities that had a long tradition of individual style. In Strasbourg, for example, a former Imperial city but a quasi-autonomous French fief since 1681, many women wore, according to a Hanoverian visitor in 1729, 'rich hats, broad over their Foreheads, and terminating on each Side in a Pick of considerable length' and gowns with a 'Multiplicity of Plaits';[13] these pleated gowns were seen by Goethe when he came to Strasbourg in 1770 but they were only worn by the elderly, French fashions having almost universally triumphed.

In fact, by this time there were only pockets of striking regional costume, kept more as tradition than law (the only sumptuary legislation taking place in the second half of the century was at the smaller courts, limiting the privileges of rank, such as the numbers of liveried servants or the displaying of coats-of-arms); such costumes were noted for their extravagance of decoration or eccentricities of head attire. A characteristic of peasant dress has always been a love of jewellery, in many cases as either portable wealth or dowry, and this often caught the eye of a commentator; in 1719, Pöllnitz, visiting a church in Lower Bavaria, was amazed to find the local girls wearing pearl necklaces and gold chains – rows of gold or silver chains, a German fashion since the sixteenth century, were widely worn in Saxony and Bavaria. It was in Munich, the capital of Bavaria, that Hester Lynch Piozzi saw in 1785 the women wearing a 'stiff gold-stuff cap, as round, and hard and as heavy as an old Japan China bason . . . clapped close round the head, the hair combed smooth out of sight, and a plaited border of lace to it made firm with double-sprigged wire'.[14] This also dated from the sixteenth century, like many regional headdresses; from an even earlier period may have derived the curious headwear seen by Nugent in Lübeck, where the women wore 'a kind of straw bonnet, or rather basket, which projects in such a manner that you cannot see their faces'.[15]

The country in which sumptuary legislation was most successfully imposed was Switzerland; the local authorities in Basel, Berne and Zürich published – on average every four years – 'acts against pride and superfluity in clothing and also other excesses and luxuries'. The main reason was religious: Switzerland had become a nation partly through its religious struggles and the Calvinist church was still a very powerful influence. However, also important was the fierce independence maintained by the Swiss in the face of events in the rest of Europe, which, paradoxically, helped to create a climate tolerant to refugees and the propagation of liberal ideas. In addition, by the middle of the century, the Swiss were large producers of textiles such as cotton, light silks (ribbons were a speciality), wool and linen. The laws encouraged people to wear locally produced linen for headdresses, collars and cuffs instead of imports from the Netherlands.

A typical act was that passed in Berne in 1708, to ban everyone from wearing smooth or flowered velvet, satin or brocatelle, except for official dress; suits made entirely of damask were to be worn only on feast days and Sundays, as were light silk gowns and suit linings. To keep abreast of the current fashion, the 1708 act legislated against the large wigs with high foretops, and those with knotted ends (campaign wigs); wigs of any sort were forbidden to those under twenty. To prevent women wearing the fashionably ornate skirts, frills and falbalas were prohibited, as were mantles decorated with ribbons and lace. Later regulations inevitably focused on hoops, but this was a case in which fashion proved too firmly implanted for the legislators, and they admitted defeat in 1737 by saying that hoops should not be 'too large and wide'.[16]

The success of the laws can be seen in the number of prosecutions: in 1727 in Basel, 210 women were prosecuted – the majority servants who had wished to dress above their station. But the regulations limited also what could be worn by upper-class women, and those fortunate enough to live near the German borders, said Keysler in 1729, '. . . impatiently wait the return of Summer, in order to their visiting Zellerbad or Teinach, Seltze, Embs and other German Spaws, where they may indulge their gay Inclinations, free from the Restraints of the Laws of their Country'.[17]

Fewer cases were reported as the century progressed, but throughout our period, sobriety in dress was the most noted Swiss characteristic. As late as 1789, a Russian visitor to Switzerland found that laws still restricted the wearing of silk, laces and jewellery and French fashions and cosmetics were

Swiss Landschape, to represent the Peasants Dwellings, and Manner of dressing

unknown. In Zürich, the men 'in general wore black coats and the women had a black woollen dress and wore hoods or veils'.[18] The regulations stipulated that black was to be worn by both sexes for church; women were to wear hoods of white linen, but after the middle of the century other forms of headdress made of black gauze or taffeta were to be seen. Servants who came to work in the cities were urged to retain their village dress for as long as possible, and this appears to have been complied with on the part of the women at least. The peasant girls' costume of dark gowns, red petticoats and jackets 'with a great superfluity of buttons' was worn with long plaited hair. Dr John Moore, travelling as tutor to the Duke of Hamilton in the late 1770s, found that the unmarried girls 'value themselves on the length of their hair, which they separate into two divisions and allow to hang at its full length braided with ribbons in the Ramillie fashion. After marriage these tresses are no longer permitted to hang down, but being twisted round the head in spiral lines are fixed at the crown with large silver pins.'[19] Both married and unmarried women wore straw hats decorated with ribbons. Although he found their dress on the whole attractive, except for the 'amazing number' of petticoats bunched up in a high waist, he could not say as much for the men, whose everyday dress consisted of black linen coat and waistcoat and linen breeches 'something like a sailor's trousers, but drawn together in plaits below the knees'[20] – these were virtually the trunk breeches of the late sixteenth century which had remained part of rural male dress along with the 'immense Beards' cultivated by some of the older men.

Outside the main fashion centres of Paris and, to a lesser extent, London, the most important capital city was Vienna, focal point for the varied nations

– the German vassal states, Hungary, Bohemia and (after 1772) Poland – that made up the Habsburg territories and the Holy Roman Empire. With a treasury drained by mercenary alliances and frequent wars, successive rulers legislated to prevent the import of foreign textiles such as English woollen cloths (for there was a flourishing woollen industry, established by Flemish weavers, in Hungary). Foreign silks were also prohibited; a typical statute of 1749 permitted clothing to be worn trimmed with gold and silver lace or braid provided it was made within the boundaries of the Empire. This was limited in 1754 to the upper classes only, but in 1766 Maria Theresa freed all classes from sumptuary legislation. Vienna was itself noted for the quality of its luxury goods like fine embroidery and, by the middle of the century, for fine silks. With the active participation of her son, the future Emperor Joseph II, the Empress Maria Theresa encouraged Italian and then French silk-weavers to work in the capital; the Austrian Florian Zeiss, who had studied in Paris, opened a drawing academy in 1758 in order to teach silk-designers. By 1765, when the revised edition of Jacques Savary des Bruslons's *Dictionnaire de Commerce* was published, silks of all qualities were listed as being produced in Vienna and exported to all areas of the Empire, and also to Turkey and its territories.

The taste within the imperial family was for private simplicity; unless it was a gala day, the empress wore simple dresses, often of Viennese silk, and only black as a widow. Her son Joseph, an admirer of Frederick the Great, preferred a uniform – in his early years that of his regiment of Hungarian hussars and later his own regiment of Light Cavalry. 'At home or on his travels he put on a simple dark-coloured dress-coat; in severe weather a green or dark blue frock-coat with a plain military cocked hat, boots and spurs.'[21] His attempts in the 1780s to achieve a healthy simplicity in women's dress by legislating against tight stays and paniers met with no success.

Within the Holy Roman Empire, Prague and Budapest had the status of semi-capital cities. Visitors commented on the mixture of quasi-fashionable clothing and the oriental elements such as fur trimming which, because of the proximity of Turkish territory, characterized dress at all social levels in central Europe. Lady Mary Wortley Montagu, on a visit to Prague in 1716, found aristocratic ladies imitating Viennese court fashions with high, decorated headdresses, excessively furbelowed petticoats and huge hoops. Later in the century, Nugent found that these ladies had begun to adopt French taste but that 'other women of the better sort wear furred caps like the Grecian women, long clokes with large necks, some of them of sattin lined with taffeta, and petticoats of the same but very short'.[22] In 1786, Mrs Piozzi found ladies attending the opera in Prague cut an odd figure in their 'rich embroidered caps or bright pink and blue satin headdresses, with ermine or sable fronts, a heavy gold tassel hanging down from the left ear'.[23] She found that ladies dressed very richly but wore no powder on their hair.

Hungarian costume, whose popularity and glamorous appeal extended beyond the confines of the country itself, was heavily influenced by Turkish elements. The Hungarian hussar troops had helped to save Vienna from the

64 J.-B. Haussart, 'Hungarian Nobleman in Hussar Costume', from the *Recueil de Cent Estampes Representant differentes Nations du Levant . . .* , 1714

Hongrois 76.

Turks at the end of the seventeenth century, and came to the aid of the new Habsburg ruler Maria Theresa when in 1740 the Austrian territory of Silesia was seized by Frederick the Great. Maria Theresa was also Queen of Hungary; not only was she herself depicted in Hungarian coronation dress, but she also dressed her sons in this costume (see pl. 132). For men, the costume is worth describing in detail, for it was to turn up not only as a popular masquerade dress but also as an influence on informal fashionable clothing.[24] It consisted of tight-fitting trousers with braided seams tucked into boots, a tunic (*dolman*) with a slanting triangular flap below the belt fastened with a twisted sash, and a pelisse (*mente*) lined or edged with fur and with a frogged or tassel fastening. Dressed in this exotic costume, the Hungarian nobility who feature in the large, painted group scenes depicting life at the Viennese court, appear like so many glamorous Hollywood extras.

For the women, the tight-fitting dress, often of the finest French silk, fastening at the front with tiny jewelled buttons, and the tiny embroidered cap, was Turkish in detail. Lady Mary Wortley Montagu early in 1717 found it 'extreme becoming'; a fashionable lady wore 'a Gown of Scarlet Velvet lin'd and fac'd with Sables, made exact to her Shape and the Skirt falling to her Feet. The Sleeves are straight to their Arms and the Stays button'd before with 2 rows of little Buttons of gold, pearl or di'monds. On their Heads they wear a Cap embroder'd with a Tassel of Gold that hangs low on one side, lin'd with sable or some other fine fur.'[25] An alternative style was to wear a sleeveless gown, heavily boned and embroidered on the bodice, laced down the front, showing huge chemise sleeves trimmed with lace and divided into three puffs of material fastened by ribbons. This latter version was more akin to the so-called 'peasant' style of costume with which we are familiar, with its emphasis on the bodice and the decorative shift sleeves. It was a costume much favoured by middle-class women, although the fabrics used were usually not the rich imported stuffs. As in all countries in this area of Europe, the middle class was tiny and of little importance; visitors commented on the gulf between the dress worn by the ruling nobility and that worn by the serfs. Johann Georg Keysler, a German visitor to Hungary in 1730, found that 'the peasants and lower sort of people dress very meanly. Among the latter the men are very proud of a furr'd mantle. Most of the women wear boots, and many of them a long furred gown, and have a kind of shift of a very coarse linen next to their skin, with a girdle round it at the waist. Their head-dress is a piece of white linen with two lappets hanging down behind. Blue is the usual colour worn here by both sexes.'[26]

Nothing much had changed by the time that Nathaniel Wraxall visited Hungary almost fifty years later. He saw that 'few of the women had any covering below the knee except boots', and the postillions who drove him in their 'black sheep skins with the wool outward . . . [had] long moustachios and fur bonnets, [that] gave them the appearance of tartars more than of Europeans'.[27]

Even greater was the disparity noted between the feudal magnates of Poland and the mass of the peasant population, a situation exacerbated by the tragedy of Polish politics (there was an elective monarchy and, for much of the century, a foreign king resident in Dresden). A Polish king, Stanislas Poniatowski, was elected to the throne in 1764. He was a cultivated man with French tastes but his preference for 'idle amusements and Gallantry' (Wraxall's phrase) did not fit him to cope with the anarchic mosaic of different peoples and religions that made up Poland, rendering it an easy prey for gradual dismemberment. Wraxall, visiting Poland in 1778, was appalled by the dirt and poverty of the cities, many of which survived only because of the artificial needs of an extravagant court; there was hardly any middle class, except for a few German merchants in the semi-German cities to the north, like Danzig. He noted also the air of indifferent despair after the First Partition of Poland (1772) which had deprived the country of one third of its territory. He found a semi-primitive country aristocracy 'living in a style almost royal amidst the ruins of their expiring country'; although French fashions were worn, especially at court, many of the nobility wore the national dress and had even tried to pass a law obliging the king to wear it.[28]

The wearing of this national dress was partly a protest at the state of their country and also a part of a long tradition of semi-oriental splendour. For men, the basic garment was a long caftan (*kontusz*) made usually of the striped silks woven near Warsaw. It fastened at the waist with a sash, had

65   D. Chodowiecki, *A Polish Family Scene with a Portrait of the Gräfin Szacka*, 1773

On the left is a good example of patrician Polish national dress, dominated by the caftan (*kontusz*) with its hanging sleeves. The other participants in the scene, including the priest on the far right, wear international fashionable dress.

hanging sleeves and the front edge cut to curve over to one side and was worn over tight trousers. Like the Hungarian nobility, the Poles shaved their heads and wore large moustaches (a Turkish mode which made them almost unique in Europe, where facial hair was very much the exception). Wraxall, again on the Polish gentleman, found: 'His head, which he shaves, is covered with a large fur bonnet. He wears a sort of hussar's dress with long hanging sleeves, a sabre that reaches to the ground, and boots. His enormous moustachios complete the fierce singularity of his figure.'[29] The powerful magnates with their retinues of servants, some in Turkish caftans with hundreds of silver buttons and some in embroidered Hungarian dolmans, were typified in the person of Karol Radziwill, Prince Palatine of Vilna, who wore

> a short pomegranate-coloured kontusz, with vest and trimmings of an amaranth hue, a silver girdle embroidered with amaranths, a sword on a sheath of costly fur, yellow boots soled with silver, the whole surmounted by a mantle (zupan) of thick grey cloth lined with fur, and fastened round the neck by a silver Radziwill eagle. His roomy pantaloons were fastened round his body by a sort of apron, so that his kontusz might not be dirtied.

Stuck at the back of his shaven head, and leaving his ears uncovered in the coldest weather, was a carmine cap trimmed with black lambskin. He wore felt shoes over his boots.[30]

Wraxall found the women's long gowns edged with fur and tied round the waist with a sash or girdle 'something Asiatic . . . which reminds me of Greek or Turkish, more than French or German modes'.[31] This dress, often with short fur-trimmed oversleeves and decorated with frogging and tassels, was a fashionable *déshabillé* with Austrian and German princesses through the century, and in the last quarter began to influence French and English modes.

In contrast to the deliberate adoption in Poland of national dress to preserve independence, if we turn to Russia in the early eighteenth century the opposite is the case: Peter the Great forced his subjects to wear the western clothes he had seen on his travels and which he himself wore. His edicts or *ukases* against the wearing of Russian dress dated from the end of the seventeenth century, when the 'general Habit which the Russes used to wear was a long Vestment hanging down to the middle of the Small of their Legs, gathered and laid in pleats upon their Hips, little differing from the Habit of Womens Petticoats'.[32] This description comes from the account of *The State of Russia under the Present Czar* (1716) by Captain John Perry, who worked in Peter the Great's service as a naval engineer; he was one of that hardy band of foreign experts who were employed in Russia throughout the eighteenth century to help bring the country into the modern world, and whose published accounts of their experiences in a country regarded as a kind of barbaric *ultima Thule* found ready ears in a Europe fascinated by the immensity of contrasts to be found within that huge empire. The nobility and the small middle class, said Perry, were ordered to wear 'handsome Cloaths made after the English Fashion, and to appear with Gold and Silver Trimming, those that could afford it. And next he commanded that a Pattern of Cloaths of the English Fashion should be hung up at all the Gates of the City of Moscow'.[33] Those daring to appear at court or to enter the city in the old-style dress were to have their coats cut off at the knees or to be fined (Peter the Great emphasized his point by mockery: when one of his court jesters married in 1701, the courtiers were made to wear the old-style Russian dress for the crude wedding masquerade, which the Emperor enjoyed). The long beards hanging down to the chest were to be trimmed except for priests and peasants, and those disobeying were to be fined 100 roubles a year. Perry noted that although there was much complaint, most became reconciled to this practice, although he found that some of his workmen kept their shaved-off beards to be buried in.

Peter the Great succeeded only too well in his injunctions to his subjects to adopt 'Gold and Silver Trimming' on their western suits. In 1714 Friedrich Christian Weber, a German traveller in St Petersburg, was turned away from a reception given by a Russian general for wearing a plain untrimmed suit, and in 1732 the English Resident at the Russian court noted that he 'never

LE MARCHAND DE GATEAU.
Dédiée à Mr. Chardin Peintre du Roi Conseiller et Trésorier
de son Académie Royale de Peinture et de Sculpture.
Par son très Humble et très Obéissant Serviteur Le Prince.

Paysanne Moscovitte
dans son Habit simple

66 (*above left*)   Title page from J.-B. Le Prince, *Première Suite de Cris et divers Marchands de Petersbourg et de Moscou*, 1765

Le Prince was in Russia from 1758 to 1763, and the several series of etchings that he produced are accurate records of the costume. Here the peasant buying cakes wears a voluminous shirt and baggy wide trousers which are pushed into fur leg coverings wrapped around with strips of cloth.

saw such heaps of gold and silver lace laid upon cloth, and even gold and silver stuffs, as are seen here',[34] many of the Russian nobles being ruined by the expense of the changing fashions where it was not unusual to pay £200 for a suit. By the end of the reign of Peter, any dislike of the edicts against Russian dress had been overcome, and the nobles were quick to adopt what many considered the excesses of Parisian styles without much taste or elegance. The unsympathetic Lord Macartney laughed at the Russians for their slavish acceptance of French modes or dress and behaviour: '. . . in France it is the etiquette of fashion to begin the spring season at Easter, and to mark it by dress; the imitative Russian does the same and flings off his winter garments whilst the earth is covered with snow . . . At Petersburg a Russ gentleman of any fashion must have a Swiss also, or some tall fellow with a laced belt and hanger, which it seems are the indispensable accoutrements of a Parisian janitor.'[35]

Lord Macartney, whose account of Russia was published in 1767, admitted that the production of textiles had increased enormously since the days of Peter the Great, who had established manufactories for linen and woollen cloth. By the middle of the century, in the reign of the Empress Elizabeth, imported raw silk was woven into 'velvets, paduasoys, tabbies, armazeens' and gold and silver lace was also produced, a sumptuary law of 1740 having failed to restrict this decoration on male clothing.[36]

Sumptuary edicts concentrated on male dress, where it was felt that imperial example needed force to back it up. Peter the Great had established assemblies on the western European model at St Petersburg, where noble ladies, dragged from their almost oriental seclusion into court and social life, could dance, converse and play cards, dressed in English and French fashions. The traditional Russian costume, consisting of a chemise with long, very wide sleeves worn under a sleeveless tunic (*sarafan*) with ornamental front closures and a band-like headdress (*kokoshnik*) of precious stones and gold or silver thread, was described in the early years of the eighteen century by an official of the Austrian embassy:

> their shapes, unimprisoned by stays, are free to grow as nature bids, and are not of so neat and trim figure as those of other Europeans. They wear chemises interwoven with gold all through, the sleeves of which are plaited up in a marvellous way, being light and sometimes ten ells in length . . .
>
> Their outer garments resemble those of Eastern women; they wear a cloak over their tunic. They often dress in handsome silks and furs, and earrings and rings are in general fashion among them. Matrons and widows cover the head with furs of price; maidens only wear a rich band round their forehead and go bareheaded with their locks floating upon their shoulders, and arranged with great elegance in artificial knots.[37]

With certain regional variations, this kind of dress was worn all over Russia by the women in the towns and the more prosperous country women; even aristocratic ladies residing on their estates continued to wear it, for it was only in the towns, Moscow and St Petersburg in particular, that western fashions were demanded. In any case, the Russian climate demanded more practical clothes than Paris could dictate. In the 1720s, an English woman, Mrs Ward, prepared for the Russian winter by adopting the native costume of a long-sleeved fur-trimmed gown called a '*foube*, or gown to travel in or to wear to any place where ceremony is not required'. For more formal occasions, she wore a crimson velvet cloak lined with ermine and 'a broad forehead cloth of black velvet lined with sattin, and a muffler under the chin, that is fastened to it on the temples, so that only eyes, mouth and nose are seen'.[38] To an English traveller[39] in Russia in 1789, the dress of the women reminded him of that worn by the Highland women, in particular the use of what he called the plaid, probably a woollen cloak in a checked pattern worn in the summer, although he admitted that 'the Russian women are . . . far more elegant and rich in their attire; nor is gold lace wanting to set off their charms'. He noticed the short jacket (often padded) worn by the poorer women, whereas those of higher class wore a silk cloak lined with fur. What he described as 'a napkin rolled about their head' was one of the great variety of linen headdresses (in winter of flannel) worn by many women of the lower classes which had charmed the French artist Jean-Baptiste Le Prince when he had sketched them in the 1760s.

By the time that Catherine the Great became Empress (1762), the court nobility and the small but growing middle and professional classes had adopted completely the western style in clothing. French was the language at court and whole libraries and art collections were purchased from the west in a process so quick that Russia seemed almost in a frenzy to catch up with the 'culture' of the civilized nations of Europe. Yet, paradoxically, this was also a period when traditional Russian costumes returned to favour: they had lost their connotations of barbarism and could now be regarded as picturesque. In her later years, visitors found Catherine in either feminine versions of the dress uniforms of her various regiments, or, as Archdeacon William Coxe found in the 1770s, 'according to her usual custom a Russian dress, namely a robe with a short train and a vest with sleeves reaching to the wrist, like a Polonaise'.[40] She was also fond of the loose-fitting *sarafan* and a dark grey or mauve dress in the Livonian style with hanging sleeves. The Empress encouraged the wearing of Russian silks but her attempts to introduce a Russian dress for court seem to have met with little success.

Livonia had been captured from the Swedes by Peter the Great and Riga, the capital, was, next to St Petersburg, the greatest commercial centre in the Russian empire, relying heavily for its prosperity on the Baltic trade. Visitors described the dress there as being very close in style to traditional Russian costume; in 1774, Wraxall found the more fashionable women wearing sleeveless, red silk gowns covered in gold lace and on their heads pearl embroidered headdresses, costing in some cases many thousands of roubles.

For all classes, keeping warm in winter was a major preoccupation. The wise foreign traveller 'dressed in furs; a fur coat or pellice, boots lined with fur, and a cap resembling a muff . . . his hands cloathed with fur gloves are likewise thrust into a muff almost as large as a French jackboot'.[41] Russians wore a range of furs from the fine sables worn by the nobility to the sheepskins of the poor. In remote Siberia, John Bell, a Scottish doctor journeying from St Petersburg to Peking in 1719–22, found both sexes in deerskin garments, the women in knee-length gown and buskins and the men in jacket and trousers, with extra protection given by a 'ruff made of the tails of squirrels to preserve the tips of the ears from the cold'.[42]

As indicated above, one of the basic working-class male garments was the functional pair of trousers. In Poland, Coxe had found in 1778 that in summer the peasants wore 'nothing but a shirt and drawers of white linen, without shoes or stockings'; continuing to Russia he saw a similar costume with the addition of 'sandals woven from strips of a pliant bark, and fastened by strings of the same materials which are afterwards twined round the legs and serve as garters to the woollen or flannel wrappers' worn for extra warmth; this was a costume uniformly worn all over the Russian territories.[43] The peasants, said Coxe, 'still universally retain their beards, their national dress, their original manners'; the beards were needed for warmth, and most wore the long shirt with wide sleeves belted over trousers in the summer, and in the winter 'the long swaddling coat either of skins or of coarse cloth lined with skins in winter, and in summer of cloth only', tied round the middle (buttons were too expensive) with a yellow or green sash.

It was a brave man who penetrated to those countries in the north of Europe that, according to Wraxall, retained 'the vestiges of Gothic ignorance' with 'not many charms to tempt the traveller'. Russia was interesting for its mixture of barbarism and civilization, astonishing the comte de Ségur, acting as French Minister Plenipotentiary at the Russian court from 1784 to 1789, for its combination of 'the manners of Asia and those of Europe, uncouth Scythians and polite Europeans!' Such surprising contrasts were not to be found in any other country, and certainly not in neighbouring Sweden where, by the late 1760s, an air of complacent self-sufficiency already characterized society. Joseph Marshall in 1769 found that although small amounts of French silks and English woollen cloths were imported, the Swedes were able to manufacture their own medium-quality silks and 'some gentlemen and nobles, through patriotism, wear Swedish cloth that is pretty fine'[44] (although this was, in fact, more expensive than imported materials). The peasants in both Sweden and Norway were reasonably well-clad in cloth of their own making, a striking contrast to the situation in Poland and Russia. In Sweden, particularly in the second half of the eighteenth century, the court, dominated by French taste, was able to encourage (and produce) a wide range of fine and applied arts of the highest quality, comparable to those in France and England. In Denmark, there was no such centre of fashion; apart from a small royal circle and an aristocratic elite adopting French and English styles, the country remained provincial, with some German influence in dress. The last period of Danish influence and prosperity had been the early seventeenth century and when Coxe visited Copenhagen in 1779 he remarked that the local costume reminded him of that worn by the Quakers in seventeenth-century Dutch paintings, the men in 'broad brimmed hats, black jackets, full glazed breeches of the same colour, loose at the knee and tied round the waist. The women were dressed chiefly in black jackets and petticoats, with a piece of blue glazed cloth bound on their heads'.[45]

Much regional costume evolved in periods of prosperity, and this was certainly the case in the Low Countries, where many of the styles were seventeenth-century in origin: in Holland in the 1760s, an English traveller found that the peasants 'change their fashions as rarely as in Spain. With regard to the dress of the men, they have neither shape nor plaits [pleats], and their long pockets are set as high as their ribs; but that of the women is still more odd, their coats coming no lower than the middle of their legs and in North-Holland only to their knees.'[46] As a seafaring nation, many of the Dutch sailors and lower classes had adopted trousers 'wide enough to make some People a whole Suit', said Pöllnitz. In 1776, Parson James Woodforde saw some Dutchmen at Yarmouth 'with monstrous large Trousers and with large wooden shoes'.[47] When Abigail Adams visited Holland in 1786 she

68 J. J. Horemans, *Winter*, mid-eighteenth century

This painting, one of a series of the four seasons, shows a good range of Dutch lower-class costume; the men wear either lumpish versions of semi-fashionable dress, or, as with the skater, traditional peasant dress with its tight-fitting doublet fastening with tiny buttons. The women wear short jackets and traditional frilled linen caps.

noted that the clothing of the country women had not changed for 200 years and they reminded her of the styles worn by the German and Dutch settlers in America: 'many of them wear black tammy aprons, thick quilted coats or russet skirts and small hoops . . . Gold earrings are universally worn by them.'[48] Many Dutch women, in fact, kept to the seventeenth-century type of headdress: under a linen cap was a metal band crossing the top of the head with ear-irons at the side, from which the wealthier hung gold pendant jewels.

For a number of complex reasons to do with the early decay of feudalism and the demands made by a more flexible society, England had very little that could be called regional costume. The red cloaks of calimanco (a kind of hard-wearing, glazed wool) were worn by fashionable and working women in the country all over the British Isles, though by the end of the century they were more a working garment. Occasionally the garments had hoods and they could vary in length. With the English settlers the hooded cloaks came to America; the imported cloaks were expensive (Anna Winslow in Boston paid £45 for a cloak and bonnet in 1772) and were probably restricted to the upper classes in the long-established and more cultivated colonies. In Virginia in 1773, Philip Fithian noted at church: 'Almost every Lady wears a red Cloak; and when they ride out they tye a red handkerchief over their Head and Face, so that whenever I saw a Lady, I thought she had the Tooth-Ach.'[49] As noted above, stuffs in patterns of stripes and checks played an important part in working-class and regional costume: the distinctive Welsh dress worn by women consisted of a tall hat, black bodice or jacket and striped skirt of Welsh cloth, though the latter fabric was also worn for aprons and short gowns by working women in England.

In the Highlands of Scotland in the early eighteenth century, the 'plaid' was almost synonymous with a checked pattern, although strictly speaking it was a type of garment. Originally, it was a long strip of fabric that had to be pleated or kilted in position on the man, the ends being thrown over the shoulder and fastened with a brooch; the kilt was later made as a separate garment and the plaid became the cloak (sometimes square, sometimes like a long scarf) worn by both sexes. Male members of the gentry wore it with matching trews, while Edward Burt, who was employed in the construction of military roads in the Highlands in the 1730s, noted: 'The Plaid is the Undress of the Ladies, and to a genteel Woman, who adjusts it with a good Air, is a becoming veil . . . It is made of silk or fine worstead, chequered with various lively colours, two breadths wide and three yards in length; it is brought over the head and may hide or discover the face according to the Wearer's fancy or occasion.'[50]

The colours of the plaids were ordered by area and not by clan (the clan tartan system was very much a product of the vogue for things Scottish in the early nineteenth century). According to Guy Miège's fanciful view in his *The Present State of Great-Britain and Ireland* (1715), 'the Colours they affect most are Purple and Blue . . . a Dark-colour resembling that of the Corps of the Heath, that they may not be discover'd while they lie in the Heaths waiting for their Game',[51] but brighter colours could be woven to fancy, particularly for women's plaids, which were usually worn over current fashionable dress. In the early 1720s, Daniel Defoe saw in Glasgow 'a Manufacture of Plaiding, a stuff cross-strip'd with yellow and red'; in various colours it was popular for morning gowns and men's waistcoats. In 1747, as a result of the Jacobite Rebellion, the use of Highland dress was forbidden except for the Highland regiments; the prohibition lasted until 1782. Smollett's novel *Humphrey Clinker* (1771) described the misery felt by the

Habit of a Lady in the Highlands of Scotland in 1745.

Dame des Montagnes d'Ecosse.

69   T. Jefferys, 'Habit of a Lady in the Highlands of Scotland in 1745', from *A Collection of the Dresses of Different Nations . . .*, 1757

poor Highlanders . . . [who] are compelled to wear breeches, a restraint which they cannot bear with any degree of patience – indeed the majority wear them, not in the proper place, but on poles or long staves over their shoulders. They are even debarred the use of their striped stuff called Tartane, which was their own manufacture, prized by them above all velvets, brocades and tissues of Europe and Asia. They now lounge along in loose great coats of coarse russet, equally mean and cumbersome and betray manifest marks of dejection.[52]

The Lowland Scots wore English dress, as did most of the Irish by the beginning of the eighteenth century. Paradoxically, while the English authorities succeeded only in stirring up feelings of patriotism in Scotland through their banning of Highland dress, in Ireland the death blow was given to the traditional forms of Irish dress not by proscription (which was virtually non-existent) but by the gradual infiltration of London fashions via Anglo-Irish society. Ireland even produced its own silks, which well-connected people like Jonathan Swift, and later Mrs Delany, tried to promote at the English court; Swift in 1726 urged his correspondent Henrietta Howard – one of the Women of the Bedchamber to the Princess of Wales – to popularize the 'Irish silk plaid' and the princess did, in fact, order some in 'purple, yellow and white silk'.[53] By the middle of the century, only the Irish remote from towns wore the old dress, the men in 'little Woollen Jackets, Breeches close to their Thighs and over them a Mantle or Shagg Rugg deeply fringed'[54] and the women in linen shifts (this was sometimes the only everyday garment), woollen dresses and, increasingly rarely, the shag-rug mantle.

Of all the countries in Europe that combined a long tradition of culture with a variety of regional customs, Italy was the most popular and most visited country in Europe. The Italians, said Teodoro Viero in his book of costume plates, *Raccolta di Stampe che rappresentano Figure ed Abiti di varie nazioni . . .* (1783–91), were not only 'la Nazione piú colta del Mondo' (the most cultured nation in the world) but they lived in the garden of Europe, blessed with a good climate, a fertile soil and magnificent cities. Among their productions were fine textiles; the northern cities like Milan and Turin wove a wide range of silks from heavy satin to fine gauzes, Genoa and Verona made high-quality velvets, and a number of cities produced various weights of woollen cloth. The peculiarities of the Italian climate, with extremes of heat in summer and cold in winter, demanded a greater range of clothing than perhaps was common in the more temperate countries of northern Europe. Since Italy was a major producer of luxury goods as well as woollens, cotton and linen, Italian gentlemen in particular were able to indulge in a love of finery that appeared to outsiders one of their noted traits. To Baretti, an Italian living in England, dress in his native country appeared rich and luxurious compared to the austerities of his adopted land: 'Gentlemen throughout Italy in the hot months dress in the thinnest silks, and use velvet in winter, besides cloth of all sorts and colours, much laced or embroidered if they can afford it, for they love finery as well as the French. In winter likewise they line their coats with costly furs; wear large muffs; and in many parts adorn their hats with feathers.'[55] Yet although the fabrics were rich, the styles were often plain; Nugent summed it up at the beginning of his third volume of travels (which took place in the 1770s) by describing the dress of both men and women as 'being a kind of medium between the stiff Spanish querpo and the fantastic French garb'.[56] By 'querpo' he meant the stiffly boned, tight-fitting style that affected Spanish dress, and to some extent that of the south of Italy where Spain was a dominant political and cultural influence. In the north of Italy generally, except for the distinctive patrician dress of cities like Venice and Genoa, men and women of the upper classes wore more restrained versions of French dress – usually not the very latest styles, for there was no enormously wealthy aristocracy as in France or England. Milan was probably closest to being a fashion centre, as it is today, with a wide range of luxury fabrics available.

The city states of Italy had, in many cases, founded their wealth on trade in the Middle Ages, but by the early eighteenth century the great merchant families had become aristocratic in taste and autocratic in rule. Nowhere was this more evident than in the rules regarding dress, particularly in Venice and Genoa, where officials regulated the magnificent clothes worn by the patricians. The costume worn by the Doge of Genoa was a soutane and robe of crimson satin (velvet in winter) with huge sleeves; the Doge of Venice wore purple, but when he appeared in public for the ceremonial occasions that made up much of Venetian life, he wore a white gown with a cloak of gold cloth faced with ermine. Nugent described his traditional headwear as 'a purple cap, almost in the form of a mitre, which is encompassed with a border of gold plate, and rises behind almost in the shape of a horn'.[57] Official regulations demanded that on reaching the age of twenty, Venetian patricians wore the *veste patrizia*, a kind of gown with huge sleeves in either black, red or violet according to rank and employment; senators usually wore red. The most common everyday colour was black; Baretti tells us that in winter this gown was made of black wool bordered with ermine and tied with a silver clasp at the waist. 'His gown has large hanging sleeves. He wears likewise an enormous periwig, but no hat or cap though formerly a black cap was part of his dress. His summer dress is likewise black, open loose and shorter than that of the winter, with a silk coat under it made after an old fashion somewhat resembling what is called a Vandyke-dress.'[58] A noted characteristic of ceremonial and official dress is the incorporation of elements of antiquity conferring tradition and dignity; the silk 'Vandyke-dress' was a tunic cut in seventeenth-century style, a period that was popular for both servants' liveries (the Doge of Genoa's pages dressed in a kind of early-seventeenth-century, red velvet doublet and hose, with a shoulder cloak trimmed with gold lace and a plumed hat) and the robes of knightly orders.

The size of the sleeve was a mark of distinction; Charles de Brosses, the first President of the Burgundian Parlement who visited Italy in the 1730s, found that 'the higher his grade, the larger the sleeve. That of the Doge is as big as a lady's hoop.'[59] With his gown the patrician wore a periwig of enormous size, adopted from the fashion of 1709 by Doge Giovanni Correr

Gentiluomo Veneto
in abito ordinario

Noble Venetien
en habit ordinaire.

Cittadina Veneziana
in Cendale.

Bourgeoise Venitienne
en Zendale.

70a and b 'Gentiluomo Veneto in abito ordinario' and 'Cittadina Veneziana in Cendale', from Viero's *Raccolta di Stampe che rappresentano Figure ed Abiti di varie nazione . . .*, 1783–91

and kept for official dress. The patrician gown or toga was, by the second half of the eighteenth century, reserved for government and for formal receptions. It was rather cumbersome when dancing at the latter – as a German visitor to Venice on the eve of the French Revolution reported, 'it really makes a most droll appearance'. Increasingly, the nobility tended to prefer the *tabarro*, a large, round cloak with a turned-back collar which was worn over ordinary dress.

Venetian elite women were governed both by traditional forms of clothing and by sumptuary laws. Over their everyday clothing they wore a kind of veil called a *zenda*, *zendale* or *zendaletta* made of fine, black silk sometimes edged with lace. It was draped over an iron wire attached to the woman's head (so as not to disturb her hair) and then hung down over her black silk or velvet dress and was tied at the waist. Mrs Piozzi, visiting Venice in 1785, was charmed by this arrangement:

A skeleton wire upon the head such as we use to make up hats, throwing loosely over it a large piece of black mode or persian, so as to shade the face like a curtain, the front being trimmed with a very deep black lace or souflet gauze infinitely becoming. The thin silk that remains to be disposed of, they roll back so as to discover the bosom; fasten it with a puff before at the top of their stomacher, and once more rolling it back from the shape, tie it gracefully behind and let it hang in two long ends.[60]

Over the dress and veil, or as an alternative covering, women wore a knee-length cloak called a *tabarrino*, usually white or a light colour and sometimes embroidered in gold if worn by a recent bride (the sumptuary regulations passed in 1707, 1709 and 1732 forbidding all women, except unmarried girls and noblemen's wives in the first two years after marriage, to wear gold and silver trimmings or any colour but black, were often flouted). According to Keysler, who came to Venice in 1730, great numbers of persons 'offend against this law, that it is not strictly put into execution';[61] in fact, the Venetian authorities wished to impress on foreigners the extent of luxury and affluence of the state. Many visitors noticed a curious mixture of finery but with no frenetic desire to keep up with the latest fashions; the fashionable wardrobe of a Venetian lady in 1744 included a 'black Patrician's mantle and petticoat, with embroidery and lace . . . a Robe of black velvet', as well as considerable numbers of sacks and other gowns in plain silks or velvets, embroidered in gold or silver.[62]

Other cities followed the lead of Venice in insisting on black for the nobility. In Genoa, for example, the nobleman wore black 'with a narrow silk cloak hanging down his back; nor is his wig so large as the Venetian's. He wears a plain hat, generally under his arm. His lady dressed often in colours; but her dress of ceremony is black silk or black velvet according to the season.'[63] By law, the wives of nobles were to wear coloured dresses for only the year after marriage, but this was not strictly observed, nor was the rule allowing jewellery to be worn only six weeks before and six weeks after the marriage.

The preponderance of black in many cities was striking to some observers, but the reasons for its widescale adoption are not clear – it may derive from sixteenth- or seventeenth-century Spanish influence (a Burgundian inheritance[64]): black dye was hard to achieve and black material correspondingly expensive. Yet in the eighteenth century black was popular for all classes in Italy: it was worn by the nobility, as noted above, and also by the middle classes, Goethe observing in Verona in the 1780s that women of this class wore the *veste* and *zendale* of black taffeta, a costume suitable for those not devoted to cleanliness. In Rome, the men were often taken for abbés, because they dressed solely in black; this was in addition the dress worn at the papal court. At Bologna, de Brosses found that the lower-class women 'look like black phantoms as they cover their bodies with black cotton shawls'.[65] Spanish influence was particularly striking in the south of Italy, in Naples and Sicily, in the first half of the eighteenth century. The French traveller Jean-Baptiste Labat, who visited Sicily in 1711, found fashionable ladies 'vêtues à l'Espagnole . . . Elles ont toutes des voiles de soye noire sur la tête,

& ne montrent qu'un oeil; mais c'est un oeil qui sçait parler à merveille' (dressed Spanish-style . . . they all have black veils over their heads, revealing only one eye, but an eye that knows how to 'speak' amazingly well).[66] In the streets, they were carefully chaperoned by lackeys dressed in the Spanish fashion with spectacles on their noses (the inexplicable fondness of Spaniards for spectacles amazed the rest of Europe), fiercely armed to protect their lady's honour and 'd'une manière qu'ils sembloient avoir étudiés sous Don Guichotte' (in a way they seemed to have studied from Don Quixote). Most men of substance wore Spanish dress: black, short doublet, breeches and the *golilla* (a plain, standing, wired collar introduced by Philip of Spain in the early 1620s). This continued as a kind of official costume for professional men until the end of the century. When the Englishman Henry Swinburne visited the Kingdom of the Two Sicilies from 1770 to 1780, he discovered that although the upper-class women were now mainly following French fashions, for church and for the purposes of incognito they continued to wear the all-embracing cloak. The netted headdresses that were a feature of Spanish dress (and had been worn in southern Italy by all classes) were worn mainly by the lower classes, but this style was occasionally to be seen worn by a woman of fashion (pl. 73); so, also, was that of wearing two black silk petticoats, one pulled over the head, which Mrs Piozzi noted in Naples in the 1780s.

Greater extremes of poverty were to be seen in the south of Italy than in any other part of the country; in the very hot weather the children went naked, and visitors from northern Europe found the absence of adult under-linen as distressing as the sunburnt complexions of the women in an age in which whiteness was preferred. In Sicily, the clothing was of poorer quality than on the mainland: the men wore rough, serge breeches, waistcoats and enormous cloaks. When the French traveller and artist Jean Houel visited Sicily at the end of the 1770s (his account is the most comprehensive in this period) he dressed like a Sicilian peasant[67] for ease of travelling, his hair in a net with ribbons, a turned-down hat (uncocked) and short boots. He noticed how Spanish influence remained in the types of cloaks worn by both sexes: the *capotto*, a vast cloak with a collar, and the *palandrano*, a cloak with a long pointed hood, both of these of black or dark brown wool. The women sometimes wore short mantles tying round the waist and falling down the back in a kind of tail.

We have already seen that the basic working costume for women through-out the eighteenth century comprised a shift, stays, petticoat and bodice. In very poor (or hot) countries, women dispensed with the bodice, or wore the type with removeable sleeves, laced at the shoulders.

In any society, distinctions are created by dress. In a relatively primitive, peasant society, where the monotony of agrarian life is punctuated by religious and secular feasts, holiday dress often assumes a great importance. It was the gala dress worn by the peasants on Sundays and holidays that many visitors to Italy found so attractive; the variety of costume displayed was enormous, some deriving from fashionable dress of the sixteenth and seventeenth centuries and much decorated with metal lace, semi-precious stones and embroidery. Mrs Piozzi found the holiday dress of the women in Naples in the 1780s to be 'a scarlet cloth petticoat with a broad gold lace at the bottom, a jacket open before, but charged with heavy ornaments and the head not unbecomingly dressed with an embroidered handkerchief from Turkey',[68] while the men appeared in 'thick blue velvet coats'. It was the variety of headdresses in particular that Mrs Piozzi found charming on a visit to north Italy in 1785; they ranged 'from the velvet cap, commonly a crimson one worn by the girls in Savoia, to the Piedmontese plait round the bodkin at Turin, and the odd kind of white wrapper used in the exterior provinces of the Genoese dominions'.[69]

A few years earlier, Swinburne had visited Genoa, giving a fuller description of the headdress worn by the countrywomen there, who 'plait and twist their coal-black hair in a round upon the crown of their head; then fasten it together with a large silver or steel bodkin. The front is cropped and kept back with pomatum. In winter they wear a veil of white linen checked with red flowers, which they throw over their heads; it falls down to their hips, and some of them hide almost all their faces behind it'.[70] In many cities, sumptuary regulations prevented the wearing of rich jewellery made with precious stones, so countrywomen wore either starched, muslin handkerchiefs (in Lucca they were arranged in turban shape) or straw hats with ribbons, as in Pisa or Florence. To Madame de Bocage in the mid-eighteenth century, the pretty country girls in Tuscany seemed like members of the chorus from the opera in Paris, and the description given some thirty years later by Mrs Piozzi conjures up the gracefulness of a costume drawing by Boquet, for they wore:

71 'Contadina del Pian de Ripoli', from Viero's *Raccolta di Stampe che rappresentano Figure ed Abiti di varie nazione . . .*, 1783–91

> a very rich white silk petticoat exceedingly full and short, to shew her neat pink slipper and pretty ancle, her pink corps de robe and straps, with white silk lacing down the stomacher, puffed shift sleeves . . . with at least eight or nine bows of narrow pink ribbon, a lawn handkerchief trimmed with broad lace, put on somewhat coquettishly, and finishing in front with a nosegay . . . the hair is drawn away from the face, tight . . . under a red velvet cushion edged with gold, which gives the small Leghorn hat lined with green a pretty perking air.[71]

The peasants in Tuscany, under a reasonably beneficent Habsburg regime, were well-off and were able to afford, said Mrs Piozzi, sets of garnet jewellery, for Italy was well-supplied with the bright semi-precious stones which formed an important part of peasant decoration. In Naples, even the very poor women would not find it incongruous to be barefooted and yet wear the locally produced red, white and black coral, emeralds and cameos. A French visitor to Rome in 1709 found the poorer women wearing large necklaces of amber and matching pendant earrings and in the late 1740s, while visiting Treviso, Casanova was attracted to a countrywoman who displayed more than 150 sequins' worth of gold pins and arrows fastening her plaits, in addition to a gold chain wound twenty times round her neck.

Italy, in spite of its natural geographical advantages and its long traditions of design, was politically chequered, where a number of independent states managed their affairs with greater or lesser efficiency, and, if not achieving the greatest happiness of the greatest number, made important cultural contributions to the life of the country. Such an example was Naples under a Spanish prince, the future Charles III of Spain (his accession took place there in 1734), where appalling poverty, superstition and a Spanish indolence occurred alongside the rediscovery of much of western Europe's heritage of classical antiquities and with major contemporary developments in architecture, painting and music.

Spain, a country that had had so much influence in earlier periods on the culture and dress of the rest of Europe, was by the eighteenth century no longer a dominant power. Its isolation was emphasized by the distinctive Spanish men's dress which had evolved in the early seventeenth century, Philip IV having banned French fashions from court in 1623. He had introduced a short, tabbed doublet and narrow knee-breeches, a *golilla* collar starched and raised on a wire frame and flat shoes. Other manifestations of Spanish dress recognized all over Europe included a ruff (as an alternative to the collar), a moustache, spectacles and, above all, 'une gravité des plus grandes & une morgue des plus fières' (the greatest gravity and the fiercest pride), noted the abbé Labat,[72] who, travelling in Spain in the first decade of the eighteenth century, found nearly all the men of quality wearing the traditional black suit and cloak in early-seventeenth-century style.

The cloak, also dating from the seventeenth century, was an essential part of Spanish dress, being worn by all classes. An English visitor to Spain in 1786–7 found how 'it is pleasing to see the genteel young Spaniard in his capa, which he throws into a thousand graceful forms, each remarkable for its peculiar ease and elegance, such as no foreigner can imitate'.[73] This cloak was usually brown, and remained as part of the dress of the upper classes when the rest of the Spanish dress was limited to court and official costume. Count Almaviva, a grandee of Spain in Beaumarchais' *The Barber of Seville* (1775) wore over his satin suit a 'grand manteau brun, ou cape espagnole' (a large, brown mantle of Spanish cloak). In the second half of the century, the old costume disappeared except for official dress, and by the early 1760s an English clergyman, the Reverend Clarke, regretted the fact that the Spanish 'have quitted that old dress, which looks so well on our English stage'; it had long been the costume of some of the popular *commedia dell'arte* characters. It remained, however, a popular masquerade costume. Dr Bartholo, Rosine's tutor in *The Barber of Seville*, wore, according to the stage directions, 'un habit noir, court, boutonné, grand perruque, fraise & manchettes relevées' (a short, buttoned, black coat, large wig, ruff and turned-up shirt cuffs),[74] but this was increasingly regarded as eccentrically conservative, especially when worn with a large wig.

In the early 1760s, Baretti visited Spain and found that most men dressed in the French manner, with the addition of the Spanish cloak and the sombrero, a 'hat with the flaps down', although this costume was frowned on by the authorities for it disguised identity and concealed weapons. Another

72 F. Bayeu, *El Paseo de las Delicias en Madrid*, 1785

This tree-lined avenue connecting the Paseo del Prado with the Canal de Manzanares was a fashionable walking place, especially in summer.

traditional feature of Spanish dress was the hair gathered up in a black net, observed by Arthur Young on his visit to Spain in 1787, worn by the middle classes and the well-off men with their French clothes. The colours of men's clothes were dark, often black, a sobriety seen at the highest levels with the Spanish kings. Charles III (1759–88) was an ugly but appealing king who played a considerable part in restoring the artistic glories of Spain. He was in no way a leader of fashion and was happiest in his hunting costume of grey cloth frock, leather breeches and boots; on gala days, according to Swinburne, 'a fine suit is hung upon his shoulders, but as he had an eye to his afternoon sport, and is a great economist of his time, the black breeches are worn to all coats'.[75] Baretti, in the 1760s, found that he preferred 'the fashion that was used in his younger days, and he always appears impatient to undress, being never easy until he resumes his grey frock and leather waistcoat'.[76] The king's grey frock was made in Segovia, a long-established centre for the woollen trade that was based on the excellent wool produced by the Spanish merino sheep. Other textile industries made Spain self-sufficient: Valencia was the centre of the silk industry, with 5000 looms by the end of the 1780s; light silks were made in Madrid and Barcelona; cotton was woven in Barcelona (the raw material came from the Spanish colonies in America);

and linen at Corunna. Spanish silks were exported to their own and to Portuguese colonies in South America, as was woollen cloth for these growing and important markets. But in spite of an appreciable increase in national prosperity in the second half of the eighteenth century, most foreign visitors were exasperated by the inability of the country to take up the possibilities offered by its range of natural resources, a failure they attributed to the inherent indolence of the people, for the peasants, said Swinburne, spent all their time 'wrapped up in a cloak, standing in rows against a wall, or dozing under a tree'.

Joseph Townsend, one of that breed of English travellers inspired by recent discoveries and improvements in agriculture and science, found the Spanish terrain inhospitable ('a good constitution' was essential for the hazards of getting round the country) when he came there in the late 1780s. He found hardly any middle-class society and a large gulf between the nobility and the poor. Like all visitors to Spain, he was attracted to the distinctive and seductive clothing worn by the women, in particular the *mantilla*, 'a kind of lace or muslin shawl, covering both the head and shoulders, and serving the various purposes of the hood, of the cloak, of the veil',[77] which, used for flirtatious display, almost became an art form. At mass, the ladies wore their normal dress (this was French in taste) but with an extra black silk petticoat, the *basquiña*, over the top. This fondness for layers of skirt coverings had been a characteristic of Spanish dress ever since the abbé Labat noted, in the early years of the century, how women had seven or eight skirts, the one covering their feet being called a 'garde pied', for a lady showing her foot to a man indicated her readiness to grant him further favours.

To foreign visitors, the most striking costume was that worn by the lower-class people of fashion, the *majo* and the *maja*; Baretti was told that the *majo* was 'a low personage between the poissard of Paris and the city-spark of London . . . a low fellow who dresses sprucely, affects the walk of a gentleman, looks blunt and menacing and endeavours after dry wit, upon every occasion'. He goes on to describe the dress, which 'consists in the man of a tight waistcoat, tight breeches, white stockings, white shoes tied with a ribband instead of a buckle, the hair in a net of various colours, and a *montéra* over, instead of a hat. The *montéra* is a cap of black velvet, and of a particular cut which fits the head exactly and covers the ears'.[78] In *The Barber of Seville*, this was the costume worn by Figaro, the scheming valet with an eye to the main chance, and it remained for many years in the popular imagination as the epitome of Spanish dress.

The *maja* wore 'a tight jacket, so open before as to form two hanging flaps under the breast, something in the form of wings, with sleeves close to the fist, a short petticoat of any colour, a black apron, a striped handkerchief carefully covering the whole net, and the *montéra* exactly such as the man. The seams of both dresses (male and female) are not sowed but kept together by interlacing ribbands'.[79] This was a popular dress for masquerades (pl. 73), and, by the 1780s, it had begun to influence the informal *déshabillé* of the Spanish aristocracy, following the general trend in costume in that decade of adopting picturesque versions of working-class dress.

73 Detail of pl. 178

This detail from Mengs's fine portrait of the marquesa de Llano demonstrates the new appealp of *maja* costume to the elite. Beneath a black velvet cap, the hair is kept in place by a silk net. The frogged jacket has a decorative reminder, at the shoulders, that the bodice and sleeves of working women were fastened together with ribbons.

As with all costume showing strong regional traits, the headdresses were both inventive and varied. A visitor to Cadiz in 1773 found that the ladies in the evening 'fixed glow-worms by threads to their hair, which had a luminous and pleasing effect';[80] in Aragon, Baretti found old women wearing the *montéra* and younger women with their hair netted; near Pamplona the hair was interwoven with coloured ribbons, and in Valencia it was fastened with a large silver pin. Usually, the dress of the poorer women was made of a brown coarse woollen mixture, in jacket and skirt style, but in northern Castile in 1760 Baretti found a vestige of the old Spanish style which 'consists of a robe, generally brown, that runs close to the neck and wrists, with several cuts along the sleeves from the shoulder to the elbow and a broad girdle round the waist'.[81]

Generally, dress for the Spanish male peasant was a jacket and breeches of dark brown, locally produced cloth; even the poorest, said Labat, possessed a cloak, which was needed for warmth and bedcovering. Whereas most poor

men in the rest of Europe would wear a wig of some kind, in Spain, Labat
noted, men grew their hair long, shaving it at the top in the form of a triangle (to distinguish it from the round clerical tonsure), a practice com-
mended by doctors for health; they then bound it up into a net at the back.

In summer, the very poor wore linen trousers and waistcoats; their feet
were clothed in what reminded Townsend of theatrical 'buskins . . . called by
them *alpargates*, which are made of the esparto rush', tying round the legs
with strings, and which lasted only two weeks. By the end of the eighteenth
century, some uniformity had set in to the dress of the poor, but in the more
remote areas individual characteristics still ruled. Swinburne, in the middle
of the 1770s, saw mountaineers in Barcelona with netted hair, a handkerchief tied round the neck, a short striped waistcoat, a red jacket with large
silver bell-shaped buttons, blue and white striped breeches and a great-coat
embroidered with white thread.

In Portugal, which had very close links with Spain, the costume worn was
very similar. Women wore a version of the Spanish *mantilla* called a *velo*, made
usually of fine black silk, over their richly embroidered dresses in the French
mode. Although there were sumptuary laws prohibiting 'all ornaments of gold
or silver lace or embroidery',[82] these were usually ignored and dress (of both
sexes) exhibited a greater luxury and opulence than in Spain. According to
Baretti, who visited Portugal in 1760, the famous Lisbon earthquake of 1755
had deprived many women of their clothing, 'and they dress as well as they
can, and have no prevalent or national fashion'. The poorer women, however,
had in some areas kept to the large, wide sleeves of the early sixteenth
century – a period when Portugal was prosperous and influential – and many
showed variety in their headdresses, some of ribbons and some with real or
artificial flowers. Both men and women of the lower classes wore 'a kind of
network silk purse over their hair, with a long tassel behind and a ribbon
tied in a bow-knot over the forehead', according to one of the few published accounts of Portugal, written by Richard Twiss in 1772–3.[83] Twiss
found, as many did in Spain, that the contrasts between rich and poor were
striking. On the one hand, he found an elegant aristocracy covered in the
precious stones from their South American colonies, listening to the Italian
opera at Belem or walking through the royal palace of Queluz which was
built and decorated in the French rococo taste; on the other hand, he found
a poor peasantry in dark, coarse cloaks and slouched hats – a vignette that
stayed in Twiss's mind was a man in Lisbon selling the services of a baboon
to pick out lice from the hair of the poor.

It is these contrasts that sum up the extremes and variety of costume that
could be seen in eighteenth-century Europe, and which should be born in
mind in any discussion of dress. Much regional costume changed only very
slowly, and at any given time one would find society built up of layers, consisting of the most recent fashions imported from France or England, middle-
class versions with local adaptations demanded by custom and law and the
virtually static traditional dress in the more remote areas where costume
varied from village to village, so tightly knit were the small communities.

4 *The Triumph of the Rococo: 1740–1770*

> The beauty of intricacy lies in contriving winding shapes . . . as the modern lappet when it is brought before. Every part of dress that will admit of the application of this principle, has an air (as it is term'd) given to it thereby; and although it requires dexterity and taste to execute these windings well, we find them daily performed with success.
>
> W. Hogarth, *The Analysis of Beauty*, 1753

THIS PERIOD ENCAPSULATES all that is graceful and elegant in clothing in the eighteenth century. It marks the change from the symmetry and geometric restraint of early eighteenth century costume to the ornamented breaking up of the surface of dress, which was such a feature of women's clothing in the middle of the period; dress moves from the sobriety of the classical to the lightness and wit of the rococo. By about 1730 in France the *style Régence* had turned into the rococo, the full development taking place in the 1740s, although in England this did not really happen until the following decade. In the late 1760s, there appeared the beginnings of the neo-classical movement in dress, the antithesis of the rococo.

Men

For men, too, mid-eighteenth-century costume was characterized by a gradual retreat from the almost sculptural heaviness of cut and material that had previously been worn, although male fashions were slower to change than were women's; the classical uniformity of the suit was international. However, from about 1740 there was a definite decrease in the amount of stuff needed for the coat: the side pleats began to be reduced in size and there was a perceptible curving away of the front edge of the coat from just above the waist. With this slight narrowing of cut, men were increasingly reluctant to fasten the buttons of their coats at waist level, and the emphasis moved to buttoning at mid-chest. This allowed more of the waistcoat to be seen and also perhaps encouraged the gesture so typical of the period, that of placing the hand through the waistcoat over the chest (pl. 83). From the end of the 1760s, the side flare of the coat had virtually disappeared, and another change to be noted from the middle of the century was the placing of pockets higher up, just below the waist. From the 1740s, the waistcoat began to change significantly: in 1740, it was only a few inches

75 J.-B. Perroneau, *Jacques Cazotte*, c.1760

This portrait encapsulates all the elegance of mid-eighteenth-century French costume, from the pink silk of the suit to the powdered and carefully dressed wig.

shorter than the coat, but by the end of the decade the discrepancy had increased so that it was only mid-thigh length, and it, too, had begun to curve away from waist to hem. By the end of the 1740s, sleeved waistcoats were worn only by the older man or the valetudinarian, the side stiffening had gone and, increasingly, the back part of the waistcoat was cut much shorter than the front; with the greater popularity of embroidery, men would often buy a pair of embroidered waistcoat fronts that would then be joined to a plain back section. From the middle of the century, a much greater range of waistcoats was available. They included the formal sleeveless waist-coat or *gilet*, and a much shorter sporting waistcoat, usually double-breasted and sometimes with an assymmetrical flap fastening. With this shortening and curving of coat and waistcoat, the breeches also had to tighten up for the new, slimmer silhouette; fastening below the knee in a buckled or buttoned band, they were closer-fitting to the thigh, the *London Chronicle* of 1762 noting 'long Trowser-like Breeches'. From the middle of the century, the central front buttoning began to be replaced by a 'fall', or flap front, cover-ing the front opening.

The total effect was to tighten up the rather heavy, triangular male figure; a smaller head (wigs tightly curled at the sides with the hair drawn off the face into a bag at the back) and neater outline with fewer projections by way of reinforced side pleats and large cuffs was the fashionable line. From about 1750, cuffs were smaller and narrower; a popular style, particularly on the frock coat, was the cuff *à la marinière*, a small, round cuff with a slightly scalloped, vertical flap edged with three to four buttons.

The idea current at the beginning of the century that 'to keep to the pro-priety of dress, the coat, waistcoat and breeches must be of the same piece' (*Guardian*, 1713), was no longer widely held. It remained, however, the rule for the patterned, flowered, velvet suits that played a part in every gentle-man's wardrobe for winter. When Boswell made his preparations for foreign travel in 1763, Lord Keith urged him to take for the more formal German courts 'against winter, a complete suit of worked flowered velvet, the buttons of velvet'.[1] In the same year, Lord Riverstone had made in Paris a suit of claret velvet – coat, waistcoat and breeches in a small, stylized design – which still exists, with its bill (it cost him £27. 10s. 3d., with £2. 5s. 6d. to have it carried duty-free), in Birmingham Museum and Art Gallery.[2] Gradually, the suit became the coat and breeches only, the waistcoat being made of dif-ferent material, usually embroidered. On the Grand Tour in 1754, the Adam brothers in Genoa bought black velvet suits 'with which we can wear all our waistcoats by turn'. Very often, the embroidery on the coat matched that on the waistcoat; in 1753, Mrs Delany admired at court the Duke of Portland's appearance in 'dark mouse-coloured velvet, embroidered with silver . . . the waistcoat Isabella satin embroidered the same as the coat'.[3] The elegant Bel-larmine in Fielding's novel *Joseph Andrews* (1742) admired himself in 'a cut Velvet Coat of Cinnamon Colour, lined with a Pink Satten embroidered all over with Gold; his Waistcoat, which was Cloth of Silver, was embroidered with Gold likewise'.[4]

76   M.-Q. La Tour, *Duval de l'Epinoy*, 1745

The sitter retains the rather conservative knotted wig and the silk hose fastening over the breeches. The coat, of superb silver watered silk, is stiffly reinforced at the side pleats, so that it echoes the width of the female hooped skirt of this period.

By the end of the 1740s, the suit could (except for court and formal wear) be made of three different colours and stuffs. In Smollett's *Roderick Random* (1748), the absurd Captain Whiffle appeared thus:

> His coat, consisting of a pink-coloured silk lined with white, by the elegance of the cut retired backwards, as it were, to discover a white satin waistcoat embroidered with gold, unbuttoned at the upper part to display a brooch set with garnets that glittered in the breast of his shirt, which was of the finest cambric edged with right Mechlin. The knees of crimson velvet breeches scarcely descended so low as to meet his silk stockings, which arose without a spot or wrinkle on his meagre legs, from shoes of blue Meroquin, studded with diamond buckles that flamed forth rivals to the sun.[5]

It is not the clothes themselves that are held up to ridicule here but the manner in which the effeminate Captain wore them. In the same novel, the hero Roderick bought a new wardrobe in London which consisted of 'five fashionable coats, full mounted, two of which were plain, one of cut velvet, one trimmed with gold, and another large plate buttons, the other of blue with gold binding; one waistcoat of gold brocade; one of blue satin embroidered with silver; one of green silk trimmed with broad figured gold lace; one of black silk with fringes; one of white satin, one of black cloth and one of scarlet; six pair of cloth breeches, one pair of crimson, and another of black velvet . . .'[6] At this period, the fashionable man appeared like a bird of brightly coloured plumage.

With formal dress, furs were an important addition both for luxury and warmth. They lined court suits in winter, the soft fine furs like ermine, squirrel and sable being the perfect complement to silk, velvet and brocade. In 1740, Mrs Delany saw Lord Baltimore in 'light brown and silver, his coat lined quite throughout with ermine'; in 1745, for the wedding celebrations of the Dauphin, the marquis de Stainville wore a coat of silver cloth lined with sable, the lining alone costing 50,000 livres.[7] The degree of bulkiness created by a fur-lined suit was permissible in the mid-eighteenth century – when, incidentally, there were some very cold winters – but by the end of the 1760s the slimmer line of fashion limited furs to edgings; only the vulgar or the effete could wear, like the duc de Villars in 1769, 'a gold stuff coat lined and turn'd up with sable in gold tassels and loops, all his diamonds & a great sable muff'.[8]

When François Mazerac entered the service of James Boswell in September 1763, he listed the wardrobe of his new master; this began with the formal suits of one colour and then the individual coats, waistcoats and breeches.[9] Boswell's favourite suit was of scarlet trimmed with gold lace which he wore 'with white silk stockings, handsome pumps . . . silver and gold sword-knot, Barcelona handkerchief and elegant tooth-pick case' at a formal assembly in October. In December 1764, he wore the coat and waistcoat with buckskin breeches and boots, a mixture of the rich and the fashionably sporting with which he hoped to impress Rousseau. Increasingly by the 1760s, suits

77 P. Batoni, *Sir Edward Dering, c.*1759

One reason for the success of Batoni was his flattery of his aristocratic sitters, not just by his lovingly rendered depiction of luxury fabrics, such as this sumptuous velvet gown lined with squirrel, but also his use of accessories from classical antiquity to create an atmosphere of learning and leisure.

were being made of cloth. For summer Boswell was urged to buy 'fine camlet with a gold thread button but no lace'. His wardrobe inventory included only one frock of brown stuff, but this may have been because Boswell was travelling to the more formal German courts where the frock was still mainly a sporting garment and because his own personal taste was for a gaudy finery.

In England by the early 1750s, the frock was the most common ordinary wear; when Peregrine Pickle, the eponymous hero of Smollett's novel (1751), met Emily he wore 'a genteel grey frock, trimmed with silver binding'. The

World (1753) noted at Newmarket that it was difficult to 'distinguish between his Grace and his Groom . . . for a pair of boots and buckskin breeches, a fustian frock, with a leather belt about it, and a black velvet cap, is the common covering of the whole town'.[10] To an English visitor in Paris in 1753, the frock was synonymous with liberty; in his 'full-dressed Coat, with hellish long Skirts, which I had never been used to, I thought myself as much deprived of my Liberty, as if I had been in the Bastile; and I frequently sighed for my little loose Frock, which I look upon as an Emblem of our happy Constitution; for it lays a Man under no uneasy Restraint, but leaves it in his Power to do as he pleases'.[11]

Frocks were made of a range of materials, usually wool or wool mixtures. The *London Chronicle* of 1762 noted the popularity of red shag frocks, shag being a worsted fabric with a long pile like velvet. Linen or cotton frocks (or fustian, a cloth with a linen warp and cotton weft) were worn in summer, close relations to the working-man's smock from which they derived. By the end of the 1760s, F.-A. de Garsault's *L'Art du Tailleur* acknowledged the existence of 'la Fraque, espèce de justaucorps leger, nouvellement en usage' (the frock, a kind of light coat, newly in fashion), but it was not truly fashionable until the 1770s outside England. With the shorter frock, a short waistcoat was worn, de Garsault's 'veston . . . espèce de Veste moderne à basques courtes' (a kind of modern waistcoat with short skirts).[12]

When Boswell made his pilgrimage to Rousseau in 1764, it was winter, so 'above all I wore a greatcoat of green camlet lined with fox-skin fur, with the collar and cuffs of the same fur';[13] in this he was painted in Rome by George Willison in 1765 (pl. 79). This greatcoat, which we have already noted as being the staple out-of-doors garment, was increasingly important as a fashionable replacement for the coat, which was no longer ample enough to serve for travelling in bad weather. It took various forms, that worn by Boswell being made in the form of a nightgown with wrap-over front; the *London Chronicle* of 1762 found that 'very spruce smarts have no buttons nor holes upon the breast of these surtouts . . . and their garments only wrap over their breasts like a morning gown'.[14] The most usual fastening was by buttoning down the front; this was what the French called the *redingote*, the original overcoat with side seams worn when riding, and an alternative to the short, buttoned, circular cape. By the middle of the century, the surtout was quite sophisticated in cut and trimming, with buttoned or turned-back cuffs, single or double-breasted fastening and often with more than one collar for extra warmth. It should, said *L'Art du Tailleur*, strictly speaking, be worn in the country but it was increasingly worn in town.

As well as being fashionable, the surtout was functional. George Washington in 1759 ordered 'a Newmarket great-coat with a loose hood to it, made of Blew Drab or broadcloth . . . let it be made of such cloth as will turn a good shower of rain'.[15] In England, umbrellas for men (which had been introduced by Jonas Hanway in 1756) were regarded as effete and detrimental to the livelihood of the hackney coachmen; when John Macdonald brought a silk umbrella from Spain to England in 1778, people shouted

78   E. Jeaurat, *Three Men at a Café*, 1760s

The greatcoat in the forefront of this drawing, with a collar of contrasting colour, has to be capacious enough to cover the flared coat beneath it.

79   G. Willison, *James Boswell*, 1765

'Frenchman, why don't you get a coach?' and Francis Place remembered in his youth the coachmen 'lashing the peoples umbrellas with their whips as they drove away'.[16]

The elegance of the fashionable man in the middle years of the eighteenth century depended on total perfection from head to toe, not just in tailoring but in the tasteful use of accessories and even a discreet use of cosmetics. The ideal masculine face was smooth and clean-shaven (only a very few soldiers, actors and those leading a deliberately bohemian existence wore beards or moustaches). The *Female Spectactor* (1744) found it necessary to poke fun at the male predilection for scents, patches, lip salves, cold cream and rouge – cosmetics widely used in the upper reaches of society until the early nineteenth century.[17] Criticism occurred when cosmetics were too heavily applied or the pursuit of a soft white complexion was taken too far: Smollett's Captain Whiffle, for example, was ridiculed for wearing a face mask and white gloves to protect his skin, and Catherine the Great told in her *Memoirs* of the Danish envoy at the Russian court in 1750, known as the 'white count on account of his complexion' which he nurtured by covering 'his face and hands with ointment before going to bed'.[18] In an age in which a hearty intake of food and drink was the norm, a rubicund complexion was often the result; the critic and journalist Friedrich Melchior Grimm found it necessary to tone down his complexion with ceruse (white lead).

As the cut of the suit changed relatively slowly, the dressing of the hair or wig assumed greater importance. The *London Magazine* for 1753 gave some advice to *Monsieur à la Mode*:

> Let a well frizzled wig be set off from his face;
> With a bag quite in taste from Paris just come,
> That was made and ty'd up by Monsieur Frisson;
> With powder quite grey, his head is complete,
> If dress'd in the fashion, no matter for wit . . .
> Then a black solitaire his neck to adorn,
> Like those of Versailles, by the courtiers there worn.[19]

Wigs, according to the *London Chronicle* (1762) 'are essential to every person's head, as lace is to their cloaths'. Although earlier in the century men could have their own hair dressed with pomatum and then powdered, by the 1740s all except the lowest classes wore wigs of some kind. The most usual wig was the bag-wig, with the side hair formed into rigid rolls of curls; the French word 'boucle' came to be the English 'buckle', and to keep the hair in buckle meant to keep to the tightness of the roll, a sign of a well-dressed wig. Frederick the Great, for example, was notoriously indifferent about his clothing and about his wig, which was 'dressed with a single buckle on each side. From their being very carelessly put up and unequally powdered, we may naturally conclude that the friseur had been greatly hurried in the execution of his office'.[20] The number and type of side rolls to the wig varied, with one being fashionable in the 1750s and two generally the rule in the 1760s: Beaumont's *Enciclopédie Perruqière* (1757) has many names for very

Next to the guitar in this Spanish still life is a back view of the formal bag-wig.

similar styles. W. H. Pyne's father, a weaver, in the 1760s 'had three wigs; two were of the same pattern, with two curls on each side; these were every-day wigs, one of which Ned regularly brought, nicely powdered, every morning when he came to shave master and my uncle; the other he took away to dress; the third was a Sunday wig: this was carried off on the Friday and returned on Saturday morning'.[21]

Wigs were an expensive item of the male wardrobe, but so essential that every man with tolerable claims to substance would have enough to ensure that while one was on his head, others were ready dressed. The best hair was human hair (which sold at about £1 a pound), but it needed constant dress-ing with pomatum to keep the curls and toupet in place and then had to be heated to retain the style: wigs were heated in ovens, but hair on the cus-tomer's head was twisted into curl papers and curled with a hot iron. Cheaper wigs were made of horsehair and goatshair (though the latter broke off too easily). Other materials included Edward Wortley Montagu's famous wig made of copper and iron wire which Walpole admired in 1751 and Dr Johnson's wig of worsted given to him in 1777 by Henry Thrale because it stayed longer in curl (for this reason, wool wigs were widely worn by sailors on long voyages).

Pomatum for the hair and hair powder made from rice flour were often perfumed (Rome was reputed to produce some of the best quality). The secret of a good barber or valet was to spread the powder evenly. The gentleman sat in a small closet, with a powdering jacket to protect himself from the rain of powder; the comte de Ségur in Vienna in 1789 found the

Englishman at Paris
1767

81   H. Bunbury, *An Englishman at Paris*, 1767

The bluff Englishman dressed in his frock and carrying a sturdy cane is surrounded by exaggerated French types; the peasant or worker in trousers and sabots, the well-fed monk, the effeminate hair-dresser carrying an umbrella or parasol and the over-refined nobleman in his carriage, who wears a powdered bag-wig and fine lace shirt ruffle.

82   Detail of pl. 75

Cazotte's wig has a curving roll of hair over the ears and a black silk bag at the nape of the neck. The black ribbon, brought round to the front *en solitaire*, is a perfect foil to the white lace of the shirt ruffle.

old Austrian statesman Count Kaunitz keeping to the elaborate wig of his youth, and to ensure that the powder was put on evenly, 'he proceeded to a closet destined for this purpose between two rows of servants, who, armed with large puffs, covered him with a cloud of hair powder'.[22] In the following year, Nikolai Mikhailovich Karamzin, a Russian visitor to London, in order to have his hair dressed went to a barber, 'who having first unmercifully flayed my face, plaistered my head with flour and tallow. "Alas, I am no longer in Paris", I said to myself with a sigh, "where the powder-puff of the ingenious lively Rulet played like a gentle zephyr around my head and strewed it with a resplendent white aromatic rime"'.[23] The French made the best barbers and hairdressers, a fact picked out by the Master Peruke-makers of London in 1763, who claimed that 'swarms of French hair-dressers' were depriving them of their business, and that men were increasingly 'beginning to dress their own hair pernicious to their [the wig-makers'] trade'. This custom was gradually to increase towards the end of the 1760s, in spite of the barbers' protests; some were able to impose their will on their customers, and the young Goethe, finishing his education in Strasbourg in 1770, was told firmly by a barber that his hair would never take a 'frisure' (that is, dressing) and he had to cut it off and wear a wig. Even Dr Johnson, visiting Paris with the Thrales in 1775 and astonishing the French with his rusty suit and his habit of speaking Latin, found it worth while to make some sartorial effort and bought a French wig, which must have been better fitting than the 'little old shrivelled unpowdered wig' that he wore when Boswell first visited his chambers in the Temple in 1763.

The wig that he purchased in Paris was probably a bob wig, for this was the most usual undress wig worn by the middle classes and by older men generally in the middle decades of the century: the hair was curled or frizzed up all round, stopping short of the shoulder. The campaign wigs with locks of hair were worn into the 1750s by older men but by the 1760s they were very old-fashioned and the young William Hickey's favourite term of abuse for anyone he regarded as out-of-date was 'a horrid perriwig bore'.

Some fashionable wigs in the 1760s copied those worn by the working classes. The best-known was the 'scratch wig' which the *London Chronicle* called 'the Blood's skull covering', 'combed over the forehead untoupeed, to imitate a head of hair, because these gentlemen love to have everything natural about them'. They were the colour of natural hair, the wearer's own hair mingling with the false hair at the front, dressed with pomatum. Smollett saw them being worn in the streets of Paris in the mid-1760s, an early example of English 'sporting' fashions being adopted by the French.

Grey or white powder was the finishing touch for formal wigs but the bob wigs were usually unpowdered, the most popular colours being black and shades of brown from the almost blonde to the very dark. Red hair was intensely disliked: when Smollett's Roderick Random came from Scotland to London in 1748, one of his first purchases was 'a good handsome bob' which cost him 10*s*., for his red hair 'was sufficient to beget an antipathy against me in all mankind'. For those who wished to keep to their own hair and not to wear a wig (which was the obvious solution), the *Gentleman's Magazine* for 1770 published a recipe for making red hair black with a dye of black lead and ebony shavings.

An essential part of the outfit of a well-dressed man was the hat, increasingly carried under the arm as the hairstyle gradually rose in the 1760s. The three-cornered style remained in vogue throughout the middle years of the eighteenth century, with slight variations in size and type of brim or trimming and often named after famous battles (Dettingen in 1743) or men of fashion (Nivernois). The Nivernois hat was named after the French ambassador to London in the 1760s, Louis Mancini-Mazarini, duc de Nivernois, a man famed for his elegance and good breeding: it had a low, round crown and a very wide brim that was rolled over at the edges into a broad triangle. When William Hickey was in Madras in 1769 he attracted a great deal of attention when he wore this hat newly brought out from England, for it was small compared to the large hats worn out there. Although hats became smaller towards the end of the 1760s, the main differences in style related to the cocking of the brims; 'some have their hats open before like a Church-spout, or the tin scale they weigh flour in, some wear them rather sharper, like the nose of a greyhound', declared the *London Chronicle* of 1762, whereas Quakers made 'a point of their faith not to wear a button or loop tight-up; their Hats spread over their heads like a pent-house, and darken the outward man to signify they have the inward light'.[24]

The loop and button fastened the hat up at one side and provided an opportunity for the display of wealth and taste, for at court diamonds and

Placing the hand between the buttons of the waistcoat was not only an approved gesture of elegance, it served also to show off the fine lace of the shirt sleeve ruffle and to keep the hat firmly in place under the arm.

other precious stones were used for the button and also for the hat-clasp, which was sometimes pinned on. One of the most famous French royal diamonds was called the Regent, bought in 1717 and, according to Saint-Simon, 'the size of a greengage plum', it was worn as a hat button by the kings of France throughout the eighteenth century. The French kings also wore another famous diamond, the Sancy, as part of the epaulette holding the cordon bleu of the order of the Saint-Esprit. Orders were an important part of the male jewellery, for precious stones surrounded the badge and held the sash in place. On gala occasions royalty sparkled like the stars they wore: to an English visitor at the court of Spain in the 1770s, the men of the royal family glittered 'like the belt of the constellation of Orion'. When Keysler visited the Saxon royal treasury in Dresden in 1730 he was amazed by the stones that he saw, which included a diamond setting for an order of the Golden Fleece which had cost 200,000 thalers. He noted also 'a set of diamond buttons for a suit of cloaths, diamond buckles and cane heads, one

84   A. Roslin, *Gustavus III of Sweden, with his Brothers Karl* [later Charles XIII] *and Fredrik-Adolf*, 1771

All three brothers wear sumptuous embroidered silk court costume *à la française* and the Swedish Order of the Seraphim. The most luxurious is worn by Gustavus III – glittering cloth of gold embroidered in gold and silver (pl. 85).

of a diamond the size of a nutmeg'.[25] For the grandest occasions, suit buttons were made of diamonds, such as those seen on the coat of the Austrian ambassador in London by Lady Mary Coke in 1768, which had cost him £7000. In the following year at Lyons, Lady Mary found that the duc de Villars even had his shirt buttons made of diamonds. Not only were suit seams covered with diamonds for occasions like royal marriages but so were swords and canes. This was particularly the case in Russia where the nobility 'were almost covered in diamonds' which formed 'their buttons, buckles, hilts of swords and epaulets'; in 1777, Catherine the Great gave Gustavus III of Sweden not only the Alexander Nevsky order in brilliants, but a cane with a knob made of a single diamond worth 60,000 roubles.

Such lavish display was rarely seen in England, where more modest jew-ellery was the rule. Except at court, buttons were made of crystal or paste

85 Detail of pl. 84

set in silver, gold or base-metal cups. Shoe buckles, which became larger in the 1740s, were very often made of materials such as steel, brass, pinchbeck and quartz, which could be worked into very elaborate designs and suited the more delicate shoe with pointed toe and smaller, slightly lower heel. From the middle of the century, the growing feeling in England that too much glitter was vulgar restricted the acceptable use of precious stones to that in small stock or breeches buckles, or in finger rings of brilliants.

★   ★   ★

Women

The rococo, with its emphasis on the ornamental frivolity of dress and accessories, is considered by many today to be the epitome of eighteenth-century elegance; its essential features were the love of surface decoration, a fondness for asymmetrical, curvilinear forms and an eroticism and succulence which can best be seen in the portraits by Boucher in the 1740s. To many contemporaries the rococo in art seemed a decadent working out of the essential lines of the baroque, but without its seriousness (the word 'rococo', first used during the very different moral and artistic climate of the French Revolutionary years, was a term of abuse), very often degenerating into meaningless superfluity of form. By the 1750s, many artists felt that domestic virtues and public morality should be upheld by art, which, as practised by Boucher (and the artists whom Clive Bell called 'upholsterers to the nobility and gentry'), was often mere decoration. Certainly the rococo was a princely and urban art form, which demonstrated a kind of opulence in taste sympathetic to absolute rule; it was thus adopted by the wealthier German princes with their admiration of French culture and their own tradition (particularly in the south and in Austria) for the more extreme forms of the baroque, but it never quite got off the ground in the more democratic and tepid climate of England. Indeed, by the time that the rococo in terms of dress came to England in the 1750s, there was already a movement towards the more restrained and classical in art, which was itself to be taken up in costume in the 1760s.

In 1745, Madame de Pompadour commenced her reign as *maîtresse en titre* to Louis XV and her fashion sense was dominant for the next decade; she summed up the elegance of the rococo which could so easily in a less practised wearer seem mere fussiness of dress and decoration. From 1752, her intimacy with the king ceased but she continued to dominate the French court until her death in 1764, even in 1752 being made lady-in-waiting to the modest and retiring queen, with whom she had the good sense always to be on the best of terms.

The sack or *robe à la française*, usually worn over small side hoops, was the dress most typical of the period; to the English it was sometimes known as a 'negligée', a slightly confusing term as, in fact, it was gradually becoming more a formal gown, more fitted to the waist and with the bodice cut separately and seamed to the skirt. It was worn as an open robe (though the English kept to the closed version until the end of the 1740s), with stomacher pinned to the sides of the bodice; the robings were, from the middle of the 1740s, carried down to the hem, increasing in size and elaboration. From about 1740, the pleated cuff was replaced by sleeve flounces, growing in number (often three at the end of the decade) and in size; these were cut to hang very short inside the bend of the arm, but long over the elbow. By the end of the 1740s, this type of sleeve was also seen on the tighter-fitting gowns preferred by the English, such as the mantua and the nightgown. The mantua, by the 1740s, was worn in England at court, but the earlier style of

86   After H. Gravelot, *A Woman with a Fan*, 1744

The cap with long lappets, and the mantua with folded-back train denote formal dress for an English lady at this period.

87   F. Boucher, *The Marquise de Pompadour*, 1759

Pompadour's dress of peach-coloured taffeta is a riot of three-dimensional decoration: frills, ribbons and flounces – the quintessence of the rococo.

skirt drapery with the train gathered to fall over the hips was no longer possible because of the huge square hoops of the period. The skirt was cut separate from the bodice at the front and folded round to the back, but by the end of the 1740s, the side pieces were removed altogether so the back panel only was cut in one with the bodice, forming a train for court dress. The train was increasingly coming to be associated with formal court wear and could in some cases be made totally separate from the dress, hooking on above the waist.

Although the sack dress was widely worn in England and Scotland (the Scottish ladies were sometimes quicker than the English to adopt French fashions), the English preferred a tighter-fitting open gown such as the nightgown, which was less formal for everyday than the mantua with its back draping; sometimes the bodice extended without a seam into the skirt, sometimes it was cut quite separately. It was a gown worn in the mornings, usually with a kerchief crossed over the bosom, an apron and a quilted petticoat. In Richardson's novel of 1748, *Clarissa*, it captivated Lovelace, who wrote to his friend Belford of Clarissa, 'Her morning-gown was a pale primrose-coloured paduasoy, the cuffs and robings curiously embroidered by the fingers of this ever-charming Arachne, in a running pattern of violets and their leaves; the light in the flowers silver; gold in the leaves . . . A white handkerchief concealed – O Belford! what still more inimitable beauties did it not conceal! . . . Her ruffles were the same as her mob. Her apron a flowered lawn. Her coat white satten, quilted.'[26]

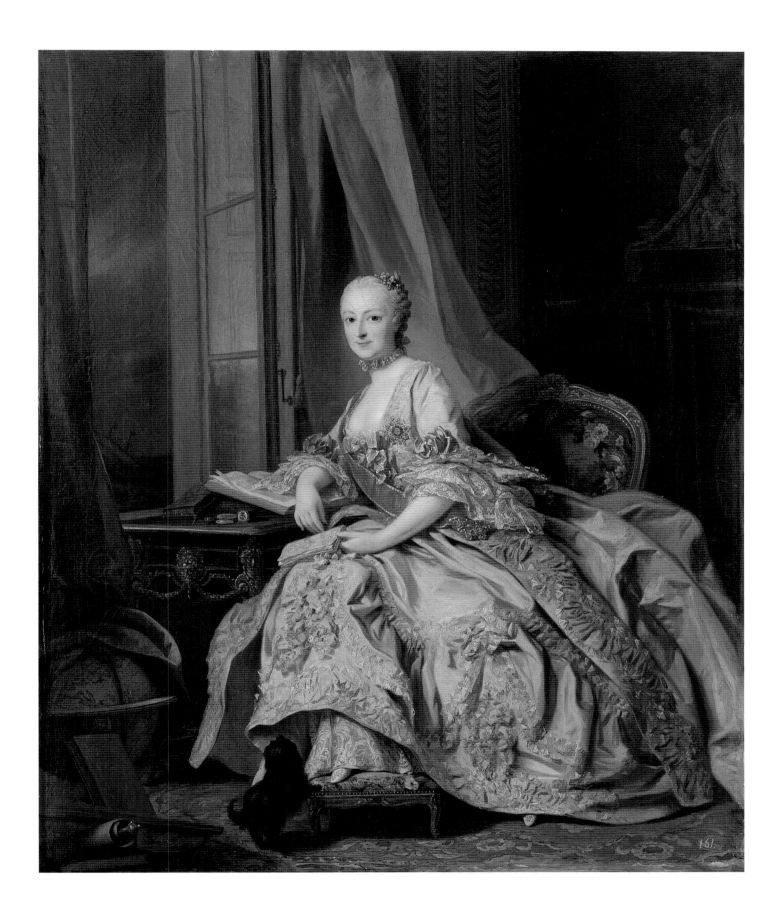

F. Hayman, *A Scene from Samuel Richardson's Novel* Clarissa Harlowe: *Robert Lovelace prepares to abduct Clarissa*, c.1753–4

In the novel, published 1748, Lovelace describes Clarissa's clothes in almost fetishistic detail, from the mob cap matching her sleeve ruffles, the yellow silk of the dress embroidered 'in a running pattern of violets and their leaves; the light in the flowers silver, gold in the leaves' (pl. 91) and white quilted satin petticoat to the braided blue satin shoes, and so on. While retaining some of Richardson's costume details, such as the yellow embroidered silk dress, Hayman brings the outfit into line with English rococo taste of the early 1750s, replacing the quilted petticoat with one matching the dress (the shoes also match the dress) and the cap with a ribbon in the hair.

92 (*page 142*)   Detail of pl. 93

93 (*page 143*)   F.-H. Drouais, *The Marquise d'Aigurandes*, 1759

At the height of the rococo period, even patterned silks like this striped and floral brocade are covered in three-dimensional trimmings – ribbons, ruffles and furbelows all decorated with metal lace.

91 (*facing page*)   Detail of pl. 90

Lovelace admired the delicate floral embroidery which Clarissa had worked herself; this type of decoration was particularly to be seen in England and Italy, where ladies were slow to adopt the three-dimensional ornamentation of the dress that was an essential part of the rococo, preferring a plainer surface on which to embroider the large flower designs in silk or wool which were popular. Embroidery may have been the inspiration for the fine botanical English Spitalfields silks of the 1740s; in 1742, Mrs Delany noted 'several very handsome flowered silks, shaded like embroidery'.[27] Any sense of the roroco in dress in England in this decade manifested itself through the serpentine lines of the delicate meandering floral designs on light grounds that were popular for woven silks and which were exported in large quantities to the fashion-conscious Americans. Silks were lighter in the 1740s and 1750s (heavy damasks and huge flowered brocades were out of fashion except at court), and small flowers often twined round trellises or meandered by the side of stripes. Much use was made of design motifs such as ribbons, butterflies, garlands and feathers: for a royal birthday in 1747, Mrs Delany had a gown made of 'a flowered silk . . . a pale deer-coloured figured ground; the flowers, mostly purple, are mixed with white feathers'.[28]

Great ingenuity was used to cover the surface of dresses with padded robings and furbelows, ribbons, feathers and garlands of artificial flowers. In 1746, Mrs Delany, attending a reception at Leicester House, the home of the Prince of Wales, found the Duchess of Portland in a gown of 'white satin, the petticoat rufed, and robings and facings'; two years later she described

94 T. Gainsborough, study of a woman seen from behind, early 1760s

Dress was meant to be as attractive in retreat as in advance, which may explain the popularity of the sack dress; one of the most characteristic gestures of the eighteenth century is the curve of the arm, allowing for the display of the treble sleeve ruffles, hoisting the dress slightly at the back. This had the additional advantage of revealing the ankle and the graceful curves of the high-heeled shoes.

95 F.-H. Drouais, *Madame de Pompadour*, 1763–4

the trousseau of Lady Frances Carteret, which included a dress of 'white, flounced, with a magnificent silver trimming all over the gown and petticoat'.[29] Such French styles, with frills and furbelows, were being worn in England by the end of the 1740s and had reached Russia by 1750, where the young Grand Duchess (and future Empress) Catherine annoyed the Empress Elizabeth by adopting the new French dresses flounced all over and with zig-zag borders.

Mrs Delany was most censorious about what she called 'the tubs of hoops' that reached an enormous width in the mid-1740s in England, although they had, as Elizabeth Montagu was told by a friend returning from Paris in 1742, disappeared from French dress except at court. In 1741, an English painter found the ladies in Rome wearing a sack 'extended on each side by a hoop, not quite six yards wide'; by the middle of the 1740s, the hoops had become huge pyramid shapes, which were to turn into squares at the end of the decade. Such extremes were bound to attract comment: a writer in the *British Magazine* of September 1746 was struck at Vauxhall by the appearance of a lady 'whose Paraphernalia fill'd up three Fourths of the Breadth of the principal Walk, and spread over almost an equal Space of Ground behind her; the Hoop extending to an enormous Distance on each Side, and a majestick Length of Sack trailing behind, and doing the Office of a Broom on the gravel Walk'.[30]

By the 1750s, fashionable English ladies had abandoned their large hoops either for small side hoops or none at all, causing their gowns to trail on the ground, more or less elegantly according to their style. In 1754, Mrs Delany could not help but admire the casual elegance of Mary Gunning Lady Coventry who wore 'a black silk sack, made for a large hoop, which she wore without any, and it trailed a yard on the ground';[31] a few years later, Oliver Goldsmith derided a bourgeoise imitation of the fashionable style when he saw 'a fat lady in a lutestring trollopee . . . how she waddles along with her train two yards behind her'.[32] The trollopee was a particularly descriptive word for the sometimes slovenly appearance that such a trailing gown, without hoops, made to the eyes of those accustomed to the tautness of silk spread over an understructure; it could also mean the original *contouche* style of sack which some preferred for comfort and convenience.

Flowers and floral designs dominated dress silks of the mid-eighteenth century, becoming more delicate in the 1760s when small flowers or bunches of flowers were mixed in with lace-like meanders or diaper frameworks or compartmented by scrolls and fronds. Painted silks from China came to Europe by way of Indian depots, their beautifully observed, naturalistic flower patterns making them both expensive and fashionable, as can be seen in Drouais's portrait of Madame de Pompadour (pls 95 and 98). General Napier advertised in 1761 for the recovery of a stolen 'painted silk Negligée and Petticoat, the ground white, a running pattern of flowers and leaves, the edges of the leaves painted in silver, and the veins gold, with some birds and butterflies painted thereon'.[33]

96 J. G. Grooth, *An Unknown Woman*, 1760s

Painted silks, such as this one, allow for a freedom in design not possible for woven silks, and contribute to the elegant informality of this morning dress, with its delicate worked muslin sleeve ruffles. A touch of German provincialism can be seen, however, in the black silk kerchief round the neck and in the lace cap with pinned up lappets.

97 Detail of pl. 37a

98 (*facing page*) Detail of pl. 95

The beautiful painted silk of Madame de Pompadour's dress and the large flounce of French needle lace (possibly Argentan) that decorates the skirt are depicted with consummate skill by Drouais.

Chinese influence showed also in chinoiserie textile designs; amusing and totally imaginary 'Chinese' landscapes with pagodas, parasols and mandarins were featured in the many pattern books published in the mid-eighteenth century, which also inspired designs for china, furnishings and wallpaper and contributed to the vogue for all things Chinese so tellingly satirized by Oliver Goldsmith in *The Citizen of the World* (1762). Just as popular as the painted silks, and cheaper, were the printed cottons. Often with Chinese patterns but versatile enough to imitate silk designs as well, they could be produced quickly to match the changing moods for allegorical designs, pastoral scenes or topical allusion. By the middle of the century, many centres in Europe had begun to manufacture polychrome printed cottons of high quality, the most famous being the Jouy factory in France established in 1760. Printed linens and cottons featured increasingly for jackets and for dresses in the wardrobes of women of all classes: an inventory of Madame de Pompadour's clothes on her death (1764) included 'indiennes', some half-mourning toilettes in black and white,[34] and in the same year Barbara Johnson paid 3*s.* a yard for eight yards of 'a Blue & White Copper-plate linnen' to make a 'Gown' (printing linen by copperplate had been invented in the early 1750s, Mrs Delany observing the process in Ireland in 1752). Many of the references in Barbara Johnson's album are to 'gowns' made of linen or cotton. These may be the informal gowns, some wrapping over and tying with a sash, that were, with the vogue for the oriental, becoming high fashion in the 1760s. Painted silks, printed fine cottons and embroidered muslins made both formal dresses (Madame de Pompadour's inventory recorded a robe and skirt of muslin embroidered with small silver bouquets[35]) and the loosely draped gowns with long sleeves which appealed to artists inspired by the neo-classical.

Another new fashion (although it had earlier been seen in workingwomen's dress) was that for long sleeves, which were first worn with informal gowns and travelling dresses. A long-sleeved version of the sack, usually three-quarter-length and with a high neck and a buttoned, unstiffened bodice, was called a 'German habit' or a 'Brunswick' and was widely worn in Germany from the middle of the century; the *London Magazine* for January 1764 noted that the going-away dress for Princess Augusta (sister of George III) was 'the German fashion, a scarlet silk buttoned before, sleeves down to her wrists and with a sack behind'. The early sleeves had a break at the elbow with a ruffle (so ingrained was the notion of a natural break there), but the sleeve of the late 1760s ended in a small ruched cuff. In Barbara Johnson's album, a three-quarter-length Brunswick ordered in 1768 had military buttoned-back revers and was used as a garment for out-of-doors; but later, in 1772, a Brunswick of blue and white checked cotton was probably more seen as an informal, indoor dress. As was customary with informal clothing, the latest textile designs were used, the tiny spots, checks and plain stripes anticipating the formal silk designs of a decade later.

Also indicative of the change in mood from large expanses of unbroken surface to the fragmented surface of the rococo in dress was the popularity

of the jacket and petticoat style, which gradually rose in the social scale during the middle years of the eighteenth century. From the 1740s, many women wore jackets made with a sackback; they were worn with a stomacher pinned on over a laced-up, boned lining, but after about 1750 the usual fastening was front-buttoning. 'Nothing is so ravishing than an easy dishabille', said the *Connoisseur* in 1754, referring to 'the short sacks (pet-en-lairs) and negligées'. Such jackets were often worn out-of-doors; Horace Walpole described his old (and dying) enemy Lady Mary Wortley Montagu in 1762 as wearing 'a kind of horseman's riding coat, calling itself a pet-en-l'air, made of a dark green (green I think it had been) brocade with coloured and silver flowers and lined with furs'.[36] But generally for out-of-doors the riding habit, which had been thought so eccentric when worn by English travellers to Europe in the early years of the century, was widely worn until the feminine versions of the greatcoat overtook it in popularity. Sometimes the riding

99 L.-G. de Carmontelle, *The Craymoyel Family*, 1760

The proud father, dressed in formal suit and bag-wig, holds the leading strings attached to the gown of the child, who wears on its head a feather-trimmed *bourrelet* as a protection against falls. The mother's hooded, sack-back Brunswick gown has the characteristic long sleeves broken at the elbow with a double, pinked ruffle.

100 P. Batoni, *Lady Mary Fox, later Baroness Holland*, 1767

The sitter wears a travelling costume, a Brunswick gown (see pls 37a and 97) of grey silk, comprising a fitted three-quarter-length hooded jacket and skirt. It is a practical yet feminine costume with its ruched trimming, striped ribbons decorating the sleeves, lace jabot and small lace headdress.

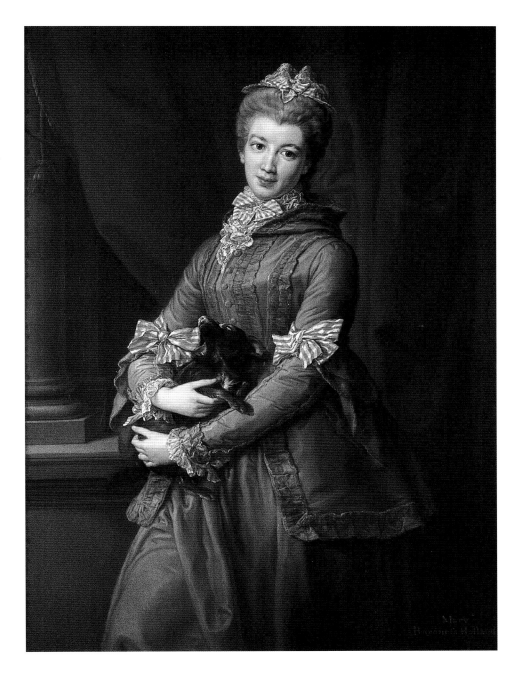

101 (*following page*) Detail of pl. 113

Fur is both decorative and practical here. The twisted fur tippet is more pretty than functional, but the fur-lined, blue velvet muffetees (arm muffs) protect the skin from the cold and help to keep it soft and white.

habit was a three-piece suit in the traditional English style; the future Catherine the Great as a fashion-conscious German princess at the Russian court wore habits of silk camlet (these were not very practical as the rain made them shrink), one in particular 'of rich skyblue material with silver braid and crystal buttons which looked exactly like diamonds. My black hat had a string of diamonds round it'.[37] Princess Ulrica of Prussia's travelling gown (when she married the heir to the Swedish crown in 1744) was 'a rose colord amazonian habit, trim'd with silver; the lappels and vest were of sea green. She had on an English hat of black velvet, adornd with a white feather'.[38]

Many German princesses rode astride and dressed like men; an English visitor to the court of Mecklenburg Schwerin in 1766 found the riding habit with cocked hat and bag-wig to be the everyday dress of the ladies except on Sundays.[39] Breeches for hunting were worn in many countries (except in England where the art of riding sidesaddle was cultivated) and the inventory of Madame de Pompadour's clothes contained 'culottes pour la chasse', some of knitted wool or silk, which could alternatively and with more propriety be worn under a riding skirt (Casanova saw, in 1758, ladies skating on the ice in Amsterdam with black velvet drawers worn under short petticoats). The idea of the riding habit as a kind of uniform based on the male suit was replaced in England in the mid-eighteenth century by the riding jacket and skirt (this is probably what Barbara Johnson meant by a 'Riding dress' that she ordered in 1757, taking seven yards of brown fustian) or a riding coat called a 'joseph', usually green in colour. In Goldsmith's *The Vicar of Wakefield* (1766) a large historical family group was to be painted, Olivia to be an Amazon 'in a green joseph richly laced with gold and with a whip in her hand'.[40]

Yet over the hoops and the fragile decorated surface of the dress a cloak was the most practical garment and also the most luxurious. To the young Catherine the Great, coming to Russia in 1744 from a penny-pinching court, Russian splendour seemed to be typified in her first present, a cloak of gold brocade lined with sable. Such full-length cloaks were lined with the most expensive soft furs such as squirrel and ermine; the fashionable beauty Lady Coventry attracted the attention of Mrs Delany in 1754 in her 'pink satin long cloke lined with ermine mixt with squirrel skins'. Shorter, hooded cloaks were less sumptuous but more functional; to an out-of-town enquiry, Mrs Delany in 1755 described the pelisse as a cloak 'made of satin or velvet, black or any colour lined or trimmed with silk, satin or fur, with slits for the arms to come out'.[41] Summer cloaks had the hood and the edge of the cloak ruched with tiny pleats; popular fabrics were dark glazed cottons, linens and silks. Even indoors small shoulder mantles made of silk, lace or feathers were needed to protect the skin and cover the décolletage; in the 1750s, black lace mantles were all the rage. They varied in shape from tiny shoulder capelets like large collars to the pelerine with front pendants crossed at the waist.

Not only was fur used to edge and line jackets and coats, but it was also used to line wrapping gowns; a 1744 Venetian trousseau included a wrapping gown of black velvet lined with marten and one of pale blue velvet lined with ermine and squirrel. However, its most rococo manifestation was for decoration on the dress; its fluffiness and the taste for sharp contrasts in fabrics (and sheer expensive impracticability) appealed to the fashionable lady, and from the 1740s fur was turned into robings, petticoat bands, stomacher ornaments, tippets and necklaces. Although it is often stated that this fashion for fur trimming came from the Polish styles introduced by Louis XV's wife Maria Lesczynska in the mid-1720s, it is more likely that it was made popular by the involvement of Central European troops – and in particular the Hungarian hussars with their glamorous, fur-lined uniforms of Oriental origin – in the War of the Austrian Succession which began in 1740; in any case, the French queen was no leader of fashion.[42] Fur was used also for the heavy swag-like decorations on court gowns. Ermine, in particular, which had once been reserved just for royalty, was a popular trimming: in 1740, Mrs Delany saw a dress at court of dark green velvet trimmed with ermine and with an ermine petticoat which must have been monstrously heavy. By the end of the 1760s, ermine was no longer a fashionable fur (soft, white furs like squirrel or Arctic fox and dyed rabbit were in vogue for edging pelisses) but it remained for the superfluity of ornament demanded at court. On one occasion in 1769, Elizabeth Montagu wore 'a corded blue tabby trimmed with Ermine which with fine lace and jewels makes a respectable figure and as I had the Ermine cost me little'.[43]

The middle years of the eighteenth century are years of show and splendour, very often superimposed on a lack of personal hygiene that we would find startling; ideas of cleanliness seem, in many cases, to have been honoured more in the breach than in the observance. A few, like Lord Chesterfield, regarded personal cleanliness as necessary for health and good manners, but many men would sympathize with Boswell who preferred to have 'a suit of clean linen every day' rather than to wash frequently, and consequently, according to the sculptor Joseph Nollekens (himself a man with a low standard of hygiene), stank. Although towards the end of the eighteenth century, with the growing emphasis on simplicity in dress and the increased use of washable fabrics, the standard of hygiene improved, there was a general acknowledgement that cosmetics and perfumes were necessary to rectify the inadequacies of plumbing (only the grandest houses had built-in baths and water supplies were erratic). Ideas of health were also involved, for many felt that it was, for example, dangerous to wash the hair because it made the brain 'humid' and so bran or ivory powder was used instead. Sweet floral perfumes were worn by both sexes to cover the lack of cleanliness and the smells of the streets.

Higher standards of physical cleanliness and appearance were expected of women throughout the century and there was no shortage of advice on skin care and cosmetics. The perfect face typified eighteenth-century ideas of regularity and proportion, being an oval shape with small straight nose, slightly rosy cheeks and lips and a white complexion. 'The Face is the chief Seat of Beauty' stated Antoine Le Camus, the author of *Abdeker, or The Art of preserving Beauty* (1754), who proceeded to list cures for skin disorders and recipes to improve its whiteness; white paint or white lead (ceruse) were used, although the dangers of the latter were recognized by the middle of the century. By this time the thicker paint was no longer needed to cover the ravages of smallpox and lighter face washes were used, such as mercury water or rice water, which were safe enough to cover the neck and bosom. In addition, parasols shielded the skin from the sun and masks protected it in bad weather. The face was as much a work of art as the costume and as much time had to be spent on it to achieve the delicate, enamelled effect that was admired in such leaders of fashion as Madame de Pompadour. With white skin, and the use of grey or white hair powder, rouge was necessary to give colour and so red lead was mixed with carmine or vermilion and painted on the cheeks to produce bright spots of colour. To appear natural was not the aim, said Casanova; he claimed that rouge emphasized the eyes and indicated an 'amorous fury'. The practice began in France, along with the use of hair powder, in the early years of the century. In Paris in 1739, John Russel found the women's faces made hideous by 'two globular spots . . . as fiery red as the orb of the sun when setting in a dusky evening'.[44] It continued to the Revolution, although after the middle of the century it was worn at court and in the evenings only. The custom rapidly spread to other countries in spite of attacks on the grounds of health and morality and, as early as 1723, Weber noted in Russia how it was a compliment to call a woman 'a red maid'. The red cheeks must have looked rather startling with the black teeth to be seen in the early eighteenth century – the wife of the English Resident was visited in Moscow in 1729 by an admiral's wife, 'her teeth being dyed black and shining as if japanned'.[45] The Russian custom for dyeing the teeth had disappeared by the mid-eighteenth century, but rouging continued until the end of the period; the comte de Ségur, accompanying Catherine the Great on a provincial tour of Russia in the mid-1780s, described how at the end of every day the Empress was covered in red from the homage of local ladies.

Wherever French fashions reigned, rouge was used; thus it was widely worn at the German courts and even at Vienna, although forbidden to the arch-duchesses and court ladies by Empress Maria Theresa. In England, rouge was not much worn except on very formal occasions; Lord Glenbervie, an inveterate collector of gossip, noted how people remembered the 'extraordinary ugliness' of the young Queen Charlotte at the English court in 1761, a plainness emphasized by her lack of rouge and powder, which she remedied eventually by adopting the latter but never the former. Italian women on the whole preferred a pale complexion: in Venice in 1785, Mrs Piozzi commented that the rest of the fashionable world, influenced by the cult of naturalism and sentimentality, had caught up with Italian taste in the vogue for a pale face. To emphasize the whiteness of the skin, the eyes were sometimes made up with lamp black or the residue of burnt ivory shavings and false eyebrows were made of fur or mouseskin. Another essential part of the female armoury (and worn also by men in the early eighteenth century) was the use of patches, made of 'black Taffety . . . cover'd with Gum Arabic'. This, too, was a French fashion, which could be taken to excess by the undiscriminating; the Russian ladies, said Weber in 1723, covered their faces in patches cut out in the shapes of trees and horses as well as the more usual suns, stars and moons.[46] The *Lady's Magazine* for 1759 stated that no woman should have more than one, 'or at the utmost one large patch and a little satellite stuck just by the greater planet'. The placing of the patch was a language of allusion. Le Camus said a patch 'at the exterior Angle of the Eye' was 'killing' and one 'in the midst of the Forehead, Majestic'; one in the

102 (*previous page*) Detail of pl. 123

In Boucher's *La Toilette* (1742), the modiste's red velvet, fur-trimmed pelisse is flung over a chair.

152

103 Detail of pl. 123

This is Boucher's ideal facial type: delicate and pert, with a perfect complexion enhanced by cosmetics (just one patch, near the eye) and lightly powdered curls.

middle of the cheek indicated gallantry, a patch near the lips the coquette, and one on the nose demonstrated daring.[47] Larger patches covered up the effects of venereal disease; the Germans called them 'Venus-blumen', claiming that this fashion was also the result of French influence.

As the face could be changed by art, so, too, could the hair or wig. With the contrariness that affects human nature, southern women preferred blonde hair, while their northern sisters desired black above all. In *The Art of Dress* (1717) the anonymous author declared:

> Not all your locks are equal in Renown,
> Red yields to Fair, and Black excells the Brown.[48]

In Italy, the women, said Thomas Nugent, 'affect yellow hair, as the Roman ladies and courtesans formerly did, and where nature denies them that colour (which it often does, their hair being generally black) they obtain it by art'.[49] The women in southern Italy used 'a lye of wood ashes' to turn their hair 'flaxen yellow'. In Venice, they dyed their hair in the sun as they had for hundreds of years; the more affluent (or less successful at dyeing) bought wigs of pale blonde hair from the convents of the Austrian Netherlands.

104 M.-Q. La Tour, *Marie-Madeleine Mazade, Madame Grimod de la Reynière*, 1751

The powdered hair, possibly a wig, is arranged in the tightly curled *tête-de-mouton* style. The sack dress is of watered silk and the separate lace stomacher bodice is front-fastening in the buttoned *compère* style. Notable aids to the elegant display of the hands are the fine painted fan and the embroidered knotting bag.

Although a greater variety of hair colouring was permissible in the fashion centres of north and western Europe, black was the most admired. In 1746, the Empress Elizabeth, with the kind of autocratic whim that ran in the family of Peter the Great, ordered all her ladies to shave their heads and wear black perukes.[50] As late as 1775, the *Lady's Magazine* gave a recipe for dyeing yellow hair; elderberries and wine simmered together would 'in time' produce 'an agreeable black colour'. By the 1780s, the uniformity of taste was breaking up; even red hair could be worn, and the changes could be rung with the use of red, blue and yellow powder in addition to the grey or white powder which had been *de rigueur* for most of the century.

The French had taken the lead in the 1720s with regard to the cutting and curling of the hair, which by the early 1740s was universally adopted. Some cut their hair short and curled it, as did Maria Theresa for the first time in 1743, for her coronation in Prague; the following year in Russia the newly arrived Catherine persuaded her ladies to adopt the new style, which they did though protesting that they looked like 'tufted birds'.[51] In England this *tête-de-mouton* style had arrived in the 1720s. Mrs Delany described it in 1727 as 'curley-murley', a style suited 'to the young and handsome', and it did not make much headway for another ten years, for many English-women preferred a longer style curling down the neck. By about 1740, the increasingly complicated small tight curls needed to be arranged by a male peruke-maker, thus beginning the masculine rule in the kingdom of female hairdressing which lasts to this day. Sometimes women wore a *tête-de-mouton* wig; 'you must cut off your Hair and get a little Periwig and a French Cap,' was the cry in Fielding's farce *Miss Lucy in Town* (1742) and the *Female Spectator* of 1744 described how an unfortunate lady, wearing a 'mischief-making hoop', tangled with a flock of sheep in the street, slipped in the rain, 'her gause cap half off her head in the scuffle, and her tête de mouton hanging down on one shoulder'.[52]

By the 1760s, hair was still curled short to the head at the back and sides, but smoothed back off the forehead; by the middle of the decade the hair was rising, often combed over a roll at the front, and set with small roll curls at the side. Lady Sarah Lennox advised a friend in 1766: 'The hair must be powdered, curled with very small curls . . . and neat, but it must be high before and give your head the look of a sugar loaf a little. The roots of the hair must be drawn straight up and not frized at all for half an inch.'[53] As the hair rose, artificial hair was needed to supplement the wearer's own. In 1766, the choleric novelist Smollett found the French women 'covered with a vast load of false hair, which is Frizzled on the forehead, so as exactly to resemble the wooly heads of the Guinea negroes'.[54] So complicated had hair-dressing become that in 1768 the first manual, *L'Art de la Coiffure des Dames Françoises*, was published; the author Jean Legros in the following year opened an Academy of Hair in Paris where ladies' maids and valets could practise on hired models and where the hairdressing was created for the dolls sent to the rest of Europe.

Caps and other hair ornaments were always considered as part of the total hairdressing. In the 1740s, the linen cap edged with lace and with lappets was increasingly a middle-class fashion, although the lappets, made of lace, continued to be worn at court until the end of our period. Other popular caps in this decade included the pinner, a circular cap edged with ruffles of linen or lace, and the round-eared cap, which curved rather like a bonnet to the level of the ears; from the mid-1740s there was a fashion for wiring the side frill of these caps – Mrs Delany called them 'vast winkers' – which corresponded to the width of the hooped skirt. The most chic of all indoor caps, popular from the 1730s to the 1780s, was the *dormeuse* or French night-cap, a version of the mob cap with a close-fitting crown decorated with a ribbon.

For more formal occasions, tiny wired caps, also from France, were the height of fashion in the 1750s; these were made of lace (the heavier Brussels lace was replaced by the lighter French and Flemish needlepoint laces, with fine mesh ground), but most often of blonde, which was lace made of white silk near Chantilly. The fashionable style for 1754 was a butterfly; the *Oxford Gazette and Reading Mercury* published a verse entitled *A la Mode* (1754) in which the lady of fashion was urged:

> Let your Cap be a butterfly, slightly hung on,
> Like the Shell of a Lapwing just hatch'd, on her Crown.[55]

That same year Mrs Delany admired Lady Coventry's 'French cap that just covered the top of her head, of blond, and stood in the form of a butterfly with its wings not quite extended'.[56] The variety of caps in the 1750s and 1760s was enormous, some named after popular whims, others after contemporary characters or historical personages. Walpole, in Paris in 1755, found a 'fureur des cabriolets' (this was a one-horse chaise currently the vogue amongst the fashionable): '. . . the men paint them on their waistcoats and have them embroidered for clocks on their stockings, and the women . . . are now muffled up in great caps with round sides, in the form of, and scarce less than, the wheels of chaises.'[57] The *London Chronicle* of 1762, amongst a list of fashionable caps, mentioned the 'Ranelagh Mob' of gauze which crossed under the chin, tying at the back of the neck, 'copied from the silk handkerchiefs which Market-women tie over their ears, roll about their throats, and then pin up to the nape of their necks'; also popular was the Mary Queen of Scots cap made of black gauze, with a peak in the front, and 'edged down the face with French beads'.[58] By the end of the 1760s, silk scarves, rolled up in a turban shape, demonstrated the new vogue for Turkish styles which was beginning to enter informal fashionable dress.

But the height of rococo delicacy in headwear was achieved by a style introduced by Madame de Pompadour in the mid-1740s and called in England, where it appeared in 1748, the pompon; it consisted of a small spray of flowers, feathers or jewels placed either centrally or to one side of the head and worn either on its own or with a small cap. Hogarth in his *Analysis of Beauty* (1755) declared that women of the best taste preferred 'a single feather, flower or jewel . . . on one side of the head'.[59] By the late 1760s, according to Lady Sarah Lennox, 'you must wear no cap, and only little, little flowers dab'd in on the left side; the only feather permitted is the black and white sultane'.[60] The most attractive pompons were made of jewels, sometimes *tremblant* on wires so that they quivered with the wearer's movements, like the one admired by Lady Jane Coke in 1752, 'a diamond bird with the wings stretched out, and in its beak held a diamond drop'.[61]

Jewellery was an intrinsic part of dress, particularly in the middle years of the eighteenth century. At court, women glittered in jewels, which were worn not just in their hair, ears, arms and necks but also on the dress itself; the inventory made on the death in 1767 of the Dauphine Marie-Josèphe of Saxony listed two *grandes parures* of jewels, which included diamond girdles, sleeve and shoulder knots, stomacher brooches and brooches for holding back the sides of the *grand habit*.[62] The petticoat was also covered in jewels, but the focal point of formal dress was the ornamentation of the stomacher made of precious stones, very often of diamonds; the stomacher was a series of interlocking brooches, frequently in bow or floral designs after the prevailing French rococo taste. For her wedding to George III in 1761, Queen Charlotte was given by her husband a stomacher of diamonds set in an openwork floral design of silver worth £70,000.

The clothes of the extremely wealthy could be covered in jewels; Russian empresses in particular liked a great show of precious stones sewn onto their court robes in addition to the formal parure and jewelled orders that were worn. When Peter the Great and his wife visited Berlin in 1717, the Czarina

105 Detail of pl. 93

The hair is tightly curled and powdered, then decorated with a floral pompon.

106 Detail of pl. 127

The plain and homely queen of France glitters in the jewellery essential for a state portrait – the diamonds and pearls that form her stomacher brooch and decorate her mantle.

(a courtesy title as she had not yet been crowned), in a famous description by an appalled hostess, 'wore a dozen orders and as many portraits of saints and relics fastened to the facing of her gown; so that when she walked, the jumbling of all these orders and portraits one against the other, made a tinkling noise like a mule in harness'.[63] By 1750, St Petersburg had 51 silversmiths and 15 goldsmiths, French and Swiss designers producing the rich and exotic jewelled objects (particularly with bright stones such as emeralds and rubies) that remained part of Russian taste until the end of the Romanov empire.

Above all, the bright glitter of diamonds was the most admired effect for the rich and fashionable, either as a brooch or necklace, or set against black ribbon at the neck. By the beginning of the eighteenth century, technical advances had led to the brilliant-cut diamond, so extensively faceted as to reflect a maximum of light. In the 1720s, fine-quality stones were coming from the newly discovered mines in Brazil (India had previously been the major source) and in *A Treatise on Diamonds and Pearls* (1750) the author, a well-known jeweller, headed a chapter: 'Of the superior worth of Diamonds over all other Jewels'.[64] Prices were high: Mrs Delany in 1756, describing a friend's wedding jewels which had cost £12,000, found that the necklace was 'most perfect brilliants, the middle stone worth a thousand pounds, set at the edge with small brilliants'.[65] Single stones made the popular pendeloque earrings worn by ladies of fashion and Madame de Pompadour's inventory contained a pair valued at 22,000 livres; the other style of earring seen in formal portraits was the girandole, with three pear-shaped drops.

Diamonds and other precious stones were used as dress buttons and to decorate hats; they also edged watches and miniatures such as those exchanged within royal families. The Dauphine Marie-Josèphe (mother of Louis XVI) had two bracelets with miniatures (one of Louis XV (her father-in-law), and the other of her husband) edged with small brilliants and set in six rows of pearls. A similar design can be seen in Lawrence's portrait of Queen Charlotte of 1789–90 (London, National Gallery). Pearls were age-old symbols of love and fidelity, suitable for miniatures; they had been fashionable since the end of the sixteenth century and in our period were most usually worn either as a single strand or as a choker of many rows, but always fastened at the back with a bow or ribbon. For those who could not afford the real thing, imitation pearls made of wax (called in England French beads) were available.

The English were in the vanguard of the movement towards simpler clothing and preferred the less expensive and less ostentatious types of jewellery. Very often, their jewellery comprised a simple brooch bow or pendant cross or clip earrings called snaps; it was not unusual for these to be made of paste, which was glass cut and polished into gem-like forms that reflected colour from foils placed at the back. Paste was the invention of G.-F. Stras, a Parisian jeweller who was well established in the quai des Orfèvres by the mid-1730s, leading a growing group of *bijoutiers-faussetiers*. Although French paste was the best quality for much of the eighteenth century, towards the end of the

109 (*below*) Detail of pl. 159

In accord with the simplicity of the costume worn by Princess Louise Augusta, the fan she carries is of plain coloured paper.

period many English ladies were buying native products, particularly the fine opaline paste made in Derbyshire.

Many of the prettiest rococo designs in jewellery were based on flowers; in Garrick and Colman's play *The Clandestine Marriage* (1766), a bride described to her sister her new brooch made in the shape of a bouquet 'of diamonds, and rubies and emeralds and topazes and amethysts – jewels of all colours, green, red, blue, yellow intermixt – the prettiest thing you ever saw in your life'. Fresh flowers were worn as nosegays, particularly at court, although keeping them fresh was a problem. By the 1750s the French wore water-filled bosom-bottles, described by Walpole as 'a tin funnel covered with green ribband . . . which the ladies wear to keep their bouquets fresh'.[66] They were adapted in the 1780s for the huge fashionable hairstyles; Baroness d'Oberkirch in 1782 wore fresh flowers in her hair in little flat bottles. Some women wore fresh flowers in the straw *bergère* hats, popular in England from the middle years of the century, and in France in the 1770s and 1780s when Marie Antoinette and her ladies played at rural simplicity. The best straw plait came from Livorno and the hats were made with a flat crown and wide brim, lined with silk and decorated with ribbons; chip hats were made of finely shaved willow or poplar, and were almost as popular for strolling in the parks, sometimes worn over a small linen cap. The correct dashing angle at which the hat was worn, particularly over the rising hairstyles of the late 1760s, was one of the distinguishing marks of the Englishwoman, Lady Mary Coke remarking, 'I never knew a foreigner that could tell how to put on an English hat.'

Accessories were an important part of dress and etiquette as well as a language suited to demonstrate good breeding and the more (or less) subtle aspects of courtship. Ribbons, for example, worn in knots at the bosom, waist and on the sleeves were, like patches, a language of gallantry. 'Knots below and knots above, / Emblems of the tyes of love,' declared a poem in the *London Magazine* of 1755. Fans were also an aid to coquetry, to hide a lady's blushes (Madame de Genlis, writing a dictionary of etiquette in 1818, felt that one of the greatest changes in manners was the new immodesty of girls compared with the blushing timidity of her youth) and to keep the heat off the face; César de Saussure, in England in the 1720s, found the ladies 'have but little talk, and the main conversation is the flutter of their fans'. These fans, in the scallop shape so typical of rococo ornament, were made in a variety of mediums including ivory, painted silk and paper, and lace. There were fans for every occasion and they were one of the earliest tourist souvenirs for they could be painted or printed with picturesque landscapes and topical allusions or they could depict pastoral and mythological scenes, some after famous paintings. Apart from a temporary fad in the middle of the 1740s for very large fans – the *Spectator* noted in 1744 that they were 'from three quarters of a foot to even two feet' in length – they were usually about eight or nine inches long. For ceremonial occasions they acted as offertory plates; the Baroness d'Oberkirch stated that it was etiquette at the court in France to give something to the queen on an open fan (the only time a

111 (*facing page*)   Detail of pl. 123

Silk thread escapes from the blue knotting bag hung on the fire screen in this detail from Boucher's *La Toilette*.

fan could be opened before her) but on the occasion when she tried to show Marie Antoinette a bracelet this way, she dropped it and had great difficulty bending in her court panier to retrieve it.

The difficulty with the many cosmetic and jewellery accessories – perfume flasks, stay hooks, patch boxes, mirrors, watches and so on – that a fashionable lady needed, was where to carry them. Some of the more decorative items were kept on a châtelaine worn at the waist; less wealthy women kept their handkerchiefs, keys and money in their pockets tied by tapes round the

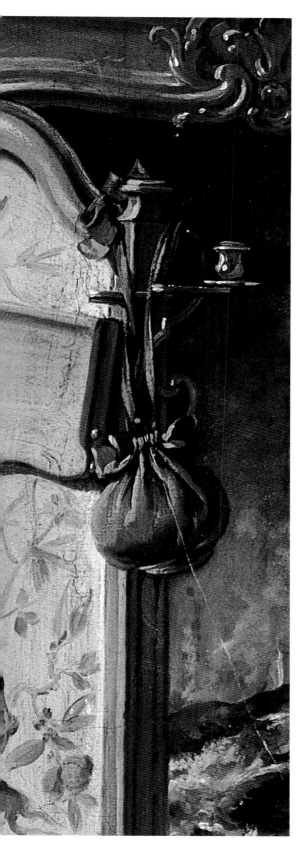

waist under the petticoat. But in the 1760s, an alternative place to hold such lightweight impedimenta was a knotting bag, made of silk and with a drawstring top. Knotting had been a popular pastime since the end of the seventeenth century and the bags were traditionally used to hold the linen or silk thread which was knotted with a small shuttle into a decorative braid which could be sewn onto fabric and small textile objects. The shuttles themselves were often a kind of jewellery, made of, for example, gold, silver, crystal, mother-of-pearl or ivory. Knotting (like the previous rage for *parfilage*, called 'drizzling' in England – the unravelling of gold and silver braid from tassels, galloons and epaulettes for the metal content which was then sold) was not so much a constructive pastime, unless one was highly skilled like Mrs Delany, but a chance to show off the gracefulness of the hands and to gossip with the pretence of work. According to Madame du Deffand, friend of Horace Walpole and hostess of a famous literary salon:

> Vive le parfilage!
> Plus de plaisir sans lui!
> Cet important ouvrage
> Chasse partout l'ennui
> Tandis que l'on déchire
> Et galons et rubans
> L'on peut encore médire
> Et déchirer les gens.

(Long live parfilage!/There's no pleasure without it!/This important employment/Chases away boredom./While one unravels [tears apart]/Braids and ribbons/One can also gossip/And tear apart other people.)

Knotting was a fashionable pastime at court and at many social occasions; Lady Mary Coke found ladies knotting at the opera in 1770 and, although she herself did not knot, she found 'the bag is convenient for one's gloves and fan'.

Formality demanded, as it still on occasion does today, that gloves were worn as part of fashionable dress; many portraits show sitters carrying rather than wearing gloves, for the beauty of the hands and arms consisted in their delicacy of shape and whiteness of skin. Gloves were on the whole rather plain in style, of light-coloured kid, cotton or silk; they were usually elbow-length, tying with ribbons above the bend of the arm, thus preserving delicate white skin. Sometimes, summer gloves (made with open ends) and mittens were worn, often of printed linen, knitted silk or a fabric matching that of the dress, all these being supplied by the milliner. They were quite cheaply produced and available to most women; Pamela, in Richardson's novel, bought from a pedlar 'a pair of knitt mittens turned up with calico', which might have been manufactured on the framework knitting machines established in the English Midlands or imported from France or Italy. An equally stylish way of keeping the hands and wrists warm was the muff, small in size until the 1770s and made of silk, feathers or fur. Small muffs or 'muffettees' came in pairs covering the hand and wrist, and made of velvet or fur (pl. 113); in Richardson's *Clarissa*, the besotted Lovelace admired Clarissa's 'black velvet glove-like muffs of her own invention'. A specifically Roman and Florentine skill was the perfuming of gloves and muffs: they were impregnated with scent by being suspended over a brazier of burning coals on which aromatic gums were sprinkled or they could be rubbed with oil of roses or musked rose-water. Very often the fur muff made of squirrel or sable matched the fur tippet twisted round the neck; both were needed for the bare arms and décolletage that were part of fashionable dress in the mid-eighteenth century but more for the sensuous contrasts of furs and textiles. Mrs Piozzi, in Milan in 1785, found a typical mixture of finery and function in the green velvet bags, adorned with gold tassels and lined with furs, that the servants of women of rank carried for their mistresses to put their feet in at church or at the opera.

For much of the century, even when women wore trained gowns, the skirts were lifted slightly at the front, so that the shoe and ankle could be seen. From the middle years of the eighteenth century, developments in knitting machines meant that more complex designs could be incorporated into stockings and by the end of the 1750s ribbed hose were widely worn, usually in white silk or cotton. The brighter colours, especially red and blue, were increasingly limited after about 1740 to the lower classes. When, at around this time, Richardson's Pamela received some of her late mistress's clothing, it included 'fine white cotton stockings, and three pair of fine silk ones', which were suitable for the fine silk dresses she was also given; but when she decided to equip herself in humbler style to return to her original station in life, 'two pairs of ordinary blue worsted hose . . . make a smartish appearance, with two white clocks'.[67]

114   Anon., *Pug Dog with Mule, c.*1730

The dog appears to be saying, 'This is my lady's shoe', as he places a protective paw on the fashionable, braided silk mule.

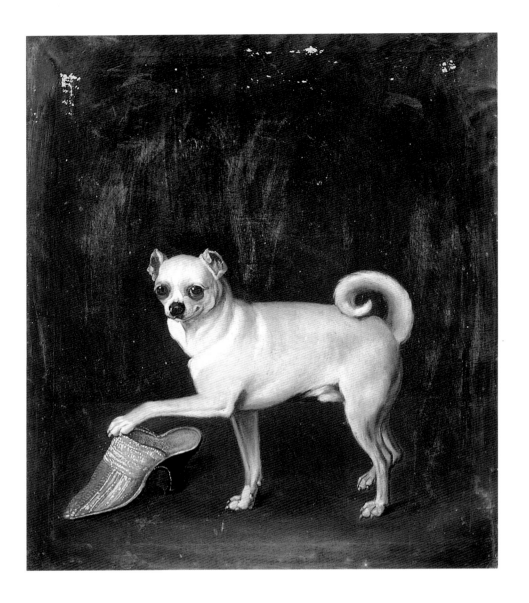

Pamela was given three pairs of fine silk shoes that had once belonged to her mistress, but we are not told if they matched the 'delicate green Mantea silk gown and coat' with which they came. Fabric shoes, made of damask, brocade or plain silk, and often trimmed with gold or silver braid, did not necessarily match the dress, except on more formal occasions. In 1771, Mrs Nollekens was married in a sack 'of the most expensive brocaded white silk, resembling net-work, enriched with small flowers' and her shoes were made of matching material with silver spangles and Bristol buckles.[68] Such fine shoes were not meant to be worn much out-of-doors, and the fashionable lady needed a variety of shoes, including leather ones for sturdy walking and clogs for bad weather; a bill in the Heal Collection (in the British Museum) dated 1766 shows Lady Winterton paying 6*s.* for a pair of 'black Calemanco Pumps', the same for a 'pair of Bath clogs', 4*s.* for red Morocco clogs and, most expensively at £1. 11s. 6d., 'Pink Sattin Pumps trim'd with a Silver Shape the heel and quarters Trim'd with silver Cox-combe and Brade'. Shoes were, by the 1740s, more delicate with a lower and slenderer curved heel, often decorated with jewellery or embroidery, an element of coquetry not missed by contemporaries who were equally aware of the erotic aspects of garters, tying above or below the knee, which were often embroidered with mottoes of a slightly risqué kind – 'No Search' was a popular phrase. The backless mule – called a slipper – made of silk with embroidery or lace, familiar through the intimate scenes by Boucher of ladies at their toilettes (see pl. 123), is perhaps the most characteristic shoe of the rococo, typifying the softness and sexual allure of this most 'feminine' period in the history of dress.

5 Dress and Etiquette

Dress is a very foolish thing, and yet it is a very foolish thing for a man not to be well dressed according to his rank and way of life.

Lord Chesterfield

Johnson had a fancy that as a dramatic author his dress should be more gay than what he ordinarily wore; he therefore appeared behind the scenes and even in one of the side boxes in a scarlet waistcoat, with rich gold lace, and a gold laced hat. He humorously observed to Langton 'that when in that dress he could not treat people with the same ease as when in his usual plain clothes'. Dress, indeed, we must allow, has more effect even upon strong minds than one should suppose, without having had the experience of it.

J. Boswell, *The Life of Samuel Johnson*, 1791

IN ANY AGE, THE DEMANDS OF SOCIAL LIFE and the exigencies of rank and status determine the type of clothing worn, and this was certainly true in the eighteenth century when the art of dressing well was not just a part of good manners but was also a necessary prop to established society. This art, and contemporary attitudes to it, must be appreciated in a consideration of eighteenth-century costume.

For most of the century, where styles did not alter dramatically, some means had to be found to identify those with good taste from those aspiring perhaps to reach a higher social position than was merited; this was particularly the case in countries like England and France where, in theory, lack of sumptuary regulations should have led to greater social flexibility. In fact, although those with no position but with money to buy rich clothes were able to do so, they were held back by the ridicule of the upper classes whose tightly knit club repelled outsiders. Barbier, in his *Chronique de la Régence et du Règne de Louis XV*, recounts the scorn poured on the head of a M. Dodun, *contrôleur-général des finances*, who bought in 1725 a marquisate, and, celebrating his elevation to the ranks of the nobility, began to dress in suits covered in gold lace (galloon). Unfortunately, it was discovered that his grandfather had been a lackey (lackeys often wore gold braid loops at the shoulders) and a song was sung about Paris, the refrain being: 'Galonnez, galonnez, galonnez-moi, Car je suis bon gentilhomme' (Cover, cover, cover me with braid, for I am a proper gentleman).[1] The moral was to dress in a way suitable to one's station in life. On the other hand, Pamela, the heroine of Richardson's novel of 1740, although of humble status (she was personal

115   Detail of pl. 133

This detail from Nattier's portrait of a nobleman in the costume of the Order of the Saint-Esprit shows part of the great ceremonial mantle with its heavy gold embroidery and fringe, the eight-pointed cross of the Order, and a glove trimmed with ribbons of silver tissue.

maid to a lady of the gentry), found that by assiduous attention to the social niceties of life – dress, deportment, conversation and so on – she was able to achieve her ambition of marrying into the family of her late mistress; her impenetrable virtue was not so attractive to the rakish Mr B. as his knowledge of her acceptability in his world, an acceptability gained through natural virtues and applied intelligence.

Clothes, as Richardson knew, were the visible emblems of social standing. When Pamela dressed in her home-spun gown and petticoat with a plain muslin tucker, instead of the cast-off fine silk gown and lace which she had been given from her mistress's wardrobe, Mr B. was literally unable to recognize his mother's maid, so accustomed was he to seeing her in clothes befitting a newly acquired gentility. This theme occurs time after time in novels and plays in the eighteenth century, with its opportunities for deceit and the comedy of manners; potential suitors mistake the mistress for the maid and women can be tricked by their lovers dressing up in fancy costume.

Foreigners were instantly recognizable by their clothes and a wise traveller quickly assumed the camouflage of the country. In Russia in the 1720s, the English wife of the British Resident had to adopt Russian dress to stop the people commenting at her appearance; some fifty years later an English clergyman in Smolensk was greeted coldly by the local governor for 'the plainness of our dresses had raised suspicion of our being tradesmen', but the governor was finally convinced that 'English gentlemen seldom wore lace on their clothes or swords in a journey'.[2] Travellers from England, where woollen cloth was widely worn by the middle of the century, were often stared at; this happened to Baretti, in Lisbon in 1760, because he was not 'dress'd in silk like other gentlemen'. Goethe, in Rome in 1787, found that 'the long clothes of the native of the north, his large buttons, his curious round hat [pl. 116], strike the fancy of the Romans'[3] who thought it like a masque costume, used as they were to the silk suit and the three-cornered hat.

In England in particular, and especially so in the first half of the century, an oafish chauvinism ruled the streets of London. 'When I first went to London,' said Baretti, 'I remember that a stranger could scarcely walk about with his hair in a bag without being affronted. Every porter and every streetwalker would give a pull to his bag.'[4] The bag-wig was the most obvious token of rank; supporters of Lord George Gordon in 1780 attacked peers thought to be sympathetic to Catholic emancipation and removed their wigs. The appellation 'French dog' greeted anyone dressed in French styles throughout the century and Henri Decremps, in London at the end of the 1780s, found that mud was thrown at men wearing the *habit à la française*, a sword and a chapeau bras, whether they were English or foreign.[5]

An awareness of the nuances of class in dress was not unique to England, but it certainly seemed more highly developed there, and continues even today. In the eighteenth century, with its firm sense of caste, there were fierce attacks made on those who presumed to ape their betters, though whether these feelings were motivated by class betrayal or sheer envy is hard to tell. When, in Smollett's *Humphry Clinker* (1771) the foolish maid Win Jenkins

116 German School, caricature of a
northern European, 1790s

put on airs and, dressed in 'faded lutestring, washed gauze and ribbons three times refreshed' with her 'frisure . . . like a pyramid, seven inches above the scalp' and her face 'primed and patched from the chin up to the eyes', walked through the streets with a valet dressed in the cast-off finery of his master, with a sword and 'his hair in a great bag with a huge solitaire', the people 'had got information of their real character and hissed and hooted them'.[6] The custom was to remove trimmings and generally simplify the clothing given to servants by their masters and mistresses; Richardson's Clarissa, feeling that she had not long to live, decided to give to her maid Mabell 'a brown lutestring gown, which, with some alterations to make it suitable to her degree, would a great while serve her for Sunday wear'.[7] When Molly Seagrim, the gamekeeper's daughter in Fielding's *Tom Jones* (1749), was foolish enough to wear to church a sack, unaltered, given to her by Sophia Western, with a laced cap and a fan, a near-riot ensued as the local women tried to tear the gown off her back. Women, with their greater sense of place in society, and at the same time their awareness of changing fashions, some-times found it hard to reconcile the two. To Goldsmith's Vicar of Wakefield, 'finery is very unbecoming in us, who want the means of decency', but this pursuit of finery was a lodestar for those who wished to be fashionable. In Goldsmith's *The Citizen of the World* (1762), Mr and Mrs Tibbs, a lower-class couple, visit Vauxhall, she in 'flimsy silk, dirty gauze . . . and a hat as big as an umbrella' and he in a coat 'trimmed with tarnished twist',[8] and yellow-ing stockings: the point was that the silk had to be of high quality, the gauze had to be new and clean (it did not wash), the trimmings on a coat had to be sparkling (ideally, the coat should be plain out-of-doors) and stockings white. Snobbery was a guiding factor, recognized early on in Bernard Mandeville's *The Fable of the Bees* (1714) for the 'poorest Labourer's Wife . . . who scorns to wear a strong wholesome Frize . . . will starve herself and her Husband to purchase a second hand Gown and Petticoat, that cannot do half the Service, because, forsooth, it is more genteel'.[9] So fashion became a race; ladies of fashion, said Mandeville, sent for mantua-makers 'so that they may have always new Modes ready to take up, as soon as those sawcy Cits shall begin to imitate those in being'.[10] The gradual evolution of a consumer society encouraged the transmission of fashion from elite to non-elite. It is, however, too simplistic to suggest emulation as the only reason for this pro-cess (although it did exist in many cases); peer-group norms and individual motivation existed alongside imitation.[11]

Although fashions were fairly slow to change in the eighteenth century, there was a heightened awareness of out-of-date styles that, particularly with regard to women's dress, often bordered on the cruel. Dress fabrics, as we have seen, were expensive and were sometimes refurbished over decades; the elderly, unmarried Tabitha Bramble (the sister of the irascible Matthew, Smol-lett's alter ego in *Humphry Clinker*) insisted on dressing for formal occasions in 'the style of 1739', appearing at a reception 'in a full suit of damask so thick and heavy that the sight of it alone . . . was sufficient to draw drops of sweat from any man of ordinary imagination'.[12] Large-patterned silks were quite out of fashion in 1771, as were the 'scanty curls, lappet-head, deep triple ruffles and high stays' that she also wore.[13] Lady Mary Coke, one of that breed of eccentric lady travellers that seems peculiarly English, spent much of her time chasing fresh air and royalty on the Continent, astounding foreign courts with the out-of-date hoops and sacks that she wore in the 1770s;[14] her riding habit, said her niece Lady Louisa Stuart in 1782, was 'shining with so much gold, I am amazed the boys do not follow her'.

By the 1780s, clothes covered in gold lace were considered absurd. Mrs Piozzi, in Munich in 1785, was astounded to see an old gentleman in a white coat, lined with red satin and 'laced all down with gold', as was the red waistcoat, which reminded her of 'the very coat my father went in to the old King's birthday five and thirty years ago'.[15] Goethe, in Palermo in 1787, found Prince Pallagonia 'frizzled and powdered, with his hat under his arm, in a silken vest, with his sword by his side',[16] a startling sight when cloth had virtually replaced silk except at court and the sword and chapeau bras were as obsolete as buckled shoes. The author, well-known and indeed famous then, was able to afford the latest fashions coming from France or England, but he remembered when, as a student in Leipzig (which was a centre for luxury and French styles) in the mid-1760s, he had been laughed at for the heavy, clumsy cut of his suits, made of cloth that had been bought many years ago for economy.

For women there was very much a sense of what was suitable for their age, thirty being the onset of middle age when the frivolities of fashion, such as pastel colours, feathers and flowers, should be abandoned. Those who failed to observe this rule were commented upon; the acid Princess Royal of Prussia remarked on her great-aunt in 1731 that 'she tricked herself off like a young person. She wore her hair in large curls with pink ribbands of a shade somewhat lighter than her face; and the stones of her jewels were of as many colours as the rainbow'.[17]

The correct arrangement of dress and accessories, and the borderline between richness and simplicity, was highly perplexing to the eighteenth-century woman, for there were many to judge and criticize. According to *The Art of Dress* (1717):

> Oft have I seen a Mantua pinn'd amiss
> Make people sneer and almost cause a Hiss;
> For Knots ill-fancy'd, or a tawdry Gown,
> Ill-natur'd Criticks; cry the Woman down.[18]

One of the purposes behind the eighteenth-century women's magazines was to teach the correct way to dress, through advice columns ('Always dress rather above your time of life than below it,' said the *Lady's Magazine* of 1783) and novelettes where the heroine was always dressed in the best of taste. One example, from the *Lady's Magazine* of 1773, had a rich heiress over-dressed in a 'pink and silver sacque, stretched over a wider hoop than was reckoned genteel' and covered in diamonds; she discovered her sartorial errors when confronted with a lady in a simple untrimmed negligée (sack) without a

117 W. Hogarth, *Before*, 1736

In spite of her last-minute resistance, the girl has anticipated events by removing her heavily boned stays which lie on a chair. The two velvet patches, one large, one small by her eye, may also indicate an invitation; the rest of her battery of patches lie spilled on the floor at her feet.

hoop, spotted gauze for linen and, instead of jewellery, a 'bouquet of orange and myrtle sprigs, mixed with Indian pinks'.[19]

Although regularity of features was admired in the female face, it was even more important to achieve the correct shape in the figure, accentuated with carefully chosen clothes and accessories. Distinctive personal charm and conscious powers of fascination were, in fact, often preferred to a regular beauty; the French, in particular, 'are gifted with such a knack of magnifying the Worth of Bagatelles and making much out of Nothing, that whatever they devise relative to the Ornament and setting off of their persons, is generally thought agreeable and becoming'.[20] In an age in which a Lovelace could go into raptures about his beloved's taste in dress and her bodily charms and not mention her face, there was a consciousness of the natural body shape that could be abruptly changed with the fashionable understructures, such as stays and hoops.

Full dress, though very splendid, made women inaccessible, and their virtue could best be undermined when wearing the loose, floating négligé styles, which to many commentators smacked of indecency. A French periodical, *La Bagatelle* in 1718, found that the new *robes volantes* gave women 'an air of coming pleasures' and their bodies 'freedom to expand and thicken'; a decree in Vienna in 1728 stated that they could not be worn in church. Even when, by the middle of the century, the sack had become more fitted, there were still moralists in England who found it 'loose, and indecent . . . calculated to hide any defects in the body'.[21] Yet, even under a loose-fitting gown, women wore laced stays; lack of stays denoted a whore (the prostitutes in *Clarissa* wore a 'shocking dishabille, and without stays . . . their gowns hanging trollopy') or at least evidence of moral delinquency. Stays were felt necessary to give support to the bust (lighter versions were sometimes worn at night) and to push the shoulders back. The shape of the bosom varied from the full protuberance of the early years of the century to the flat effect, created by the stays laced high, of the middle years and, in the 1780s, a pouter-pigeon look was fashionable, the natural bosom being eked out by layers of starched muslin or even 'bosom friends' of wool or flannel. Stiffly boned stays laced high up the bosom contributed to the rigidity and antique appearance (noted by foreigners) of Englishwomen in the early eighteenth century, but gave way by the 1760s to a more natural shape. This development was attributed by Pierre-Jean Grosley to the newly fashionable country pursuits such as riding and also to the fact that young girls were not put in 'armour but in a lightly boned waistcoat' that kept 'the body in a slight compression'.[22] High lacing was a sign of the more modest middle class throughout the century; in Laclos's *Les Liaisons Dangereuses* (1784) Présidente Tourvel, an attractive bourgeoise, has 'a tolerable shape' but is dressed without elegance with 'her stays up to her chin'.[23]

The stays, whether cut low or high, and the hooped petticoat, presented a smooth, taut appearance that was essential for formal dress. The correct manipulation of the hoop, particularly when it was very wide in the 1730s and 1740s and for court throughout the century (when the lady had to move backwards from the royal presence), was a sign of good breeding. The *Female Spectator* of 1744, when hoops were huge, found women 'do not walk, but straddle, and sometimes run with a kind of frisk and jump, and throw their enormous hoops almost in the faces of those who pass them by'.[24] When hoops were flattened in front, there was more decorum in movement (women could sit down with more decency) but the excessive width made women move sideways through doors and sit like puppets, with feet sticking out. The greater negligence in dress with the softer fabrics of the last quarter of the century meant that for the first time in the century, women were seen to have knees.

118 S. F. Patton after L.-P. Boitard, *Taste A-La-Mode*, 1745

Set in the fashionable rendezvous of the Mall, this satire pokes fun not just at the ungainly wide hoops of the fashionable female promenaders, but also at the exaggerations of men's clothes, such as their flared coats and large hats and bag-wigs.

Men were also expected to demonstrate gentility through their clothes, and in particular through the accessories of formal elegance, the sword and the chapeau bras. The sword was the traditional emblem of gentility and was necessary to cope with the violence that was part of life in the streets of any city: '. . . all the World here wear Swords, and Paris resembles the Utopia of Sir Thomas More, where there is no Distinction of Persons,' was the comment of an English visitor in the early eighteenth century.[25] As late as 1786, Jean-François Sobry noted that all French gentlemen thought they had a right to wear a sword that it was difficult to make them renounce. In Bath in the early years of the century, Beau Nash fought hard to prevent swords being worn at the Assembly Rooms and his influence helped to popularize the cane instead;[26] by the middle of the eighteenth century in England, duels ceased to be such an important way of deciding quarrels and, except on the most formal occasions, men no longer wore swords. Yet, in countries where French influence was paramount, where the nobility held on to this privilege, or where duelling remained in vogue, the sword continued to be worn. In Verona in 1786, the observant Goethe noted that men of rank swung their right arm as they walked, being accustomed to holding the left arm still, even when they were not wearing a sword. The correct stance was to hold the hilt of the sword to prevent it entangling in the legs or, worse still, in women's clothing, an occupational hazard at dances and polite assemblies and even in the street. Boswell, in Holland in 1763, wished Hogarth had been there to record the sight of a Dutchman in a blue nightgown, 'with a wig of amazing size and a sword at right-angles to his body'; not only should the sword have been held close to the side but it was by this date properly worn only in full dress, along with the bag-wig and chapeau bras. The *London Magazine* of 1774 had great fun with those who did not know how to keep the black silk bag fixed to short hair or to deal with the chapeau bras: 'a country boor' did not know which arm he was to put it under: '. . . sometimes he has it in his hand, sometimes in his mouth, and often betrayed a great inclination to put it on his head, concluding that it was a dammed troublesome, useless thing'.[27] Elegance of deportment was crucial for the man of fashion and had to be taught by the dancing master; had Dr Johnson been so instructed, he might not have had his body in continual agitation, see-sawing up and down as Fanny Burney described it, but might have assumed the 'affected delicacy' of Horace Walpole, who entered a room 'chapeau-bras under his arm, or compressed between his hands, knees bent and feet on tiptoe, as if he were afraid of a wet floor'.[28]

Civilization was often only veneer-thin in a violent society, and dancing (at public assemblies established in fashionable towns all over Europe) helped people to participate in social functions and to conduct themselves with gentility and without affectation. The dancing master was needed, said Lord Chesterfield to his lumpish son, 'not so much to teach you to dance, as to walk, dance and sit well'. For this purpose, he employed Denoyer, a popular French dancing master of the 1740s who also taught at Westminster School, where the subject was as much an essential part of the syllabus as was Greek or Latin. In an age in which entry into company had to be performed like a minuet, with grace and elegance, men, said an English visitor to France, had to learn 'savoir vivre' which he defined thus: 'to make a Bow, enter a Room, or offer any Thing gracefully; to accost a Lady, or run over the Alphabet of Compliments with an Air of Facility and without the least Appearance of Bashfulness or Inexperience.'[29]

Minuets, allemandes and quadrilles were danced at court, but the most popular dances at assemblies were increasingly the so-called 'English' or 'country' dances, where participants ranged themselves opposite ('contre') their partners in long lines. The aim, it was felt, of a civilized society was for the sexes to dance together, although a visitor to Edinburgh in the mid-1770s found the men preferred their traditional dances which they performed 'with gestures so uncouth and a vivacity so hideous that you would have thought they were acting some midnight ceremonies or enchanting the moon' (this was before Sir Walter Scott had made Highland customs romantic). When they did dance with women, it was without looking at their partners, and regarding it as 'a field of exercise'.[30] Dancing masters found a ready audience for individual lessons: a Mr Dukes of Cheapside, announcing his services in the *Public Advertiser* of 17 October 1759, emphasized that 'Grown Gentlemen or Ladies are taught in so private a Manner as to be seen by none but myself', successful pupils being 'fit to appear in the genteelest Assemblies'. He also sold, for 10*s. 6d.*, a book of instructions, one of the many manuals produced throughout the century that taught dancing by numbers, men and women practising before a mirror.

119   Attributed to T. Hudson, *An Unknown Gentleman*, c.1745

The almost balletic stance and the hand inserted in the waistcoat are no doubt the work of the dancing master. This is formal, possibly court dress, with a lace-trimmed brocade waistcoat and chapeau bras.

Dressing was a ritual as complicated as the manoeuvres of the stately French dances, a rigid dividing line being driven between formal and informal dress. As formal dress was often rich and uncomfortable and took, in some cases, so long to prepare, it was generally the custom to dress for dinner, the main meal of the day, which took place at about 2 p.m., although often as late as 4 p.m. by the end of the period. To Arthur Young in the 1780s, formal dressing was a nuisance that he hoped would eventually take place in the evening: 'What is a man good for after his silk breeches and stockings are on, his hat under his arm, and his head bien poudré. Can he botanize in a watered meadow? Can he clamber the rocks to mineralize? Can he farm with the peasant and the ploughman? He is in order for the conversation of the ladies . . . an excellent employment; but it is an employment that never relishes better than after a day spent in active toil or animated pursuit . . .'[31]

When Pamela managed to capture Mr B., among the list of duties expected of her as his wife was 'to be dressed by dinner time . . . and whomsoever I bring home with me to my table, you'll be ready to receive them'. Lady Mary Coke tells us she was always dressed by 11.30 a.m. and Clarissa dressed after breakfast, 'when I have no household employments to prevent me'. For household tasks a skirt and jacket were often worn, the bodice being unboned for ease and comfort, or worn over a lightly boned and decoratively laced stomacher; for those not involved in the supervision of servants, a fashionable *déshabillé* or undress could be worn in the parks and gardens that every city possessed and that were places to display the latest styles. In London, St James's Park and especially the Mall were places in which to be seen walking. Jacob Friedrich von Bielfeld found the dress of the ladies in the Mall 'extremely neat; instead of a large hoop, they have short pettycoats; their gowns are elegant but not gaudy; they have short cloaks trimd with lace and little hats either of straw or beaver, or els feathers in their hair'.[32] When dressed for the day, a hooped, formal open robe would have been worn, suitable for all occasions except appearance at the opera, formal assembly or court. In Paris, people of fashion in the early eighteenth century loved the Tuileries gardens, where 'you may see display'd in Attire every thing that Extravagance can invent, the most tender and the

120   T. Gainsborough, *The Mall in St James's Park*, 1783

This is the painting that Walpole aptly described as 'all a-flutter like a lady's fan'. The floating layers of silk gauze for the dresses emphasize the soft, rounded outline of the fashionable lady.

121 J.-B. Pillement, *Les Jardins de Benfica*, 1785

These gardens provided a fashionable promenade for the citizens of Lisbon. The ladies have adopted French and English modes, with, in the background, the addition of wide, light shawls. Talking to two officers in the foreground is a fashionable lady wearing a *polonaise*, and with her ribboned cap tilting forwards over her high coiffure.

most touching. The Ladies in Fashions ever new, with their Adjustments, their Ribbons, their jewels, and agreeable Manner of dressing in Stuffs of Gold and Silver, declare the continual Applications of their Magnificence.'[33] Later, the gardens of the Palais Royal became the fashionable promenade.

In France, the morning toilette was a fine art and a leisurely procedure at which friends could be present and business affairs discussed. Louise Fusil, in her *Souvenirs d'une Actrice* (1841), described how a lady of fashion on the eve of the French Revolution performed her toilette with an almost sexual lingering on its pleasures, reflected in the importance of underwear and négligé garments.[34] (Chérubin, in *The Marriage of Figaro*, confessed to Suzanne his envy at her intimacy with the Countess Almaviva, 'L'habiller le matin et la déshabiller le soir, épingle à épingle' (to dress her in the morning and undress her in the evening, pin by pin).) On awakening, the fashionable lady rang for her maid who handed her a lace-trimmed *manteau de lit* for her early ablutions, after which she was dressed in a *négligé du matin*, a loose robe worn over chemise and stays. Then she was ready to receive visitors in her *cabinet de toilette*; these could include men, and very often abbés, who acted the part of *cicisbei* and were always there with the latest news and gossip.

177

122 After P. Longhi, *Le Lever*, mid-eighteenth century

The sensual elements of the morning toilette, with its appreciative male audience, can be seen here as the lady is helped by her maid into her *négligé du matin*. The husband, or at least a man whose open shirt, loose gown, unbuttoned breeches and negligent hose indicate an intimacy with the central figure, has his patrician wig and gown on stands by the bed.

123 (*facing page*) F. Boucher, *La Toilette*, 1742

In this teasingly erotic scene of dressing, a woman of the *demi-monde* ties up her garter with a silk ribbon, an act which reveals her white under-petticoat beneath the blue silk dress; a powdering mantle protects her clothes from cosmetics, hair powder and pomade. While dressing, a fashionable woman transacted business with her modiste; here the backview of the *marchande de modes* demonstrates how the sack dress or *robe à la française* could be tucked into the pockets of the petticoat to achieve a swagged look, very much in harmony with rococo taste.

It was then that her hair was done, either by a personal maid or a male hairdresser, and the finishing touches applied to the face; the French hairdresser, said Smollett in 1766, 'regulates the distribution of her patches and advises where to lay on the paint . . . If he sees a curl or even a single hair amiss, he produces his comb, his scissors and pomatum and sets it to rights'.[35] The light-hearted intimacy of the lingering toilette was an essential part of dressing in the eighteenth century: 'Une femme, pour être jolie, emploie plus de raffinement & de politique à sa toilette, qu'il n'y en a dans tous les cabinets de l'Europe,' (A charming woman uses more subtlety and politics in her dressing than there are in all the governments of Europe) stated the *Petit Dictionnaire de la Cour* (1788). By this time, the art of undress was a witty and subtle language of its own. A *négligé de malade* (a muslin peignoir trimmed with lace) could, according to Louise Fusil, announce 'une indisposition, ou une convalescence, à inspirer enfin un grand intérêt'.[36]

Informality for men was the keynote for the early morning, and nightgowns could be worn at breakfast and in the street. When, in 1750, Sir Thomas Bottle, Chancellor to the Prince of Wales, visited Cliveden, Walpole noted that he took with him 'a night-gown, cap and slippers of gold brocade in which he came down to breakfast the next morning'.[37] So popular was the nightgown for street wear, particularly for students, that in some university towns there were regulations against its use out-of-doors; in 1781, for example, the Count Palatine of Bayreuth had to issue an order that students and young men in the street should wear 'decent dress' and not slop around in gowns. It was permissible to wear the gown in male company, in coffee houses and for morning business meetings, but not before ladies, and Beau Nash forbade their wear in Bath.

As noted above, England was the first country to adopt the frock coat for morning undress. In this, and sometimes with his hair rolled up in paper clay rollers (which curled the hair before it was dressed by the barber), the fashionable Englishman walked in the park. In Fielding's *Joseph Andrews* (1742), a foppish young man described his day to the accompaniment of groans from Parson Adams: 'In the Morning I arose, took my great Stick and walked out in my green Frock with my Hair in Papers (a Groan from Adams) and sauntered about till Ten.'[38] From 2 to 4 p.m. was spent in dressing, then came two hours dining, followed by a number of visits and finally to the theatre. By the end of the century, Englishmen had begun to form exclusive clubs, which largely took the place of the earlier coffee houses, and where formal dress was required.

For men, the morning toilette was an occasion for business affairs as well as for formal dressing. Madame d'Epinay found her husband's mornings rather a trial: while he was being dressed by his valets-de-chambre, with lackeys and a secretary waiting for orders, and discussing business with his

124 After J.-M. Moreau, 'La petite toilette', 1789, from *Monument du Costume Physique et Moral de la fin du dix-huitième siècle*

While the nobleman's hair is being dressed (the assistant barber on the far right heats up the curling papers with tongs), the tailor with a new coat is received in audience. In the background stands the running footman, with his traditional feathered cap, ready to deliver messages from his master.

La petite Toilette.

horse-dealer, an opera singer and other callers, she had to deal with the credi-tors.[39] One of Restif de la Bretonne's moral and entertaining stories to illus-trate life and manners in the late 1780s recounts the morning toilette of the marquis de L., 'who receives his tailor while his hair is being done. Although the tailor and his assistant dwell on the elegance of cut and the refinement of the embroidery on the suit that they have made, the marquis insists on different buttons, like those that he has seen worn by the 'Duke of F.', the alterations to take place within the hour.

In England, said Madame du Bocage in 1750, 'it is not thought necessary to dress except to appear at the Opera, or at the places where they are invited to dine'.[40] For the theatre and for formal entertainment, full dress was *de rigueur*; this consisted of a suit with matching coat and breeches, usually of silk and sometimes embroidered, and an embroidered waistcoat, hair dressed with a bag at the back, chapeau bras and sword. At the opera, said J. T. Smith in *Nollekens and his Times*, men wore 'swords and bags in full dress', and he particularly noted the miniaturist artist Richard Cosway, a well-known dandy, who appeared 'full dressed in his sword and bag with a small three cornered hat on the top of his powdered toupee and a mulberry silk coat profusely embroidered with scarlet strawberries'.[41] By this time, full dress was, accord-ing to the *Fashionable Magazine*, 'too antiquated for any other place than court' (1786). The court in England was 'the residence of dullness', accord-ing to foreign visitors; the nobility paid their respects at the levées and drawing-rooms (and, in fact, any well-dressed person could see the royal family even if they were not officially presented), but the real centres of fashion were aristocratic assemblies or fashionable watering-places such as Bath. On the Continent, and particularly in the smaller German states, the court was the sum of fashionable people. It regulated existence and orga-nized entertainments such as hunting, dances, card assemblies, sleighing parties in winter, promenades in summer, the French theatre and the Italian opera. Choosing the correct dress for the day, and for the many functions at court, required care and attention. The Saxon minister Count Brühl 'had at least 300 suits of clothes; each had a duplicate, as he did not choose that his dress should appear different in the afternoon from what it had been in the morning. A painting of each suit, with the particular cane and snuff-box belonging to it, was very accurately drawn in a large book, which was pre-sented to his Excellency every morning by his valet-de-channbre, that he might fix upon the dress in which he wished to appear for the day.'[42]

The greatest ritual of the formal toilette took place at court, where for most of the century monarchs and their families were on display, dressing, dining and undressing in public. The process of dressing (*lever*) and undress-ing (*coucher*) had become formalized in the reign of Louis XIV, a tradition that was continued by his heirs, for personal attendance on the monarch was a sign of political favour. Louis XV, although interested in dress, performed the boring ritual of the formal *lever* and *coucher* with a dignified indifference. Before the formal dressing in the morning, he received the queen, the royal children and the princes of the blood in bed for the *grandes entrées*; then his

125 N. Dupin, 'Le Seigneur et la Dame de Cour', 1776, from Le Père's *Les Costumes François Representans Les differents Etats du Royaume, avec les Habillemens*

The nobleman wears court dress with the sash and badge of the Order of the Saint-Esprit. The lady is in the full *robe de cour*, or *grand habit*, with tightly boned bodice, hooped skirt and train.

LE SEIGNEUR ET LA DAME DE COUR.

On qualifie du nom de Seigneur, les personnes de haute naissance, ou celles qui sont revetus des plus hautes dignités de l'etat ; pour l'ordinaire ils sont décorés de l'Ordre de leur Souverain ; il n'appartient qu'à eux d'être très recherchés dans leurs ajustemens ; les talons rouges qu'ils portent sont la marque de leur noblesse et annoncent qu'ils sont toujours prêts à fouler aux pieds les ennemis de l'Etat. Il faut distinguer du Seigneur, l'homme riche et fat qui par des dehors trompeurs cherche a surprendre le peuple toujours ébloui par l'éclat d'un habit magnifique sans cesse on le voit ramper auprès des gens en place pour en obtenir quelque marque de distinction ; il n'est point de souplesses et d'intrigues qu'il ne se suggere pour venir à ses fins, et sçait bien se vanger sur ses Vassaux des mortifications qu'il reçoit.

On entend par Dame de cour, une Femme de haute consideration, attachée à la Reine ou à quelque Princesse ; elle est toujours obligée de paroitre dans l'éclat le plus brillant, les etoffes les plus riches, l'Or, les pierreries, les Equipages les plus elegants sont de son apanage ; on la distingue aisément à son air, de ces Coquettes qui la copient et même la surpassent quelquefois, la Coëfure de ces dernieres varie à l'excès, tantôt elle est haute, tantôt basse ; aujourdhui en avant, demain en arriere ; on voit construit sur leur têtes des compartimens de jardins à fleurs et à fruits ; les plumes, simbole de la legereté, n'y sont point épargnée surtout dans ces derniers tems, elles ne pouvoient faire un meilleur choix pour exprimer leur vrai caractere ; enfin leur toilette est une vraie etude, on pourroit faire un assés gros Dictionnaire des mots employés pour designer chaque chose qui sert à leurs parures.

personal officers such as the Grand Master of the Wardrobe and the Gentlemen of the Bedchamber were allowed the *premières entrées* to watch him wash, shave and dress for the day. In the evening at the *grand coucher* he retired publicly in the bedroom that had once belonged to Louis XIV, afterwards dressing to return to his private suite or that of his current mistress; after a time he no longer kept up the pretence of taking off his clothes.

Louis XVI was far less interested in what he wore, but readier to comply with the custom. His own taste was for simplicity, but the Wardrobe ordered for him six full-dress suits a quarter, in addition to hunting suits, uniforms and the *habits de cérémonie* supplied by Dargé, master-tailor in Paris. One of his pages, Félix d'Hézecques, left an account of his *lever* and *coucher*, occasions of formality mixed with touches of buffoonery, a tradition that had become totally meaningless.[43] The king rose at 7 or 8 a.m., but as the formal *lever* did not take place until 11.30 a.m., he dressed in a simple grey or brown suit; then he had to undress, put on a morning gown and leave his private apartments for the bedroom of ceremony, where those such as the princes of the blood and the Knights of the Saint-Esprit watched him being dressed in shirt and stockings. The Grand Master of the Wardrobe put on the breeches, waistcoat and the cordon bleu of the Saint-Esprit, then the coat (those lesser courtiers such as tutors, equerries, chaplains and even distinguished foreigners were by now present) and, finally, the two Masters of the Wardrobe gave him his handkerchief, hat, gloves and sword. His hair, which had been prepared on rising by his *valet-de-chambre barbier*, was then given the finishing touches and powdered. For the *coucher*, there was an equally ceremonial disrobing; the holding of the sleeves of the coat as it was taken off was a particularly prized privilege, as was that of presenting the king with his nightshirt. When the robe was put on, the breeches were unbuttoned and fell to the ground, and 'thus attired, hardly able to walk so absurdly encumbered, he began to make the round of the circle' (that is, to talk to those watching him) before the final stages of his undressing were completed in privacy.

Marie Antoinette had an equally elaborate morning ritual, her morning toilette being, according to Jeanne-Louise Campan, her First Woman of the Bedchamber, a 'chef-d'œuvre d'etiquette'.[44] The public *lever* took place at noon, after the queen had had her hair dressed; the first lady of honour handed her water to wash her hands and then her chemise (this was also an honour and was claimed by a princess of the blood if she were present, which led to squabbles which Marie Antoinette found tiresome). The Mistress of the Robes handed the queen her petticoat and robe and the accessories that went with it, then her handkerchief and gloves were presented to her on a gold or silver salver. Later in her reign, the queen abandoned the formal dressing in her bedchamber, because she preferred Rose Bertin to be with her while this took place (and the modiste, not being of noble blood, was not allowed at the *lever*), so, after having had her hair done, she withdrew to her private closet to dress.

The queen's expenditure on clothes was huge. Officially, said Madame de Campan in her memoirs, she had every winter and summer twelve *grands habits*, twelve *robes parées* (formal robes with paniers) and twelve undress robes, all of which were discarded at the end of the season. There were, as well, informal muslin or linen gowns that were bought when required and which were, paradoxically, kept for several years, being re-trimmed if especially liked. The 120,000 livres allowed by the government did not cover the cost of this extravagance: in one year alone 172 new gowns were ordered and in 1786 Marie Antoinette earned the sobriquet of Madame Deficit for spending more than twice what was allocated to her. Clothes had to be managed so that the correct colours and accessories were matched, and a dress for a gala occasion was worn only once. Every day the queen was presented with a book of samples of dress materials that corresponded to items in her wardrobe. From this she marked with a pin those she needed for the various functions of the day, which could include a formal morning dress, an afternoon *déshabillé* and a full dress for an evening card or supper party in the private apartments, as well as a *grand habit* for a court presentation. The book was then taken back to the wardrobe and all that was needed for the day was brought in large baskets covered in silk; the wardrobe woman who had the care of the linen brought in the *prêt du jour* which contained a daily supply of chemises and kerchiefs, and in the evening the *prêt de la nuit* for nightgown and cap. The sample book for 1782, now in the Archives Nationales, still contains 78 samples (some have vanished and the original total may have been over 100).[45] These range from *grands habits* and *robes parées*, to *robes turques*, *lévites* and redingotes, but not jackets, skirts, cloaks, mantles, the hundreds of other accessories or the intimate gowns of the boudoir.

Other courts in Europe used Versailles as a model, but while formal dressing in public was an accepted idea, many rulers were more modest in their ritual or reluctant to spent their time on such a restrictive etiquette. Philip V of Spain, for example, although French by birth, spent only fifteen minutes a day dressing, the main royal event being the toilette of the queen (Elizabeth Farnese, Philip's second wife), who was the real ruler of the country. The *lever* and *coucher* of the Swedish king, Gustavus III, was based on that of Versailles,[46] the courtiers entering to see his formal dressing.[46] Once a week the royal couple dined in public and played cards in state; the afternoons were spent in reading and other entertainment, the king occasionally embroidering belts and scarves for the ladies of the court. To Catherine the Great, the French pomp adopted at the Swedish court was the sign of an effeminate ruler, and she herself, late in her reign, evolved a toilette that was comfortable rather than glamorous. One of her secretaries, Adrian Gribovsky,[47] listed the events of her day, which began with a morning spent on affairs of state, dressed in a heavy, white silk dress and crêpe cap, followed by a simple toilette at noon which consisted of wiping the face with iced water and having her hair dressed with small curls behind the ears and a cap pinned on while a selected circle of visitors chatted to her. She then retired to her private bedroom and with the help of her ladies dressed for the day, usually in Livonian dress or another informal gown. Unlike the Empress Anna, who changed her dress six times a day, Catherine's tastes were simple, although for formal court occasions, French splendour and lavish jewellery were worn.

Perhaps the simplest court in relation to its size and importance was that of England. George I brought with him in 1714 a German staff (and two Turkish *valets-de-chambre*) who dispensed with the more formal dressing and undressing by sinecured courtiers, though the right of putting on the shirt remained a privilege of the groom closest to the king. The Office of the Robes, under a Master and a Yeoman, provided official robes, mourning and liveries, as well as furnishing for state apartments. Although George I was dressed by his personal body servants, both George II and George III reverted to the original custom of being dressed by the Master and the Yeoman, but formal dressing was a simple affair without the squabbling for precedence that marred the French court.[48]

The English queen's morning toilette was also simple in comparison with that of her French counterpart. The most famous account was provided by the novelist Fanny Burney, who was appointed Assistant Keeper to Queen Charlotte in 1786. She found it interesting but exhausting, for she had to be dressed by 7 a.m., when the queen would call her to help Mrs Thielky, her wardrobe woman: 'Mrs Thielky hands the things to me and I put them on. 'Tis fortunate for me I have not the handling them – I should never know which to take first, embarrassed as I am, and should run a prodigious risk of giving the gown before the hoop, and the fan before the neckerchief'.[49] Fanny then had to help prepare the formal dress for the queen, who dressed at 12.45 p.m. in the State Dressing Room. The queen's gown was removed, a loose peignoir put on while she had her hair dressed and powdered (she read the newspapers while this was being done) and the robe was presented by the Keeper of the Robes, Mrs Schwellenberg.

Courts had, from the earliest times, been sources of power and wealth, and magnets for the ambitious; in addition, they were arbiters of taste and culture. This was particularly so at the court in France, which was, in La Bruyère's phrase, the 'centre du goût et de la politesse', personified by the brilliance of the ruler. Under Louis XIV, a system of controlled admission to the court and the king was introduced, a complicated set of rules called 'les honneurs de la cour', which governed who could sit in the presence of the king and the royal family (and the kind of chairs they could sit on), who could dine or play cards in the royal apartments, assist at the *lever* and *coucher*, ride in the royal carriages, hunt with the king and be present at the *débotter*, (when he returned from hunting, for example). Under Louis XIV, no man who was not a *fils* or *petit-fils de France* could be admitted to the king's table, although on campaigns this was sometimes relaxed. By the reign of Louis XV, however, some favourites were admitted not by birth but as 'une faveur de choix', leading to the unedifying squabbles over trifles that marked the eighteenth-century French court.[50]

For men, court dress consisted of 'des habits à grands paremens, brodés sur toutes les tailles'; cloths of gold and silver stuff, with embroidery and precious or semi-precious stones on the coat and waistcoat made up court formal dress of unparalleled splendour. With the suit went red-heeled shoes, which remained as distinctive a mark of the aristocracy as the bag-wig or the sword.

For women, rules for admission to court were stricter, as they had to prove a title of nobility reaching back to 1400, although there could be a

126 Detail of pl. 133

The silver ribbon rosettes at the knees and on the red-heeled shoes are inspired by seventeenth-century styles, in accordance with the rest of the ceremonial costume of the Order of the Saint-Esprit. The elegant pose of the legs derives from the ritual of formal dance steps.

dispensation for favourites; in any society the laws regulating the conduct of women have always been more rigid, and sharp eyes were constantly on the lookout for any infringement of court etiquette. For presentation at court, women had to wear the *grand habit*, which was the fashionable dress of the 1670s, with short sleeves, heavily boned bodice and elaborately draped train, but worn over a large hoop; with no alterations, this lasted until the French Revolution. 'Le grand habit de Cour', said *L'Art du Tailleur* (1769), 'consiste en un corps fermé, plein de baleines, & un bas de robe; le corps se couvre d'étoffe; le bas de robe se fait de mêmes étoffes, ainsi que le jupon' (Full court dress consists of a heavily boned bodice and a train; the bodice, train and skirt are made of the same fabric).[51] The *tailleur de corps* made the whale-boned bodice and the train (*bas de robe*), the *couturière* made the skirt and the *marchand de mode* provided the elaborate trimmings that covered the dress as well as the lace for the flounced sleeves and the lappets for the head. On the day of presentation, the dress had to be in black, with matching trim-ming (*agréments*) and a little tippet (*palatine*) of black decorated with black ornaments (*pompons*) as were the lower sleeve bands (*bracelets noirs*); the fol-lowing day the lady had to appear at court in a *grand habit* made of colours and covered in jewels. For the presentation of Madame de Villedueil in 1787, Madame Eloffe made her a dress in black and silver decorated with fringes and ribbons, with court sleeves and lappets of Alençon lace; for the next day she wore a dress of white and pistachio-coloured satin, decorated with embroidered gauze, over a skirt of white crêpe.[52]

The presentation was often an ordeal, for the lady had to curtsy with a large hoop to kiss the hem of the queen's gown (having taken off her glove to do so); after a brief conversation, she then retired backwards, with three curtsies, having to cope not only with the huge hoop but also with the enormous train. This was where the services of a dancing master were so useful; when the marquise de La Tour du Pin was presented a few days after her marriage in 1787, she had lessons from M. Huart, who impersonated the queen at one moment and then the actions of the lady who was being presented to her.[53] Not only did the boned bodice straps cut into the shoulders, but, according to the marquise, the weight of the dress made it impossible to raise the foot in heels three inches high, so the correct movement was to take little gliding steps, the lady with huge hoop looking like a ship in full sail. Not only did the train and hooped skirt take vast amounts of material (twenty to twenty-two yards, according to the comtesse de Genlis) but the decorations on the paniers, she said, were an indescribable sight en masse: 'Leurs énormes paniers formoient un riche espalier, artiste-ment couvert de perles, d'argent, d'or, de paillons de couleur et de pierreries. L'effet de toutes ces brillantes paniers réunies, ne peut de décrire. On portoit alors non-seulement des fleurs mais de fruits, des cerises, des groseilles, des fraises avec leurs fleurs. L'art imitoit ces fruits à s'y méprendre' (Their enor-mous hooped skirts formed a richly decorated surface, tastefully covered in pearls, silver, gold, coloured spangles and precious stones. The effect of all those brilliant hooped skirts gathered together can hardly be described.

127 L. Tocqué, *Queen Maria Lesczynska*, 1740

The queen wears her ermine-lined coronation mantle embroidered with fleur-de-lis, over the *grand habit*; the bodice is trimmed with gold lace and a huge stomacher brooch with pendant pearls. Attached to her powdered hair can be seen the false ringlets that were customarily worn for coronations.

There were not only flowers, but fruits – cherries, currants, strawberries with their flowers – in the designs of these skirts. Art imitated these fruits to the life).[54]

The *grand habit* was worn not only for court presentations, but also for ceremonial occasions such as the chapters of the order of the Saint-Esprit, baptisms and marriages of members of the royal family and the *grands bals parés*, the court balls. From about 1783, the *grande robe à la française*, worn over a medium hoop, replaced the *grand habit* on all but the most formal occasions, being acceptable for services in the royal chapel, receptions, court mourning and when the court travelled to Marly or Fontainebleau.

With varying degrees of imitation, court dress at Versailles was followed by the rest of Europe, notably at the German courts and in Russia. In Italy, courts were fairly poor and women did not wear the *grand habit* except for the grandest occasions. Men wore black suits, though the style of wig varied from court to court; Boswell, in Turin in 1765, hired a valet (their advice regarding individual court regulations was invaluable to the travellers to whom they hired themselves) who stated that the hair had to be dressed in a 'horse-tail', which Boswell, after abusing the fellow, complied with. It was also possible at court to wear a uniform; Casanova, having renounced the clerical profession, went to Bologna in 1745, where he wore a uniform invented by himself of 'white, the vest blue, a gold and silver shoulder knot and a sword knot of the same material . . . I procured a long sword, and with my cockade and wearing a long false pigtail, I sallied forth'.[55] When Boswell was in Dresden in 1764 he wished to attend the court, but was at first frustrated for it was in mourning and he did not have a black suit; eventually he decided to go as an army officer, but with his unerring talent for doing the wrong thing chose a white cockade for his hat, a Jacobite emblem which was hardly tactful.

In England, private, frugal tastes at court contrasted with public show. The *grand habit*, or the English version of it, the 'straight-bodied gown', was worn only by members of the royal family and on occasions of exceptional splendour such as royal marriages and coronations. Most ladies at court wore the mantua with train, described by the *Magazine à la Mode* of 1777 as 'a close body without pleats or robings; and a train descending from the waist, two and a half, or three yards long, and containing two breadths of silk . . . The stays are cut low before and shaped like a heart. The Hoop is French resembling the shape of a bell.' The queen's train, three yards in length, was borne by a page, but those of the other ladies were 'looped up to the left side of the hoop by a button and a loop at the end of which is a large tassel'.[56] Abigail Adams, in London in 1785, chose 'a white lutestring, covered and full trimmed with white crape, festooned with lilac ribbon and mock point lace over a hoop of enormous extent',[57] which she wore with treble ruffles, lace lappets and white plumes. As a staunch republican she found the ceremony tedious (guests stood in a circle while the king walked round to the right, the queen and princesses to the left) and the royal conversation limited.

128 J. Gillray, *Temperance enjoying a Frugal Meal*, 1792

A caricature of the frugal habits of George II and his consort, this shows the king wearing the Windsor uniform.

TEMPERANCE enjoying a Frugal Meal.

129 (*below*) Noble, 'View of the Court at St James's with the Ceremony of introducing a Lady to Her Majesty', late 1770s–early 1780s

Although this engraving dates from the late 1770s or early 1780s, a period during which, in theory, women at court were beginning to adopt the sack dress, illustrated here is the elaborately decorated, tight-bodied gown or mantua, with the treble sleeve ruffles that etiquette demanded. Most ladies wear the long lace lappets pendant.

View of the COURT at St JAMES's with the Ceremony of introducing a Lady to her Majesty. — Noble sculp. —

From the early 1780s, the customary court dress was the sack (it had for some years been out of high fashion), also worn over a large hoop and with treble ruffles. The novelist Fanny Burney noted a conversation in 1782 between two ladies complaining about the court dress required for the Duchess of Cumberland's Drawing Room: 'How disagreeable these sacques are! I am so incommoded with these nasty ruffles.'[58] The actress Sarah Siddons went with some trepidation to read to the king and queen at Buckingham House, wearing 'a Sacque or Negligée with a hoop, treble ruffles and Lappets, in which costume I felt not at all my ease';[59] the hoop, in fact, was to stay as part of court dress until 1820, looking increasingly odd as the waistline rose during the neo-classical period.

In England, men's court dress was influenced by the move towards simplicity. By the end of the 1770s, the French frock, which was more stylish and tighter-fitting than the English frock and embroidered, was admitted at court on all but very solemn and grand occasions.

In Spain at the beginning of the eighteenth century, a French-dominated court meant that for women the *grand habit* was worn, with slight differences, such as a panel of lace worn as a background to the many orders that royal ladies and others wore on occasions of ceremony. Although men continued to wear the slashed trunk hose and doublet with ruff, which had not changed since the end of the sixteenth century, by the end of our period this was only for the most formal occasions, such as court investitures and receptions.

During the first half of the eighteenth century, Spanish influence lingered in the dress worn by men at the court in Vienna.[60] This consisted of black doublet and breeches with a short black cloak, the whole decorated with lace; a hat turned up on one side and surmounted by a plume; red stockings and red shoes. On gala days, the king wore a Spanish suit either in gold or in black, the latter with 'small cuffs of purple embroidered with silver; his shoe ribbons are also embroidered, and he wears a red feather in his hat'.[61] The only item of French clothing was the long periwig. The greatest ceremony, where Spanish formality predominated, took place at the court in Vienna, the Hofburg, but at the summer palaces of Laxenburg and Schönbrunn, French elegance was permitted. Maria Theresa, who preferred a bourgeois intimacy in her private life, to a large extent dispensed with Spanish formality in clothing, although some of the older courtiers adhered to it: in 1788, the marquis de Bouillé met the aged Count Kaunitz wearing the short Spanish mantle that he kept to for warmth in winter,[62] with the traditional black suit that he always wore with the star of the Toison d'Or and the diamond star of the Order of St Stephen, established by Maria Theresa in 1764. Formal occasions were still, however, regulated by the movements of Spanish etiquette (even men had to curtsy to the empress) until Joseph II in 1780 abolished all surviving remnants of it. The only fixed gala day was New Year's day, the others to be as he was moved to call them, which was unsettling to a court used to the old ways. After 1768, Joseph II and his successors always wore uniform at court and on most formal occasions.[63]

130 M. S. Maella, *Infanta Carlota Joaquina, Queen of Portugal*, 1785

This portrait celebrates the ten-year old infanta's marriage to Don Juan de Braganza, later João VI of Portugal. Holding a pet canary, the young princess wears a pink silk court dress which largely follows the French style, with long pointed bodice and wide hoop; it is trimmed with delicate embroidery and blue and white tassels. The stiffness of the dress (and the pose) is complemented by the elaborate headdress of flowers, ribbons and lace, perched on top of a highly frizzed and powdered coiffure.

131   A. Roslin, *Gustavus III in Coronation Costume*, 1777

132 (*above*) After M. van Meytens, *The Empress Maria Theresa and her Family*

The Empress, in ermine-lined robes of state, is enthroned with her husband Franz Stephan who wears the Spanish-influenced gala court costume of gold, covered with embroidery, lace and ribbons. On his mother's left hand stands the future Emperor Joseph II wearing the Order of the Golden Fleece; two of the younger princes wear Hungarian costume which was popular at the Austrian court.

For women, Spanish black remained for some years as part of Austrian court dress; Lady Mary Wortley Montagu in 1716 found ladies wearing black velvet gowns embroidered with gold and silver and worn over coloured skirts. By the middle of the century, trained sacks in the French style were worn; Lady Mary Coke found in 1770 that the only difference was that along with the black lace lappets, 'you are permitted to wear the ribbon of the colour of your robe & as many diamonds as you please'.[64]

To a large extent, the power of a court depended on its formal splendour (only exceptional princes like Frederick the Great could afford to dispense with pomp); where a king was personally insignificant, ceremony acted as a rampart to royal authority. This was particularly true at the court of Louis XVI, where the king appeared gauche against the pomp of pageantry. One

of his pages, Félix d'Hézecques, writing in 1804, in echo of Figaro's famous statement about the basic equality of all men if accidents of birth were set aside, said: 'Dépouillez le prince de l'état qui l'environne, il ne sera plus aux yeux de la multitude, qu'un homme ordinaire' (Strip the prince of the ceremony that surrounds him, and he will in the eyes of the people be but an ordinary man).[65]

Ceremonial costume reinforced the historic rights of monarchs and the privileges of aristocracy. Coronation costume could emphasize the religious and traditional base on which a prince governed; Louis XV, for example, wore in 1722 the violet mantle sewn with gold fleur-de-lys and lined with ermine over a violet silk tunic and dalmatic also sewn with gold fleur-de-lys, religious vestments which dated in style from the early Middle Ages. In 1772, Gustavus III of Sweden (a king who recognized the political and social significance of clothing[66]) deliberately strengthened a somewhat dubious historical continuity when he designed for his coronation tunic a copy of that worn by his predecessor, Karl XI, in the late seventeenth century, under a mantle of purple velvet lined with ermine and embroidered with crowns in gold thread and pearls. Imperial splendour also marked the coronation costume of Catherine II of Russia (1762) – a gown of silver silk embroidered with eagles, and the customary purple velvet mantle (which had been made in Paris for the coronation of Catherine I in 1724) encrusted with hundreds of double-headed gold eagles.

The ceremonial processions and investitures of knightly orders formed an important part of court display, from the black embroidered with gold flames of the Saint-Esprit, to the gold-embroidered crimson habits of the Toison d'Or. A prince's standing was also demonstrated by the appearance of his envoys at foreign courts and by the splendour of his liveries. As French ambassador to Vienna in 1725, the duc de Richelieu entered in state in regal style with sixty-nine carriages, the horses of his own carriage being shod in silver, and surrounded by running footmen in red velvet covered in silver braid and fringes, twelve pages on horseback in red and silver, and fifty foot valets in scarlet embroidered in purple and silver galloon.

Richelieu knew that he had to make a considerable effort to impress the court in a city accustomed to a wide range of glamorous uniforms and exotic liveries. For in Vienna, a visitor could see the German guard in red with facings of black velvet, embroidered in gold, the Galician guard in Polish cavalry costume and the Hungarian guard in scarlet hussar uniform;[67] in addition, many of the magnates who made up the Austrian empire had large contingents of *heyducks* (liveried personal servants, originally Hungarian or Polish) dressed in Turkish caftans covered in gold or silver lace or embroidery. Joseph II followed the German fondness for wearing uniform as an alternative to court dress; this could be as rich as the *habit à la française* when worn with diamond-encrusted orders and demonstrated independence from France.

By the second half of the eighteenth century, many courts had begun to develop personal liveries exclusive to the royal family and their circle. These

133 (*previous page*) J.-M. Nattier, *A Nobleman in the Costume of the Order of the Saint-Esprit*, 1732

It would be impossible to imagine a more sumptuous costume in the eighteenth century than the lavishly trimmed ceremonial dress of this knightly order (founded in 1578). The silver, ribboned trunk hose, the short black cloak and the feathered hat derive from the fashionable dress of the seventeenth century, for nearly all official or ceremonial dress is in part the fossilized dress of the past. The page, dressed in the royal red livery, gathers up the huge train embroidered with interlaced knots, fleur-de-lis and flames.

very often began as uniforms to be worn at royal places away from the main court centre. In France, for example, Louis XV instituted a *uniforme des petits châteaux*, of green braided with gold, to be worn by his intimate circle (later, each royal château required a uniform of a different colour). In 1750, Madame de Pompadour invented a livery for her château of Bellevue:[68] the men wore a purple, gold-embroidered, suit lined with white satin, with a grey-white waistcoat embroidered in purple and gold; the women, a dress of grey-white silk with the same purple and gold embroidery. This was, in fact, almost as expensive as court wear, for although the marquise donated the material, the guests had to pay for the costly embroidery and equip their valets in the correct livery of green cloth with gold braid. At other summer courts or hunting palaces, similar liveries were worn; at Laxenburg Maria Theresa introduced a red cloth frock with green waistcoat and golden tassels and for women a red gown with gold trimming; at Nymphenburg (the summer palace of the Bavarian royal family) guests were to wear a uniform of green and white; and at Oranienbaum (a Russian royal hunting lodge) in the 1750s, men wore a blue coat with grey breeches and women a blue gown with grey petticoat.

In England in about 1777, George III created the Windsor uniform[69] of blue with red collar and cuffs and gold braid (see pl. 128); by this date blue and red were fashionable uniform colours as well as being used for servants' liveries and made popular hunting and riding outfits (in 1779 the queen and princesses were wearing riding habits of blue faced and turned up with red). The Windsor uniform, as worn by a small royal circle, was very plain compared with the more lavish European styles, but it occasionally inspired elaborate feminine versions for special occasions. One such occasion was a ball given at Windsor to celebrate the king's recovery from his illness in 1789, when ladies wore 'a Garter blue body trimmed with a scarlet and gold edge, the stomacher white, laced with gold cord, the sleeves white with a crêpe festoon on the shoulders, tied up with gold tassels, a scarlet and gold band round the arm. The petticoat was white crêpe with a flounce trimmed at top and bottom with a white and gold fringe, and the same of scarlet and gold.'[70]

In 1778, Gustavus III established a national uniform to be worn by the elite and the middle classes (the clergy and peasantry were exempt). Regulations for this uniform encompassed not only the royal households, but all government officials, legal and military officers, university and medical staffs, and so on. The uniforms were based on early-seventeenth-century styles, arising perhaps out of the king's admiration for the fashionable Henri IV styles that could be seen at the French court, or his recollection of a period when Sweden was a dominant power in Europe. Gustavus also had a collection of costumes (from the reign of Gustavus Adolphus in the early seventeenth century) that inspired the court theatricals in which he took part as author, actor and designer. An English visitor in 1784 found the women at court wearing black dresses with puffed and slashed sleeves, red sash and central rosette: 'The dress of the men resembles the old Spanish, and consists of a short coat, or jacket, a waistcoat, a cloak, a hat with a feather à la

134a, b and c J. Gillberg after J. E. Rehn,
Swedish National Costume, 1778

Svenska Nationella Mans Klädedräkten
med Allernådigste Tilstånd graverad af
J.Gillberg 1778.

Svenska Nationella Fruntimmers Klädedräkten
med Allernådigste Tilstånd graverad af
J.Gillberg 1778.

Svenska Nationella Fruntimmers Klädedräkten
med Allernådigste Tilstånd graverad af
J.Gillberg 1778.

135   P. Hilleström, *A Conversation at Drottningholm*, 1779

All the courtiers in this salon of the Swedish summer palace are shown wearing the court uniform devised by Gustavus III, who is seated to the left on a sofa.

Henry IV, a sash round the waist, a sword, large and full breeches, and roses in the shoes; the cloak is of black cloth edged with red satin; the coat or jacket and breeches are also black, ornamented with red stripes and buttons; the waistcoat, the sash, the pinks at the knees, and roses for the shoes, are of red sattin.'[71] For more formal occasions, there was a uniform of white and red and a gala costume of pale blue and white, trimmed with braid. The latter favoured by the royal family, although, said Archdeacon Coxe, the king 'while he has limited his subjects to particular colours, assumes the liberty of varying his own dress with all the tints of the rainbow'.

Any examination of the etiquette of dress is incomplete without discussing weddings for, in royal circles, they demonstrated courtly splendour as well as cementing international alliances. A French queen as bride wore a *grand habit* covered with jewels and a purple velvet state mantle; in 1725, for example, Maria Lesczynska, according to La Motraye, had 'the Fore-Sides of her Stays and of her Peticoat shinn'd with divers pretious Stones' and her 'Royal Mantel was of Purple Velvet spread with gold Flower de Luces, linn'd with Ermine'.[72] When, in 1761, Princess Charlotte of Mecklenberg-Strelitz came to England to be the bride of George III, she was married in the court 'stiffen-body'd Gown' of 'Silver Tissue, embroidered & trimmed with Silver, on her head a little Cap of purple Velvet quite covered with Diamonds, a Diamond Aigrette in the form of a Crown, 3 dropt Diamond Earrings, Diamond Necklace, Diamond Sprigs of Flowers in her Sleeves and to clasp back her Robe, a diamond Stomacher, her purple Velvet Mantle was laced with Gold and lined with Ermine'[73] (she wore the same dress for her coronation). At coronations, it was the custom for royal ladies and peeresses to wear false ringlets, and this applied also to royal brides (the origin was probably in the long hair worn by brides on their wedding day). Frederica Sophia Wilhelmina, the Princess Royal of Prussia, was in 1731 compelled to wear 'the royal crown . . . with four and twenty locks as thick as my arm . . . I could not hold my head up, it was too weak to sustain such a weight. My robe was of a very rich silver brocade, with a Brussells gold lace and my train was twelve yards long. I had well nigh died under this attire.'[74] As weddings were state occasions, the bride and groom were ceremonially conducted to the state bed, where the formal undressing took place in public; dynastic considerations outweighed royal privacy. Etiquette also demanded that a foreign royal bride should be disrobed on the borders of her future country and dressed anew from head to foot in the clothes of her new kingdom as a symbolic gesture of commitment to the interests and loyalties of her adopted state.

Royal brides and grooms could, in the early eighteenth century, wear colours and gold; Louis XV wore gold brocade with diamond buttons for his wedding in 1725 and in 1734 Princess Anne of England married in 'a manteau and petticoat, white damask with the finest embroidery of flowers intermixed in their various colours'. By the middle of the century, white with gold or silver was the rule; in Denmark, Christian VII's wedding suit (1766) was cloth of silver with gold embroidery, and in 1744 Princess Sophie of Anhalt-Zerbst (the future Catherine the Great) was ordered by the Empress Elizabeth, who was determined to follow the customs of Versailles, to wear a French dress of cloth of silver, embroidered in silver and with a cloak of silver lace. In the Livrustkammaren in Stockholm is the wedding dress worn by Princess Sophia Magdalena of Denmark, the bride of Gustavus III of Sweden, on her marriage in 1766; the dress, a French *robe de cour* (possibly ordered in France), is white and silver damask brocaded with sprays of roses. The style, with separate boned bodice, train and petticoat worn over a huge hoop, is identical to her coronation dress – the fabric of which, a silver brocade with gold crowns, was designed by Jean Eric Rehn and woven by a French weaver, Peyron, who had settled in Stockholm in 1740. The latter dress was originally woven for the coronation of Queen Louisa Ulrica in 1751 and is also preserved.[75]

The idea of a gown reserved for just the wedding ceremony was a nineteenth-century notion, when clothes, comparatively speaking, were cheaper. In the eighteenth century even the most richly elaborate dress (except for the *grand habit*) had to serve more than one occasion. In England, brides were often presented at court in their wedding dress and, particularly in the first half of the century, a heavily embroidered mantua would be suitable, later to be replaced by a sack dress. Emphasis was laid more on

136 and 137 (*following pages*)   Details of pl. 135

the pre-marriage financial settlement than on the actual ceremony in the eighteenth century; the marquise de La Tour du Pin, for example, tells us in her memoirs more about the white gauze gown that she wore at the signing of the marriage articles than about the robe of white crape with Brussels lace that she wore for her wedding in 1787. This was because the first dress was the latest fashion, the chemise gown, tied round the waist with a blue silk ribbon; the wedding dress was more conservative in style.[76]

Weddings were very often private affairs, taking place in the afternoon or evening; in England, the 1753 Marriage Act stated that weddings should take place in church but even after that date licences for private weddings could be obtained for many, like Fanny Burney in 1768, believed that a public display at church was an affront to the sensibilities of the bride – 'I'm sure I trembled for the bride. Oh, what a gauntlet for any woman of delicacy to run.'[77] Modesty and informality were important aspects of the bride's attire; Walpole's niece Maria married Lord Waldegrave in 1759 'in a white and silver night-gown with a hat very much pulled over her face',[78] and in the anonymous novel *Harcourt* (1780), the bride wore a negligée of white lustring with flounces of embroidered gauze, a short apron and a chip hat. White and silver were, in the second half of the century, the customary colours for upper-class brides, and could also be worn by their grooms. Earl Ferrers, for example, on his way to Tyburn in 1760 to be executed for the murder of his steward, wore his wedding suit of white and silver. However, men could also wear other light colours: Mr B. in *Pamela* wore a blue paduasoy waistcoat, a 'pearl-coloured fine cloth, with gold buttons and button-holes and lined with white silk',[79] and Lord Stormont in 1776 chose 'embroideries with foils upon Brown Cloath, and lined with couleur de paille, with a waistcoat paille embroidered with gold and foils'.[80] Lower down the social scale, the bride's dress was often her best and had to last. Mrs Primrose, wife of the Vicar of Wakefield, chose her gown 'not for a fine glossy surface, but such qualities as would wear well'; the sculptor Nollekens's bride in 1771 wore 'a sacque and petticoat of the most expensive brocaded white silk, resembling network, enriched with small flowers, which displayed in the variation of the folds, a most delicate shade of pink';[81] the groom himself wore a suit bought in Rome of 'Pourpre de Pape', probably the only formal suit that he possessed during his life and which survived at his death in 1823.

As in all centuries before our own, death was an ever-present fact of life, to be prepared for and to be accorded an important place in the rituals of society. It is sometimes hard to imagine how dismal and widespread full mourning could be, with its depressing effect on trade, for court mourning had to be observed for all reigning princes and sometimes their families. In France, Barbier's journal records many times the protests of Parisian tradesmen and suppliers of luxury fabrics at the repeated orders for black. For example, when the Dauphine Marie-Thérèse d'Espagne died in August 1746 there was the customary six months' mourning, terminated in February by the festivities for the re-marriage of the Dauphin to Marie-Josèphe de Saxe. In March 1747, however, the Queen of Poland (mother of the French queen) died, and Louis XV decided that the whole court should wear 'un très grand deuil', even the army officers having to dress in black. This mourning, beginning so soon after the conclusion of the previous one, 'ruine totalement le commerce des marchands de soie, qui étoient déjà changés des habits de printemps et des taffetas de couleur' (totally ruined the business of the silk mercers who had already introduced the spring styles and coloured taffetas).[82] In some of the Italian states that relied on the textile industries, mourning was limited by sumptuary legislation; the most important was Milan, which specified that six months was the maximum length of time when black should be worn.

Court mourning was a sign of the international brotherhood of princes, and its diplomatic observance was necessary even when contending politics made this difficult; mourning was regulated less by the status of the deceased than by their closeness in blood to the sovereign and ranged from six months for a consort to a few days for a minor princeling. In France in 1740, the court mourned three weeks for the Empress Anna of Russia, a similar period of time for the Austrian Emperor Charles VI and, in 1760, only two days for a mere Landgrave of Hesse-Cassel. In an age in which communications were poor, there could be occasional confusion: in 1748, the Grand Duchess of Tuscany died and her great-nephew the Young Pretender, who had completed his mourning by the time the French court were officially informed, was to be seen conspicuous among the black-dressed courtiers at the theatre in France in his 'habit rouge brodé d'or' (red coat embroidered with gold).[83]

The actual ceremonial of royal funerals, with formal lying-in-state and the draping of apartments and mirrors with black, dated back to the Middle Ages. By the beginning of the eighteenth century, the medieval gown and hood had given way to a long cloak and hat adorned with black streamers; Baron Bielfeld attended the funeral in 1740 of the King of Prussia, Frederich William I, and found 'all the princes and noblemen were in the deepest mourning with trailing cloaks and long crapes in their hats'. Walpole, with his unfailing talent for finding something amusing on the most melancholy occasion, noted that on the death of George II (1760), the king's brother, the Duke of Cumberland, 'in a cloak of black cloth with a train five yards . . . felt himself weighed down, and turning round found it was the Duke of Newcastle standing upon his train to avoid the chill of the marble'.[84]

Purple was traditionally the colour worn by the sovereign for mourning, but otherwise the gloom was unrelieved. Mrs Delany found that the one topic of conversation in the pump-room in Bath was of the death of George II: '. . . the public mourning will make every place appear dismal till the eye is used to it.' Although the details of mourning dress varied from country to country, it generally graduated from the matt, untrimmed cloth of deep black, through black silk with touches of ornament, to shades of grey and white with black. Full mourning for men was the currently fashionable suit made of black cloth without buttons on the pockets or the sleeves, but with a black sword, sword-belt and buckles and black crape bands in the hat. Linen was plain, sometimes edged with black, and 'weepers', white linen or muslin cuffs, were added to the coat, varying in size according to the stage of mourning. For second mourning, men could wear black silk coats (or dark grey frocks for undress), their linen could be fringed and swords and buckles could be silver.

Women's mourning was more complicated and extreme, particularly that of widows; it generally followed current fashion, but for first mourning they wore the widow's cap and pleated white collar with a black veil. A large proportion of widows (particularly royalty) wore mourning for the rest of their lives. In 1716, Lady Mary Wortley Montagu in Vienna found the Dowager Empress with 'not the least bit of linnen to be seen; all black crape instead of it, the neck, ears and side of the face cover'd with a plaited piece of the same stuff; and the face that peeps out in the midst of it looks as if it were pillory'd'.[85] When the Empress Maria Theresa lost her husband (1765) she stayed in black for the rest of her life, Lady Mary Coke finding her some years later 'still in deep mourning . . . Her own private apartment is hung with black Cloth, & in the room She sits in She has the pictures of the Emperor & all the Children she has lost.'[86] As with court mourning for men, the first stage was black woollen cloth, black accessories including a crape hood and plain linen; then black silk, with fringed and embroidered muslin or net, and diamonds, with white or grey for undress wear.

As the prince was supposed to be a father to his people, there was, at least among the upper levels of society, widespread observance of mourning for members of ruling families, even though the prescribed stages might be omitted in favour of token black. César de Saussure found, in London in 1727, on the death of George I that 'nobles, gentlemen, officers, merchants and citizens' were in black; inevitably, however, the impact made on society further away from the immediate court was slighter. Court mourning abroad was an expected hazard for the gentleman on the Grand Tour; the British envoy in Dresden told Boswell 'never to be without a black coat, as so many accidents can happen'.[87]

Personal family bereavements for those outside a court circle followed an equally hierarchic system. An ordinance in 1716 in France declared the period of mourning should range from one year six weeks for a widow (widowers mourned for only six months) to two months for brother or sister and eight days for a distant cousin; widows wore black for the first year (and could not attend court for the first six months) and white for the last six weeks. Although many wore fashionable dress, some middle-class women wore a long-sleeved gown with little or no trimming even when out of first mourning. There are constant references in the letters of Mrs Delany to her mourning preparations, not just for members of the royal family but also relatives; for the death of her mother in 1747, both formal and informal mourning was needed: 'I think black bombazeen will do very well in a sack. I have one in a manteau and petticoat which I wear when in full dress, at home a dark grey poplin, and abroad, undrest, a dark grey watered tabby.'[88] In addition, she put her housekeeper and personal maid into mourning, which for female servants consisted of black silk (if they were close to their mistress)

138 T. Gainsborough, *Maria Walpole, Lady Waldegrave*, c.1764

For second mourning, Lady Waldegrave has followed current fashion, in her black silk sack trimmed on the sleeve with fly fringe and with blonde lace for tippet and ruffles.

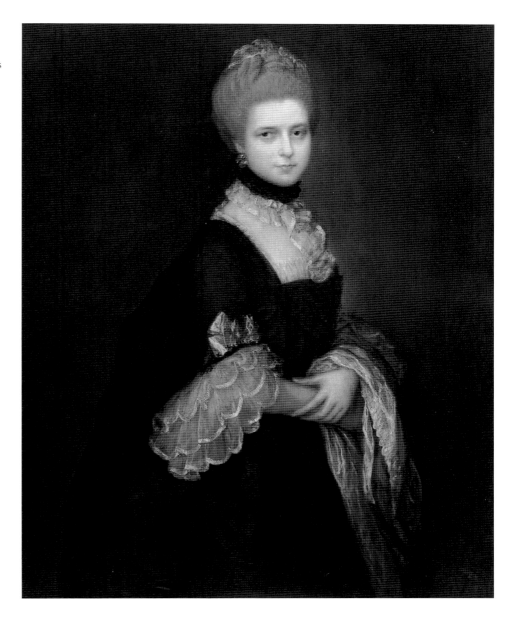

or cloth and for men a suit of black cloth or dark grey material. Parson James Woodforde, on the death of his father in 1771, gave to his servant 'a black crape hatband and buckles and a black broad cloth Coat and Waistcoat';[89] this was suitable for a clerical household, but many men wore for mourning just a black hatband and black gloves, which were relatively inexpensive items even for those who could not afford full black.

6   Frivolity and Freedom: 1770–1789

De La Mode

Figurez-vous une infinité de Ministres, dont le règne ne s'étendoit pas au-delà d'un jour, & qui, chaque matin, changeroient à leur lever les habillements, les usages, les esprits, les moeurs, & meme les caractères de tout un peuple.

L. S. Mercier, *Tableau de Paris*, 1782

THE LAST TWO DECADES BEFORE the French Revolution were years of transition, with a new informality in clothing contrasting with the rich restrictions of full dress.

For men, the French suit with elaborate embroidery and equally highly decorated waistcoat was identified with an increasingly ossified court circle and the privileges of aristocracy. The *Fashionable Magazine* found by 1786 that 'gentlemen's full dress [was] too antiquated for any other place than court'; by then, frock coats were the most widely worn, not just the English plain frock, but, more formally, the more elegantly cut and embroidered French version. Formality gave way to English 'country clothes' with their emphasis on sober simplicity of material and cut; finery was out and 'democratic' informality was in vogue.

In women's dress, two themes predominated. On the one hand, there was a change in the female silhouette from the triangular rigidity imposed by boned stays and hooped petticoats, to a softer line where bulk was created by hip pads, bustles and layers of linen at the bosom, so that women, by the 1780s, looked like downy pigeons, this feeling emphasized by the popular white, blues and greys of fashionable clothing. On the other hand, in contrast to this billowing femininity, there was a growing emphasis on more functional dress, including the adoption of masculine garments such as the greatcoat, which could be worn over the newly fashionable long-sleeved gowns. The most important new development in the 1780s was the extreme popularity of dresses made all in one piece and based on the chemise, which could be put on over the head; this was a revolutionary change from the dress into which, so to speak, the lady stepped sideways, and the chemise gown (which in various versions was to dominate the revolutionary period and the Napoleonic aftermath) was the real ancestor of the dresses worn today. The increased momentum of change and the almost frenzied adoption of every fashion whim was partly due to the enormous popularity of fashion magazines and considerably improved communications.

139   Detail of pl. 145

Mrs Coltman 'feminizes' the severe lines of her riding habit with a lace ruff at the neck and her beaver hat with gold ribbon and white ostrich feather.

141 A. von Maron, *Unknown Gentleman,* late 1760s

This portrait by an Austrian artist in Rome shows a fashionable tourist in a gold-trimmed frock suit of the vivid red so popular in Italian male dress of this period; it seems to have been a popular choice, also, for foreigners on the Grand Tour who would have suits locally made.

140 After C.-L. Desrais, 'Jeune Officier en Habit de Zèbre', 1787, from *Gallerie des Modes et Costumes Français*

Men

The two decades leading up to the Revolution were the swan-song of the *ancien régime* and were the last time that the formal French suit with its superbly decorated silk fabrics was the accepted dress for high society.

By the beginning of the 1770s, the coat was being cut quite narrow across the back; it began to curve away sharply at the sides with a corresponding reduction in the reinforcement of the side pleats. By 1789, some coats were turned over at the sides, so that the back took the form of 'swallow-tails', and by this date many men had their coats cut straight across at the waist, following the line of the fashionable sporting or informal waistcoat.

During the 1760s, a small, standing collar had been added to the formal coat. This gradually increased in height and was embroidered to match the small cuffs, the pocket flaps and the side and back pleats. For court functions, the embroidery remained sumptuous and expensive; in May 1782, one of the coats ordered for Louis XVI was of lilac moiré silk, with silver and diamond embroidery costing 1400 livres. Seventy-eight livres was spent on the silver buttons, diamonds and green and white spangles alone.[1] Buttons were increasingly *objets de luxe*, for the coat was cut away at the sides so much that the front panels met only at chest level and fastened at the level of the third button down with hooks and eyes; the buttons remained very large in the 1770s and were jewelled, embroidered or enamelled with topographical; political or theatrical scenes – a style set by the leader of fashion in France, Charles, comte d'Artois, younger brother of Louis XVI.

At court and formal assemblies in England, suits were made of silk (cloth was also acceptable provided it was trimmed as richly as silk), the colours varying with the season. For winter, either bright or dark colours were in vogue; at the queen's birthday, in January 1777, there were, said the *Magazine à la Mode*, 'many suits of velvet and cloth . . . trimmed with a rich appliqué, a term given to shapes of rich embroidery intermixed with gold and silver, and coloured spangles and foil, green, red and crimson . . . The plainer suits were Irish rateen lined with feathered velvet or sattin, of different colours from the coat, with gold spangled buttons . . . the plain suits were chiefly puce or flea colour, damson or chocolate lined with white, blue, green pink or rose-colour feathered velvets or sattins.'[2] For summer, the lighter silks were used with pale colours such as pink, light blue, buff and lilac; Horace Walpole's summer visiting costume in the early 1770s was 'a lavender suit, the waistcoat embroidered with silver or tambour-work, ruffles and jabot of lace, partridge silk stockings'.[3] For woven silks, patterns were small stylized floral designs, or spots, stripes and chevrons; Mercier, in Paris in 1787, found a popular source of inspiration was the king's zebra: '. . . coats and waistcoats imitate the handsome creature's markings as closely as they can. Men of all ages have gone into stripes from head to foot, even to their stockings.'[4]

The new fashionable male silhouette of the 1770s was tall and slim, with short waistcoat and tighter-fitting breeches. The coat was made very tight

142 P. Dawe, *The Pantheon Macaroni*, 1773

The exaggerated styles of dress worn by
the macaronis were popular masquerade
costumes at places like the Pantheon in
Oxford Street. A certain Lord P★★★ at one
masquerade (1773) wore a 'club of hair . . .
of such a prodigious size, that it covered
both his shoulders . . . his foretop was of
an uncommon height, . . . and upon this
amazing structure was placed a remarkable
small hat . . . which he could not possibly
reach without the help of his sword'.

PANTHEON MACARONI.

across the back, with narrow sleeves that pulled the arms back; in a play
called *The Pantheonites* (1773), an unhappy man complained of his French
tailor that 'the French son of a cabbage has made sleeves as if I have no more
giblets than a goose . . . I have no more use of my arms than an Egyptian
mummy'.[5] And poor Henry Angelo at court in 1775 in his summer suit of
lilac poplin lined with yellow found to his embarrassment that the coat had
split under the arms, which with presence of mind he covered with his
chapeau bras and then fled to his sedan chair.[6]

Young men-about-town, such as the macaronis in England and the *élégants* in France, exaggerated their lean figures with striped suits and stockings and their height with toupets that rose to six inches and more. The macaronis, latest in the long line of fashionable empty-headed young men, took their name in the 1760s from a dish they had tasted on their Italian grand tour; they formed a club, 'the members of which were supposed to be the standards of taste in polite learning, the fine arts and the genteel sciences; and fashion, amongst the other constituent parts of taste, became an object of their attention. But they soon proved, they had very little claim to any distinction, except in their external appearance.'[7] Their influence was out of proportion to their number, though society and fashion papers in the 1770s and a few men of importance, such as Charles James Fox, helped to popularize their fashions in clubs such as Almacks. These fashions consisted of towering wigs with tiny hats, very tight coats (to achieve the fashionable unbroken line an inside pocket (1777) replaced the outside flapped pocket) with huge buttons, nosegays in their buttonholes and vast shoe buckles. Inevitably, they were a godsend to the first great age of caricature, particularly when artists could linger on the effeminate side of the costume – the parasols, the powder, the large muffs, the perfume and the light colours – which were, except for court, becoming old-fashioned. The styles may have originated in France (possibly to try to stem the flood of English outdoor fashions that would, in the following decade, sweep all before them), but in England the frivolity and richness of macaroni clothes was attributed also to the wealth of nabobs returning from India to England. William Hickey, who spent some years in India, described the transformation of a friend, who 'Instead of the plain brown cloth suit we had last seen him in, with unpowdered hair and a single curl, we now beheld a furiously powdered and pomatumed head with six curls on each side, a little skimming dish of a hat . . . His coat was of a thick silk the colour sky blue and lined with crimson satin, the waistcoat and breeches also of crimson satin . . . The cut too was entirely different from anything we had seen, having a remarkable long waist to the coat with scarce any skirts.'[8]

Ridiculous though many of the more exaggerated macaroni styles were, their emphasis on a slim figure helped to improve the quality of tailoring and the shape of the average man. No longer, by the 1780s, could a moderately fashionable man be pot-bellied in baggy breeches, for, said the *Fashionable Magazine* (1786), they 'are made excessively high-waisted, long over the knees and to set very tight'; they had to be cut high, for by this time the waistcoat was 'exceedingly short', usually double-breasted and with 'small lappels'.[9] Braces or 'gallowses' (which before then had been limited to working men to keep up their often ill-fitting breeches or trousers) now entered the fashionable man's wardrobe and helped to hold up the breeches that could no longer cling to the hips for support.

The macaronis and their followers represented the last gasp of the bright, highly decorative clothing that to many is so typical of the eighteenth century. The mood by the 1770s, and even more so in the following decade,

143   After P.-T. Le Clère, 'Fraque à la Polonaise', 1779, from *Gallerie des Modes et Costumes Français*

This newly fashionable slim male figure is accentuated by the frock with its braided seams and skimpily cut skirts.

was for 'the agreeable negligence in dress' typical of the English country gentleman. It was Dr Johnson in his 'rusty-brown' suit, rather than Oliver Goldsmith in his 'bloom-coloured coat', that fitted the mood of the last quarter of the century.[10]

Plain cloth frocks in either dark blue, black or buff, buffskin or leather breeches and boots had been, throughout the century, almost a uniform for the English gentleman, more content to live and work on his estates than to hover round a court looking for royal favour. A return to the supposed simplicities of country life had for long been advocated in the works of the French philosophers, who saw and admired what they thought was its highest expression in the relatively liberal climate of England. Many could find in the pleasant informality of country life and clothing a practical expression of their tentative movements towards democracy. Not for the first time was homespun equated with egalitarianism and when, in 1789, George Washington was inaugurated as President of the United States, he was careful to wear a suit of dark brown woollen cloth of American manufacture (though in 1793 aristocratic black velvet was deemed appropriate, with powdered hair in a bag).[11] Joseph Wright of Derby's portrait of Sir Brooke Boothby (1781) (pl. 144) shows him lying somewhat uneasily in a wooded glade with a volume of Rousseau in his hand; he wears a sober brown cloth suit comprising frock coat, knee-breeches and double-breasted waistcoat, and plain linen. By the early 1780s, plain linen had replaced lace, other than at court; fine, white, crisp linen made the neckcloths, sometimes stiffened, that were folded closely round the neck and buckled behind. An alternative form of neckwear from the mid-1780s was the cravat (a revival of an earlier fashion) which was a long muslin scarf, knotted in front, and known in France as a 'cravate à l'anglaise'.

The impetus that made many fashionable men on the Continent adopt English styles was the publication, in Leipzig in 1774, of Goethe's *succès fou, The Sorrows of Young Werther*. Werther, the hero, was depicted in a romanticized version of English country clothing: dark blue coat, yellow waistcoat and buff breeches with boots. He was deliberately shown as a contrast to the aristocrats who spurned him, in their 'gothic dress' which 'made a still greater contrast to our modern coats'. When Richardson's novel *Pamela* appeared in 1740, it, too, was a runaway success, with foreign translations, imitations and parodies. But where *Pamela* made little, if any, impact on the readers' appearance, Goethe's novel set a vogue for young men to dress *à la Werther*, for the mood of the moment, the beginnings of *Sturm und Drang*, were already stirring the minds of young readers rebelling against the Augustan canons of reason and control. Werther, in fact, turns away from Homer to Ossian, whose poems he translates, and his suicide at the end of the novel even inspired imitators to follow suit out of pure sensibility of feeling.

Towards the last quarter of the eighteenth century, the idea of the suit made of one fabric was breaking up among the fashionable elite, the *Gentleman's and London Magazine* (1777) noting that 'an entire suit of cloth is hardly ever seen except upon old people, physicians, apothecaries and

144 J. Wright, *Sir Brooke Boothby*, 1781

lawyers'. William Hickey, on his return to London in 1780, found that he needed a completely new wardrobe, so the tailor 'advised my having a dark green with gold binding, dark brown with the same, a plain blue, and for half-dress a *Bon de Paris* with gold frogs, all of which he spoke as being much worn and of the highest ton'.[12] These were dark-coloured frocks, some plain in the English style, the others trimmed in the French mode; the French took to the frock with enthusiasm (by 1778, Louis XVI wore one) and, with typical ingenuity, produced different versions of it, including one with a sloping shawl collar and one *à la polonaise*, i.e. without a back vent. Dark blue and black were popular colours for the frock, the latter especially so in France, giving, said commentators, an air of gloom to the streets in contrast to the natural gaiety of the French. In England by the early 1780s, most Englishmen wore 'a short white waistcoat, black breeches, white silk stockings, and a frock, generally of a very dark blue cloth which looks like black'.[13] By the end of the decade, a Russian visitor, Nikolai Mikhailovich Karamzin, found almost half the men in the streets wearing this dark blue, and even his ambassador wore a similar garment but with a small hair bag 'which distinguishes him from every other inhabitant of London'.[14]

Hickey's new wardrobe in 1780 included 'Rymer's for boots, Wagner for hats and Williams of Bond Street for leather breeches. In three days I was to come forth a proper Bond Street Lounger, a description of person then just coming into vogue.'[15] The full panoply of English sporting wear rightly included leather breeches or stockinette pantaloons (tight-fitting trousers), the latter being rare until the 1790s, but occasionally seen. As well as the frock, the buffskin breeches, the riding coat and the jockey cap, the French enthusiastically adopted English aristocratic sports like driving and racing, in a wave of Anglomania which, transmitted by the duc de Chartres (duc d'Orléans in 1785 and later Philippe Egalité) who was a crony of the Prince of Wales, swept over Paris. The *Petit Dictionnaire de la Cour et de la Ville* (1788) commented sourly: 'Bientôt Paris sera tout Anglois. Habits, voitures, chevaux, bijoux, boissons, spectacles, jardins & morale, tout est à l'angloise. Nous avons pris de ce triste peuple le vauxhall, le club, les jocqueis, les fracs, le vishk, le punch, le spleen, & la fureur du suicide' (soon Paris will be completely English. Clothes, carriages, horses, jewellery, drink, entertainments, gardens and morals, all is *à l'anglais*. We have taken from this gloomy country Vauxhall, the club, jockeys, frock coats, whist, punch, low spirits, and the craze for suicide).[16]

Hickey's newly acquired London hat was probably a round hat with flat-topped crown and wide uncocked brim, which was originally a functional out-of-doors hat, taken up along with leather breeches by young bloods in the middle of the century. This round hat had, by the 1770s, replaced, except for court and formal assemblies, the three-cornered hat, though the latter was preferred by the more conservative and the professional and middle classes. Francis Place (born 1771) wore as a child a round hat with a gold band and tassel, and although his father 'said none but thieves and persons who were ashamed to show their faces wore them' he too wore one 'covered with fine canvas and painted by himself' in bad weather.[17] Although the formal three-cornered hat was black, other, more fashionable hats, according to Mercier in the 1780s, could be coloured or white, the latter a popular choice for summer. Once the tyranny of the three-cornered hat was ended, hats assumed a variety of forms, some with brims turned high up in front and behind, some with high crowns and some jockey caps.

But is was the footwear that distinguished the fashionable man in the north of Europe from his counterpart in hotter southern countries: Goethe, in Verona in 1787, found the townspeople staring at his boots, which to Italians were purely for riding. The fashion for wearing soft leather jockey boots reaching to the knee and turned down at the top often with a contrasting colour had begun, as noted earlier, in the middle of the eighteenth century in England. They became, by the 1770s, fashionable for walking and for indoors (even for polite assemblies, although frowned on) and so remained until the beginning of the next century: 'The number of walking jockies is very numerous and the rage for boots by no means over,' said the

145 J. Wright, *Mr and Mrs Thomas Coltman, c.*1769

Painted soon after their marriage in 1769, Mr and Mrs Coltman are shown in informal country costume. Seated side-saddle, Mrs Coltman wears a riding habit comprising matching jacket and skirt, and a buttoned waistcoat trimmed with braid. Mr Coltman wears a light riding frock and breeches, jockey boots and a waistcoat with frogging *à la* hussar.

Ipswich Journal for June 1786. An alternative style in the 1780s was the hussar buskin, a calf-length boot dipped in front with a tassel at each side.

Formal occasions, however, demanded shoes and buckles (shoe strings or laces were in vogue for plain leather shoes from the mid-1780s). These buckles were large oblongs or ovals and a gentleman of fashion had vast numbers – the comtesse de Boigne, visiting Maria Fitzherbert in 1789, was astounded to see a large cupboard full of buckles belonging to the Prince of Wales (they had married in secret in 1785), a different pair for every day of the year. At court, precious stones were used but these were increasingly replaced by cut steel to suit the English taste; this was what the *Petit Diction-naire* meant when it referred to English jewels being all the rage in Paris in the 1780s. This cut steel (which could be faceted to a high degree of brilliance) was used to make not only shoe and breeches buckles, but *breloquets* (decorative chains hung with enamel plaques, intaglios and cameos which jangled as the dandy walked) and watches. There was a temporary fashion in the mid-1780s for two watches to be worn on either side of the waist, a false watch matching the real and containing a mirror, a miniature or a vinaigrette. Suit and waistcoat buttons were also made from cut steel. According to the *Magasin des Modes Nouvelles* of 1789 'les habits de couleur sombre et sur les gilets de drap on ne porte guère que des boutons d'acier travaillé' (one hardly wears anything but buttons of cut steel on sombre-coloured coats and cloth waistcoats).[18]

The overcoat or surtout had, by the 1770s, become a triumph of tailoring based on sober materials excellently cut (its apotheosis was to be achieved in later years under Beau Brummell); it was cut close to the body, with small cuffs and a variety of collar styles. The *Cabinet des Modes* for February 1787 stated that the most fashionable men were wearing 'un habit redingote de drap couleur de suie des cheminées de Londres' (a long coat of cloth of the colour of soot from London chimneys), with scarlet collar and cuffs *à la marinière*; this was so close-fitting that it was worn straight over a waistcoat of grey satin and with boots and a *chapeau jockey*.[19] For very cold weather, the magazine recommended redingotes of plush (a velvet-like fabric of wool or cotton), which was obtained from such specialists as Jubin at the Trois Mandarins in the arcades of the Palais Royal.

Surtouts could be plain and untrimmed; when, in 1784, Gustavus III came to Paris (travelling under the name of the Count of Haga), he drove about the city streets dressed in a plain grey surtout, being mobbed by the crowd as 'the commons' king' – perhaps another example of the equation made between simplicity of clothing and liberal accessibility to the sovereign. Some surtouts were made in the wrapping style that had been especially popular in the middle of the eighteenth century. When Mrs Piozzi was in Milan (1785), she saw the men in 'an odd sort of white riding coat, not buttoned together, but folded round their body after the fashion of the old Roman dress that one has seen in statues, and this they call Gaban'.[20] This is probably what Goethe wears in the famous portrait by Tischbein painted on his trip to Italy in 1786 (pl. 146); after the romanticism of Werther, Goethe had

146   J. H. W. Tischbein, *Goethe in the Roman Campagna*, 1786

Goethe, in romantically pensive mood, 'on a fallen obelisk viewing the ruins of the Campagna di Roma', has chosen, to echo the classical mood, what an English visitor called, 'an odd sort of white riding coat . . . folded round [the] body after the fashion of the old Roman dress that one has seen in statues'.

turned to classicism, the drapery of the *gaban* being particularly suitable for this mood as 'enveloped in a white mantle' he sits 'on a fallen obelisk viewing the ruins of the campagna di Roma'.[21] The most popular surtouts or great-coats had collars of contrasting colours, sometimes more than one – an idea taken from the English coachmen, who wore, said Pierre-Jean Grosley, seeing them in the 1760s, 'an upper coat adorned with a long cape of two or three rows'. In 1775, Sir Joshua Reynolds's nephew (Samuel Johnson, son of the artist's sister Elizabeth) in London chose a greatcoat of 'a light colour with a light green collar, made in the new fashion; the colour of the coat depends on one's own fancy, but the green capes are almost universal'.[22] In the 1780s, triple capes were the usual style both in London and Paris; in the latter a popular version was the *redingote à la lévite*, with buttoned revers and the requisite three collars.

Although a convinced Republican, Mercier was first a patriot, and argued fiercely against the collared coats, which to him were the epitome of a slovenly if easy-going English style; foreigners attending the House of Commons were astounded by the behaviour of M.P.s, who came in dressed in boots and greatcoats and lay on the benches eating nuts and oranges. Horace Walpole claimed that his good health and longevity was due to the fact that he never wore a greatcoat, though the real reason for his dislike of an overcoat might have been that it spoiled the line of his suit or the elegance of his gait. Although the cloak continued to be worn by such old-fashioned or conservative gentlemen, it was increasingly being limited in England to professional men, army officers and for funerals. In colder

Rédingotte à trois colets et Croisée par devant, dite Rédingotte en Lévite.

147 (*above left*) F. Bayeu, *An Unknown Man*, c.1785

With his formal pose and wig, this Spanish gentleman is dressed for winter in fur-lined coat; a fashionable touch is the wearing of two decorative chains suspended from the waist.

148 (*above right*) Vogsard after P.-T. Le Clère, 'Redingotte à trois colets', 1781, from *Gallerie des Modes et Costumes Français*

This triple-collared style of overcoat was the height of fashion in the 1780s both in London, from whence it was derived, and Paris. With it is worn a muslin cravat *à l'anglaise*.

climates, however, fur-lined mantles were both necessary and luxurious: in Frederick the Great's inventory there were mantles of wolf-skin and lynx lined with silk, and important visitors to Russia were given fur pelisses – Gustavus III, in St Petersburg in 1777, had as a gift from Catherine the Great one of blue fox.

Perhaps one of the greatest demonstrations of the new feeling of simplicity in men's appearance was a rejection of the long-established wig in favour of the natural hair. True, the macaronis in the early 1770s wore high, powdered wigs, but this was the exception rather than the rule, and from the end of the 1760s some men had begun to wear their own hair either unpowdered or dressed formally. In Fanny Burney's novel *Evelina* (1778), a foolish young man of fashion was urged after an accident (a monkey had bitten his ear) to wear a wig. '"A wig?" repeated the affrighted Mr Lovel, "I wear a wig? – no! not if you would give me a thousand pounds an hour."'[23]

For court, the hair had to be dressed and then powdered in stiff styles (with black silk bag at the back); Henry Angelo in his *Reminiscences* recalled how, in the mid-1770s, 'many a night (I then sported four curls on each

149 Attributed to J. M. Moreau, *The Hairdresser*, early 1770s

From the late 1760s, an alternative to wearing a wig was to have one's own hair dressed with pomade and powder, a messy business which necessitated a protective cloth over the client. This rapid and economical drawing shows an artist familiar with his subject: Moreau's father was a master wig-maker.

150 (*following page*) A. Labille-Guiard, *Madame Adélaïde de France, Daughter of Louis XV*, c.1787

Madame Adélaïde wears the formal sack with embroidered robings; a similar star and floral design can be seen in the embroidery on the skirt. The wide, frizzed hairstyle supports an elaborate 'pouf' or confection of lace and ribbons.

side), previous to going to bed, my time has been long employed plaistering each curl with a mixture of powder and pomatum; I then had to roll them up separately preparatory to the hairdresser's visit the next day to add his embellisments . . . with maréchal powder'.[24] Paradoxically, far more bother was needed to have the hair dressed than to wear a wig; the *London Magazine* of 1772 had already commented unfavourably on 'the plaistered pyramid of scented pomatum . . . those immoveable buckles that destroy the grace of the flowing curls', and even in the 1780s, when the rolled curls gave way to a more natural profusion of curls, the fashionable look was still acquired by curl papers and grease to create the necessary bulk and width. The *Art of Hairdressing or the Gentleman's Director* by Alexander Stewart (1788) discusses the byzantine complexities of dressing and papering the hair ('a frise is put in the root of the curls') so that the fashionable frizz was achieved – this was a style known as *à l'hérisson* – then it was powdered (a range of light colours was permissible). Even when, at the end of the 1780s, hairstyles were more natural and had lost the frizzed look in exchange for a more wind-blown appearance, powder continued to be used for formal wear. Some men wore with their own hair a vestigial black silk bag, often with a fancy rosette and sewn to the back of the coat collar. The proper bag-wig, like the hoops and the chapeau bras, remained as correct court wear into the nineteenth century, but the hair powder (except for the army, the church and some of the more learned professions) was abandoned in England in 1795 with the tax on powder; those who wished to pay to continue this privilege were called 'guinea-pigs' after the amount of tax they had to pay.

Women

Apart from the *robe de cour*, the most formal dress worn by fashionable women in the 1770s was the sack dress (it went out of fashion towards the end of the decade, except for at court). For formal occasions it demonstrated an *embarras de richesse*, stomacher, robings and petticoat being covered in padded furbelows, silk flowers, tassels and chenille trimmings. One such robe in silver, ordered by Madame du Barry from Rose Bertin in 1782, had 'large puffed pleats all down the front in Italian gauze edged with big ruchings of cut crape, a garland of silver rope placed over the puffs each separated by bunches of golden wheat-ears and fastenings in catkins of blue stones mixed with white pearls . . .' and the petticoat was flounced with Italian gauze with a decoration of fringe, gold corn-ears, shells and silver ropes.[25] A more modest version was worn at the English court, the Duchess of Cumberland appearing in 1773 in 'a full dress'd sack of Rose Colour'd Lutestring trimm'd with Point';[26] it was 'full dress'd' because the duchess wore not only point lace (which was out of fashion other than at court) but also her diamonds.

To achieve a tight fit thought suitable for a formal gown, the bodice lining was laced at the back so that it fitted tightly under the flowing pleats. Less formally, the stomacher, with its elaborate trimmings, was replaced by a

151 (*previous page*) R. Ducreux, *Self-Portrait with a Harp*, c.1790

Stripes are the dominant design motif in this ensemble. The artist is fashionably dressed, in a silk *robe à l'anglaise* and a striped silk gauze kerchief which crosses the breast and ties at the back at the waist.

front-fastening bodice, hooked with an edge-to-edge closure. It was probably this kind of sack that the Duchess of Northumberland found Voltaire's niece (and mistress) Marie-Louis Mignot, Madame Denis, wearing in 1772, 'a sack of dark grounded chintz, brodée au tambour'.[27] Printed cotton was, by this time, an unusual fabric for a sack, though the combination probably continued in hot climates where even the most formal gowns needed to be washed. Occasionally, the pleats were cut loose from the bodice at the back, forming a connecting bridge from the shoulders to the hips where the pleats again merged into the overskirt. This style was known as the *robe à la piemontaise*, the name deriving from a dress popularized by a fashionable actress in Lyons for the wedding of Madame Clothilde, the sister of Louis XVI, to the Prince of Piedmont in 1775.

By the 1770s the hoop, over which the sack was originally meant to be worn, had disappeared except for court. To create soft bulk at the sides, very small paniers or hip pads were worn, or as an alternative, the excess skirt material of the overgown was fastened up with inside tapes or loops and tassels. When the sack was worn at court, the sleeves had long double or treble flounces, but otherwise in the 1770s a small winged or round cuff could be seen, similar to those worn in the more popular *robes à l'anglaise*. The fitted gown had long been the favourite in England and, in the 1770s, it had a new lease of life with a closed front fastening, usually worn over a skirt of a different colour. It was, in a sense, a hybrid gown – a marriage of the fitted mantua with the back pleats of the sack, but so reduced in size that they eventually became seams; the central section of the back bodice was sewn down with seams curved into the small of the back, extending without a waist seam into the skirt – this style was known as the *fourreau* back, and could even, by skilled seamstresses, be made from the sack dress. By the 1780s, there was a complete division at the waist and the skirt was set with tiny pleats into the bodice. These pleats (sometimes worn over small hip pads attached to the stays, or small crescent-shaped bustles, called 'rumps') created the side width and bounce that were so characteristic of dresses in this decade. The *robe à l'anglaise* was versatile enough to be regarded as a semiformal ('half-dress') or informal gown, and is probably synonymous with the nightgown. Although it is difficult for us to disentangle contemporary terms, it would appear that the 'Italian nightgown' was more formal than the English version, which was usually of light silks or chintz and was often worn with an apron. Queen Charlotte liked both styles: Lady Mary Coke found her in 1769 in the park, walking 'in an English nightgown and a white apron', and some years later Mrs Delany admired her on a more formal occasion in 'an Italian nightgown of purple lutestring trimmed with silver gauze'. The English nightgown was a walking dress, but in the hands of a lady of fashion it could be fairly elaborate; Georgiana, Duchess of Devonshire, and her sister wore to Carlton House (the London home of the Prince of Wales) in 1785 'nightgowns of my invention. The body and sleeves black velvet bound with pink and fastened with silver buttons. The petycoat light pink and the skirt, apron and handkerchief crape bound with light pink, and large chip hats

155   Detail of pl. 120

In this back view of a fashionable woman, the floating layers of the drapery are fastened up in the jaunty triple loops of the *polonaise*.

154 (*facing page*)   C. J. Vernet, *A Sea Shore* (detail), 1776

In this detail from a fanciful Mediterranean scene, a man in hussar uniform points out to sea, while next to him stand two fashionable ladies, one showing from the back the looped-up *polonaise* skirt.

with feathers and pinks'.[28] The Italian nightgown very often had a train and the *Magazine à la Mode* said that for winter 1777 they were 'made with whalebone in the back to fit quite close to the stays' with a very long train 'drawn up for walking'.[29] Very often the skirt had tapes inside so that it could be looped up to create the *polonaise* styles so popular in the 1770s and 1780s.

The name *polonaise* or *polonese* derives obviously from Polish styles – whether it referred originally to the fur trimming or the kilting up to one side of the skirt of the dress (a Polish fashion which came from Turkish costume) is not really clear. The *polonese* in the mid-eighteenth century was a small hooded cloak trimmed with fur, but by the early 1770s the term usually meant a dress on which the back drapery of the overskirt was arranged (through tapes or rings sewn to inside seams) in three puffs of material, in varying lengths. There had, since the beginning of the eighteenth century, been various impromptu ways of lifting up the skirt of the over-gown, a necessary feature of walking dress as worn by middle-class women in the streets of cities, but the *polonaise*, cut in four parts, two at the front and two at the back, was a fashionable version of this bourgeoise style. The petticoat was quite short at the end of the 1770s and, with the bunches of the *polonaise* overgown, it created a bouncy bulkiness which was at the same time light, for the silks were the thinnest and the aprons that were often worn as part of the dress were of fine muslin or silk gauze. In the same way that the sack could be adapted for a jacket, so the half-*polonaise* was a shorter version of the dress, worn for travelling.

A characteristic feature of both the *robe à l'anglaise* and the *polonaise* was the way the bodice was designed to close at the top of the centre front and then slope away to the sides, leaving a triangular gap that was filled by a false waistcoat or 'zone' sewn to the lining of the sides of the bodice and laced, hooked or buttoned down the front. The sleeves were either three-quarter-length finished with a small double ruffle, or long to the wrist fastening there with a frill. According to the *Lady's Magazine* (1774), the Irish *polonaise* 'buttons down half the arm', but the other types of *polonaise*, Italian, French, and so on, although identifiable to contemporaries, were probably only distinguished by slight differences in size of skirt puff or type of trimming.

The variety of fashionable dress in the 1770s and 1780s was immense, a confusion not helped by a host of names – some after aristocratic customers, or modish watering places such as Bath, or Spa, some following the mood for historic revivals and oriental fantasy (these were prevailing themes in dress in the years before the Revolution and are discussed in the following chapter) and some based on masculine garments such as the greatcoat.

However, the style of dress that was to have the most profound influence on future developments in clothing was the gown known as the *chemise à la reine*. This name derived from a controversial portrait by Vigée-Lebrun of Marie Antoinette exhibited at the Paris salon in 1783, and which depicted the queen in a simple, white muslin gown rather reminiscent of a chemise or shift (pl. 156). The picture itself had to be withdrawn, but the attendant fuss helped to popularize a style of dress that had already been in the

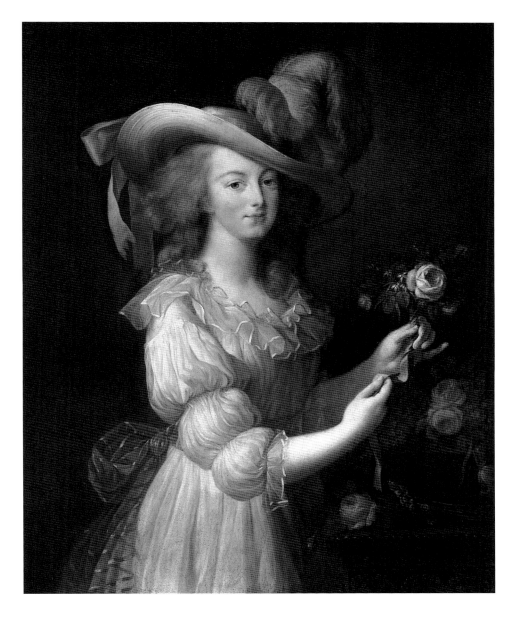

wardrobes of some fashionable women, including the French queen, for some years. The dress of white muslin with sleeves to the elbow or wrist, sometimes tied with ribbon, was put on over the head; it was gathered in on a drawstring round a low neckline, and the soft fullness was drawn in with a sash at the waist. Marie Antoinette preferred white dresses of Italian taffeta or muslin for the summer, particularly at Marly or the Petit Trianon. Jean-Louis Soulavie in his *Mémoires Historiques et Politiques du Règne de Louis XVI* (1801) blamed the decline of the Lyons silk industry on the queen's taste for white muslin; it would have been unwise in 1801 to claim otherwise, but the queen was merely following current taste, copying the simple tubes of white muslin that had for some time been worn by ladies on the plantations of the French West Indies; from the West Indies came also the indigo that blue-rinsed the muslin to a startling whiteness. Not only was taste moving towards the informal (all over Europe silk industries began to feel the pinch) but there was also the beginnings of a movement towards dress reform, a desire to free women from the restrictions of tight-lacing and clothes that did not reflect the natural body shape. Throughout the century there had been protests against the harm done to women by their clothing and this gathered momentum in the 1780s, especially in Germany. In 1783, the Emperor Joseph II tried to pass a ban corsets and hoops but, like most sumptuary legislation, it was ineffectual (by the time such edicts became law, fashion has usually moved on) and they remained for court and formal dress. In 1785, Franz Ehrenberg, the publisher of the magazine *Frauenzimmer-Almanach* gave the artist Daniel Chodowiecki the task of designing a reform dress; the resulting gowns, very much in the classical Greek taste, were based on the simple chemise gown.

As soon as the French queen had made the chemise popular, it was taken up by ladies of fashion: Georgiana, Duchess of Devonshire, in 1784 'went to a concert in one of the muslin chemises with fine lace that the Queen of France gave me'.[30] Three years later (such was the increased change of fashion and the comparative cheapness of the style), the *Lady's Magazine* noted 'all the Sex now, from 15 to 50 and upwards . . . appear in their white muslin frocks with broad sashes'.[31] The original chemise was pulled on over the head, but later versions had a front bib opening or were fastened with buttons or ribbons down the front. A popular English chemise (sometimes called the 'Perdita' chemise after the actress 'Perdita' Robinson, mistress to the Prince of Wales in the early 1780s) had a low neck with falling double collar with vandycked edge and closed down the front with ribbon bows. The dress gradually became more complex, with a separate skirt and bodice and a general tightening up at the waist.

A number of dresses in the 1780s derived from a mixture of sources – the neo-classical chemise gown, the oriental or theatrical styles and the masculine greatcoat. The wrapping gown was given a new lease of life in this period, made of light material and fastened at the waist with a sash. Walpole saw one of these garments, newly named the *lévite* (the name taken from the habits worn by actresses playing the Jewish priests in Racine's *Athalie*) on Lady Ossory in 1779 and exclaimed, 'where the deuce is the grace of a man's nightgown bound round with a belt?'[32] By the mid-1780s, they had become more formal, often worn as an open robe over a skirt, but retaining the sash and the simplicity of style and fabric; Vigée-Lebrun tells us in her Memoirs that Madame du Barry's favourite dresses when she was in her forties were *lévites* of cambric or white muslin. As well as disguising *embonpoint*, the *lévite* in its earlier form was a useful robe for pregnancy, the French queen herself favouring them in 1778. Other popular open robes that incorporated elements of the oriental were the 'circassiennes,' sometimes with a *polonaise* skirt and short sleeves trimmed with fur and decorated with tassels, and the *robes à la turque*, a name covering a multitude of meanings which ranged from the simple white robes with fringing and sash to a grand

157   A. Kauffmann, *Lady Elizabeth Foster*, 1786

This is another version of the chemise, with double falling collar and three-quarter-length sleeves edged with a ruffle.

158 'Woman in a Redingote', fashion plate from *Cabinet des Modes*, 1786

The caped collar of the masculine greatcoat is imitated in this fashionable tight-waisted redingote, the most popular outdoors garment of the 1780s. The design of spots on a plain background is characteristic of silks of this decade.

159 J. Juel, *Princess Louise Augusta*, 1787

By the late 1780s, the chemise gown was *de rigueur* for fashionable informal wear all over Europe. Here the Danish princess wears such a dress, of white muslin tied around the sleeves and at the waist with pink silk ribbon. An air of Arcadian simplicity is created by the flowing muslin veil, the sprig of roses at her breast and the plain paper fan.

semi-formal gown. For 'la grande parure', said the *Cabinet de Modes* (1786), one could wear 'des Robes à la Turque de velours de differentes couleurs, doublées de satin' (*robes à la turque* of velvet in different colours, lined with satin).[33]

One of Queen Charlotte's favourite gowns in the late 1780s, said Fanny Burney, was a 'dimity greatcoat', popular 'from the quickness with which they enable her to finish her toilette'.[34] This may have been a morning lévite gown, but it was more likely to have been an indoors version of the redingote or masculine greatcoat, a popular style of the 1780s. It could either close down the front with buttons, or, more usually, be worn open over a waistcoat. Sometimes it had the caped collar of the male coat and a fashionable feature was the large revers or lapels, very often a contrasting colour to the main body of the gown. The French wore it, very often made in silk, as a *robe à l'anglaise* made tightly fitting at the waist, the fullness flaring out at the back and over the hips. It was a fashionable walking dress for the mornings and the *Lady's Magazine* stated that for the summer of 1783 the most popular colour combinations were 'the Perdita's pearl colour with jonquil yellow facings, and the dark brown with a scarlet waistcoat'. In the same issue, the editor published a letter from a tradesman complaining of his wife's predilection for the riding dress that she 'whips on . . . as soon as she gets out of bed, sets down to breakfast in her beaver and goes to market in her boots', even though she had never mounted a horse in her life and there were no redcoats, that is, military men, in her family.

The masculine/military influence in women's clothing was particularly strong in the 1780s and it was noted earlier that the greatcoat had been adopted from men's wear in the 1760s, when it was worn out-of-doors; in 1767 at Spa, the fashionable summer watering place in the Austrian Netherlands, Lady Mary Coke was extremely irritated when her maid forgot to pack her greatcoat, for she needed it as protection from the continual rain. When, in the 1770s, women began to wear long-sleeved dresses, the greatcoat was an obvious choice for turning into a fashionable garment, worn with caped collar and lapels and fastening with large buttons like the man's coat. In the 1780s, both the greatcoat and the riding habit (the latter by then comprising a jacket and skirt of matching material, with a satin waistcoat) were decorated with braid, frogs, loops and tassels, and fashionable ladies, like men, carried canes. Boots were the fashionable walking footwear and the *Ipswich Journal* (1786) noticed that: 'The ladies begin to wear morocco half-boots and Hussar riding habits.' According to the *Gentleman's Magazine* (1781), the unthinkable happened when ladies even began to wear breeches and watches on fobs tucked into their belts. This is a surprising statement, for although breeches were common riding wear on the Continent, and some men in England had urged their use rather than 'silly and perilous modes' (that is, riding habits with skirts), conventional opinion would have been outraged had they been worn in the streets.[35] But to many people, the times were out of joint, and the new liberty given to women by their adoption of masculine clothes caused a freedom of gait that the more

160 Detail of pl. 161

conservative, like Elizabeth Montagu, found at best unappealing and at worst potentially immoral: in Bath in 1780, she found 'the misses waddle and straddle and strut and swagger about the streets here, one arm akimbo, the other swinging'.[36] The more natural look also demanded shoes with a low heel and, except at court, women no longer looked like galleons, with hoops and high heels and that curious titupping walk that so many recalled as typical of the *ancien régime*.[37] Instead, dresses without hoops clung to the body and allowed its shape to be seen and the new shoes gave women an unaccustomed freedom of movement.

Informality grew in the 1770s to include hitherto lowly garments such as the jacket and skirt, the staple wardrobe of the working woman throughout the century. The 'caraco', originally a hip-length jacket with a sack back, first appeared as an informal toilette négligé at the end of the 1760s and by the 1770s it could be seen as a *déshabillé galant*, worn on the Champs Elysées. In England, the caraco was a close-fitting, three-quarter-length jacket, the back sometimes longer than the front, usually worn closed and sometimes made of fashionable printed linen or cotton.

The most popular jackets by the end of the 1770s were worn open over the corsage, fastening at the centre front, sloping down at the sides and cut short to flare over the hips and back. The *Gentleman's and London Magazine* for February 1777 stated:

> The most fashionable morning dress and home undress for all day is a dishabille which consists of a short jacket and petticoat. The coat is generally puckered round the bottom about a quarter of a yard deep, with gauze or the same silk. But the fur is more in vogue this month than any other trimming. The jacket is short, not above a quarter of a yard on the hip; it is neatly shaped in the back with four quarters; the front resembling the polonese, fastens at the top with two frogs and tassels. The waistcoat is generally ornamented with frogs and tassels.[38]

Small distinctions of style or trimming, or of the colour and fabric from which they were made, provided a variety of names – the *pierrot* and the *juste à la suzanne* (which was white) to name just two – and these jackets, being newly popular, demonstrated the latest textiles and designs.

The 1770s and 1780s were decades of change both for textile design and fabric, with a shift from silks to cottons and linens. For woven silks, the large, self-confident patterns that had dominated design for most of the century gave way to small flower patterns, spots and stripes. Only those conservative or middle-class ladies (whose outlay was limited, and whose silks had to last) kept to the large natural flowers; Mrs Nollekens, for example, had in 1771 as part of her trousseau 'a dress of lavender silk brocaded with white and enriched with bouquets of carnations, auriculas and jessamins the size of nature'.[39] Much more fashionable were stripes; Lady Stormont in 1776 wrote to Mary Graham that her 'birthday gown is to be Lilac with a little silver stripe', and a few years later Abigail Adams, visiting London and Paris, noted a wide use of the fine Chambéry gauze with satin stripes. The changing

161   J. Zick, *The Remy Family*, 1776

Prominent in this mainly middle-class musical conversation piece are two ladies in the popular informal costume of flared jacket and skirt of matching material.

shape of women's gowns, with a newly narrow silhouette and long, tight sleeves demanded tiny patterns. Silks were ribbed to imitate stripes; they were patterned with spots, specks, random dots or with zodiac designs;[40] and even imitated the new neo-classical motifs such as laurel wreaths and medallions which were being printed successfully on linen and cotton. So desperate were the silk-weavers to keep their declining trade that, by the end of the 1780s, they were imitating printed cotton designs.

In the 1770s there was a preference for strong colours. In 1775, puce (flea colour) was all the rage: '. . . dos de puce or ventre de puce – the only colour that can be worn,' said Lady Spencer in a letter from Paris, prompted by a chance remark, made by the king to Marie Antoinette about an item of dress, that was taken up by the fashionable modistes. Stripes of varying thicknesses were woven into silks and printed onto linens, the latter also stamped and spotted and decorated using copperplate or woodblock designs. Barbara Johnson's account book has increasing references to chintzes and calicoes throughout the second half of the eighteenth century; in 1771 she had a

162 'Caraco et jupon de mousseline rayé', fashion plate from the *Cabinet des Modes*, 1786

Ideally, says the accompanying text, this caraco and skirt of striped muslin is 'une toilette du matin', worn before one is ready to dress for the day, and suitable 'pour faire un tour de promenade avant midi' (to take a walk before noon).

163 J.-L. David, *Anne-Marie-Louise Thélusson, Comtesse de Sorcy*, 1790

Daughter of a rich financier, the revolutionary austerity of her costume – a plain cotton chemise with drawstring neckline – is softened by the beautiful and expensive cashmere shawl, a luxurious novelty in France at this date.

'purple and white copper-plate linnen Gown', and in 1776 a yellow spotted linen dress. The restrictions in England on the wearing of all-cotton printed fabrics were removed in 1774 – they had been unworkable for many years and ingenious manufacturers had found many ways to evade the strict letter of the law.

White was the most fashionable colour in the 1780s, both for silks and, even more, for fine muslin. The Duchess of Devonshire in 1784 chose for a ball-dress 'an English night-gown of muslin with small silver sprigs and all white',[41] and even Queen Charlotte, usually conservative in her tastes, wore for the king's birthday in 1787 'a very beautiful dress, of a new manufacture of worked muslin, thin, fine and clear as the Chambéry gauze'.[42] Muslin could be embroidered using the tambour (introduced from Turkey in the 1760s and becoming a fashionable diversion) or painted; in 1784 J. T. Smith helped the Misses Wyatt paint butterflies on a muslin dress.

To Abigail Adams, in London in 1784, 'everything [was] as light and thin as possible', the dress pleasing her best: 'a delicate blue and white copper-plate calico with a blue lutestring skirt flounced, a muslin apron and a hand-kerchief.[43] Whether this was because it reflected American styles (a French visitor had seen in New Haven in 1788 the girls 'galloping boldly with an elegant hat on the head, a white apron, and a calico gown'[44]) or was just admirable in its informality, the blue and white colour combination was *de rigueur* for the whole decade and subtle effects could be created by wearing transparent muslin over coloured underskirts. Also noticeable was an excess of trimming: dresses were decorated with ribbons ('white ribbon in the Vandyke style', noted Abigail Adams in the mid-1780s), floss silk and steel beads 'which are much in fashion and brought to such perfection as to resemble diamonds'. Sophie von la Roche, in England in 1786, admired the mixture of luxury and 'country informality' that she found in one dress of pink and white striped taffeta with painted trailing roses on the hem, pearls on the seams and real roses in the straw hat. She was less taken with the sight of two ladies at the theatre with 'their neckerchiefs . . . puffed up so high that their noses were scarce visible, and their nosegays like large shrubs, large enough to conceal a person'.[45] For amplitude was in vogue in the 1780s, particularly at the bosom; *buffons* were large, diaphanous, sometimes starched handkerchiefs puffed up over the bust. Softness replaced crispness when lace gave way to silk gauze and muslin; the short silk mantles of the mid-eighteenth century gave way during the 1770s to the long scarf or stole, crossed over the bosom; and by the mid-1780s cashmere, 'more costly than silk, much lighter and also much warmer', was being imported for the most expensive shawls.

Paradoxically, as some styles of dress were becoming simpler in cut and fabric, so hairstyles were increasing in height and complexity. From the beginning of the 1770s, the hair on the forehead rose high, built up over pads; at the side were large stiff rolls placed diagonally; and at the back a wide flat loop of hair hung to the nape of the neck: the chignon. The height of the hairstyle sometimes exceeded the length of the face; the twelve-year-

164 'A la Zodiaque', 1777, from the *Lady's Magazine*

The hair is dressed with diamond stars, and the *bandeau* is decorated with the signs of the Zodiac.

165 H. Kingsbury, *A Side Box at the Opera*, 1792

Kingsbury satirizes every aspect of female fashion here, from the starched amplitudes of the *buffon* to the large frizzed hairstyles and the towering headdresses; feathers even adorn the top of the columns in the theatre box.

old Anna Winslow, sent from home in Nova Scotia to be 'finished' in Boston, proudly noted in her diary in 1772 that 'I mesur'd above an inch longer than I did downwards from the roots of my hair to the end of my chin'. The gum (gum Arabic, pomatum, tallow or hog's grease) needed to keep the style in place, and the powder, made her 'head itch, & ach, & burn like anything', and to get the required bulk a 'cushion' of false hair included 'a Red Cow tail . . . and horse-hair very coarse, and a little human hair of yellow hue';[46] the arrangement once concocted could not easily be disturbed, although it was dangerous to health and a source of endless satire. So full and tall did hairstyles become that an English lady, Eliza Fay, when attacked at Calcutta by the troops of Hyder Ali in 1779, was able to hide her own and her husband's watches in her hairstyle.[47]

By the middle of the 1770s, hair was piled enormously high and very large and elaborate hats were impossible to wear. In order to cover the hair out-of-doors a 'calash' was needed, a large hood built up on cane arches, sometimes quilted, and often collapsible so that it could be more easily stored. Women therefore concentrated on the decoration of the hair itself and, very often, covered it with feathers – a fashion set in England by the Duchess of Devonshire (a shocked German visitor in 1775 found the most popular colours to be red, white and black, and the cost to be a guinea each) and in France by Marie Antoinette (though her mother Maria Theresa thought they were more suitable for actresses). Other forms of headcovering included jewels – the hair being gummed to such an extent that pins could be stuck there; the *Lady's Magazine* for July 1777 illustrated a hairstyle 'representing the hemisphere, interspersed with jewels representing stars' (pl. 164).

In the 1780s, hair became very wide. The stiff side rolls were unravelled to fall into a frizz of tiny curls and loose ringlets, but this slight disorder had to be equally carefully arranged, gummed and powdered, even when a seemingly nonchalant and natural air was aimed at. As hair flattened on top, so hats became more important, and this was a decade of enormous hats, covered with ribbons, tulle, feathers and flowers. Never was millinery more subject to the whims of the moment, whether political or fashionable: the first flight in a hot-air balloon, from the Bois de Boulogne on 1 November 1783, inspired ballooning hats, *poufs à la Montgolfier*, and a grimmer event, the storming of the Bastille in 1789, produced *bonnets à la Bastille*, a strange flirting with danger that, during the Terror, made some women adopt red ribbons round their necks in imitation of the cut made by the guillotine. Many of the most fashionable hats were made of straw, turned up at the side, lined with silk and covered with flowers; others were inspired by the countryside – Mercier, in the early 1780s, spoke of 'the English Park, the Windmill and the Grove . . . Shepherds and Shepherdesses, the Huntsman in Covert', declaring his inability 'to fix a likeness of anything so fleeting'.[48] By the end of the 1780s, the very large hats were on their way out – their last form was the 'lampshade' style with a curtain of lace all round the brim which sloped like a roof – and the magazines were describing smaller caps and turbans that were, with their classical and exotic influences, to be the headwear for the revolutionary years and well into the nineteenth century.

Charlotte Louisa Papendiek was Assistant Keeper of the Wardrobe to Queen Charlotte, her memoirs being a useful source of information on the court of the time. When Lawrence was at Windsor in the autumn of 1789 painting the queen (now in the National Gallery, London) he did this drawing of Mrs Papendiek (who sat in lieu of the queen for some of the details of the dress and jewellery in the royal portrait). In her memoirs she mentions the 'black bonnet' made by a 'Miss Pohl' that she wore and her muslin dress that she had had made for the King's Birthday in June, of 'a new Scotch manufacture, chequered, made round with a short train, . . . a broad sash pinned in a peak in front'. Her son Frederick wears the white unisex frock tied round the waist with a sash, of the kind worn by boys and girls in their early years.

Children

We have so far looked at children's clothes only in relation to those of adults, for, with some exceptions, the one was a miniature version of the other. But the word 'revolutionary' reminds us that it was in the third quarter of the eighteenth century that English ideas of sensible and functional clothing for children were gradually adopted by the rest of Europe. Many of the ideas regarding the education and general upbringing of children, popularized by eighteenth-century philosophers, had already been discussed by John Locke in his *Thoughts on Education* (1693): man, being born free, he said, should not have his limbs swaddled (this practice was on the wane in England by the middle of the eighteenth century, though still common in Europe), nor

There is a characteristically English sense of individuality, freedom and informality in this image of a group of children. Pride of place in the centre is the seven-year-old boy in perhaps one of his first grown-up suits, but his shirt is worn without the adult stock or necktie and his own hair falls to his shoulders in the English style. The eldest girl (on the left) wears a dress of silk brocade, whereas the two younger sisters are still in their plain, back-fastening stiffened bodice and skirt costumes suitable to their age.

should he be confined by strait-lacing. Rousseau, in his *Emile* (1762), with the ardour of one who preaches rather than practises, enthusiastically popularized Locke's ideas, advocating breastfeeding and a regime of loose-fitting clothes, cold water and fresh air for children from their earliest years. A few years later, Grosley noted how the English, even when not endowed with natural beauty, appeared lithe and healthy as a the result of 'the free and easy manner in which the bodies of children of the present generation have been formed and the little use made of swaddling cloaths or constraint of any sort'.[49]

Babies of both sexes wore linen shirts, over which were worn stays, sometimes boned but very often corded or quilted (some reinforcement was considered necessary for the correct deportment that was so much a part of the eighteenth-century credo). Although the stiffened bodice was worn only for approximately the first year by boys, girls continued to wear some light form of reinforced bodice that kept the back flat by pushing back the shoulders. Mrs Delany disapproved strongly of the new front-buttoning gowns of the 1760s, for she felt they dragged the shoulders forward and spoilt the upright carriage that young girls were taught to observe.

At about a year old, children were put into short frocks. Girls wore simple frocks of linen or muslin with a sash and fastening at the back, a linen cap or coif and an apron. Boys' frocks varied from the simple linen gown with a sash (see pl. 166) to a more formal front-fastening gown, sometimes trimmed with frogging or braiding. When the child started to walk, leading strings, strips of material sewn to the back of the armholes, were needed to control movement. It was at this age, too, that children wore head-protectors in the form of padded rolls (the English called them 'puddings', the French *bourrelets*), for it was felt that the head was the most vulnerable part of the body and needed extra protection (this might explain the reluctance to wash the hair and the universal practice of wearing a nightcap). Nollekens recalled that in his youth (he was born in 1737), 'I wore a pudding when I was a little boy . . . This pudding consisted of a broad black silk band which went round the middle of the head, joined to two pieces of ribband crossing on the top of the head and then tied under the chin; so that by this most excellent contrivance children's heads were often preserved uninjured when they fell.'[50] In England, such puddings were rarely worn in the later years of the century, but Madame de Genlis says that the practice continued in France until the Revolution, except for the royal children, whose surroundings were well-enough upholstered to prevent damage being caused by a fall.

From the age of three or four, girls and boys were dressed differently. Girls continued to wear the frock unless greater formality was needed (for much of the eighteenth century, particularly the first half, upper-class parents on the whole did not see much of their children and their sometimes strained relationships were reflected in rather formal encounters), on which occasions they wore adult styles. Nathaniel Wraxall, on a visit to Vienna in 1779, found girls of seven or eight 'with powder, a high head, a Chignon and a hoop', such 'absurdities' being common in all countries other than England. In England, where family contacts were sometimes more relaxed, little girls wore either a simplified version of adult dress, with boned back-fastening bodice and separate skirt, or, particularly by the 1760s, a white muslin gown and sash worn over a lightly boned corset. This was worn by girls up to their

The little girl in blue silk, a matching
ribbon in her hair, carries a doll, which is
fashionably clothed in Dutch or German
style and possibly made from her mother's
cast-off dress.

mid-teens and, of course, anticipated the chemise dress of the 1780s, an early
example of the young setting trends in dress. However, by the age of about
twelve, girls were expected to begin to learn adult accomplishments such as
dancing, and at practice assemblies there was an opportunity to learn how
to manage the intricacies of adult attire. Anna Winslow, in Boston in 1772,
aged twelve, attended a 'constitution' to learn dancing and good deportment
and proudly recorded in her diary her 'yellow coat, black bib & apron, black
feathers on my head, my past comb, & all my past garnet marquesett & jet
pins . . . black collar round my neck, black mitts . . . striped tucker and
ruffels'.[51] Although this was her finest outfit, it still included the childish bib
and tucker and the jewellery was imitation paste and marcasite. Americans
adopted English ideas on children's dress and Abigail Adams, visiting France
in the mid-1780s, was horrified at girls of seven being dressed like twenty-
year-olds. She echoed the feelings of Baretti, who commented in 1760 when
in Portugal: 'Here, as in France and Italy, they have the absurd custom of
dressing their children too much. I hate to see a little girl with a tupee and
a little sword at the side of a little boy . . . In England, boys and girls, even
when they are sons and daughters of Earls and Dukes are never made to
look like dwarfish men and dwarfish women; and this may be the reason
that England abounds less with fops and coquets than either France or Italy.'[52]

Boys were breeched at the age of about four (although it could be as late as seven years). In Europe, and particularly at court, little boys often wore adult styles: embroidered velvet suits, wigs and swords. Even Mercier, fiercely anti-English in most respects, granted that the French way of dressing children was absurd (a boy of seven 'n'avoit ni poingts, ni bras, ni jambes, mais il savoit s'asseoir & danser le menuet' (had no hands, arms or legs, but he knew how to sit and how to dance the minuet)) in comparison with the freedom granted in England. In some cases, a compromise was reached between adult styles and childish behaviour: the Germanisches National-museum in Munich has a mid-eighteenth-century boy's coat (for a child of about three) of red wool trimmed with silver braid and with two waistcoat fronts joined in so that from the front the child looked like a tiny adult, but turning to the back one notices not just leading strings, but the whole coat completely open, fastening with hooks and eyes to the waist.[53]

In England, it seems to have been the custom from early in the century for boys to wear easier-fitting coats, with the more functional slit cuff, and instead of the formal stock or cravat, they wore a frilled shirt collar tied up high to the neck with a black ribbon. Compared with the Continent, where quite small boys were put into wigs in the first half of the century, in England this was the exception rather than the rule. Lord Chesterfield in 1748 refused to allow his sixteen-year-old son (who had complained of headaches) permission to cut his hair and wear a wig, for the latter, however well-made, was a 'disguise' and took away from the natural air which should be affected by the young.

From the 1760s, foreign visitors to England admired the distinctive national informality in boys' dress (some of which must be attributed to the influence of sport both in and out of school): the frock suit with waistcoat cut straight across; shirt with open collar; simply styled hair, left to grow naturally and usually with a fringe. For the middle class or the prosperous artisan class, there was less of a gap between adult and boy, partly because of reliance on the second-hand trade, which prolonged the life of any style, and partly because the new notions of a separate existence for children manifested through their clothing seemed a privileged fantasy in an age in which every member of a household had to contribute to the finances of the family. Francis Place, remembering his childhood in the 1770s, described the dress of the reasonably well-to-do apprentice boy as 'a cloth coat without any collar to it, and wide skirts . . . single-breasted . . . a waistcoat of the same material and a pair of sheepskin breeches, sometimes of a yellow, sometimes of a leaden colour, with four buttons at the knees . . . sometimes the breeches were of cloth the same as the coat and waistcoat, worstead stockings, sometimes white cotton stockings, shoes with buckles and a cocked hat'.[54] In fashionable terms, this dress with its skirted coat and cocked hat was out-of-date for both adults and boys by the time that Place was wearing it, with the exception of the leather breeches, which were just about to be taken up by young men such as William Hickey.

A compromise between Spanish formality and the new, more relaxed and functional styles for children's wear can be seen in this little boy's red silk skeleton suit, fastened round the waist with a wide lace-trimmed silk sash.

It was in this decade, the 1770s, that a new style for young boys took shape: trousers, made in various forms from the baggy to the tight-fitting, from calf-length to ankle-length. Loose-fitting trousers had been worn for many years by sailors and peasants, and there are a few examples of upper-class boys in the middle years of the century wearing calf-length trousers, but with the new trend for informality in the 1770s, those worn by young boys foreshadowed the fashionable pantaloons of the 1790s and early nineteenth century. With these new nether garments went a short jacket, sometimes double-breasted (the logical extension of the cut-away adult coat without its tails). By the end of the 1780s, the shortened jacket (which anticipated the rising waist of a few years later) had the trousers buttoned on to it. This new garment, called the 'skeleton suit', was ideal for a young boy when he abandoned his childish frock; Mrs Papendiek described in 1790 the breeching of her four-year-old son:

> A total change of dress it was then for a boy. The shirt was made like a man's except that the collar was large and frilled and turned over the jacket instead of being buttoned up. The jacket and trousers were of cloth, the latter being buttoned over the jacket and the trousers only to the ankle bone. Boots for children being then unknown they had gaiters which went over the end of the trousers, and these with strong shoes equipped them very properly for walking . . .
>
> Underwaistcoats and drawers were not then worn, so I had the linings of the trousers made separate which ensured proper cleanliness.[55]

By the end of the 1780s, the prevalence of English styles in children's dress was an accepted fact; even young princes, said the *Journal des Luxus und der Moden* (1786), were being brought up under the principles first established by John Locke a century before. The short jacket and tight-fitting trousers, the open shirt collar and the long, casually arranged hair bespoke early-nineteenth-century Romanticism, the last flicker of male elegance before the black dreariness of the Victorian age (already presaged in the dark suits worn by English businessmen of the 1780s helping the Industrial Revolution on its way).

The simple white frocks worn by girls were worn also by women by the end of the 1780s. Although the chemise gown as such came into fashion via a route other than as a child's dress, it too reflected new ideas of a natural informality that were to have a temporary sway over female dress during the revolutionary years.

7 *Fantasy and Fancy Dress*

I must tell you how fine the masquerade of last night was. There were five hundred persons, in the greatest variety of handsome and rich dress I ever saw ... There were dozens of ugly Queens of Scots ... the Princess of Wales was one, covered with diamonds, but did not take off her mask ... Lady Conway was a charming Mary Stuart; Lord and Lady Euston, man and woman huzzars. But the finest and most charming masks were their Graces of Richmond, like Harry the Eighth and Jane Seymour, excessively rich and both so handsome ... there were quantities of pretty Vandykes, and all kinds of old pictures walked out of their frames.

H. Walpole, on a masquerade at Vauxhall, 1742

He therefore, who in his practice of portrait painting wishes to dignify his subject, which we will suppose to be a lady, will not paint her in the modern dress, the familiarity of which is sufficient to destroy all dignity. He ... therefore dresses his figure something with the general air of the antique for the sake of dignity, and preserves something of the modern for the sake of likeness.

Sir J. Reynolds, *Seventh Discourse*, 1776

170   Detail of pl. 197

This detail from Morland's enigmatic *The Fair Nun Unmasked* displays the erotic possibilities of eighteenth-century ideas about dress as disguise – the plunging décolletage and the mask (with far more patches than a respectable woman would wear). The masquerade provided opportunities for rôle-playing and the subversion of propriety in defiance of the conventions of society.

'AVANT TOUT ... LE XVIIIe SIÈCLE EST UN SIÈCLE DE MASQUES.' This statement, made by Edmond Pilon and Frédéric Saisset in their book *Les Fêtes en Europe au XVIIIe Siècle* (1943) refers to the obvious fascination with masquerades and courtly *fêtes galantes* among the upper reaches of society in the eighteenth century. But no less an important part of this fondness for private theatricals and dressing up is the kind of portraiture through which people projected an image of fantasy, whether real or imaginary. Not only were people of every class accustomed to colour and pageantry, whether at court balls or in the many official and religious processions that marked the year, to an extent that has been lost, but in many of the portraits showing sitters in fancy dress, there is an almost Romantic interest in the exotic present and the historic past. This was influenced at least in part by carnival and masquerade and even inspired fashionable costume in the last quarter of the century.

Although in previous ages court masquerades were magnificent, they reached their apogee in the eighteenth century, along with the more democratic manifestations of the street carnival, from which the history of masking derives. 'The Italians', said Johann Georg Keysler, 'are excessively fond of masquerades', and the idea of the carnival began in Italy, although the custom of masking or disguise goes back to antiquity; blended with the lower-class theatrical masked mummeries went the Renaissance processional pageant, combining to form weeks of carnival festivity held just before the austerities of Lent. Every Italian city was *en fête* from the end of December to the start of Lent: the streets were decorated; pageants and *tableaux vivants* took place; private and public masked balls were held; regattas (in Venice), horse races (in Rome and Florence) and firework displays were provided; and the *commedia dell'arte* troupes performed their carefully impromptu stories to the crowds.

The masquerade reached an art form, most of all in Venice, from whence the rest of Europe took the all-embracing black silk gown, the 'domino' (possibly of ecclesiastical or oriental origin), whose ample folds made it an ideal garment for 'intrigues, trifling gallantries . . .' and disguising 'wanton syrens', according to Keysler. The domino, like the mask and the three-cornered hat, was worn by both men and women, giving an androgynous effect which struck outsiders as curious and even gloomy, with so much black in a season of jollity. Madame du Bocage, in Venice in the middle of the eighteenth century, found 'men and women wear the same sort of clokes, hoods and hats, all black with white masks; so that, when they lie down in their black gondolas, as they frequently do, you may guess what sort of appearance they make'.[1] With the domino was worn a mask, either of black velvet (*moreta*) or a white grotesque mask, the *gnaga*; as masks covered only part of the face, a piece of black silk or lace, the *bauta*, was placed on the head and drawn across the lower jaw. When the three-cornered hat was placed on top of the head, the incognito was complete and respected to the extent that those

171a and b   L. Carlevarijs, studies of carnival costume, early eighteenth century

One of the most popular carnival costumes was that of Punch, seen here in these lively drawings made during the carnival in Venice in the early eighteenth century. The women depicted here have merely added the characteristic carnival mask, *bauta* (a silk or lace scarf covering the lower jaw) and three-cornered hat, to their everyday costume. Some element of disguise, however, is created by the capacious mantle (*zendaletta*) and there is even a slight sense of transgression in the use of the masculine coat, although many working women wore this as a more practical alternative to the cloak.

172 G. Zompini, 'The Return from the Ridotto', from *Le Arte che vanno per via nella Citta di Venezia*, 1753

Carnival costume was worn also to the theatres and in the Ridotto, the public gaming house in Venice. This fashionable couple being lighted home wear hat, scarf, mask and lace *mantellina* over their everyday dress.

De notte, ora ai teatri, ora al Redutto
Son quel che col feral serve de lume;
E pur che i pagù mi so andar per tutto.

7

wearing black or white masks were admitted everywhere, even to the Ridotto, the public gaming house in Venice usually open only to patricians.

Venice, above all, was the city of masquing; not only at the carnival but at various other times of year, from October 5 to December 16, and on the many public holidays that made up the life of the city: the feast of San Marco, the election of the Doge or Procurator, and the ceremony of the Bucintoro, the wedding of Venice with the sea by the throwing of a ring into the harbour and an occasion for splendid regattas.

The upper classes generally wore the domino and mask, or occasionally the short net or lace cloak, the *mantellina*; cloaks were so light and floating that (although people's identity was preserved by their headcovering) 'their usual clothes, their hoops and even large nosegays . . . a quantity of precious stones and lace' could be observed. In any case, the prevailing aristocratic blackness was relieved by the costumes worn by the citizens and by the coloured dominoes worn by foreign visitors (Venice in particular was used to welcoming royalty), for it was an essential part of the Grand Tour to take part in the carnival at masquerade time. Foreign visitors often wore very elaborate coloured dominos with capes and huge sleeves; the egregious Baron Pöllnitz, in Venice in 1730, was immediately recognizable by his 'scarlet Domino embroider'd with Silver', and was delighted to be accosted by two girls in St Marks'.

Most Italians opted for fancy dress, the most popular styles being characters from the *commedia dell'arte* (Casanova, in Venice for the 1754 carnival, chose for a masquerade a Pierrot costume of light calico), shepherds and shepherdesses, orientals and the dress of the opposite sex – for a considerable amount of licence was allowed, a source of some complaint to visitors. Dr John Moore found Rome completely taken over for the carnival:

> The citizens then appearing in the streets, masked, in the characters of Harlequins, Pantaloons, Punchinellos and all the fantastic variety of a masquerade. This humour spreads to men, women and children; descends to the lowest ranks and becomes universal. Even those who put on no mask and have no desire to remain unknown, reject their usual clothes and assume some whimsical dress. The coachmen . . . generally affect some ridiculous display. Many of them chuse a woman's dress, and have their faces painted and adorned with patches . . .
>
> The peculiar dresses of every nation of the globe, and of every profession, besides all the fantastic characters usual at masquerades are to be seen on the Corso. Those of Harlequin and Pantaloon are in great vogue among the men. The citizens wives and daughters generally affect the pomp of women of quality; while their brothers, or other relatives, appear as train-bearers and attendants. In general they seem to delight in characters the most remote from their own. Young people assume the long beard, tottering step and other concomitants of old age; the aged chuse the bib and rattle of childhood; and the women of quality and women of the town appear in the character of country maidens, nuns and vestal virgins. All endeavour to support the assumed characters to the best of their ability; but none in my opinion succeed so well as those who represent children.[2]

In 1741, an English painter, John Russel, had found that dressing *en travesti* was the favourite costume of the women: 'the breeches, with gold clock'd stockings, shoes buckled to the toes, a laced coat and a hat cocked à la mode de Paris'[3]. This cross-dressing was noted by writers as diverse as Casanova and Goethe, the latter's famous account of the carnival in Rome in 1787 describing how the sexes changed clothes (some women even wearing uniform), raiding the second-hand clothes stalls for suitable costumes; some dressed as ghosts in white linen.

There was still a faint echo of Renaissance learning in some of the carnival entertainments. In Milan, the masquerades were events organized by the members of the academies of gentlemen and artists, who wore their own uniforms with grotesque masks; and in Rome, balls and pageants with classical, theatrical and exotic scenes were organized, very often by the famous noble families. Goethe, in 1787, attended a masked ball in the Aliberti theatre where he was impressed by the costumes and the masks 'taken from various art-epochs and imitating in a masterly way various statues preserved in Rome . . . Egyptian Gods, Priestesses, Bacchus and Ariadne, the Tragic Muse, the Historical Muse . . . Vestals'[4] – this was the period of the great antiquarian discoveries (the neo-classical artist Ennemond Alexandre Petitot was

173 D. Allan, *The Carnival in Rome*, 1775

This is one of a series of drawings done by this Scottish artist in Rome in 1775. Romans and foreigners, dressed in a variety of fashionable and fancy dress, parade in the street, while pageant floats, exhibiting masquerade themes, drive by.

employed to design the costumes for a Roman tournament celebrating a royal marriage in the Duchy of Parma in 1769).

The carnival in Rome in 1763 had a number of pageant floats: that of the Colonnas had *commedia dell'arte* characters representing the towns in Italy from which each had derived and the Orsini float representing a Hindu sacrifice, the 'priests' in turbans and the 'priestesses' in pink or blue silk with bare arms. The inhabitants of the floats pelted the crowds with sugar plums, which, according to Russel, were quite hard, and 'terribly discompose a well-powdered perruque'.

Some of the most popular carnival themes were oriental, and some of the best masquerades were organized by the students of the French Academy in Rome; in 1735, they put on a *mascarade chinoise*, but their most famous effort (which was thought worth recording by one of the participants, J. M. Vien) was in 1748 when a Turkish procession travelled through the streets in triumphal cars, the students dressed as members of the court at Constantinople.[5] It was the great popularity of this cavalcade that inspired the carnival masquerade in Naples in 1778, 'representing the return of the Grand Signor from Mecca, all performed by the noblesse about Court, and the king's guards', the king and queen taking part too.[6] Italy was, of course, the most popular place for tourists in the eighteenth century and there is a correspondingly large number of accounts of the splendour of carnival masquerades. But it was a practice common all over Europe, in northern Protestant countries as well as in Catholic countries where it was a last fling allowed by the church before Lent. Depending on the climate and tradition, masquerades could revolve around the court or be more democratically open to a greater section of society, either in the streets or in the public pleasure gardens that most large cities possessed.

Masked balls were introduced into France in 1715, when the first was held at the Opéra; it was no accident that the new atmosphere of indulgence under the Regent was highly suitable for the spread of this form of intriguing and pleasurable entertainment – the phrase 'l'esprit de bal' came to be the fashionable jargon for the adventures and indiscretions carried on at masked balls. *Fêtes galantes*, rural masquerades immortalized by Watteau, Pater and Lancret, were occasions when courtly love and social graces were displayed, when courtiers dressed as shepherds and shepherdesses, or Harlequin and Columbine (the Italian players, after a long banishment, were allowed to return to France in 1716). At times it appeared that the whole of the French court in the middle of the century was in masquerade and the reality is hard for us to disentangle from the fantasy. Not only were fashionable sitters painted as inhabitants of an Arcadian countryside, but the court, led by Madame de Pompadour (who had to devise ways of amusing an easily bored king), performed in plays put on in her private theatre, le Théâtre des Petits Cabinets. Boucher, who had decorated the theatre, helped with the costumes. Many of the plays were slight rococo pastorals in which the ladies, in particular, could appear in delightfully fashionable and frivolous versions of theatrical dress, with short skirts and bare arms. Madame de Pompadour herself loved to dress up in private life; she could appear as 'une villageoise . . . une gracieuse odalisque présentant du café à la turque . . . une piquante espagnole . . . un charmant page en travesti, ou même un Pierrot enfariné' (a village girl . . . a gracious odalisque offering coffee Turkish style . . . a piquant Spanish girl . . . a charming page *en travesti*, or even a Pierrot with white, floury face).[7]

Louis XV loved attending the masquerades held at the Opéra, where the element of incognito, though present, was not sufficient to prevent his being mistaken for anyone other than the king. Dressed as a pilgrim in 1739, his costume comprised 'velour bleu ciselé, garni de boutons de diamans et doublé de satin blanc. Sa veste était d'une riche étoffe brodée d'or et il portait le Saint-Esprit en diamants' ([a suit] of cut blue velvet decorated with diamond buttons and lined with white satin. His waistcoat was of a rich material embroidered with gold, and he wore the Saint-Esprit in diamonds).[8]

Though the major cities in France, including Paris, held masked balls or street processions (Townsend in 1786 found in Paris that there were thousands in the streets, all masked, some in the clothes of the opposite sex, and many 'Popes, cardinals, monks, devils, courtiers, harlequins and lawyers, all

174   A. Watteau, *Fêtes vénitiennes*, c.1718

A sense of elusive narrative and a mixture of fantasy and everyday dress is typical of the beautiful and mysterious *fêtes galantes* that Watteau pioneered as an art form (the term was first used in 1717 when Watteau was admitted to the Academy). The female figure in the centre, wearing a white satin bodice and skirt and a blue silk mantle may be the actress Charlotte Desmares, and her dancing partner is probably the Flemish artist Nicolas Vleughels (with whom Watteau lodged in 1718–19) dressed in masquerade Polish costume.

DECORATION DU BAL MASQUÉ DONNÉ PAR LE ROY

Dans la grande Gallerie du Chateau de Versailles, à l'ocasion du Mariage de LOUIS DAUPHIN DE FRANCE *AVEC* MARIE THERESE INFANTE D'ESPAGNE, *la nuit du XXV au XXVI Fevrier* MDCCXLV
Cette Feste Ordonnée par M.Le Duc De Richelieu Pair de France en exercice de Premier Gentilhomme de la Chambre DU ROY. a été conduite par M. De Bonneval Intendant et Controlleur-general de l'Argenterie Menus Plaisirs et affaires de la Chambre de Sa Majesté

175   After C.-N. Cochin the Elder, 'Décoration du Bal Masqué Donné par le Roy . . .', 1745

At this famous masked ball to celebrate the marriage of the Dauphin with the Infanta Maria Teresa of Spain, Louis XV and a group of courtiers came dressed as clipped yew trees; they can be seen on the right. In the centre (see detail, pl. 176) the Dauphin and his bride are dressed as shepherd and shepherdess, surrounded by crowds of masqueraders, some also dressed in pastoral costumes and others in the traditional hooded domino; one woman carrying a staff is dressed as a pilgrim, her shoulder cape trimmed with cockle shells.

mingled in one promiscuous crowd'[9]), the grandest balls were arranged for great court celebrations, such as royal marriages. When, in 1745, the Dauphin was married to an Infanta of Spain, the Galerie des Glaces at Versailles provided the setting for a glittering masked ball. The French queen (who usually led a retired life) appeared in a dress studded with pearls and with the two crown diamonds, the Régent and the Sancy, and the Dauphin and his new wife came as a shepherd and shepherdess. Louis XV, along with seven attendant courtiers, came in the disguise of a yew tree clipped to the shape of a pillar, with a vase on top. It was at this masquerade that the king met Madame le Normant d'Etioles, later the marquise de Pompadour (some thought her costume as Diana the huntress was apt), and they were publicly seen together at a masked ball given a few days later at the Hôtel de Ville, when both wore light silk dominoes as a disguise.

Although Marie Antoinette inspired a number of masquerades, Louis XVI lacked the necessary repartee and fondness for amorous intrigue, which was the sine qua non of the masked ball. The ambiguous morality of such entertainments inevitably led to criticism of the queen when she was seen to participate in them at the Opéra.

In some countries where the court was not so much a leader of fashion, the masquerade was a more democratic process. In Holland, for example, the masquerades were held in May at the traditional fairs, or kermesses, which lasted a week, when all wore masks and fancy dress, even the nobility riding masked about the streets in chaises. In Spain, Baretti, in the middle of the century, found that at carnival time all the population attended the masquerades held twice a week in Madrid (an amphitheatre had been built by the king for these occasions, open to all, with the price of admission twenty reals, about five shillings), and for dress 'everybody follows his own fancy' (although gold and silver were forbidden), some wearing the mask and domino, some the regional costumes of Spain, and some of the upper classes choosing the *majo* and *maja* styles (see chapter three).[10]

In England, the masquerade had been brought from Italy at the beginning of the eighteenth century, and set on a firm footing by a Swiss, Count Heidegger (later Master of the Revels to George II) at the Opera House in the Haymarket in 1708.[11] This innovation fell on fertile ground, for not only had there long been a tradition for court masques (as there had been in many other countries) but there were well-established pleasure gardens so that all classes of society could take part in summer masquerades. There were thus splendid masquerades with musical entertainment at the theatres, which provided the kind of lavish spectacle that the English court was unwilling to arrange itself, and the pleasure gardens of Vauxhall and Ranelagh which, said

177 After A. Canaletto, 'A View of the Canal, Chinese Building, Rotundo &c, in Ranelagh Gardens, with the Masquerade', *c.1750*

This is one of the many engravings of the masquerades held in 1749 to celebrate the Peace of Aix-la-Chapelle. A group of masqueraders – one can easily pick out such perennial favourites as Punch, Harlequin and a mixed bag of 'orientals' – strolls by the water in which is placed the 'Chinese Building'.

178 A. R. Mengs, *Isabel Parreno, Marquesa de Llano, c.1773*

The wife of the Spanish ambassador to the court of Parma is shown here dressed in an elegant version of *maja* costume, probably for a masquerade.

Grosley, were more noted for their 'splendor and magnificence' than any other places in the kingdom. Vauxhall Gardens re-opened in 1732 (they had been in existence at the end of the seventeenth century, visited by Pepys, and found by Addison's Sir Roger de Coverley (*Spectator*, 20 May 1712) to be 'a kind of Mahometan paradise', but shortly after they had been closed due to their unsavoury reputation); they were extended and improved with long vistas, lawns, fountains, statuary and temples, and even supper boxes in the Chinese style and a 'Gothic' structure to house the orchestra. At Ranelagh Gardens in Chelsea, where the famous rotunda opened in 1742, there were also formal gardens, canals and 'Chinese' or 'Venetian' buildings. It was at Ranelagh in 1749 that a famous series of masquerades was held, celebrating the Peace of Aix-la-Chapelle that had, the previous year, ended the War of the Austrian Succession. One of the most extravagant of these events was 'a jubilee-masquerade in the Venetian manner' (the Venetian aspect seems to have consisted of a gondola 'adorned with flags and streamers and filled with music' on the canal). Walpole, whose comments on all the major English masquerades are an important source of information, found the gardens full of

masks and spread with tents . . . In one quarter was a Maypole dressed with garlands and people dancing round it to a tabor and pipe and rustic music, all masked, as were all the various bands of music that were disposed in different parts of the garden; some like huntsmen with French horns some like peasants, and a troop of harlequins and scaramouches in the little open temple on the mount . . . All round the outside of the amphitheatre were shops, filled with Dresden china, japan &c and all the shopkeepers in mask.[12]

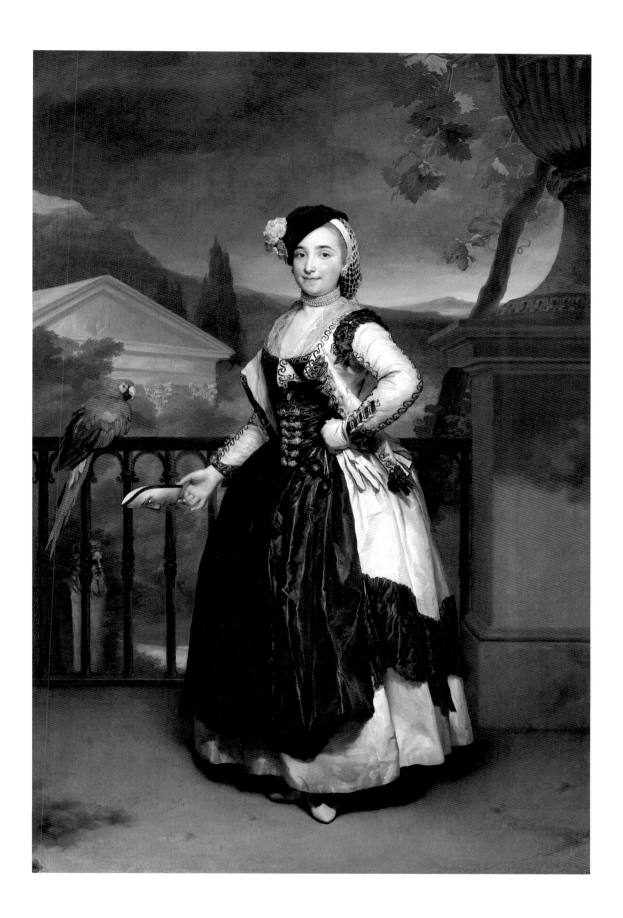

At a masquerade some weeks later, Walpole found the king enjoying himself 'in an old-fashioned English habit'; the Duke of Cumberland, victor of Culloden, had grown so fat that he reminded Walpole of a drunken captain in a Jacobean play[13] – the early seventeenth-century costumes that many of the participants wore reflected English interest in this romantic period, further evidenced by the number of portraits in this style of dress which will be discussed later.

The English pleasure gardens were popular partly because of their accessibility, but mostly because of their amenities; they were quick to follow prevailing trends in taste, such as the mid-century love of chinoiserie (the only English interpretation of the rococo) and the later fondness for the neoclassical. A 'Chinese regatta' was held on the Thames in 1749, possibly inspired by a similar entertainment held in 1716 in Venice for the Elector of Saxony; *fêtes chinoises* were held in the Colisée, the Parisian imitation of Vauxhall; and at the Swedish summer palace of Drottningholm a 'Chinese' village was built for Queen Louisa Ulrica,[14] who even dressed her son, the future Gustavus III, as a Chinese prince, and his gentlemen as mandarins, thus inculcating a taste for the theatrical which was to have lasting effects. As well as in buildings, gardens and follies, the Chinese taste could also be seen in Carlisle House in Soho, the fashionable place for winter masquerades in London in the 1760s; there, Teresa Cornelys, an adventuress of dubious reputation (she had at one time been the mistress of Casanova) but with a sense of theatrical display, built a room for dancing, tearooms, a grotto and a 'Chinese Room . . . so decorated as to afford the most enchanting coup d'oeil'. She arranged rural masquerades where whole suites of rooms were decorated with flowers, shrubs and trees, 'under whose embowering shade the masks will sup'.[15] By the time that this description, taken from a newspaper of 1776, was published, Mrs Cornelys' masquerades were being eclipsed by those held in the Pantheon in Oxford Street (this had opened in 1772 and was to Walpole 'so glorious a vision that I thought I was in the old Pantheon or in the Temples of Delphi or Ephesus').[16] The idea of *rus in urbe*, or the countryside indoors, was a popular theme for masked balls in places where the climate was uncooperative. In Russia, Mrs Ward attended a masquerade in 1734 (to celebrate the capture of Danzig) given at the Summer Palace on the banks of the Neva. The imperial family dined in a grotto under a pavilion of green silk supported by pillars, round which twined flowers (in winter, the Winter Palace was heated so that orange trees and myrtles could bloom); the ladies were in 'stiffened bodied gowns of white gause with silver flowers, their quilted petticoats were of different colours'.[17]

Arcadian themes had been popular since the Renaissance for court masques and they provided a suitable source for the *fêtes champêtres* that many countries adopted in the eighteenth century, particularly in the second half of the period when 'picturesque' English landscaped gardens and the cult of open-air simplicity were in vogue; it was becoming the fashion, said Walpole in the 1770s, 'to make romances rather than balls'. A very expensive and elaborate *fête champêtre* was held in the grounds of Lord Stanley's house, The

Oaks, near Epsom, in 1774:[18] a temporary amphitheatre, designed by Robert Adam, housed the guests, who were expected to dress in 'pastoral habits', although Lord Stanley and his fiancée chose to appear as Rubens and his wife and, from the surviving illustrations, many interpreted the rural to include orientals and vandyke costumes. Some of the most lavish *fêtes champêtres* were held in Poland in this decade; Archdeacon Coxe attended one near Warsaw in 1778 where mock peasants' cottages were erected (this rather grates on our modern susceptibilities when we consider the wretched state of the poor), along with Turkish tents, and the guests were entertained by dancers in Cossack and Polish costumes and by ladies 'in Grecian dresses of the most elegant simplicity'.[19]

In the same vein, there were courtly entertainments in Germany, called 'Wirtschaften', where the guests, dressed in the romanticized costumes of peasants, shepherds and shepherdesses, acted the verses of the court poet – one of Geothe's tasks when he was first employed by the court of Weimar in 1775 was to provide such entertainments.[20] In the Residenz in Munich, the Elector and Electress of Bavaria, dressed as village inn-keepers, received guests who had driven from the summer palace of Nymphenburg dressed in peasant costume.[21] Regional costumes and pastoral subjects provided the themes for some of the rural masquerades popular in Vienna, many designed by Antonio Bertoli, who worked for the court from 1707 to 1743. During this period, masquerades at carnival had been forbidden, but when Maria Theresa came to the throne, her own taste was for enjoyable public displays (though she became increasingly puritanical after the death of her husband in 1765). She organized sleighing parties in winter where the ladies, dressed in fur-trimmed velvets covered in diamonds, rode on gilded sledges shaped like swans, horses, griffins or unicorns. A popular court activity was the carousel, a cavalry tournament where the riders performed elaborate equestrian dances, dressed in splendid, often exotic uniforms. One such was held in the winter riding school in 1743 to celebrate the recapture of Prague from the French, and Maria Theresa led the first quadrille on horseback, dressed in gold-embroidered purple, followed by her ladies in carriages.[22]

Masquerades were held at the opera house in Vienna, and at the palace of Schönbrunn, where in 1775 Dr John Moore saw 4000 guests watching a ballet, danced by some of the imperial family and the nobility, 'all of them dressed in white silk fancy dresses trimmed with pink ribbons and blazing with diamonds'.[23] The Germans generally, said Moore, 'being so much harassed with ceremony and form . . . are glad to seize every opportunity of assuming the masque and domino, that they may taste the pleasures of familiar conversation and social mirth'.[24] This was certainly the case at the Austrian court, where Lady Mary Coke found in the 1770s that the popularity of the masquerade was unabated; light lustring dominos were the rule, decorated with ribbons (the Emperor appeared in a white domino trimmed with gold), or an alternative dress for the ladies was a Polish costume 'made tight to the waist . . . commonly of sattin trimmed with fur, and silver or gold'.[25] To Baron Bielfeld, the monotony of the court at Hanover was only lightened by the winter masquerades in the opera house and the summer masked balls held at Herrenhausen, where, seeing the white dominos walking down the lamp-lit allées, 'they gave the Gardens the appearance of the Elisian fields'.[26] In Russia, masquerades had begun in the reign of Peter the Great, as part of his imposed westernizing policy; according to some commentators, they were more like burlesques than the elegant masked balls of other courts. Aubry de La Motraye found when he went to court in 1719 that there was a masquerade to celebrate the taking of four Swedish men-of-war. The Czar was dressed as a Dutch sailor, the Czarina and her ladies 'like country-women of Frizland and Zealand', 'and the rest in old Russian fashion . . . & attended with a great number of Vizars in peculiar habits, some playing upon Instruments and others dancing as they march'd'.[27] By the 1770s, masquerades were held twice a week in winter in St Petersburg, thousands attending at a time and the dresses a mixture of Russian regional costume or court dress under a domino; in the winter of 1778, William Coxe found Catherine the Great dancing masquerade quadrilles with a number of partners dressed in such exotic costumes as Roman habits with diamond-studded helmets.[28]

Many masquerades were theatrical in inspiration, some deriving directly from the staged *tableaux vivants* of the Renaissance; the Margravine of Bayreuth gave to her husband for his birthday in 1736 an entertainment where Mount Parnassus was erected: 'A very good singer whom I engaged represented Apollo; nine ladies magnificently attired, were the muses, and underneath Parnassus we had a theatre'[29] where the performers danced a ballet. Classical themes dominated some of the expensive tournament fêtes which seemed a particularly popular entertainment for absolute princes. Month-long celebrations occurred at the Bavarian court in 1722 for the marriage of the Electoral Prince to the Archduchess Maria Amelia; at one of the evening carousels, the court dressed up as Greeks and Romans, in gold-embroidered costumes decorated with diamonds, for a mock tournament.[30] Such classical military combat was a particularly apt choice for the martial Prussian court and in August 1750 a fête was held at Potsdam in honour of a visit made by the king's favourite sister, Fredericka Sophia Wilhelmina, during which princes of the blood led contingents of courtiers dressed as Romans, Carthaginians, Greeks and Persians.[31] The entertainment was taken very seriously, and a month was spent in practising military manoeuvres and the torchlight processions that, since medieval times, had been an important part of German court festivities. The costumes were distinguished more for their glamorous appearance than for accuracy and were very similar to those worn for the courtly opera-ballet: light glittering fabrics with stiffened skirts, helmets, feathers and asymmetrically draped mantles. The Romans were distinguished by their feathered headdresses, gold cuirasses and gold-decorated blue mantles; the Carthaginians, imitating Moors, were clothed in black satin with feathered skirts, pearl collars and turbans of silver cloth and were led by the king's brother Frederick, who was dressed in a costume of cloth of silver, embroidered with a golden sun on the front, and a tiger-skin cloak.

179 Detail of pl. 182

Costume *à l'antique* adopted by the participants on horseback in this court entertainment at Drottningholm in 1778.

The Greeks and the Persians proved more difficult to dress: the former wore a version of Roman dress with one-sided mantles edged with fringe, and the latter came in a kind of Turkish dress (some of them were called 'Janissaries' after the famous Turkish palace guard) with turbans, their leader wearing a cloak of green satin lined with ermine over a tunic of silver brocaded with gold flowers and a bonnet *à la Persanne* (a turban decorated with precious stones). After the ceremonial parades to music, the tournaments took place at specially erected barriers; later, masked balls were held, those taking part in the carousel wearing the clothes they had worn for the tournaments. It was all very costly, with elaborate and contrived allegory, the kind of courtly entertainment with which a Olivier de la Marche in fifteenth-century Burgundy, or Inigo Jones in early Stuart England, would have instantly been familiar.

In Spain, the mock battles with attendant processions were closely linked to the Moorish tradition. Henry Swinburne in the mid-1770s described the *parejas*, 'a kind of dancing on horseback', where the courtiers 'arrayed in the ancient Spanish dress' tilted in the grounds of the royal palace of Aranjuez.[32] The ancient Spanish dress, which Baretti described in the 1760s as 'made fine with many ribbonds of various colours, with feathers on their hats', was also worn for bull-fighting both in Spain and Portugal.[33]

In the last quarter of the eighteenth century, the idea of the theatrically inspired tournament reached new heights of elaborate display. Medieval themes, precursors of the rage for the 'Gothic' that had begun by this period and which were temporarily halted by the European wars, were to emerge in the early nineteenth century as a decisive cultural influence. Again, these could be organized only by courts oblivious to expense. In 1775, a medieval tournament was held at Choisy in honour of Marie Antoinette in which knights in full armour jousted – the first glimmerings of the *style troubadour*,[34] or the romantic harking back to the Middle Ages and the Renaissance. The apogee of the fancy dress entertainment arrived with Gustavus III of Sweden, who initiated a series of tournaments and carousels at court between 1776 and 1785. Not only did he write a number of pageants, but he acted in them and probably helped with the design of the costumes.[35] One such fête was held in the grounds of Drottningholm in 1779, the theme being from the *chanson de geste, Amadis de Gaul*; Gustavus took the part of the enchanter Arcelaus and the music was composed by Gluck. The king also helped to design costumes and stage sets for plays performed at the court theatre in Gripsholm Castle, and it is ironic that he should have been shot at a masquerade in 1792 at the Stockholm Opera House which had been built at his expense and inspiration.

Masquerades celebrated occasions of national rejoicing but in many cases their full splendour could not be appreciated by the mass of the people, who were not admitted. What the populace could see were the civic and religious processions that formed an important part of everyday pageantry, and which were descended from medieval clerical and mercantile power. In Rome, for example, the richest entertainments were provided by the papal processions,

180 (*following page*) L.-J. Le Lorrain, *Before the Masked Ball*, late 1750s

Le Lorrain's masterpiece may depict an actual episode from one of the sumptuous masquerades held by the Russian court at St Petersburg, or a fantasy on the theme of the *bal masqué*. Set against an imaginary architectural background, the sitters wear theatrical versions of Central European costume, trimmed with fur, feathers, gold braid and glittering jewelled decoration.

attended by retainers in the deliberately archaic costumes of the previous
century. In 1730, Pöllnitz saw Pope Clement XII in his litter surrounded by
pages 'in an antique Dress of white Sattin, with a great many red and
silver'd Ribbands, and black cloaks lin'd with white and silver Mohair,
and enriched with broad Gold Lace',[36] and accompanied by clerics, the
Roman nobility and drummers and trumpeters in red and gold.

City authorities provided much of their own pageantry. This ranged from
the Lord Mayor's processions in London (with a cavalcade of City companies and a ceremonial progress up the Thames) to the staged *tableaux vivants*
with speeches and dances arranged by cities to welcome important events,
such as those held by Strasbourg in 1744 to celebrate the recovery of Louis
XV, who had fallen ill at Metz while on campaign. In Strasbourg, the city
companies formed themselves into battalions imitating the uniforms of the
regiments of the French army. Young boys dressed like the French king's
Swiss Guard, in sixteenth-century costumes of blue camlet slashed with red,
white muslin ruff and black hat with a white feather. A number of young

181 (*previous page*) Detail of pl. 180

182　P. Hilleström, *A Tournament*, 1778

This painting of a carousel held at Drottningholm Palace gives a good indication of the elaborate theatrical divertissements that were so much a part of Swedish court life under the cultivated Gustavus III. The king and his courtiers have adopted 'classical' costume, the king in a red and white Roman dress with ermine-lined mantle being received by 'Diana' (Duchess Hedvig Elisabet Charlotta) who wears a flower-trimmed version of fashionable costume and a crescent in her hair. The spectator courtiers are in the Swedish national costume, itself an amalgam of a fashionable contemporary dress with elements of the Henri IV styles of the late sixteenth century. Walpole's comment that it was the fashion 'to make romances rather than balls' in the 1770s was particularly true of absolutist courts with unlimited funds to provide the kind of fantasy entertainments that were so popular. In this decade, it is not surprising that fashionable dress was itself so strongly influenced by the historic past.

183 (*following page*)　Detail of pl. 154

Fancy dress versions of hussar costume (see also pl. 184) were popular for masquerades.

girls wore their *habits de cérémonie* with the traditional headdress of black velvet and lace and there were young couples dressed as shepherds and shepherdesses in costumes of white taffeta, decorated with garlands of flowers and rose-coloured ribbons.[37]

It is in the eighteenth century that we get a last glimpse of the medieval *joyeuse entrée*, originally the formal acknowledgement by a city of the sovereignty of its prince but by this time merely an official, if elaborate, welcome. Strasbourg was in a special position in this respect, a former imperial city but with a certain degree of independence under French rule; it was there that foreign brides were welcomed to French territory, such as Marie-Josèphe of Saxony (1747) and Marie Antoinette (1770). On the latter occasion, children dressed as shepherds and shepherdesses greeted the Austrian princess; Goethe saw the triumphal arches that decorated the city on these occasions and the future French queen making her entry in a glass coach. In Spain, clinging to royal traditions, the king still formally entered his capital: in 1760, Charles III made a public entry into Madrid (where the balconies along the route were lined with people) attended by his knights in old Spanish dress and his guard 'in liveries of Moorish habits of silk, richly and elegantly ornamented with lace and embroidery'.[38]

It was no wonder that in such a climate, where pageantry and masquerade were accepted parts of everyday existence, fancy dress played an important role. Dressing *en travesti* was part of this masquerade and it is not surprising that Casanova changed clothes with his mistress on such occasions. For women there was a respectable operatic tradition of appearing as boys – Mozart's Cherubino in *The Marriage of Figaro* (1786) is the best example – and at masquerades male costume was very popular; the Empress Elizabeth of Russia in the 1740s organized masked balls called Metamorphoses, where men and women adopted the costume of the opposite sex – men in wide hooped dresses, and the empress herself in a robust selection of male clothing either as a cossack or as a Dutch sailor.[39]

Apart from a few notorious examples (and in spite of the attacks directed against the macaronis for their effeminacy and the popularity of women's dress at masquerades), there was not much perceptible female influence on male costume. For women there have been, on the other hand, constant attacks on their propensity for borrowing from men's clothing, and this was true of the eighteenth century. When, in 1728, Augustus the Strong of Saxony went to Berlin, accompanied by his daughter, she amazed the Prussian court with a large number of male outfits for dancing and for riding – not surprising given the masculine influence on the female riding habit and the great-coat discussed earlier. Other trends – historical and exotic – which played their part in fashionable costume and as fancy dress will be considered, although the subject is so vast (and the range of costumes so great) that only the major points can be mentioned.

It has already been noted to what an extent exotic and flamboyant liveries were worn at some of the German and Central European courts. A royal marriage taking place at the Saxon court in 1719 included cavalcades of attendants in Saxon and Polish liveries, hussars and twenty-four Moors 'dressed in Turkish habits' of scarlet edged with blue, and feathered turbans on their heads.[40] These costumes were everyday wear in Saxony, which also ruled Poland, where, in turn, as discussed earlier, clothing was influenced by Turkey. By the middle of the century, such exotic styles had made an impact all over Europe.

The popularity of the Hungarian hussar costume in England was based on sympathy for the Empress Maria Theresa who enlisted the help of her Hungarian subjects to ward off Frederick the Great's invasion of her territory in 1740; not only did English Catholics (who were refused commissions in the British army) fight in Austrian regiments, but fashionable men-about-town, according to the *Female Spectator*, swaggered about London 'like warriors for the Queen of Hungary'. No doubt they wore a version of hussar dress that had slight acquaintance with the original dolman, pelisse and fur-edged cap. At masquerades, fashionable gentlemen turned up in what Thomas Jefferys described as 'the Modern Dress of a Hungarian Hussar . . . rose-coloured Sattin trimmed with Silver', which was not very martial, but incorporated the frogged trimming that came to be synonymous with 'hussar'.

The costume was further popularized by the actor David Garrick, when, for no conceivable reason except that it was in vogue, he wore it playing a twelfth-century ruler of Sicily in James Thomson's play *Tancred and Sigismunda* in 1745.[41] Not only were servants put into hussar liveries (they were particularly, if inappropriately, worn by fashionable and highly prized negro servants) but children also wore them. Little hussars paraded the streets of Italian cities at carnival time and even George III (who was later to disapprove of his sons' attendance at masquerades) attended a masque organized in 1769 by the governess of his two eldest sons who wore 'rich Hussar Habits of white sattin embroidered with Gold & trimm'd with Sable'.[42] Just as in the 1880s velvet Lord Fauntleroy suits adorned small boys, so from the middle of the eighteenth century 'Hussar Dresses' were advertised for sale; this jacket and calf-length trouser style was particularly suited to the new kind of boys' clothing pioneered by the English in the 1770s and 1780s. By the 1770s, elements of hussar dress, notably the trimming and the fur, decorated men's coats. William Hickey (who put his Indian servant into a hussar livery) admired a particularly dashing friend in 1772: 'His dress then being a white coat, cut in the extremity of ton, lined with garter-blue satin, edged with ermine, and ornamented with rich silver frogs; waistcoat and breeches of the same blue satin, trimmed with silver twist à la hussar, and ermine edges.'[43] The Prince of Wales, the future George IV, loved fancy dress and uniforms, the two influences combining to create a fascination with hussar uniform, which was gradually being adopted by armies all over Europe. By the late 1780s, along with other fashion leaders, he was beginning to adopt the tight-fitting pantaloons and tasselled boots that were originally part of hussar costume. Like many other princes, the Prince of Wales loved to dress up in Turkish costume, a style of dress with long flowing robe/caftan and turban, which was not only 'very proper for a prince because it disguises well and has a commanding aspect',[44] but it also provided an opportunity to display jewelled ornaments and an exotic, if conventional, taste.

The influence of Turkey on the taste and culture of eighteenth-century Europe was immense. The Ottoman Empire, declining as a military power since the end of the seventeenth century, began to open out to western European travellers who had long been intrigued by the secret, autocratic and above all exotic court in Constantinople. Turkey had since the Renaissance exported fine silks and embroideries to the west via Venice, and such trading links were further strengthened by the establishment of diplomatic facilities granted in particular to France, England and Holland in the late seventeenth century. From about that time, too, Turkish embassies appeared at European courts, a notable visit to France in 1721 inspiring artists, writers, interior designers and the theatre.[45]

From the beginning of the century, a number of foreign artists had settled in Constantinople, painting members of the merchant and diplomatic communities and their families and an increasing number of young men who extended their Grand Tour to include the newly fashionable East. Perhaps the most famous was the artist J. B. Vanmour (who had worked in Turkey since the end of the seventeenth century), who was commissioned by the French ambassador, Charles de Ferriol, to paint a series of scenes depicting the life and costumes of the Ottoman empire; these were engraved and were published in Paris in 1714 under the title *Recueil de Cent Estampes representant differentes Nations du Levant*. The accuracy of detail and quality of design meant that this collection inspired artists throughout the eighteenth century to produce similar costume pieces, and a number of artists who had never been to Turkey, such as Aved, Cochin and Boucher (who illustrated one of the most popular works, Jean-Antoine Guer's *Moeurs et Usages des Turcs*, published in 1747), painted their sitters in the newly fashionable oriental dress. The Swiss artist Jean-Etienne Liotard (who himself dressed like a Turk for comfort and self-advertisement) painted sitters in Constantinople and in fashionable western European capitals, dressed *à la turque*.

Courtly entertainments were inspired by Turkey also, perhaps the most impressive *mise-en-scène* being at Dresden, where Augustus II in the early eighteenth century 'kept a kind of seraglio of the most beautiful females of his dominions'; the Saxon court, said a contemporary, 'was the seat of all pleasures; it might justly be styled the island of Cythera'.[46] There were Turkish gardens, portraits of court beauties in Turkish costume and Turkish entertainments were provided at court, where the Elector appeared as the Sultan; Keysler, the indefatigable Hanoverian traveller, saw, in 1730, an astonishing array of 'rich habits' that belonged to the royal wardrobe, including many Turkish costumes which had been used at masquerades.[47] When, in 1787, Catherine the Great visited the recently annexed Crimea, Prince Potemkin designed in her honour a whole series of Turkish delights, banquets and regattas, dressed in his favourite costume of richly embroidered caftan and loose trousers. A prince's income was also needed for the party held in 1781 to celebrate the coming-of-age of William Beckford; Fonthill was transformed by the stage designer Philippe-Jacques de Loutherbourg into a Turkish palace for three days of oriental entertainments.[48]

Anything oriental was in vogue for fancy dress; 'Turks pour'd by hundreds,' said a poem commemorating a masquerade held at the Haymarket Theatre in 1768 in honour of the visiting King of Denmark. Also present on this occasion were the Duke of Northumberland 'in a Persian habit with a turban richly ornamented with diamonds . . . Lord Clive in the dress of a Nabob very richly ornamented . . . An East India director was dressed in the real habit of a Chinese Mandarin'.[49] Some of the costumes were obviously brought back from eastern travels, some hired and some no doubt made from the 'Indian' nightgowns that had long been a staple item in the fashionable wardrobe; loose silk gowns often lined with fur were worn by European travellers to the East and worn by them in commemorative portraits.

Two years after the publication of the set of engravings after Vanmour, the most famous eighteenth-century traveller, Lady Mary Wortley Montagu, set off with her husband on an ambassadorial visit to Turkey. During her eighteen months there she set herself to discover as much as possible about the life and customs of the Turks, the women in particular, whose relaxed and elegant clothing she compared to the 'slavery' suffered by Englishwomen with their tight-lacing and hooped skirts. Like previous male travellers, she found it convenient to dress *à la turque*, recording her clothing in great detail for her sister Lady Mar in Paris in 1717:

> The first part of my dress is a pair of drawers, very full, that reach to my shoes and conceal the legs more modestly than your petticoats. They are of a thin rose-coloured damask, brocaded with silver flowers . . . Over this hangs my smock, of a fine white silk gauze edged with embroidery. This smock has wide sleeves, hanging half-way down the arm, and is closed at the neck with a diamond button; but the shape and colour of the bosum are very well to be distinguished through it. The antery is a waistcoat made close to the shape, of white and gold damask, with very long sleeves falling back and fringed with deep gold fringe, and should have diamond or pearl buttons . . .
>
> My caftan, of the same stuff with my drawers, is a robe exactly fitted to my shape, and reaching to my feet, with very long strait falling sleeves. Over this is my girdle, of about four fingers broad, which all that can afford it have entirely of diamonds or other precious stones . . . The curdee is a loose robe they throw off or put on according to the weather, being of a rich brocade (mine is green and gold) either lined with ermine or sables; the sleeves reach very little below the shoulders.[50]

With this dress noble Turkish ladies wore on their heads either a small velvet cap decorated with pearls or diamonds, an embroidered silk handkerchief or an aigrette of feathers or jewelled flowers.

Through these letters (which were circulated in manuscript before being published in 1763 and serialized in fashionable magazines thereafter) and a number of portraits, a vogue for Turkish fancy dress spread through England.

185 J. B. Vanmour, *Lady Mary Wortley Montagu and her Son Edward* (detail), *c*.1717

Lady Mary's travels were commemorated by a number of portraits of her dressed *à la Turque*, both while she was in Turkey, and after she returned to England. This portrait, painted during her Oriental sojourn, shows her in a gold silk caftan, tucked up into a jewelled girdle, and worn under a gold-trimmed *curdee* trimmed with ermine.

It had an immediate appeal to a public ready for novelty; rich, glamorous, even erotic – to a later English traveller Turkish women's 'breasts are at full liberty under their Vest without any restraint of Stays or Boddice . . . in a word they are just as Nature has form'd them' – it was worn for masquerades and entered the vocabulary of the fashionable portrait-painter. The tremor of indecorum associated with it made it an ideal costume for the masquerade; the 1724 *Dialogue betwixt a Prude and a Coquet* describes a lady's surprise at her rival's choice of costume:

O Jesu – Coz – why this fantastick dress?
I fear some Frenzy does your Head possess;
That thus you sweep along a Turkish tail,
And let that Robe o'er Modesty prevail . . .
Why in this naughty Vestment are you seen?
Dress'd up for Love, with such an Air and Mien,
As if you wou'd commence Sultana Queen.[51]

At the King of Denmark's masquerade (1768), the Duchess of Richmond 'appeared as the Fatima described in Lady Mary Wortley Montagu's letters',[52] but the most admired dress was that of the Duchess of Ancaster in 'a robe of purple satin bordered with ermine'.[53] Turkish costumes came to mean all or any of the following: fur (usually ermine) trimming, a long gown or caftan (with short or hanging sleeves) one side of which was kilted up and held by an elaborately jewelled girdle over baggy trousers, and either a turban or asymmetrically placed aigrette of feathers or jewels.

For both masquerade-goers and artists there were a variety of sources of ideas; these included collections of engravings (such as Ferriol's), or records of famous masquerades such as the *Caravanne du Sultan à la Mecque* performed by the students of the French Academy in Rome in 1748 and depicted by one of the participants, J. M. Vien.[54] Both these sources were used in Thomas Jeffreys's masquerade pattern book of 1757, *A Collection of the Dresses of Different Nations both Ancient and Modern, and more particularly Old English Dresses after the designs of Holbein, Vandyke, Hollar and others*, an important publication for the spread of certain fancy dress costumes. Turkish costumes were also popularized by fashionable plays with oriental themes (the actress Marie Favart wore a genuine Turkish costume for her rôle in Solinian in 1767) and Liotard, as well as painting his sitters *à la turque* also designed costumes, at least one for the actress Adrienne Lecouvreur at the request of her lover Maurice de Saxe.[55] Both the demi-monde and society ladies wished to appear in their portraits in Turkish costume; in 1755, Madame de Pompadour commissioned Carle van Loo to paint a series of portraits of her as a sultana for her chateau of Bellevue, and Liotard's clients included ladies as different as the beautiful Countess of Coventry and the Empress Maria Theresa.

In England, the link between the masquerade and the popularity of 'oriental' fashionable dresses was clearly perceived by contemporaries; the *Magazine à la Mode* (1777) noted how far 'The dresses of our ladies have inclined very much to the Persian and Turkish, since the taste for masquerades as a

186   J.-E. Liotard, *Mary Gunning, Countess of Coventry*, c.1753–4

In one of Liotard's most accomplished and ravishing portraits, the sitter is shown in a flower-embroidered caftan and a cream-coloured smock, with the merest hint of loose trousers beneath it.

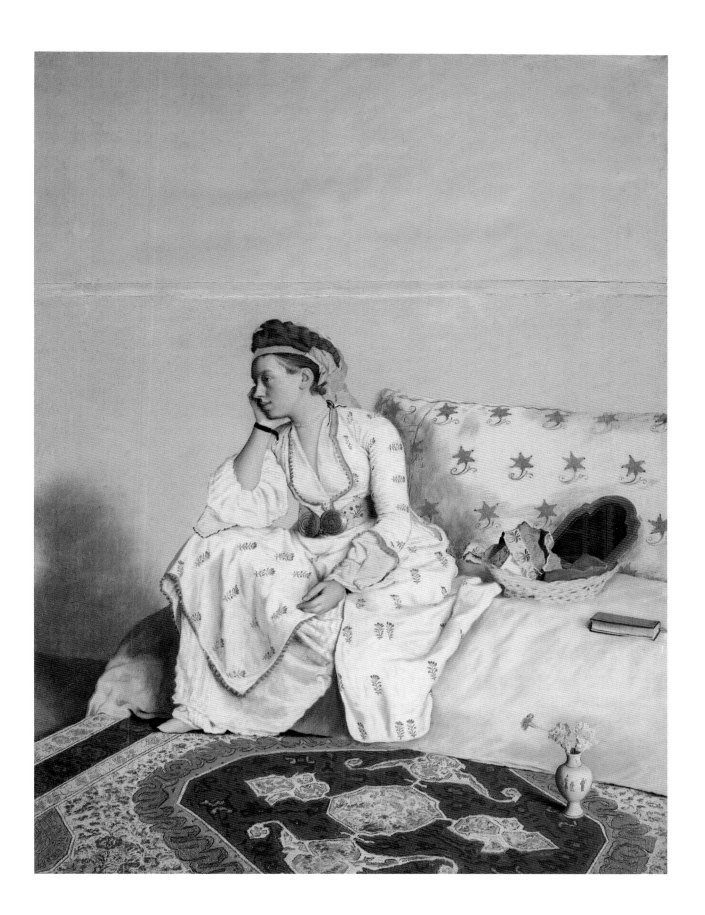

187   E. Aubry, *Mlle Rosalie Duthé*, 1779

Western European etiquette and
deportment do not allow this sitter to
lounge like an odalisque on her sofa, but
a moderately successful Turkish *mise-en-
scène*, as to setting, pose and costume,
is achieved. With regard to the dress, a
compromise between east and west can be
seen. The high-piled hair of the 1770s is
trimmed with white feathers *à la mode*, but
with a small lack feather aigrette in the
Turkish style, and a striped silk 'oriental'
scarf. A similar, transparent silk covers the
satin skirt, but the embroidered gown with
short over-sleeves (possibly a circassian
dress) is worn over a firmly structured,
European, boned bodice.

fashion amusement has prevailed . . . The resemblance of the headdress and
robe will be seen at first view, and it will be found that, with little or no
alteration, an English lady, taken from one of our polite assemblies and conducted to Constantinople, would be properly dressed to appear before the
Grand Signior.'[56]

During the 1760s, the tambour frame was imported into western Europe
from Turkey, to embroider the semi-transparent muslins used for dresses,
turbans and sashes, and from this time the number of 'oriental' gowns
increased, though their exact meaning varied. The *sultane* (a term used from
the end of the seventeenth century) was a popular informal gown (Mrs
Delany described a bride's trousseau in 1748 as containing a 'white satin
sultane with embroidered robings of natural flowers . . . and a pink and white
sprigged sultane')[57] which was either tied back at the sides or decorated with
fur; the *Lady's Magazine* for 1783 noted that it was fashionably made of white
lustring tied up at the sides, and in the following year the same magazine
found that the currently fashionable 'Westmoreland sultane' was of 'boue de
Paris' coloured satin trimmed with sable. Equally popular were 'circassians'
(the name taken, said the *Gallerie des Modes*, from the grand Sultan's favourites
in the seraglio), gowns decorated with tassels and fur, often with short sleeves.
They could be quite informal; Mrs Montagu, attending a ball at the Mansion
House in Newbury (1780) was upset to find a tailor's wife 'only dressed in
a Circassian Robe and a Queen's night cap on her head'.[58] By the end of
the 1780s, there were even circassian corsets, which were lightly boned and

188   A. Kauffmann, *Morning Amusement*, *c*.1773

This may be the painting referred to by Mrs Powys when she visited Stourhead in 1776: 'a lady in a white and gold Turkish habit working at a tambour'. The mood is one of exotic informality which in some ways anticipates later neo-classical styles. Embroidery done on the tambour frame was used both for masquerade and for fashionable dresses.

short to accommodate the rising waist, and circassian cosmetics to improve the complexion.

Some aspects of Turkish costume were approved of by artists who preferred the flow of drapery to the minutiae of fashion with all its trimmings. Angelica Kauffmann, for example, painting fashionable sitters in the 1770s, found that the modish oriental *déshabillé* of loose-fitting, cross-over muslin gown decorated with braid and fringe and worn with a sash, fitted in with her ideas about the simple styles of classical Greece. To her friend Sir Joshua Reynolds, however, such 'eastern dresses', although rich and dignified, had 'a mock dignity in comparison with the simplicity of the antique'.[59]

Poor Reynolds had great trouble with the costume of his female sitters, for he had to contend not only with their desire to be painted in fashionable

189 Sir J. Reynolds, *Philippa Rooper, Lady Sunderlin*, 1788

This is some way removed from Turkish costume, but shows how aspects of Turkish dress were incorporated into fashionable wear. The hanging sleeve has become a sleeve looped up with gold cord and fringed on the shoulders, the jewelled girdle is replaced by a fringed sash and the turban by a bandeau.

dress, but their choice of whatever was currently in vogue with regard to fancy dress; the resulting compromise costumes were often uneasy mixtures of the fashionable *déshabillé* and unreal drapery. The Duchess of Rutland, painted by Reynolds in 1781, had to try on eleven different dresses before the artist chose to paint her in a 'bedgown', a simple dress of white with a sash round the waist, which best accorded with his idea of a 'timeless' dress.[60] For the President of the Royal Academy, Greece and Rome were 'the fountains from whence have flowed all kinds of excellence . . . We voluntarily add our approbation of every ornament that belonged to them, even to the fashion of their dress'.[61] He was not alone in his view: from the 1760s, the neo-classical was a theme popular with artists, partly as a reaction against what was seen as the over-decorative and meaningless prettiness of the rococo, and partly owing to growing interest in published accounts of the classical discoveries at Herculaneum and Pompeii – it was the civilization of the Greeks in Italy that at this date inspired artists, and writers such as Winckelmann. Although in 1763 (the year that Winckelmann's *Geschichte der Kunst des Altertums* was published) Diderot was writing to Grimm that 'tout se fait aujourd'hui à la grecque' (everything today is *à la grecque*), no such influence penetrated the world of fashion until the late 1780s, although artists such as Romney and Vigée-Lebrun had tried to persuade their sitters to adopt a classical costume of simple white gown (worn without stays or hoops), unpowdered hair and entwining scarves.[62] Vigée-Lebrun organized 'Grecian evenings' in the 1780s and created a suitable Grecian dress merely by adding a chaplet of flowers to her usual costume of white linen or muslin chemise; her guests were lent draperies from her studio.[63] Until the waist rose appreciably in the 1790s and the startling political developments in France caused parallels to be drawn between the heroic days of classical Greece and Rome, classical dress (other than on the stage where it had been worn intermittently throughout the eighteenth century, but especially in the 1780s) was no more than a self-conscious pose, or an artist's ideal.[64] In the former category, Lady Hamilton, seen by Goethe in 1787, had a Greek costume made for her by her husband in which, 'letting her hair loose, and taking a couple of shawls, she exhibits every variety of posture, expression and look'.[65] The artist J. W. Tischbein (who was later to publish four volumes of engravings taken from vases in Sir William Hamilton's collection), in Naples in 1789, admired the grace and beauty of Lady Charlotte Campbell, whom he likened to 'the swaying dancers of the paintings at Herculaneum', and he painted her in a white chemise with gold-embroidered gauze scarf, and white satin shoes also embroidered in gold.[66]

Certain mythological characters were favoured for masquerades, such as the goddess Diana; the costume chosen could incorporate the classical with the ever-popular pastoral. White, however, was the only common factor in 'classical' or 'pastoral' costumes: a 'Diana' masquerade costume noted in the *Covent Garden Magazine* (1773) was 'a short kind of jacket and petticoat of white gauze . . . and a small white turban of gauze striped with silver',[67] and some years earlier at the 'sylvan theatre' at Herrenhausen, the Princess of Hesse, said Bielfeld, 'was drest in the habit of a rural nymph, made of white sattin, and ornamented with Italian flowers. Her habit was made in the form of a vest, which finely marked her shape'.[68]

Flowers, floating scarves, tinsel trimming and feathers could be added to provide suitably romantic or pastoral costumes. In Richardson's novel *Sir Charles Grandison* (1753) the heroine, Harriet Byron, was most uneasy about her costume as an 'Arcadian Princess', which 'falls not in with any of my notions of the pastoral dress of Arcadia', for it comprised a white net cap with spangles, artificial flowers and a white feather, a blue satin waistcoat and skirt trimmed with silver braid and fringe, and 'a kind of scarf, of white Persian silk, which gathered at the top, is to be fastened to my shoulders, and fly loose behind me'. The only concession, she felt, was that 'I am not to have a hoop, for 'they wore not hoops in Arcadia'.[69]

Tight-fitting waistcoats or riding jackets (such as Olivia's 'green joseph' in *The Vicar of Wakefield*) made popular rural costumes in the middle of the century; later, in the 1770s and 1780s, the whole of fashionable, informal dress was affected by a rather stylized simplicity and the *polonaise* gowns with their bunched-up drapery and the white chemises with straw hats and flowers could make passable costumes for shepherdesses. Playing at rural simplicity was an eighteenth-century pastime and fashionable ladies queued up to be painted as milkmaids, dairymaids, hay-makers and shepherdesses. This vogue

190 J. W. Tischbein, *Lady Charlotte Campbell*, *c.*1789–90

This portrait of a noted beauty was painted in Naples in about 1789–90. In the artist's autobiography, he describes how her grace and beauty brought to life classical art, 'the lovely, youthful, fleeing figures on bas-reliefs and the swaying dancers of the paintings at Herculaneum'. For her costume, Tischbein has chosen the suitably classical white chemise, with rolled-up sleeve; an embroidered mantle is draped about her, and as a headdress Lady Charlotte wears a wreath of roses, an attribute of the goddess Aphrodite.

191 C.-L. Desrais, design for a ball dress, *c.*1779

This design, engraved for the *Gallerie des Modes*, shows the popular Henri IV costume that was worn at court balls in 1774–6 at the request of Marie Antoinette and made up by 'Sarrazin, Costumier de la Famille Royale'. Claude-Louis Desrais was one of the principal artists working for the *Gallerie des Modes*.

gathered popularity in the 1770s with new enthusiasm for the 'picturesque' in nature and its potential for both drama and simplicity. Gardens in the English style, with carefully arranged wildness and, often, hamlets with shepherds and shepherdesses, formed an essential part of many royal and princely courts. At the Petit Trianon, Marie Antoinette could relax away from the formality of the palace of Versailles and with her intimate circle, dressed 'à la jardinière' or 'en belle fermière', could play in the miniature village with its lake and artificially aged farm buildings, dairy, barns and dovecots.

The classical past was far enough away in time for a multitude of fashionable interpretations in dress to occur and the pastoral could be easily adapted from whatever was the current *déshabillé*. The vogue for fancy dress based on more recent historical periods is harder to fathom. In England, particularly, the range of historical costumes was enormous: in 1768, the Countess of Moira's masquerade guests included 'Vandykes, Hussars . . . Spaniards, ancient Frenchmen . . . the Rubens' wives, the Mary of Medici, the Isabella of Spain, Jane Seymour . . .'[70] Much of the interest in the fifteenth and sixteenth century was doubtless created by the popularity of stage plays with such themes; Nicholas Rowe's play *Jane Shore* (1713) about the mistress of Edward IV, was performed throughout the eighteenth century and probably inspired Lady Waldegrave's choice of masquerade costume in this role, 'a dress richly trimmed with beads and pearls' (1770). Tragic heroines are always popular, and at Lady Moira's masquerade the Jane Seymour costume consisted of 'a stiff bodice and farthingale with silver gauze beads and ermine made of black and white Persian'.[71]

Shakespearian characters from the history plays were a frequent choice; Henry VIII and Anne Boleyn made a romantic pair (the play was a favourite of George II) and Anne Boleyn's costume was chosen by the bluestocking Mrs Montagu for her portrait by the miniaturist Christian Friedrich Zincke in 1740. No doubt such interest in the past was also inculcated by the popularity of Salmon's Royal Wax-works, near Temple Bar, which displayed such tableaux as Henry VIII introducing Anne Boleyn at court and Charles I giving his blessing to his three children the day before his execution; a number of museums also displayed collections of historic costume.[72] Growing interest in the past (helped by the increased verisimilitude of stage costumes from the mid-eighteenth century onwards)[73] was furthered by scholarly research into the history of dress and by a number of books that brought together engravings after a wide range of images, including fashion prints, Old Masters and famous historical portraits. One such important publication was Thomas Jefferys's *A Collection of the Dresses of Different Nations . . .* , which came out in two volumes in 1757 (with 240 plates) and a further two volumes in 1772 (also with 240 plates). Not only was this comprehensive book a boon to the masquerader and shops selling or hiring fancy dress so that the costumes need 'no longer be a torture to the invention', but it was also an invaluable source book for artists and their drapery painters. The emphasis in the text on sixteenth- and seventeenth-century artists was no accident. Walpole noted that for a masquerade to be given by the French ambassador

192 P. P. Rubens, *Helena Fourment* (or her sister, Susanna), early 1630s

193 T. Gainsborough, *The Hon. Mrs Graham*, 1777

A celebrated beauty, Mrs Graham is shown in the artist's interpretation of the costume of Rubens's wife, a *tour-de-force* in the depiction of satin, ruched silk, pearls and feathers.

in 1773, 'being antiquarians or historians, one is set to appear like the court of Henri Quatre', and the quadrilles were danced by a group of society ladies 'in blue satin with blond and collets montées à la reine Elizabeth'.[74] Raised collars, often with 'vandyked' lace edging, looped-up, often ruched overskirts, sleeves either slashed or decorated with ribbons, and feathered hats characterized the outfits worn by many of Gainsborough's fashionable sitters in the 1770s and 1780s and at the court of Marie Antoinette. The French queen, helped by the royal tailor P.-N. Sarrazin, popularized the Henri Quatre costume for court balls; she herself appeared as Gabrielle d'Estrées (mistress of Henri IV) in a dress of white and silver gauze with puffed slashed sleeves and a black hat with white feathers and diamonds at a ball held in honour of the Grand Duke and Duchess of Russia in 1782.[75]

In England, no costume was more popular from the 1730s to the 1770s than that worn by Helena Fourment, Rubens's second wife, for a painting by the artist in the early 1630s (pl. 192) which, for much of the eighteenth century, was in the collection of Sir Robert Walpole (it was sold to Catherine II of Russia and now hangs in the Gulbenkian Museum in Lisbon); it was earlier in the century attributed to Van Dyck, although correctly identified by Thomas Jefferys in his 1757 collection of engravings. The dress of black silk with bunched-up overskirt, the open sleeves revealing the chemise and a gauzy over-sleeve tied with lilac ribbon, the asymmetrically placed jewelled chain looking over the shoulder from a central brooch, the raised collar, the hat fastened up to one side and adorned with white feathers – all these features from the original portrait were copied both by a large number of artists and for fancy costume for balls. For example, at the *fête champêtre* held by Lord Stanley in 1774, discussed earlier, his fiancée Lady Betty Hamilton chose to appear in this costume and at Lady Moira's masquerade there were so many that they could not all be listed. The Duchess of Ancaster was painted in a 'Rubens's wife' dress that she wore for a masquerade at Ranelagh, but many other ladies merely wished to wear an artist's version of this dress, sometimes faithful to the original, or sometimes modified to suit the taste of the eighteenth century. The 'art historian' George Vertue noted in 1732 that the painter John Vanderbank had recently painted a portrait of his wife 'in a habit somewhat like a picture of Rubens' wife'.[76] This idea, from being limited to an artistic circle, caught on with the fashionable world, primarily owing to the drapery painters, in particular Joseph van Aken who worked in the 1730s and 1740s for such well-established artists as Hudson and Ramsay.[77] The more exact copies of the original dress date from the middle years of the eighteenth century, but by the 1770s, although many of the essential features were still there, they had become subdued in the generalized romantic flavour of the period. Gainsborough's 'Hon. Mrs Graham' (1777), for example, wears a dress that is a successful blending of the style of Rubens's wife's dress (overskirt, spiky collar, tied-up-ribbon sleeves and feathered hat) with fashionable fabrics such as white satin, ruched or puckered silk for the skirt and white satin edged with pearls for the hat. Fashion had caught up the past, for the eighteenth-century *polonaise* was a

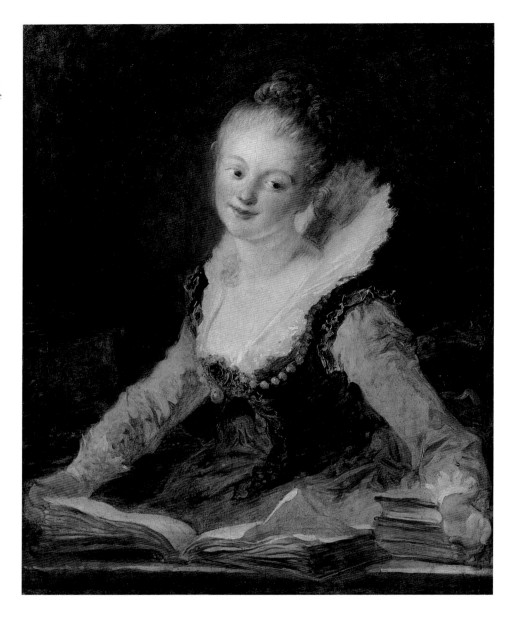

194 J.-H. Fragonard, *L'Etude*, 1769

The influence of the early seventeenth
century can be seen in this dress, with its
sleeves of contrasting colour to the bodice,
the tabbed shoulder-wings and the baroque
pendant jewel with attached pearl chain.
The raised, lace-edged 'Medici' collar and
'Vandyke' cuffs indicate the extent of the
penetration into fancy dress of the
Henri IV styles in France.

revival of the draped overskirt of the early seventeenth century, as worn, for
example, by Helena Fourment in the portrait by Rubens. The feathered hat
worn by Rubens's wife inspired the large picture hat of the 1780s, often
referred to as a 'Rubens hat' in the fashion magazines of the period.

The 'Rubens's wife' costume was just one of the many versions of Vandyke
dress popular in the eighteenth century (it was, after all, from the same period
as Van Dyck's painting career in England). During the early to mid-
eighteenth century, it seems to have been an English fad, noted by Walpole
and others at masquerades as worn by both sexes: 'there were quantities of
pretty Vandykes and all kinds of old pictures walked out of their frame,'[78]
commented Walpole at a masquerade at Vauxhall (1742). Mrs Montagu had
her picture painted in the costume she wore at the jubilee masquerade at

Ranelagh in 1749, 'my dress white satin, fine new point for tuckers, kerchief and ruffles, pearl necklace and earrings and pearls and diamonds on the head, and my hair curled after the Vandyke picture'[79] – meaning that of Henrietta Maria, Charles I's queen. Most portraits of sitters in Vandyke dress adapted it to suit the fashionable style of long pointed waist and hooped skirt, but Ramsay's portrait of Lady Mary Coke (in a private Scottish collection) (1762) is a serious attempt to follow early-seventeenth-century fashion with its wide ribbon giving an impression of a high waist. Again through the offices of the drapery painter, the height of the popularity of the Vandyke style was in the middle years of the eighteenth century, when plain heavy silks and ringleted hairstyles echoed the 1630s. The *Lady's Magazine* for 1759 urged a return to the dress of this period with the 'short waste of our great-grandmothers' and the 'free dress of the hair', which was 'preferable to the prim and close curls we have adopted from the French'.[80]

Although patriotism may have been one of the reasons why fashionable English dress should have been inspired by the early rather than the current French modes, more important, probably, was a nostalgic hankering after a period just distant enough in time to be romantic but close enough to recall, through literature, the theatre (where Vandyke dresses had been worn from the early eighteenth century) and the many portraits copied by both professional and amateur artists. It was a great period for Sweden, too, under the patriotic king Gustavus Adolphus, and, as previously discussed, Vandyke dress formed the basis for the national costume adopted by Gustavus III.

But the success of the early seventeenth century as a theme for fancy-dress portraiture must be owing not just to the English taste for the romantic and picturesque, with an appreciation of the subtlety of historical allusion, but also to the popularity of the masquerade. Many young men were recorded in their Vandyke masquerade suits, such as Viscount Powderham at his coming-of-age party in 1790 (pl. 196); some on the Grand Tour in the 1760s and 1770s, may have taken with them a favourite Vandyke costume for the fashionable portraitist Batoni to copy in Rome. In addition, such costumes could easily be the stock-in-trade of certain artists; when Sylas Neville sat for a portrait in 1770 (to an artist called Sykes, a pupil of Thomas Hudson) he informed a correspondent that 'I am drawn in the Vandyke dress, the colour dark grey, sleeves and breast slashed with crimson', and he was gratified later to be told that 'two gentlemen have desired to be drawn in the same dress I am drawn in'.[81] Some artists were especially expert in depicting early-seventeenth-century satin and lace; Zoffany painted the English royal family (1770) and the Grand Duke of Tuscany and his family (1776) all in Vandyke dress.

By the 1770s, many fancy dress elements had entered fashionable costume: in 1774, Walpole wrote to Sir William Hamilton that, 'If you were to come over, you would find us a general masquerade. The macaronis, not content with producing new fashions every day, and who are great reformers, are going to restore the Vandyke dress'.[82] It is hard to estimate how far this was typical hyperbole on the part of Walpole, or whether, in fact, the romantic

This magnificent Vandyke costume of silvery white silk embroidered in silver, dark pink cloak lined with ermine, and white silk hat trimmed with ostrich feathers, hints at the wealth and status of the sitter, whose handsome and fashionable appearance was often noted by his countrymen abroad. This is probably the costume that he wore to a masquerade given in Rome in 1773 by the Countess of Albany, the wife of the Young Pretender.

196 R. Cosway, *William, third Viscount Courtenay*, 1791

Lord Courtenay was one of Cosway's patrons, and – like the artist – was noted for his extravagance and flamboyant behaviour. He is pictured here in the black and gold Vandyke costume that he wore during his coming-of-age festivities at Powderham Castle in 1790.

fever that was dominating women's fashions had begun to affect male costume; certainly the lightness and delicacy of early Stuart costume would have appealed to the macaronis. It was also a period when adult costume was being influenced by new developments in children's clothes: some boys wore Vandyke suits for sport (in particular for archery)[83] and some young men adopted this style as evidence, perhaps, of a precocious romantic 'sensibility', the forerunner of late-nineteenth-century aestheticism.

Many great artists had ambivalent attitudes towards fancy dress. Gainsborough, whose paintings sometimes achieve a sense of haunting melancholy typical of the work of Watteau, whom he so much admired, painted many of his young male sitters in a kind of composite Vandyke/Watteau/*commedia dell'arte* costume, but at the same time expressed his disapproval of 'the foolish custom of dressing people like Scaramouches'[84] (a character from the Italian comedy). On the subject of Vandyke dress, Reynolds noted in his *Discourse* of 1776 that: 'We all very well remember how common it was a few years ago for portraits to be drawn in this fantastic dress; and this custom is not yet entirely laid aside',[85] but he himself had attended masquerades, had even been painted in Vandyke dress (by Angelica Kauffmann in 1767) and knew the stubborn English preference for a familiar fancy dress rather than the 'timeless' classical allegories that he wished to promote.

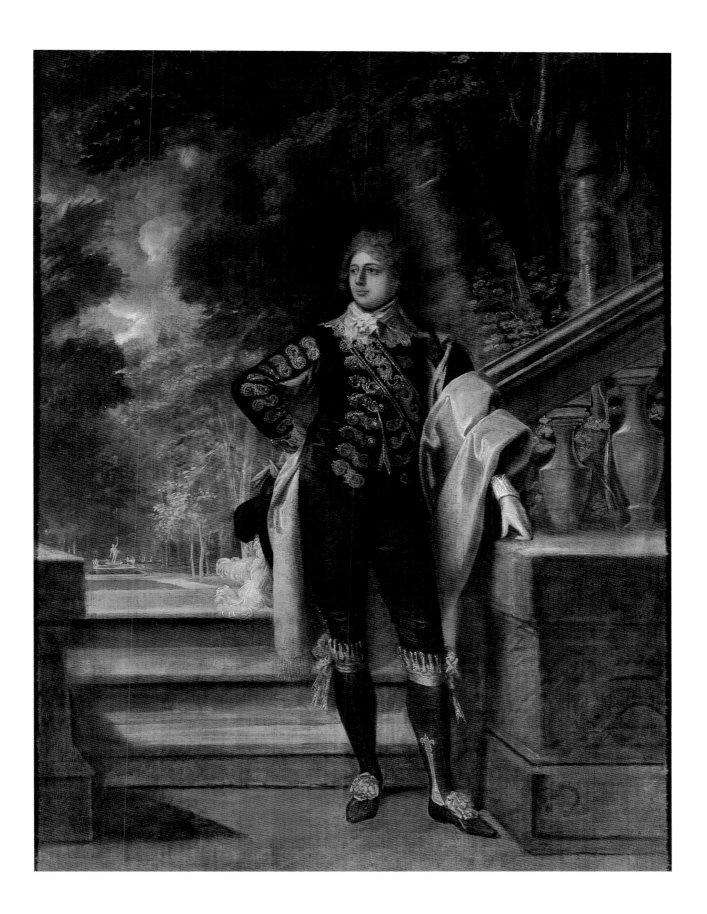

197 H. Morland, *The Fair Nun Unmasked*, c.1769

This beautiful painting may be an actual portrait, or it may be a comment on the scandalous reputation of the masquerade itself – the word 'nun' was eighteenth-century slang for a prostitute. Whatever its origin, it sums up the seductive appeal of this kind of fancy dress where 'disguise' served only to heighten the seduction of the image.

'L'histoire des modes n'est pas si frivole qu'on le croit; elle est en partie celle des moeurs' (The history of fashion is not as frivolous as people think; it is to a considerable extent the history of manners and morals), said Madame de Genlis; among fashions and the manners, the liking for dressing up, in fact and through the medium of the arts, is important in any consideration of the eighteenth century. It reflects a mood of optimistic romanticism, a sense of the attraction of the past and the exotic present, with no feeling of escape from the conventions of formal dress, but with an awareness of the possibilities of fantasy.

Conclusion

Paris is no longer what it was formerly. A threatening storm overcasts its horizon and darkens the splendour of this city, so magnificent formerly. Golden luxury, which resided here on its favorite spot, has covered its face with a sable veil, and has fled to distant regions.

N. M. Karamzin, 1790

ALTHOUGH ONE MUST AVOID presenting the eighteenth century as the last flowering of the *ancien régime*, leading inexorably to the French Revolution, there is much to be said for ending a study of the period with the year 1789.

In May of that year, Louis XVI was forced to convoke the States General, the historical representatives of the French people, which had last met in 1614. No hint of any alteration in the status quo was expressed in the orders that were sent out by the marquis de Brézé, the grand Maître des Cérémonies de France, for the costume to be worn by the three Estates at the opening of the formal proceedings. The nobility (the First Estate) wore black silk suits and cloaks embroidered with gold, white stockings, plumed hats in the style of Henri IV and swords, the insignia of their rank. The costume of the Second Estate ranged from the simple soutane and 'manteau long et bonnet carré' of the parish clergy, to the scarlet and violet of cardinals and bishops. The Third Estate, which comprised half of the deputies and represented the vast majority of the population, wore plain black cloth suits and cloaks, untrimmed hats, black stockings and thick muslin cravats.

The States General spent almost two months arguing about whether they were to vote by order, which would have meant that the Third Estate would have been outvoted automatically by the other two privileged orders; finally, on 17 June, the Third Estate seized power and proclaimed itself the National Assembly, setting in motion the gradual collapse of the old order.

Arthur Young was in Paris for the first historic meeting of the National Assembly and his account of the appearance of the newly powerful deputies reflects the links, which contemporaries had noted, between the discarding of the formal clothing of the old society and a brave new world of political freedom. 'Many of them', he noted, were 'without powder in their hair and some in boots; not above four or five were neatly dressed. How times are changed. When they had nothing better to attend to, the fashionable Parisians were correctness itself in all that pertained to the toilette, and were therefore thought a frivolous people; but now they have something of more importance than dress to occupy them, and the light airy character that was usually given them will have no foundation in truth.'[1]

Yet in 1789 there was a curious juxtaposition between the formal and the informal, between the present and the future. The court continued as before with formal presentations, and the marquise de La Tour du Pin entertained at Versailles the members of the National Assembly who were in full dress, including Robespierre, nattily attired in an apple-green suit, with a carefully powdered white wig.[2]

It has been noted that no abrupt change in clothing marked the 1789 revolution. For women, the modes set in Paris continued to be as inconstant and expensive as if the storming of the Bastille had never taken place; for men, although the *habit français* continued as formal wear, from the 1780s a kind of informality in dress had entered France and the rest of Europe from England. After 1789, no major developments in dress occurred until the mid-1790s. Nathaniel Wraxall, writing his memoirs in 1815, remembered that his first winter in London (1776–7) was a period 'which is now so distant, and the Manners, as well as the Inhabitants of the Metropolis have undergone since that Time so total a change, that they no longer preserve almost any similarity'. For him, it was in 1793, the year of the execution of the French monarchy and the 'Æra of Jacobinism', that significant changes occurred: 'Pantaloons, cropped Hair, and Shoe-strings . . . the total abolition of Buckles and Ruffles . . . the disuse of Hair-powder' for the men, and for the women the cutting of their hair and the wearing of a 'Drapery more suited to the Climate of Greece or of Italy than to the temperature of an Island situate in the fifty-first Degree of Latitude'.[3]

The events of 1789 not only quickened the pace of the change in clothing but also men's perceptions of how dress was linked to the rapidly altering face of politics; for the next few tumultuous years, continual change became a normal part of human existence, and contemporaries realized that the break with the feudal tradition was final.

The Persian or Chinese philosopher, the alter ego of so many eighteenth-century writers, would have had no difficulty in recognizing that the Europe of 1715 was fundamentally the same political and social entity until the Revolution. He would have agreed with the Frenchman J.-F. Sobry, who, writing in 1786, emphasized how far clothing 'est mis au rang des choses publiques' (is part of public welfare); clothes played the most vital role in defining man and his part in society, to an extent that we cannot contemplate today. Every period has its negative aspects, and the potential for greater social and political fulfilment was unrealized for the mass of the population in the eighteenth century. However, the eighteenth century, in its essentially urbane, civilized and moderate way, attained a perfection never since achieved in all the decorative arts, including dress. Anyone regretting its vanished grace would agree with Ben Jonson (talking of the Stuart masque) that: 'Only the envie was that it lasted not still, or (now it is past), cannot by imagination, much lesse description, be recovered to a part of that spirit it had in the gliding by.'

Notes

Introduction

1 G. Rudé in *Europe in the Eighteenth Century* (1972) calculates that in the eighteenth century between seventy and eighty per cent of the population gained their living from the land.

2 Although the first official portrait of Philip V, painted in France by Hyacinthe Rigaud, shows him in the *golilla*, which he wore until 1703. See H. Kamen *Philip V of Spain*, New Haven and London 2001, p. 9.

3 N. Boyle, *Goethe: The Poet and the Age*, 1: *The Poetry of Desire 1749–1790*, Oxford 1991, p. 8.

4 Nugent, 1778, II, p. 1.

5 [Frederick the Great], *Memoirs of the House of Brandenburg From the Earliest Accounts to the Death of Frederick I, King of Prussia, By the Hand of a Master*, London 1751, p. 241. The author noted that under Frederick I, Berlin was the Athens of the North, but under his successor Frederick William I, it became the Sparta (p. 243).

6 Caraccioli, 1772, p. 420.

7 Baretti, 1770, I, p. 10.

8 *The Present State of the Court of France, and City of Paris, in a Letter from Monsieur M★★★ to the Honourable Matthew Prior*, London 1712, p. 43.

9 Quoted in Bruford, 1935, p. 48.

10 Quoted in George, 1953, p. 29.

11 *Present State of the Court of France*, 1712, p. 21.

12 Chesterfield, 1901, I, pp. 305–306.

13 Ségur, 1803, III, p. 7.

14 Quoted in Glenbervie, 1928, I, p. 39.

15 Bermingham and Brewer, 1995, p. 3.

Chapter 1

1 *Mercure de France*, Paris 1729, p. 619.

2 Boehn, 1921, II, p. 487.

3 Delany, 1861–2, I, p. 193.

4 *Mercure de France*, 1729, p. 619.

5 Delany, 1861–2, II, p. 28.

6 Boehn, 1921, II, pp. 487–8.

7 The term 'bizarre' was first coined by W. Sloman in his *Bizarre Designs in Silks*, Copenhagen 1953.

8 Saint-Simon, 1967–72, p. 123. The order was that of Saint Andrew, founded by Peter the Great in 1699 to celebrate victory over Sweden.

9 Saint-Simon, 1967–72, p. 326.

10 H. Walpole, *Reminiscences written in 1788 for the Amusement of Miss Mary and Miss Agnes Berry*, London 1805, p. 6. The 'blue ribband' was the sash of the Order of the Garter.

11 J. Macky, *A Journey through England*, London 1722, p. 238.

12 Saussure, 1902, p. 112.

13 Pöllnitz, 1745, III, p. 289.

14 Gay, 1716, p. 4.

15 Defoe, 1724–6, I, p. 93. On the popularity of cottons in England, see B. Lemire, *Fashion's Favourite: The Cotton Trade and the Consumer in Britain 1600–1800*, Oxford 1991.

16 Campbell, 1842, II, p. 459.

17 The gown is in the collection of the Wadsworth Atheneum, Hartford, Conn. The portrait is owned by the Connecticut Historical Society, Hartford, Conn.

18 Northumberland, 1926, p. 173.

19 See M. Swain, 'Nightgown into Dressing Gown, A Study of Men's Nightgowns', in *Costume*, 6, 1972, pp. 14–15.

20 Pöllnitz, 1745, III, p. 200.

21 Baretti, 1770, I, p. 326.

22 Purefoy 1931, II, p. 304.

23 The word 'cravat' has attracted some attention. One theory regarding its origin is that it represents the adoption by French soldiers in the Thirty Years War of a central European style (as worn by Croats). However, it seems more likely that this kind of neckcloth was already in use in western Europe, and that the name comes from the French 'rabat' lace collar.

24 R. Holme, *An Academy of Armory*, 2 vols, Chester 1688, II, p. 17.

25 *The Present State of the Court of France, and City of Paris, in a Letter from Monsieur M★★★ to the Honourable Matthew Prior*, London 1712, p. 56.

26 Ibid., p. 36.

27 Mrs Delany, 1861–2, I, p. 193.

28 Saussure, 1902, p. 112.

29 La Motraye, 1732, p. 108.

30 Holme, *Academy of Armory*, II, p. 19.

31 *Present State of the Court of France*, 1712, p. 16.

32 Orléans, 1970, p. 235.

33 Number T 2594.C.1 in the Germanisches Nationalmuseum.

34 Orléans, 1970, p. 238.

35 Delany, 1861–2, II, p. 452.

36 P. de Marivaux, *Pièces détachées écrites dans le goût du Spectateur François*, 2 vols, Paris 1728, II, p. 510.

37 Mercure de France, 1729, p. 611.

38 Purefoy, II, p. 303.

39 The Second Eclogue (Tuesday); there were six eclogues, one for each day of the week from Monday to Saturday. There is some doubt about the authorship; the author of a recent biography of Lady Mary Wortley Montagu thinks they were probably hers, but 'more than one mind went to their shaping'. See Grundy, 1999, p. 104.

40 R. Halsband, *Lord Hervey, Eighteenth Century Courtier*, London 1973, p. 219.

41 'An Inventory of Margaret Cavendishe, Duchess of Portland's weding cloaths and linen, July 11th, 1734', in *Calendar of MSS of the Marquis of Bath, Longleat*, Historical Manuscripts Commission, London 1904, I, p. 361.

42 Delany, 1861–2, II, pp. 27–8.

43 Ward, 1775, p. 39.

44 Delany, 1861–2, I, pp. 427–8.

45 *Ibid.*, p. 198. On the subject of lace-patterned silks, it has been noted that there was also some evidence of silk designs influencing the design of lace; 'bizarre' elements, for example, can be traced in some Brussels lace. See S. Levey, 'Lace and lace-patterned silks: some comparative illustrations', in *Studies in Textile History in memory of H. B. Burnham*, ed. V. Gervers, Royal Ontario Museum, 1977.

46 Delany, 1861–2, I, p. 99.

47 N. Rothstein, 'God Bless this Choye', in *Costume*, 11, 1977, p. 99. For eighteenth-century silk design in general, see N.

Rothstein, *Silk Designs of the Eighteenth Century in the Collection of the Victoria and Albert Museum*, London 1990; also G. Vrignaud, *Vêture et parure en France au dix-huitième siècle*, Paris 1995.

48 Delany, 1861–2, I, p. 428.

49 *Mercure de France*, 1729, p. 611.

50 Barbier, 1857, II, p. 37 *et seq.*

51 There were also stays called 'jumps', lightly boned up the front and thus allowing self-lacing, obviating the need for the help of a lady's maid; these were worn by women in pregnancy.

52 Pöllnitz, 1745, III, p. 287.

53 Nisbet Bain, 1897, p. 109.

54 On riding habits in England, see C. Blackman, 'Walking Amazons: The Development of the Riding Habit in England during the Eighteenth Century', in *Costume*, 35, 2001.

55 T. Smollett, *Memoirs of a Lady of Quality* (incorporated into the novel *Peregrine Pickle*), 1751, III, p. 108.

56 *Present State of the Court of France*, 1712, p. 16.

57 *The Art of Dress*, London 1717, p. 25.

58 Gay, 1716, p. 14.

59 Pöllnitz, 1745, V, pp. 221–2.

60 *Mercure de France*, 1729, pp. 613–4.

61 Montagu 1965–7, I, p. 265.

62 The Fifth Eclogue (Friday).

63 T. Scott (ed.), *The Prose Works of Jonathan Swift*, London 1897, II, p. 285.

64 Saint-Simon, 1972, p. 230.

65 D. de Marly, 'The Vocabulary of the female headdress 1678–1713', in *Waffen-und-Kostümkunde*, 17, 1975.

66 Saussure, 1902, p. 204. Ribbons were often thought of as particularly French; Mrs Delany remarked in 1729 that the Duchess of Richmond had returned from Paris in the French mode, 'her head (i.e. headdress) was yellow gauze and lappets tied with puffs of scarlet ribbon' (Delany, 1861–2, I, p. 224).

67 *Mercure de France*, 1729, p. 615.

Chapter 2

1 *The Present State of the Court of France, and City of Paris, in a Letter from Monsieur M*** to the Honourable Matthew Prior*, London 1712, p. 45.

2 Karamzin, 1803, II, p. 223.

3 Pyne, *Wine and Walnuts*, London 1823, I, p. 89.

4 *Ibid.*, pp. 90–91.

5 Mercier, 1782–8, VI, p. 112.

6 Saussure, 1902, p. 74 and p. 79.

7 Roche, 1933, p. 262.

8 Nugent, 1768, II, p. 316.

9 In some countries, Jews were obliged to wear yellow badges; Nugent's travel book for those undertaking the Grand Tour (1778) stated that along with other cities in Germany, the Frankfurt Jews 'are obliged to wear a piece of yellow cloth to distinguish them from the other inhabitants'. In the territories of the Holy Roman Empire, the badge was abolished by order of Joseph II in 1765, but it was worn in Italy until 1816. In eastern Europe, the Jews adopted as another distinguishing mark the caftan and fur-trimmed hat, which had been traditional Russian costume until abolished by Peter the Great; but in western Europe, most Jews wore versions of fashionable dress. In Holland and England there were no restrictions on dress, but many Jews wore long beards; Francis Place (Place Collections, B.M. Add. MS 27827, p. 144) recalled that Jewish sellers of old clothes were easily recognizable by their shabby clothes and beards and were often baited in the streets until Daniel Mendoza set up in about 1787 a boxing school where they could learn to defend themselves.

10 Grundy, 1999, p. 128.

11 Thornton, 1965, p. 80.

12 Stirling, 1911, I, p. 325.

13 Eloffe, 1885, I, p. 325.

14 For information (not always accurate at times) about Rose Bertin's life and clients, see Langlade, 1911. For an up-to-date analysis of Bertin's career, see the forthcoming Ph.D. by K. Chrisman 'Minister of Fashion: Marie-Jeanne "Rose" Bertin 1747–1813', University of Aberdeen 2002.

15 Lady Mary Wortley Montagu was amazed at the vast hooped skirts worn at court in Vienna: 'Their whalebone petticoats out-do ours by several yards Circumference and cover some Acres of Ground', she declared in a letter to her sister Frances (Grundy, 1999, p. 123).

16 Owned by the Victoria and Albert Museum (T.219.1973). Published as *Barbara Johnson's Album of Fashions and Fabrics*, ed. N. Rothstein, London 1987.

17 See M. S. Boyce, 'The Barbier Manuscripts', in *Textile History*, 12, 1981.

18 Coke, 1889, II, p. 117.

19 Smollett, 1766, I, p. 60.

20 Smollett, 1753, I, p. 215.

21 Coke, 1889, II, p. 288.

22 Mercier, 1782–8, II, p. 125.

23 Brosses, 1897, p. 69.

24 Vaussard, 1962, p. 202.

25 Quoted in Winslow, 1894, p. 115. One such doll was thrown into the sea at the Boston Tea Party in 1773, and is now in the collection of the Bostonian Society. Most dolls were thoroughly used by metropolitan and then local dress-makers; they were then often passed on to children and consequently only a relatively small number have survived.

26 *Lady's Magazine*, 1773, p. 199.

27 For information on the *Gallerie des Modes et Costumes Français*, and other French fashion plates of the eighteenth century, see R. Gaudriault, *Répertoire de la gravure de mode française des origines à 1815*, Paris 1988.

28 Fielding, 1967, p. 108.

29 Russel, 1750, I, p. 4.

30 D. Yarwood, *Robert Adam*, London, 1970, p. 53.

31 R. Campbell, *The London Tradesman*, London 1747, p. 1992.

32 See M. Ginsburg, 'The Tailoring and Dressmaking Trades 1700–1850', in *Costume*, 6, 1972, p. 64 and p. 67.

33 Purefoy, 1931, I, p. 297.

34 See P. A. Parmal, 'Fashion and the Growing Importance of the Marchande des Modes in Mid-Eighteenth-Century France', in *Costume*, 31, 1997.

35 Langlade, 1911, p. 36.

36 Oberkirch, 1852, II, p. 102.

37 A. Varron, 'Great Paris Fashion Artists', *Ciba Review*, XXV, 1939, p. 898.

38 La Tour du Pin, 1951, p. 40.

39 White, 1895, II, p. 36.

40 Coke, 1889, II, p. 57 and p. 61.

41 Campbell, *London Tradesman*, 1747, p. 207.

42 See P. Clabburn, 'A Provincial Milliner's Shop in 1785', in *Costume*, 11, 1977. This article lists some of the goods in an inventory made when the owner went bankrupt; they include a wide range of fabrics and some ready-made items such as stays, shirts, cloaks and cardinals that could have been made up on the premises from the shop's stock.

43 Campbell, *London Tradesman*, 1747, pp. 224–5.

44 *Ibid.*, p. 147.

45 C. G. de Saint-Aubin, *L'Art du Brodeur*, Paris 1770, p. 10.

46 Barbier, 1857, I, p. 200.

47 Delany, 1861–2, II, p. 72.

48 Richardson, 1768, II, p. 28.

49 Banks Collection, British Museum. In recent years, scholars have begun to pay more attention to the growth of the ready-to-wear industry in England. See, for example, A. Ribeiro, 'Provision of Ready-Made and Second-Hand Clothing in the Eighteenth Century in England', in *Per una storia della moda pronta: Problemi e Ricerche*, intr. G. Butazzi, Florence 1991. An article by J. Styles, 'Product Innovation in Early Modern London', *Past and Present*, 168, 2000, touches upon this subject.

50 J. Arnold, 'A mantua *c.*1708–9', *Costume*, 4, 1970, p. 27.

51 White, 1895, II, p. 36.

52 For information on the trousseaus of German princesses, see Boehn, 1921, II, p. 498. It was customary for female members of the imperial Austrian family to donate their wedding clothes to religious foundations; the silver brocade dresses of the archduchesses Maria Josepha (1720) and Amalie (1723) were given to the Heimsuchung Mariae Cloister in Vienna, to be made into liturgical vestments. See D. Heinz, *Meisterwerke Barocker Textilkunst*, Osterreichisches Museum für angewandte Kunst, Vienna 1972.

53 Piozzi, 1789, I, p. 102.

54 Delany, 1861–2, III, p. 400.

55 Wraxall, 1799, I, p. 109.

56 Nugent, 1768, II, p. 295.

57 Smollett, 1766, p. 97.

58 P. J. Grosley, 1772, I, p. 106.

59 Hickey, 1913, II, p. 253.

60 Smollett, 1766, p. 97.

61 Eloffe, 1885, I, p. 136.

62 Casanova, 1940, III, p. 192. Casanova, who was in gaol in Venice at this time (1756), was able from this tinder to make a lamp to lighten his captivity.

63 Grosley, 1772, I, p. 45.

64 Smollett, 1771, I, p. 84.

65 McClellan, 1904, reprinted 1969, p. 154.

66 A. Mansfield, 'Dyeing and cleaning clothes in the late eighteenth and early nineteenth centuries', in *Costume*, 2, 1968, pp. 26–7.

67 Campan, 1823, I, p. 284.

68 In a discussion of the hierarchy of the second-hand clothes trade in Paris, Daniel Roche in his book *The Culture of Clothing: Dress and Fashion in the Ancien Régime*, Cambridge 1994 makes a distinction between the *fripiers* who cleaned garments as well as dealing in second-hand and ready-made garments, and the *revendeurs/*

revendeuses, of lower status, who could only buy and sell old clothes, which had often been stolen (p. 343 et seq.). An accepted perk of body servants (personal maids and valets) in the eighteenth century was the money raised from the sale of their masters' or mistresses' clothes when they were dispensed with. Madame de Pompadour left nine trunks of clothes to her servants; see J. Cordrey (ed), *Inventaire des Biens de Madame de Pompadour*, Paris 1939. Perhaps some of these garments fetched up at the fashionable fripier for elite second-hand clothes, Longprix's shop in the rue Saint-Honoré in Paris.

69 On the second-hand clothes trade in England, see B. Lemire, 'Peddling Fashion: Salesmen, Pawnbrokers, Taylors, Thieves and the Second-hand Clothes Trade in England, *c.*1700–1800', *Textile History*, 22, 1981. See also E. C. Sanderson, 'Nearly New: The Second-hand Clothing Trade in Eighteenth-Century Edinburgh', in *Costume*, 31, 1997.

70 Gay, 1716, p. 57.

71 Campbell, *London Tradesman*, 1747, p. 301.

72 Adams, 1848, p. 221.

73 *Ibid.*, p. 107.

74 Richardson, 1740, I, p. 60. See also A. Buck 'Pamela's Clothes', in *Costume*, 26, 1992.

75 Delany, 1861–2, III, p. 371.

76 Coxe, 1790, III, p. 135.

77 Such hard-wearing gowns were often the 'undress' wear of impoverished clergymen and schoolmasters; Smollett's novel *Roderick Random* (1748) has a description of a poor schoolmaster 'dressed in a nightgown of plaid, fastened about his middle with a serjeant's old sash'. John Holker's sample book of about 1750 (Musée des arts décoratifs, Paris) includes a collection of linen and cotton checks and plaid of twilled worsted, which could be used for Scottish regimental uniforms as well as men's dressing gowns.

78 Macartney, 1768, p. 42.

79 See, for example, the archives of the 'Florida' parishes (the name given to a section of Louisiana which from 1779 to 1810 was under Spanish rule), transcribed copies of which are deposited at the Louisiana State University, Baton Rouge.

80 Bocage, 1770, I, p. 61.

81 Smollett, 1767, p. 35.

82 British Library, Add. MS 27827, Place Collections, vol. XXXIX, pp. 50–52.

83 For a discussion of short gowns, see C.

Kidwell's article 'Short Gowns', *Dress*, 4, 1978. On the use of such short gowns by members of the middle-class and gentry, see C. Rose, 'A Group of Embroidered Eighteenth-Century Bedgowns', *Costume*, 30, 1996.

84 Eden, 1797, I, p. 557. Eden's work is very useful for the amount and breadth of data he collected, but there is a moral agenda implicit in his discussion of the differences, in terms of clothing, between the north and the south of England, a somewhat exaggerated claim for self-sufficiency by the former, and an over-reliance on outside commerce and extravagance on the part of the latter. See J. Styles, 'Clothing the North: The Supply of Non-elite Clothing in the Eighteenth-Century North of England', in *Textile History*, 25, 1994.

85 R. Cobb, *Death in Paris 1795–1801*, Oxford 1978, p. 73 et seq.

Chapter 3

1 Campbell, 1842, I, p. 90.

2 Boehn, 1921, II, p. 486.

3 Prussia, 1812, I, p. 119.

4 *Idée de la personne, de la manière de vivre et de la Cour du roy de Prusse*, London 1752, p. 4.

5 La Motraye, 1732, p. 107.

6 Nugent, 1768, I, p. 58. The garment was called a *huik* or *heuke*.

7 Nugent, 1778, II, p. 56.

8 *Ibid*.

9 Montagu, 1965–7, I, p. 255.

10 Bruford, 1935, p. 220.

11 Nugent, 1768, p. 61.

12 Boehn, 1921, p. 506.

13 Keysler, 1758, I, p. 126.

14 Piozzi, 1789, II, p. 279.

15 Nugent, 1768, p. 122.

16 For detailed account of Swiss sumptuary legislation, see J. M. Vincent, *Costume and Conduct in the Laws of Basel, Bern and Zurich, 1370–1800*, Baltimore 1935.

17 Keysler, 1758, I, p. 4.

18 Karamzin, 1803, II, p. 9.

19 Moore, 1779, I, p. 322.

20 *Ibid*.

21 Vehse, 1856, II, p. 308.

22 Nugent, 1778, II, p. 255.

23 Piozzi, 1789, II, p. 318.

24 A useful summary of Hungarian costume can be found in the catalogue of an exhibition held at the Whitworth Art

Gallery, University of Manchester, June–August 1979, *Historic Hungarian Costume from Budapest*.

25 Montagu, 1965–7, I, p. 303.

26 Keysler, 1758, IV, p. 73.

27 Wraxall, 1799, I, p. 377.

28 *Ibid*, II, p. 10 *et seq.*

29 *Ibid.*, I, p. 396.

30 Nisbet Bain, 1909, p. 33.

31 Wraxall, 1799, II, p. 113.

32 Perry, 1716, p. 197.

33 *Ibid.* Caftans, of embroidered or woven silks (damasks, brocades), were still worn by members of the court and nobility; some belonging to Peter the Great survive in The Hermitage, St. Petersburg.

34 Nisbet Bain, 1897, p. 196.

35 Macartney, 1768, p. 50.

36 *Ibid.*, p. 147.

37 J. G. Korb, *The Diary of an Austrian Secretary of Legation, at the Court of Czar Peter the Great*, trans. C. MacDonnell, London 1863, II, p. 206.

38 Ward, 1777, p. 39. The author, a clergyman's daughter, married first Thomas Ward, Consul General to Russia (1728), and secondly Claudius Rondeau, the English Resident at the Russian Court (1731).

39 Swinton, 1792, p. 227.

40 Coxe, 1790, I, p. 488.

41 Swinton, 1792, p. 195.

42 J. Bell, *A Journey from St Petersburg to Pekin, 1719–22*, ed. and intr. J. L. Stevenson, Edinburgh 1965, p. 66 *et seq.*

43 Coxe, 1784, I, p. 253 and II, p. 95.

44 Marshall, 1772–6, III, p. 98.

45 Coxe, 1784, II, p. 527.

46 Nugent, 1778, I, p. 41.

47 Woodforde, 1924–31, I, p. 188.

48 Adams, 1848, p. 303.

49 Fithian, 1900, p. 58.

50 E. Burt, *Letters from a Gentleman in the North of Scotland to his Friend in London*, London 1754, p. 100.

51 Miège, 1715, p. 38.

52 Smollett, 1771, III, p. 20.

53 Melville, 1924, p. 147.

54 Miège, 1715, p. 5.

55 Baretti, 1769, II, p. 208.

56 Nugent, 1778, III, p. 17.

57 *Ibid.*, III, p. 79.

58 Baretti, 1769, II, p. 206.

59 Brosses, 1897, p. 31.

60 Piozzi, 1789, I, p. 184.

61 Keysler, 1758, III, p. 274.

62 Molmenti, 1908, I, p. 215.

63 Baretti, 1769, II, p. 206.

64 See Harvey, 1995.

65 Brosses, 1897, p. 69.

66 Labat, 1730, V, pp. 206–7.

67 J. Houel, *Voyage Pittoresque des Isles de Sicile*, 4 vols, Paris 1782, I, p. 3.

68 Piozzi, 1789, II, p. 31.

69 *Ibid.*, I, p. 40.

70 White, 1841, II, p. 265.

71 Piozzi, 1789, II, p. 306.

72 Labat, 1730, II, p. 271.

73 Townsend, 1791, I, p. 333.

74 P.-A. C. de Beaumarchais, *Le Barbier de Séville*, Paris 1775.

75 Swinburne, 1779, p. 334.

76 Baretti, 1770, II, p. 92.

77 Townsend, 1791, I, p. 335. On the subject of the dress of Spanish women, see the essay by A. Ribeiro 'Fashioning the Feminine: dress in Goya's portraits of women', in *Goya: Images of Women*, National Gallery of Art, Washington 2002.

78 Baretti, 1770, II, p. 103.

79 *Ibid.* On the dress of the *majo/maja*, see S. Worth, 'Andalusian Dress and the Image of Spain 1759–1936', Ph.D., Ohio State University 1990.

80 Twiss, 1775, p. 281.

81 Baretti, 1770, II, p. 410.

82 Twiss, 1775, p. 28.

83 *Ibid.*, p. 33.

Chapter 4

1 Boswell, 1952, p. 270.

2 See Buck, 1979, p. 157.

3 Delany 1861–2, III, p. 250.

4 Fielding, 1967, p. 108.

5 Smollett, 1895, p. 239.

6 *Ibid.*, p. 311.

7 M. Sexé, *Histoire d'une Famille et d'une Industrie pendant deux siècles 1723–1923*, Paris 1923, p. 12.

8 Coke, 1889, III, p. 176. On the eighteenth-century use of fur, see A. Ribeiro, 'Furs in Fashion' in *Connoisseur*, 202, 1979.

9 Boswell, 1952, pp. 395–6.

10 *World*, London 1753, 17, p. 101.

11 *Gray's Inn Journal*, quoted in C. W. and P. Cunnington, revised ed., 1972, p. 17.

12 Garsault, 1769, p. 9 and p. 18.

13 Boswell, 1953, p. 217.

14 *London Chronicle*, 1762, II, p. 167.

15 McClellan, 1969, p. 228.

16 British Library Add. MS 27827, vol. 39, p. 167. On Hanway and the history of umbrellas, see A. Ribeiro, 'Men and Umbrellas in the Eighteenth Century',

in *Royal Society of Arts Journal*, CXXXIV, 1986.

17 See, for example, the accounts of George, Prince of Wales, later George IV, which indicate his extensive purchases of scents, perfumed powder and so on; see C. Hibbert, *George IV, Prince of Wales*, London 1972, p. 175.

18 Catherine II, 1955, p. 179.

19 Fairholt, 1849, p. 233.

20 Moore, 1779, II, p. 246.

21 Pyne, 1823, I, p. 30.

22 Ségur, 1825–7, III, p. 463.

23 Karamzin, 1803, III, p. 212.

24 *London Chronicle*, 1762, p. 167.

25 Keysler, 1758, IV, p. 103.

26 Richardson, 1768, III, p. 28.

27 Delany, 1861–2, II, p. 200.

28 *Ibid.*, p. 447.

29 *Ibid.*, p. 487.

30 *British Magazine*, London 1746, I, p. 257.

31 Delany, 1861–2, III, p. 300.

32 O. Goldsmith, *The Bee*, London 1759, II, p. 39.

33 *Female Tatler*, London 1761, p. 439.

34 J. Cordrey, ed., *Inventaire des Biens de Madame de Pompadour*, Paris 1939, p. 76.

35 *Ibid.*, p. 75. In the same trunk was a gown with 'Turkish' embroidery, 'une robbe de chambre et son tablier, broderie de Turquie, fond blanc, bordé d'un petit lizeré d'or' (a *robe de chambre* with Turkish embroidery on a white ground, with a border of figured gold).

36 Walpole, 1903–15, V, pp. 167–8. This edition of Walpole's letters has largely been replaced by the Yale edition (1937–83), which is arranged by Walpole's correspondents. However, the chronological sequence of Paget Toynbee's edition, while containing a number of inaccuracies and omissions, is still useful for the narrative of Walpole's life and times.

37 Catherine II, 1955, p. 181.

38 Bielfeld, 1768–70, I, p. 190.

39 Nugent, 1768, II, p. 254.

40 Goldsmith, 1766, p. 121.

41 Delany, 1861–2, III, p. 321.

42 Ribeiro, 'Furs in Fashion', in *Connoisseur*, 202, 1979, p. 229.

43 R. Blunt, ed., *Mrs Montagu, Her Letters and Friendships 1762–1800*, London 1923, I, p. 218.

44 Russel, 1750, I, p. 3.

45 Ward, 1777, p. 31.

46 Weber, 1723, I, p. 148.

47 Le Camus, 1754, p. 151.

48 *The Art of Dress*, 1717, p. 18.

49 Nugent, 1778, III, p. 16.

50 Catherine II, 1955, p. 113. Even the women from the city had to wear black perukes when they appeared at court; they wore them over their own hair, which 'pushed the perukes upwards', in contrast with those worn by the ladies of the court that at least 'were better fitted to their heads'.

51 *Ibid.*, p. 67.

52 *Female Spectator*, London, 1744, III, p. 161.

53 Lennox, 1901, p. 178.

54 Smollett, 1766, I, p. 105.

55 *Oxford Gazette and Reading Mercury*, 456, 29 July 1754.

56 Delany, 1861–2, III, p. 300.

57 Walpole, III, p. 314.

58 *London Chronicle*, 1762, p. 167.

59 W. Hogarth, *The Analysis of Beauty*, ed. J. Burke, Oxford 1955, p. 174.

60 Lennox, 1901, I, p. 177.

61 Coke, 1899, p. 123.

62 For a complete list of the jewellery belonging to the Dauphine, see The 1767 *Inventaire de Marie-Josèphe de Saxe, Dauphine de France*, ed. G. Bapst, Paris 1883.

63 Prussia, 1812, I, p. 43.

64 D. Jeffries, *A Treatise on Diamonds and Pearls*, London 1750; 'diamonds', he says in his introduction, 'are the chief ornaments of great and distinguished personages'. See also A. Ribeiro, 'Eighteenth-century Jewellery in England', *Connoisseur*, 199, 1978.

65 Delany, 1861–2, III, p. 400.

66 Walpole, 1903–15, III, p. 264.

67 Richardson, 1740, I, p. 61.

68 Smith, 1829, I, pp. 16–17.

Chapter 5

1 Barbier, 1857, I, p. 379.

2 Coxe, 1784, I, p. 247.

3 Goethe, 1892, p. 495.

4 Baretti, 1770, I, p. 43.

5 Decremps, 1789, I, p. 89. See also A. Ribeiro, 'Fashion in the Eighteenth Century: Some Anglo-French Comparisons', in N. Harte (ed.), *Fabrics and Fashions: Studies in the economic and social history of dress*, Pasold Research Fund, London 1991.

6 Smollett, 1771, II, p. 202.

7 Richardson, 1768, IV, p. 92.

8 Goldsmith, 1762, I, p. 235.

9 B. Mandeville, *The Fable of the Bees*, London 1714, p. 105.

10 *Ibid.*, p. 106.

11 See Weatherill, 1988. Daniel Roche posits a struggle 'between a society of civility, in which clothing revealed a person's social and moral condition, and a society of consumption, in which emulation undermined hierarchical representations . . .'. (*France in the Enlightenment*, trans. A. Goldhammer, Cambridge, Mass. 1998, p. 559).

12 Smollett, 1771, II, p. 237.

13 *Ibid.*, I, p. 98.

14 'Say what she would, protest, argue, and harangue, sacks were left off, ostrich-feathers worn, and a thousand fantastic dresses invented . . . the hoop vanished after the sack, and like Tilburina's confidante, everybody ran mad in white linen', J. A. Home (ed.), *Lady Louisa Stuart, Selections from her Manuscripts*, Edinburgh 1899, p. 143.

15 Piozzi, 1789, II, p. 280.

16 Goethe, 1892, p. 238.

17 Prussia, 1812, I, p. 347.

18 *The Art of Dress*, London 1717, p. 21.

19 *Lady's Magazine*, London 1773, pp. 140–1.

20 Andrews, 1770, II, p. 36.

21 *Connoisseur*, London 1754, p. 5.

22 Grosley, 1772, p. 253.

23 P. C. de Laclos, *Les Liaisons Dangereuses*, Paris 1782, English trans. London 1784, I, p. 19.

24 *Female Spectator*, London 1744, I, p. 241.

25 *The Present State of the Court of France, and City of Paris, in a Letter from Monsieur M★★★ to the Honourable Matthew Prior*, London 1712, p. 36.

26 Nash, said Goldsmith, 'was the first who difused a desire of society and an easiness of address among a whole people'; this he achieved at Bath by a series of regulations regarding conduct and clothing, and by his own example. See Barbeau, 1904.

27 *London Magazine*, London 1774, p. 213. So much were the bag-wigs and swords an essential part of formal dress that they were worn even in hot climates for 'state' occasions; Hickey, in Bengal in 1777, found that on the king's birthday, 'everybody, malgré the extreme heat, appeared in full dress with bags and swords'.

28 Hawkins, 1926, p. 32. In all fairness to Dr Johnson, infirmity helped to produce his peculiar gait.

29 Andrews, 1770, I, p. 78. Goethe found when he went to university at Strasbourg in 1770 that there were a number of aristocrats from all over Europe who 'have come to "perfect" themselves before they

can be allowed on the floor of the great metropolis, where every step, every gesture, every slightest trait is observed and ridiculed'. See Friedenthal, 1965.

30 Topham, 1776, p. 262 *et seq.*

31 Young, 1793, I, p. 53.

32 Bielfeld, 1768–70, IV, p. 162.

33 *Present State of the Court of France*, 1712, p. 48.

34 Fusil, 1841, I, p. 102 *et seq.*

35 Smollett, 1766, I, p. 114.

36 Fusil, 1841, I, p. 109.

37 Walpole, 1903–15, III, p. 13.

38 Fielding, 1967, p. 204.

39 *Memoirs and Correspondence of Madame d'Epinay*, trans. J. H. Freese, London 1897, II, p. 305.

40 Bocage, 1770, I, p. 37.

41 Smith, 1829, II, p. 402. On Cosway's personal use of dress, and dress in his art, see A. Ribeiro, 'Portraying the Fashion, Romancing the Past: Dress and the Cosways', in S. Lloyd, *Richard and Maria Cosway: Regency Artists of Taste and Fashion*, Scottish National Portrait Gallery, Edinburgh 1995.

42 Moore, 1779, II, p. 287. When the Prussians came to Dresden during the Seven Years War, they found his huge wardrobe, which included 1500 wigs, calling forth the comment from Frederick the Great, 'Wieviel Perrüquen für einen Menschen, der keinen Kopf hat!' (What a lot of wigs for a man who hasn't got a head on his shoulders!).

43 F. d'Hézecques, *Souvenirs d'un Page de la Cour de Louis XVI*, Paris 1873, p. 164 *et seq.*

44 Campan, 1823, I, p. 308 *et seq.*

45 Archives de France, No. AE16, No. 2. For a discussion of this sample book and Marie Antoinette's wardrobe, as well as the Queen's patronage of art and industry, see the exhibition catalogue *Les Atours de la Reine. Art et Commerce au service de Marie-Antoinette* Centre Historique des Archives Nationales, Paris, 2001.

46 Nisbet Bain, 1894, I, pp. 213–15. For the influence of French taste on Gustavus III, see B. Scott, 'Gustave III's love of Paris', *Apollo*, 92, 1970.

47 Cronin, 1978, p. 289 *et seq.*

48 J. M. Beattie, *The English Court in the Reign of George I*, Cambridge 1967, p. 51 *et seq.* Little in detail has been written on court dress in England in the eighteenth century. For a general survey, see N. Arch and J. Marschner, *Splendour at Court:*

Dressing for Royal Occasions since 1700, London 1987.

49 Burney, 1842–6, III, p. 28.

50 See Brocher, 1934.

51 Garsault, 1769, p. 55.

52 Eloffe, 1885, I, p. 98.

53 La Tour du Pin, 1951, p. 45 *et seq*.

54 Genlis, 1818, II, p. 40.

55 *The Memoirs of Jacques Casanova de Seingalt, 1725–1789*, trans. A. Machen, Edinburgh 1940, I, p. 270.

56 *Magazine à la Mode*, London 1777, p. 4.

57 Adams, 1848, p. 254.

58 Burney, 1842–6, II, pp. 190–1.

59 S. Siddons, *Reminiscences, 1773–1785*, ed. W. van Lennep, Cambridge, Mass. 1942, p. 21.

60 Vehse, 1856, II, p. 122 *et seq*.

61 Keysler, 1758, IV, p. 28.

62 L.-J.-A. de Bouillé, *Souvenirs et Fragments pour servir aux Mémoires de ma Vie et de mon Temps*, ed. P-L. de Kermaingant, Paris 1906–11, I, p. 72.

63 See P. Mansel, 'Monarchy, Uniform and the Rise of the Frac 1760–1830', *Past and Present*, 96, 1982, p. 111.

64 Coke, 1889, III, p. 344.

65 d'Hézecques, *Souvenirs d'un Page*, 1873, p. 189. In 1791, all the French orders of chivalry, including the Saint-Esprit, were abolished, except for the Order of Saint-Louis, awarded for bravery.

66 Not only did Gustavus design some of his own clothes, but he made a deliberate selection of garments that commemorated notable events in his life to be preserved in the Royal Wardrobe; these include his coronation tunic. See Rangström, 1997.

67 S. Sitwell, *German Baroque Art*, London 1927, p. 18.

68 Barbier, 1857, IV, p. 484.

69 See O. Morshead, 'The Windsor Uniform', *Connoisseur*, 95, 1935. More recent research by Sacha Llewellyn is briefly outlined in an article 'George III and the Windsor Uniform' in *The Court Historian: Newsletter of the Society for Court Studies*, 2, 1996. Examining the Accounts of the Master of the Robes at the Public Record Office, Llewellyn discovered that the idea of the Windsor uniform was first contemplated in July 1777, and it was ordered in the October of that year.

70 Stuart, 1926, p. 100.

71 Coxe, 1784, II, p. 328.

72 La Motraye, 1732, p. 399.

73 Northumberland, 1926, p. 31.

74 Prussia, 1812, I, p. 351.

75 See J. Arnold, 'A wedding dress worn by the Danish Princess Sophia Magdalena in 1766', *Costume*, 1, 1967.

76 La Tour du Pin, 1951, p. 38 *et seq*.

77 Burney, 1889, I, p. 16.

78 Walpole, 1903–15, IV, p. 265.

79 Richardson, 1740, II, p. 420.

80 E. M. Graham, *The Beautiful Mrs Graham*, London 1927, p. 92.

81 Smith, 1829, I, pp. 16–17.

82 Barbier, 1857, IV, p. 234 *et seq*.

83 *Ibid.*, IV, p. 326.

84 Walpole, 1903–15, IV, p. 457.

85 Montagu, 1965–7, I, p. 268.

86 Coke, 1889, III, p. 317.

87 Boswell, 1953, p. 129.

88 Delany, 1861–2, II, p. 478.

89 Woodforde, 1924–31, I, p. 109.

Chapter 6

1 See M. Delpierre, 'Marie Antoinette, reine de la mode', *Versailles*, 1975.

2 *Magazine à la Mode*, London 1777, p. 49.

3 Hawkins, 1936, p. 32.

4 *The Waiting City: Paris 1782–88* (translation from Mercier, 1782–8), ed. and trans. H. Simpson, London 1933, p. 88.

5 *The Pantheonites*, London 1773, p. 17.

6 Angelo, 1828, II, p. 379.

7 *Town and Country Magazine*, London 1772, p. 242. On the subject of the macaronis, see A. Ribeiro, 'The Macaronis', in *History Today*, 28, 1978 and V. Steele, 'The Social and Political Significance of Macaroni Fashion', in *Costume*, 19, 1985.

8 Hickey 1913, I, p. 139.

9 *Fashionable Magazine*, London 1786, p. 43.

10 In 1768, Goldsmith bought a coat of 'Tyrian bloom satin' (what the colour was is not clear, but he ordered the coat to wear with 'garter blue silk breeches' – see J. Prior *Life of Goldsmith*, London 1837, 2 vols). Boswell records in his *The Life of Samuel Johnson* (1791), that when Goldsmith bragged of his coat, he was crushed by Dr Johnson, whose description of the offending garment was 'strange-colour'!

11 McClellan, 1904, reprinted 1969 with intr. by R. Riley, p. 234.

12 Hickey, 1913, II, p. 261.

13 Moritz, 1924, p. 83.

14 Karamzin, 1803, III, p. 217.

15 Hickey, 1913, II, p. 261.

16 *Petit Dictionnaire de la Cour et de la Ville*, London 1788, no pagination.

17 Place, 1972, pp. 62–3.

18 A. R. d'Allemagne, *Les Accessoires du Costume et du Mobilier depuis de treizième jusqu'au milieu du dixneuvième siècle*, Paris 1928, I, p. 40. In 1776, a French jeweller, Dausse, obtained the monopoly of making cut-steel jewellery, and selling it.

19 Quoted in Eloffe 1885, I, p. 48.

20 Piozzi, 1789, I, p. 93.

21 'I am to be drawn of the size of life, enveloped in a white mantle, and sitting on a fallen obelisk viewing the ruins of the Campagna di Roma' – Goethe, 1892, p. 141.

22 *Sir Joshua's Nephew, Being letters written 1760–1778 by a young man to his sisters*, ed. S. M. Radcliffe, London 1930, p. 40.

23 Burney, 1778, III, p. 256. In the same year that Evelina was published Benjamin Franklin was received at the French court wearing a simple brown suit, and his own unpowdered hair. In a previous period the lack of a wig would have horrified the French, but by this date they accepted it as an amiable eccentricity; some were, in any case, sympathetic to the struggle of the American colonists against English power, and Franklin seemed to typify all that was noble in the New World as against the artificialities of the Old.

24 Angelo, 1828, II, p. 379.

25 Langlade, 1911, p. 92.

26 Northumberland, 1926, p. 204.

27 *Ibid.*, p. 174.

28 Devonshire, 1955, p. 95.

29 *Magazine à la Mode*, 1777, p. 416.

30 Devonshire, 1955, p. 91.

31 *Lady's Magazine*, London 1787, p. 331.

32 H. Walpole, *Letters addressed to the Countess of Ossory, 1769–1797*, ed. R. V. Smith, London 1848, p. 379.

33 *Cabinet des Modes*, Paris 1786, p. 4.

34 Burney, 1842–6, III, p. 170.

35 See A. Jardine, *Letters from Barbary, France, Spain, Portugal etc.*, London 1788, where the author urges women to ride side-saddle. 'They ought to wear drawers under their present, or some more graceful, long dress . . . the sex would certainly gain by shewing a little more of their legs' (I, p. 321).

36 Montagus, 1923, II, p. 82.

37 In Mary Russell Mitford's famous account *Our Village: Sketches of Rural Scenery, 1824–32*, she recalled 'early in the present century' two old ladies whose style of dress dated from the 1770s: 'Their motion out of doors was indescribable; it most

nearly resembled sailing.' It was probably rather like that of the French émigrées whom Miss Milford mentions later in the book, 'with the peculiarly bad, unsteady walk, something between a trip and a totter, that Frenchwomen of rank used to acquire from their high heels and the habit of never using their feet'. (I, p. 38, and II, p. 213).

38 Quoted in Cunnington and Cunnington, 1972, p. 297.

39 Smith, 1829, I, p. 17.

40 The Warner Collection of textile patterns (part of the Warner Archive in the Victoria and Albert Museum) of the 1770s and 1780s shows a wide range of silk designs, many on dark grounds like the fashionable cottons. In the 1770s (T. 374–1972), there are small laurel wreaths surrounding spots (e.g. f. 137 1777), loops of 'frogspawn' on light and dark grounds (f. 158ᵛ, f. 159 1777), flowers in medallions and tiny florals and garlands. In the 1780s (T. 377–1972 and T. 378–1972), patterns include random spots, various kinds of doodles, checks, stripes and bands and, by the end of the decade, large circles, perhaps copying the large buttons in vogue in costume. By this time, there appear to be far more winter patterns, possibly because in the spring and summer months, muslin and printed cottons/linens were dominating the market.

41 Devonshire, 1955, p. 91.

42 Burney, 1842–6, III, p. 368.

43 Adams, 1848, pp. 182–3.

44 J. P. Brissot de Warville, *Nouveau Voyage dans les Etats Unis*, trans. J. Barlow, Paris 1791, I, p. 134.

45 Roche, 1933, p. 208 and p. 95.

46 Winslow, 1894. p. 71, *et seq.*

47 Mrs Fay, *Original Letters from India*, Calcutta 1821, p. 142.

48 Simpson, *The Waiting City*, 1933, p. 239.

49 Grosley, 1772, I, p. 255.

50 Smith, 1829, I, p. 218.

51 Winslow, 1894, p. 17.

52 Baretti, 1770, I, p. 95.

53 Number T. 4588 in the Germanisches Nationalmuseum.

54 Place, 1972, pp. 62–3.

55 Papendiek, 1887, II, pp. 230–1.

Chapter 7

1 Bocage, 1770, I, p. 140.

2 Moore, 1781, II, p. 81.

3 Russel, 1750, I, p. 44.

4 Goethe, 1892, p. 509.

5 See F. Boucher, 'Les Dessins de Vien pour la Mascarade de 1748 à Rome', in the *Bulletin de la Société de l'Histoire de l'Art Français*, 1963, pp. 69–76, and, by the same author, 'An Episode in the Life of the Académie de France à Rome', in *Connoisseur*, October 1961.

6 White, 1841, II, p. 202.

7 Carré, 1937, p. 231.

8 *Ibid.*, p. 230.

9 Townsend, 1791, I, p. 39.

10 Baretti, 1770, II, p. 104.

11 See A. Ribeiro, 'The Exotic Diversion, the Dress worn at Masquerades in Eighteenth Century London', in *Connoisseur*, January 1978.

12 Walpole, 1903–15, II, p. 369.

13 *Ibid.*, p. 371.

14 On the taste for chinoiserie in the eighteenth century, see O. Impey, *Chinoiserie – The Impact of Oriental Styles on Western Art and Decoration*, Oxford 1977.

15 See A. Ribeiro, 'Mrs Cornelys and Carlisle House', in *History Today*, January 1978.

16 Walpole, 1903–15, VIII, p. 162.

17 Ward, 1777, p. 99.

18 This fête champêtre was so popular that there are many accounts of it, most notably in the letters of both Walpole and Mrs Delany; there was also a play, by J. Burgoyne, entitled *The Maid of the Oaks*, performed at the Theatre Royal, Drury Lane (1774), with Mrs Abington as the female lead. See A. Ribeiro, 'Rural Masquerades', in *Antique Collector*, September 1983.

19 Coxe, 1784, I, p. 178 *et seq.*

20 See G. H. Lewes, *Goethe's Life at Weimar, 1775–9*, London 1904.

21 Bruford, 1935, p. 89.

22 A. S. Levetus, *Imperial Vienna*, London 1905, p. 96.

23 Moore, 1779, II, p. 379.

24 *Ibid.*, II, p. 80.

25 Coke, 1889, II, p. 350 and IV, p. 10.

26 Bielfeld, 1768–70, II, p. 236.

27 La Motraye, 1732, p. 231.

28 Coxe, 1784, I, p. 497.

29 Prussia, 1812, II, p. 280.

30 See P. de Bretagne, *Réjouissances et Fêtes Magnifiques qui se sont faites en Bavière l'an 1722 . . .*, Munich 1723.

31 See *Journal Historique des Fêtes que le Roi a donné à Potsdam . . .*, Berlin 1750.

32 Swinburne, 1779, p. 348.

33 Baretti, 1770, I, p. 88.

34 On le style troubadour, see the exhibition catalogue *Le Style Troubadour*, Bourg-en-Bresse 1971, and F. Pupil's *Le Style troubadour, ou la nostalgie du bon vieux temps*, Nancy 1985.

35 See Rangström, 1997. The Drottningholms Teatermuseum has a collection of designs for theatre costume, and some surviving theatre costumes, including some of those worn by Gustavus III at tournaments and carousels.

36 Pöllnitz, 1745, II, p. 187.

37 P. Martin, 'Les Costumes de fêtes portés à l'occasion de l'entrée du roi Louis XV à Strasbourg en 1744', in *Waffen-und-Kostümkunde*, 12, 1970.

38 Clarke, 1763, p. 322.

39 R. Nisbet Bain, *The Daughters of Peter the Great*, London 1899, pp. 152–4.

40 Pöllnitz, 1745, V, p. 66 et seq. This marriage, that of the Elector, Augustus II, in 1719, was the occasion for many pageants and festivities. Visiting Dresden in 1730, Keysler saw the royal wardrobes crammed with all kinds of costumes, including that worn by the Elector at his 'nuptial feast', when 'he represented the element of water'.

41 See A. Ribeiro, 'Hussars in Masquerade', in *Apollo*, 105, 1977.

42 Northumberland, 1926, pp. 93–4.

43 Hickey, 1913, I, p. 280.

44 Bielfeld, 1768–70, II, p. 236. Bielfeld refers here to a masquerade held in 1740 at the opera house in Hanover, where the Elector wore 'a Turkish dress, the turban of which was ornamented with a magnificent egret of diamonds'.

45 A visit by a Turkish embassy to Louis XIV in 1669 inspired Molière to include a Turkish episode (M. Jourdain adopts the costume of a Turkish dignitary and becomes a 'mamamouchi') in his comedy *Le bourgeois gentilhomme* (1670). See S. V. Dock, *Costume and Fashion in the plays of Jean-Baptiste Poquelin Molière: A seventeenth-century perspective*, Geneva 1992, pp. 240–2.

46 Prussia, 1812, I, p. 104.

47 Keysler, 1758, IV, p. 118.

48 See G. Chapman, *Beckford*, London 1937, pp. 104–6. From his childhood, Beckford had been interested in the Orient, and on his return from the Grand Tour (1781) he immersed himself in the study of the East, working on manuscripts once in the possession of Edward Wortley Montagu, the rackety son of Lady Mary Wortley

Montagu, and a man who loved to dress up in Turkish costume, leading a Baron Corvo-like existence in exile from England.

49 See A. Ribeiro, 'The King of Denmark's Masquerade', in *History Today*, 27, 1977.

50 Montagu, 1965–7, I, p. 326. Between 1719 and 1724 Lady Mary Wortley Montagu wrote up her travel experiences, using her journal and her letters to produce 'an Enlightenment travel treatise'. Using a literary convention of the time, she chose fourteen individuals as addressees (ten of whom she had actually written to), and made the content of the 'letters' fit the recipients' interests; thus her sister Lady Mar received the letters on exotic costume. See Grundy, 1999, p. 199.

51 J. Arbuthnot, *The Ball, Stated in a Dialogue betwixt a Prude and a Coquet*, London, 1724, p. 1 and p. 3.

52 Delany, 1861–2, II, p. 185.

53 *Oxford Magazine*, 1768, p. 161.

54 See above, note 5.

55 J-L. Vaudoyer, 'L'Orientalisme en Europe au XVIIIe Siècle', in *Gazette des Beaux Arts*, 6, Paris 1911, p. 98. Liotard had a collection of Turkish dresses in his studio from which his sitters could choose.

56 *Magazine à la Mode*, London, 1777, p. 367. For the influence of Turkish dress on mainstream fashion, see A. Ribeiro, 'Turquerie: Turkish Dress and English Fashion in the Eighteenth Century', in *Connoisseur*, 200, 1979.

57 Delany, 1861–2, II, p. 487.

58 Montagu, 1923, II, p. 103.

59 C. R. Leslie and T. Taylor, *The Life and Times of Sir Joshua Reynolds*, 2 vols, London 1865, I, p. 398.

60 *Idem*.

61 E. Malone, *The Works of Sir Joshua Reynolds*, 2 vols, London 1798, I, p. 237. This is from Reynolds's Seventh Discourse, delivered to the students of the Royal Academy in 1776. For a brief discussion of some aspects of classical dress in portraiture, see A. Ribeiro 'Muses and mythology: classical dress in British eighteenth-century female portraiture', in *Defining dress: Dress as object, meaning and identity*, ed. A. de la Haye and E. Wilson, Manchester 1999.

62 For a discussion of the use of 'classical' dress in portraiture by Romney, Vigée-Lebrun, and other eighteenth-century artists, see A. Ribeiro, *The Art of Dress: Fashion in England and France 1750–1820*, New Haven and London, 1995.

63 Vigée-Lebrun, 1926, p. 74.

64 By the late 1780s, some French writers were anticipating the curious hybrid 'classical' costumes advocated during the French Revolution, and depicted by – among others – J.-L. David. J. F. Sobry, for example, in *Le Mode François* (1786) suggested that men should wear short tunics, and officials should wear a long gown (*simarre*); both sexes, for reasons of health, were advised to wear sandals. For a discussion of this aspect of dress, see A. Ribeiro, *Fashion in the French Revolution* London 1988, especially Chapter III, 'Brave New World: People and State 1789–1794'.

65 Goethe, 1892, p. 199.

66 J. W. Tischbein, *Aus Meinem Leben*, quoted in *Van Dyck in Check Trousers: Fancy Dress in Art and Life 1700–1900*, Scottish National Portrait Gallery, Edinburgh 1978, p. 37.

67 *Covent Garden Magazine*, London 1773, II, p. 245.

68 Bielfeld, 1768–70, II, p. 235.

69 Richardson, 1753–4, I, p. 43.

70 *Report on the MSS of the late Reginald Rawdon Hastings*, ed. F. Bickley, Historical Manuscripts Commission, London 1928, III, p. 150.

71 Montagu, 1923, I, p. 171.

72 Sir Ashton Lever's house in Leicester Fields, for example, housed in the 1770s and 1780s a collection of historic costumes, including 'the dress worn in Charles Irst's time', according to Fanny Burney.

73 For a discussion of the growth in accuracy in theatre costumes, see R. J. Pentzell, 'New Dress'd in the Ancient Manner: The Rise of Historical Realism in Costuming the serious Drama of England and France in the Eighteenth Century', Ph.D., Yale University 1967.

74 Walpole, 1903–15, VIII, p. 251, pp. 262–3.

75 Langlade, 1911, p. 138. In the 1780s, Marie Antoinette ordered from Mme Eloffe a number of 'cherusques en fraise', standing vandyke collars either pleated or embroidered.

76 *Vertue Notebooks*, III, pp. 5–7, Walpole Society, London 1933–4.

77 See J. Steegman, 'A Drapery Painter of the Eighteenth Century', in *Connoisseur*, June 1936.

78 Walpole, 1903–15, I, p. 182. For a general discussion of the causes and the spread of Vandyke dress in England, see J. L. Nevinson, 'Vandyke Dress', in *Connoisseur*, November 1964.

79 Montagu, 1906, I, p. 264.

80 *Lady's Magazine*, London 1759, p. 128.

81 Neville, 1950, p. 82.

82 Walpole, 1903–15 and 1918 (Supplement to the Letters), p. 233.

83 See J. L. Nevinson 'The Vogue of the Vandyke Dress', in *Country Life Annual*, 1959.

84 *Letters of Thomas Gainsborough*, ed. M. Woodall, London 1963, p. 52.

85 Malone, *Works of Sir Joshua Reynolds*, 1798, I, p. 234. Unlike his rival, Reynolds's style was not suited to the rendering of the rich glowing satins and spiky, gauzy lace of Vandyke costume; 'Sir Joshua's draperies represent clothes, never their materials,' noted Walpole with reference to Reynolds's *Eleventh Discourse* in 1782, when the artist quoted 'Vandyck, who at least specified silks, satins, velvets' (1903–15, XII, p. 403).

Conclusion

1 A. Young, *Travels in France and Italy during the Years 1787, 1788 and 1789*, London 1915, p. 325.

2 See the *Journal d'une Femme de 50 ans, 1778–1815* by the marquise de La Tour du Pin, written in 1820, and published in Paris, 1951. In 1789, her father-in-law was made Minister of War, the War Department being at Versailles, and the marquise was responsible for the entertaining of government officials and delegates from the Assembly. Full dress was demanded at Versailles, and court presentations continued until 1790; even after that date the queen continued to order clothes from Rose Bertin (who had supplied many of the presentation dresses). Rose Bertin's accounts end on 7 August 1792; three days later the Tuileries was besieged and the mob pillaged the queen's wardrobe. Both the king and queen's wardrobes were later sold.

3 Wraxall, revised ed. 1836, I, p. 142.

Appendix A
A Note on European Currencies
in the Eighteenth Century

It IS DIFFICULT TO ESTABLISH AN EXACT EXCHANGE RATE for the eighteenth century and to estimate what money would have purchased. However, the following notes may serve as a very approximate guide when prices of clothes or textiles are mentioned in the text.

In France, the value of money was fixed by a decree of 1726 and remained virtually unaltered until the Revolution. The basic unit was the livre tournois or franc; a louis d'or was 23 livres and an écu was 6 livres. In about 1760, an artisan might earn about 500 livres per year, a country gentleman might have an income of 10,000 livres, and a grand seigneur or rich city merchant might have revenues of considerably more than 10,000 livres.

In England, the pound sterling was, in about 1760, worth roughly one louis d'or or 23 livres. Arthur Young's table of conversion in 1788 was:

$$50 \text{ livres} = £2 \ 3s. \ 9d.$$
$$100 \text{ livres} = £4 \ 7s. \ 6d.$$
$$500 \text{ livres} = £21 \ 17s. \ 6d.$$
$$1000 \text{ livres} = £43 \ 15s. \ 0d.$$

By the end of the 1780s, less than fifteen per cent of British families had an income of more than £50 a year; of this fifteen per cent only about one quarter earned more than £200 a year.

Outside France and England, the situation with regard to currency is very confused. In America, for example, not only did the various states have different currencies (American dollars, Spanish pesos, English and French money), but within one currency the exchange could vary. Brissot de Warville found on his American journey that a French écu of 6 livres was worth 8s. 9d. in New York, 6s. 8d. in Massachusetts and Connecticut and only 5s. 5d. in Georgia and South Carolina. An English guinea varied in price from its face value (£1. 1s. 0d.) to almost £2.

In Italy, Thomas Nugent found that 'every little state and principality . . . coins its own money', but perhaps the most common currency was the Florentine scudo (of 7 lire, each lira worth 20 soldi) worth (around 1760) 5.68 livres.

In Germany, the situation was as confused as in Italy; states had their own currencies, based usually on the thaler and mark, and, in addition, the imperial currency, the reichsthaler (worth twice the value of the thaler). This was valued (in about 1760) at 1 écu.

Finally, it should be noted that Wraxall, visiting Russia in 1774, states that 1 rouble was worth 4s. 6d.

Appendix B
A Chronology of Significant Events in Politics and Culture, 1713–1789

1713 Peace of Utrecht ends the War of the Spanish Succession and French political predominance in Europe.

1714 Accession of the Hanoverian dynasty in England, with George I.

Alexander Pope's *The Rape of the Lock*.

1715 Death of Louis XIV; Philippe, duc d'Orléans, is Regent during the minority of Louis XV.

1718 Voltaire's first tragedy, *Oedipus*.

Quadruple Alliance formed by Britain, France, Holland and the Austrian Empire against Spanish aggrandisement and to defend the Utrecht settlement.

1719 Daniel Defoe's *Robinson Crusoe*.

1720 Collapse of speculative financial schemes in France and England.

1721 In England, Robert Walpole winds up the South Sea Bubble, restoring national credit, and begins a twenty-one-year tenure as principal Minister of State.

Treaty of Nystadt ends Swedish claims to predominance in northern Europe, with the ceding of territory to Russia.

Montesquieu's *Lettres Persanes*.

1723 Death of the Regent in France; Louis XV assumes full control.

J. S. Bach becomes music director in Leipzig.

1725 Death of Peter the Great in Russia.

1726 Cardinal Fleury becomes principal adviser to Louis XV.

Jonathan Swift's *Gulliver's Travels*.

1731 Abbé Prévost's *Manon Lescaut*.

1733 Voltaire's *Lettres Philosophiques*.

1738 Treaty of Vienna ends the War of the Polish Succession.

Augustus III, Elector of Saxony, confirmed as ruler of Poland, Stanislas Leszcynski given in compensation the duchy of Lorraine, which is to revert to the French crown on his death. Austria cedes Naples and Sicily to Spain and is awarded in exchange Parma, Piacenza and the Grand Duchy of Tuscany.

1739 David Hume's *Treatise of Human Nature*.

1740 Accession of Maria Theresa to Habsburg throne.

Accession of Frederick the Great in Prussia.

Prussian invasion of Silesia begins the War of the Austrian Succession; the main protagonists are Prussia and France versus Austria and England.

Samuel Richardson's *Pamela*.

1742 First performance of Handel's *Messiah* in Dublin.

1743 Battle of Dettingen, an English victory over the French.

1744 Anglo-French hostilities spread to North America and India.

1745 Maria Theresa's husband, Franz Stephan of Lorraine, crowned Emperor.

1746 Rebellion of the 'Young Pretender', to restore the Stuarts to the English throne, crushed at the battle of Culloden.

1748 Treaty of Aix-la-Chapelle ends War of Austrian Succession; Prussia keeps Silesia and France and England reciprocally restore all colonial conquests.

1750 Accession of Joseph I of Portugal; the real ruler of the country for the next quarter of a century is the Marquês de Pombal.

1751 Voltaire's *Le Siècle de Louis XIV*.

Diderot's *Encyclopédie* begins to appear in instalments.

1755 Dr Johnson's *Dictionary*.

Lisbon earthquake.

1756 Re-arrangement of European alliances; an Anglo-Prussian agreement is followed by the diplomatic alignment of France and Austria, the latter the work of Wenzel Anton, Count von Kaunitz, Maria Theresa's main adviser on foreign affairs.

Seven Years War begins.

1757 In England, the ministry of William Pitt the Elder begins.

At the battle of Rossbach, the Prussians defeat the French army. In India, Clive is victorious over the French at the battle of Plassey.

1759 English capture Quebec from the French.

Accession of Charles III of Spain.

Voltaire's *Candide*.

The British Museum in London opens.

1760 Accession of George III in England.

1762 Accession of Catherine II in Russia.

Rousseau's *Du Contrat Social* and *Emile*.

Gluck's *Orfeo ed Euridice* performed in Vienna.

1763 Treaty of Paris ends Seven Years War.

Prussian conquest of Silesia finally acknowledged, as is British supremacy in the New World and India.

Winckelmann's *Geschichte der Kunst des Altertums*.

1765 Joseph II becomes Emperor and Co-Regent of the Habsburg possessions with Maria Theresa; his brother Leopold becomes Grand Duke of Tuscany.

1768 James Cook begins his circumnavigation of the globe in the *Endeavour*.

1771 Accession of Gustavus III of Sweden.

1772 First partition of Poland by Russia, Prussia and Austria.

1774 Accession of Louis XVI of France.

Goethe's *Die Leiden des Jungen Werthers*.

1776 Americans issue Declaration of Independence.

Adam Smith's *Wealth of Nations*.

First volume of Gibbon's *The History of the Decline and Fall of the Roman Empire*.

1781 Emperor Joseph II frees the serfs in the Habsburg dominions.

Kant's *Kritik der reinen Vernunft*.

1783 Peace of Versailles.

American independence achieved.

Russia annexes the Crimea.

1784 First performance of Beaumarchais's *The Marriage of Figaro*.

1787 Mozart's *Don Giovanni*.

1788 Jacques Necker becomes Director-General of Finance in France.

1789 The meeting of the Estates General sets in motion the events which lead to the storming of the Bastille and the French Revolution.

Glossary

Terms that appear in the text without explanation

Armosin/Armazeen   taffeta.

Bag   'an ornamental purse of silk tied to men's hair' (Johnson's *Dictionary*, 1755).

Bas de robe   detachable court train.

Bazin/Basin (Fr.)   dimity (q.v.).

Beaver   amphibious broad-tailed soft-furred rodent of genus Castor, chief raw material for hats in the eighteenth century; the fur fibres were combed out of the skin and made a glossy waterproof fabric.

Bombazine   cloth of silk and worsted.

Broadcloth   best woollen cloth.

Bristol stone   kind of colourless quartz used for buckles and buttons.

Brocade   'a stuff of gold, silver or silk, raised and enriched with flowers, foliages and other ornaments' (*A New and Complete Dictionary of Arts and Sciences, 1754–5*).

Brocatelle   'a kind of coarse brocade, chiefly used for tapestry' (*A New and Complete Dictionary of Arts and Sciences, 1754–5*).

Buckram   'a sort of coarse cloth made of hemp, gummed, calendered, and dyed several colours. It is put into those places of the lining of a garment, which one would have stiff and to keep their forms' (*A New and Complete Dictionary of Arts and Sciences, 1754–5*).

Buckskin   leather made from the skin of a buck, or sheepskin prepared in a particular way.

Buffskin   velvety dull-yellow ox leather, or any leather of a similar buff colour.

Bugles   tube-shaped glass beads.

Calico   cotton cloth with patterns printed in one or more colours; the name comes from Calicut, a port on the west coast of Malabar, south of Madras.

Calimanco   'a sort of woollen stuff manufactured in England and in Brabant. It has a fine gloss . . . Some calamancos are quite plain, others have broad stripes adorned with flowers; some with plain broad stripes, some with narrow stripes, and others watered' (*A New and Complete Dictionary of Arts and Sciences, 1754–5*).

Cambric   fine white linen from Cambrai.

Camlet   'a kind of stuff originally made by a mixture of silk and camel's hair; it is now made with wool and silk' (Johnson's *Dictionary*, 1755). According to the *New and Complete Dictionary of Arts and Sciences, 1754–5*, camlets could be made of all silk, all wool, or mixtures such as goat's hair and silk, silk and thread, and 'some are striped, some waved or watered, and some figured'.

Cardinal   hooded cloak, originally made of scarlet wool.

Cashmere   very soft fine wool or woollen material made from the fleece of the Kashmir goat.

Chenille   velvety cord with short threads or fibres of silk woven standing out at right angles from a core of thread or wire, like the hairs of a caterpillar. It decorated women's dresses and men's waistcoats.

Chintz   printed or painted calico.

Chip   wood or woody fibre split into thin strips for making hats.

Crêpe/Crape   thin silk gauze; or a silk and worsted fabric used for mourning.

Damask   'a silk stuff with a raised pattern so that the right side of the damask is that which hath the flowers raised or sattined' (*A New and Complete Dictionary of Arts and Sciences, 1754–5*). Damasks could also be made of wool and were manufactured in France and Flanders.

Dimity   fine cotton, usually white, with a raised woven design, also white.

Ermine   the winter fur of the northern stoat; its black tail tip was used to 'powder' the white fur at regular intervals.

Floss   untwisted silk.

Frieze   a coarse woollen napped cloth.

Furbelow   'a piece of stuff plaited and puckered together, either below or above, on the petticoats or gowns of women' (Johnson's *Dictionary*, 1755).

Fustian   cloth with a linen warp and cotton weft.

Galloon   ribbon of thread, or gold or silver tissue.

Gauze   very fine, open-weave silk.

Harden   coarse fabric made from the hards of flax or hemp.

Indiennes   name given in France to all Eastern painted and printed stuffs, whatever their country of origin.

Kersey coarse woollen cloth, possibly from Kersey in Suffolk.

Lawn very fine linen.

Linsey–woolsey cloth made with linen warp and wool weft.

Lutestring/Lustring plain weave silk with glossy finish; very popular for summer wear.

Marten members of the weasel family with much-valued fur.

Mechlin fine bobbin lace from Mechlin (Malines) in Flanders.

Meroquin Morocco leather.

Mob a woman's cap with gathered crown and frill.

Mohair 'the hair of a kind of goat, frequent about Angoura in Turky; the inhabitants of which city are all employed in the manufacture of camblets, made of this hair. Some give the name Mohair to the camblets or stuffs made of this hair' (*A New and Complete Dictionary of Arts and Sciences, 1754–5*).

Muslin very fine, semi-transparent cotton.

Nankeen plain closely woven cotton, usually buff colour.

Paduasoy a strong silk, often figured.

Paillettes, paillons spangles.

Parements 'sont des garnitures dont on décore le devant des robes & des jupons, sous le nom de falbala, volans, etc.' (*Encyclopédie Méthodique, 1785*).

Persian thin, plain silk.

Point d'Espagne metal lace.

Pomatum scented ointment, in which apples are said to have been originally an ingredient, used to dress the hair.

Poplin mixture of silk and worsted.

Rateen thick twilled cloth, usually friezed.

Russet coarse woollen homespun, usually brown or grey.

Sable small fur-bearing animal of the marten family; the best sable came from Russia.

Serge hard-wearing twilled worsted.

Shalloon a light-weight woollen worsted.

Stuff plain or twilled woollen stuff.

Swanskin closely woven flannel.

Tabby a thick silk of taffeta weave with a slight nap, calendered by passing it in folds under a hot cylinder to produce an uneven or moiré effect on the surface of the material.

Taffeta plain weave flossy silk.

Tambour a circular frame formed of one hoop fitting within another, in which silk, muslin or other material is stretched for embroidering.

Tammy a twilled worsted.

Tissue a woven textile of gold, silver or silk thread.

Toupet elevated front section of the wig or natural hair.

Warehouse a large shop selling goods not usually made on the premises.

Bibliography

This includes most of the works referred to in the footnotes (except where they are of specialist interest, such as certain articles, or newspapers and magazines), and other, more general works. It does not claim to be a comprehensive list.

Adams, A., *Letters of Mrs Adams*, intr. C. F. Adams, Boston 1848.

Andersen, E., *Danske Dragter: Moden i 1700-årene*, Copenhagen Nationalmuseet, 1977.

Anderson, M. S., *Europe in the Eighteenth Century 1713–1789*, London 2001.

Andrews, J., *An Account of the Character and Manners of the French*, 2 vols, London 1770.

Angelo, H., *Reminiscences*, 2 vols, London 1828.

Archenholz, F. W. von, *A Picture of England*, 2 vols, London 1789.

—— *A Picture of Italy*, 2 vols, London 1791.

Barbeau, A., *Life and Letters at Bath in the Eighteenth Century*, London 1904.

Barbier, E.-J.-F., *Chronique de la Régence et du Règne de Louis XV, ou Journal de Barbier*, 8 vols, Paris 1857.

Baretti, J., *An Account of the Manners and Customs of Italy*, 2 vols, London 1769.

—— *A Journey from London to Genoa, through England, Portugal, Spain and France*, 2 vols, London 1770.

Bermingham, A., and J. Brewer (eds), *The Consumption of Culture 1600–1800*, London 1995.

Besant, W., *London in the Eighteenth Century*, London 1902.

Bielfeld, Baron, *Letters of Baron Bielfeld . . . containing original Anecdotes of the Prussian court for the last Twenty Years*, trans. Mr Hooper, 4 vols, London 1768–70.

Bocage, K. F. du, *Letters Concerning England, Holland and Italy*, 2 vols, London 1770.

Boehn, M. von, *Deutschland im 18 Jahrhundert*, 2 vols, Berlin 1921.

Boswell, J., *Boswell in Holland, 1763–4*, ed. F. A. Pottle, New York 1952.

—— *Boswell on the Grand Tour, 1764*, ed. F. A. Pottle, New York 1953.

—— *The Life of Samuel Johnson*, 3 vols, London 1791.

Boucher, F., *Le Costume Français vu par les artistes, XVIIe, XVIIIe, XIXe siècles*, Paris 1949.

—— *A History of Costume in the West*, London 1967.

Brissot de Warville, J.-P., *Nouveau Voyage dans les Etats Unis*, trans. J. Barlow, 3 vols, Paris 1791.

Brocher, H., *Le Rang et l'Etiquette sous l'ancien Régime*, Paris 1934.

Brosses, C. de, *Selections from the Letters of De Brosses*, trans. Lord Ronald Sutherland Gower, London 1897.

Bruford, W. H., *Germany in the Eighteenth Century: The Social Background of the Literary Revival*, Cambridge 1935.

Buck, A., *Clothes and the Child: A Handbook of Children's Dress in England 1500–1900*, Bedford 1996.

Buck, A., and C. Cunnington, *Dress in Eighteenth-Century England*, London 1979.

Burney, F., *Evelina*, 3 vols, London 1778.

—— *Cecilia*, 5 vols, London 1782.

—— *Diary and Letters of Madame d'Arblay*, edited by her niece, 7 vols, London 1842–6.

—— *Early Diary, 1768–1778*, ed. A. R. Ellis, 2 vols, London 1889.

Byrde, P., *The Male Image: Men's Fashion in Britain, 1300–1970*, London 1979.

Campan, J.-L.-H., *Memoirs of the Private Life of Marie Antoinette, Queen of France*, 2 vols, London 1823. (Originally published as *Memoires sur la vie privée de Marie Antoinette*, 3 vols, Paris 1822.)

Campbell, T. (ed.), *Frederick the Great, his Court and Times*, 2 vols, London 1842.

Caraccioli, L. A. de., *Voyage de la Raison en Europe*, Paris 1772.

Carré, H., *Jeux, Sports et Divertissements des Rois de France*, Paris 1937.

Casanova, J., *The Memoirs of Jacques Casanova de Seingalt, 1725–1798*, trans. A. Machen, 8 vols, Edinburgh 1940.

Catherine II, *The Memoirs of Catherine the Great*, trans. M. Budberg, London 1955.

Cherry, D., and J. Harris, 'Eighteenth-century portraiture and the seventeenth-century past: Gainsborough and Van Dyck', *Art History*, vol. 5, no. 3, 1982.

Chesterfield, Earl of, *Letters of the Earl of Chesterfield to his son*, ed. and intr. C. Strachey, 2 vols, London 1901.

Clark, J., *The Great Eighteenth-Century Exhibition*, National Gallery of Victoria, Melbourne, 1983.

Clarke, E., *Letters Concerning the Spanish Nation, Written at Madrid during the Years 1760 and 1761*, London 1763.

Coke, Lady J., *Letters from Lady Jane Coke to her friend Mrs Eyre, 1747–1758*, ed. A. Rathbone, London 1899.

Coke, Lady M., *Letters and Journals of Lady Mary Coke*, ed. J. A. Home, 4 vols, Edinburgh 1889.

Coppens, M., *Le Costume au XVIIIᵉ siècle*, Musées royaux d'art et de costume, Brussels, 1978.

Coventry, F., *Pompey the Little*, London 1751.

Coxe, W., *Travels into Poland, Russia, Sweden and Denmark*, 2 vols, London 1784, and 3rd vol. 1790.

—— *Memoirs of the Kings of Spain from the Accession of Philip the Fifth to the Death of Charles the Third, 1700–1788*, 3 vols, London 1813.

Coyer, Abbé, *Voyages d'Italie et de Hollande*, 2 vols, Paris 1775.

Cronin, V., *Catherine, Empress of all the Russias*, London 1978.

Cunnington, C. W., and P., *Handbook of English Costume of the Eighteenth Century*, revised ed., London 1972.

Dahlbäck, B. (et al.), *1700-tal Tanke och form i rokokon*, National-museum, Stockholm, 1979–80.

Davenport, M., *The Book of Costume*, New York 1948.

Decremps, H., *Le Parisian à Londres, ou Avis aux Français qui vont en Angleterre*, 2 vols, Amsterdam 1789.

Defoe, D., *A Tour Thro' the whole Island of Great Britain*, 3 vols, London 1724–6.

Delany, M., *Autobiography and Correspondence of Mary Granville, Mrs Delany*, ed. Lady Llanover, 6 vols, London 1861–2.

Delpierre, M., *Dress in France in the Eighteenth Century*, New Haven and London 1997.

—— 'Costumes français du XVIIIᵉ siècle', *Bulletin du Musée Carnavalet*, Paris 1962.

—— (et al.) *Elégances du XVIIIᵉ siècle, costumes français 1730–1794*, Musée de la mode et du costume, Paris 1963.

—— 'Robes de Grande Parure du Temps de Louis XVI', in *Bulletin du Musée Carnavalet*, June 1966, no. 1.

—— 'L'élégance à Versailles au temps de Louis XV', in *Versailles*, no. 55, 1974.

—— 'Marie Antoinette, reine de la mode', in *Versailles*, no. 59, 1975.

Devonshire, Duchess of, *Extracts from the Correspondence of Georgiana, Duchess of Devonshire*, ed. Earl of Bessborough, London 1955.

Dickens, A. G. (ed.), *The Courts of Europe, Politics, Patronage and Royalty, 1400–1800*, London 1977.

Eden, Sir F., *The State of the Poor*, 3 vols, London 1797.

Einberg, E., *Manners and Morals: Hogarth and British Painting 1700–1760*, Tate Gallery, London 1987.

Eloffe, Mme., *Livre-Journal de Madame Eloffe Marchande de Modes, Couturière Lingère de la Reine et des Dames de sa Cour*, ed. le comte de Reiset, 2 vols, Paris 1885.

Fairholt, F. W., *Satirical Songs and Poems on Costume*, London 1849.

Fielding, H., *Joseph Andrews*, 2 vols, London 1742, ed. M. C. Battesin, Oxford 1967.

—— *Tom Jones*, 6 vols, London 1749.

—— *Amelia*, 4 vols, London 1751.

Fithian, P. V., *Journal and Letters, 1767–1774*, ed. J. R. Williams, Princeton 1900.

—— *Journal, 1775–1776*, ed. R. G. Albion and L. Dodson, Princeton 1934.

Forster, R., and E., *European Society in the Eighteenth Century*, London 1969.

Fox, C., *Londoners*, London 1987.

Fox, C., and A. Ribeiro, *A Masquerade*, Museum of London 1983.

Friedenthal, R., *Goethe – His Life and Times*, London 1965.

Fusil, L., *Souvenirs d'une Actrice*, 2 vols, Brussels 1841.

Gallerie des Modes et Costumes Français, Dessinés d'après Nature, 1778–1787, intr. P. Cornu, Paris 1911–1914.

Garsault, F.-A. de, *L'Art du Perruquier*, Académie Royale des Sciences, Descriptions des Arts et Métiers, Paris 1767.

—— *L'Art du Tailleur*, Académie Royale des Sciences, Descriptions des Arts et Métiers, Paris 1769.

—— *L'Art de la Lingerie*, Académie Royale des Sciences, Descriptions des Arts et Métiers, Paris 1771.

Gay, J., *Trivia; or The Art of Walking the Streets of London*, London 1716.

Genlis, S. F., comtesse de, *Dictionnaire critique et raisonné des Etiquettes de la Cour et des Usages du Monde*, 2 vols, Paris 1818.

—— *Mémoires Inédits*, 8 vols, Paris 1825.

George, M. D., *London Life in the Eighteenth Century*, London 1925.

—— *England in Transition: Life and Work in the Eighteenth Century*, London 1931, 2nd edn 1953.

Glenbervie, Lord, *The Diaries of Sylvester Douglas, Lord Glenbervie*, ed. F. Bickley, 2 vols, London 1928.

Goethe, J. W. von, *Goethe's Travels in Italy*, trans. A. J. W. Morrison and C. Nisbet, London 1892.

Goldsmith, O., *The Citizen of the World*, 2 vols, London 1762.

—— *The Vicar of Wakefield*, London 1766.

—— *She Stoops to Conquer*, London 1773.

Goncourt, E., and J. de, *La Femme au dix-huitième siècle*, Paris 1862.

—— *L'Amour au dix-huitième siècle*, Paris 1875.

Grosley, P.-J., *New Observations on Italy and Its Inhabitants*, trans. T. Nugent, 2 vols, London 1769.

—— *A Tour to London, or New Observations on England and Its Inhabitants*, trans. T. Nugent, 2 vols, London 1772.

Grundy, I., *Lady Mary Wortley Montagu: Comet of the Enlightenment*, Oxford 1999.

Hamilton, M., *Letters and Diaries, 1756–1816*, ed. E. and F. Anson, London 1925.

Harvey, J., *Men in Black*, London 1995.

Haumant, E., *La Culture Française en Russie, 1700–1900*, Paris 1913.

Hawkins, L. M., *Gossip about Dr Johnson and Others*, ed. F. H. Skrine, London 1926.

Hedley, O., *Queen Charlotte*, London 1975. d'Hézecques, F., comte, *Souvenirs d'un Page de la Cour de Louis XVI*, Paris 1873.

Hickey, W., *Memoirs of William Hickey*, ed. A. Spencer, 4 vols, London 1913.

Hutton, C., *Reminiscences of a Gentlewoman of the Last Century*, ed. C. H. Beale, Birmingham 1891.

Johnson, S., *Sir Joshua's Nephew, being Letters written 1760–1778 by a Young Man to his Sisters*, ed. S. M. Radcliffe, London 1930.

Kalm, P., *Kalm's Account of his Visit to England on his Way to America in 1748*, trans. J. Lucas, London 1892.

Karamzin, N. M., *Travels from Moscow through Prussia, Germany, Switzerland, France and England*, 3 vols, London 1803.

Keysler, J. G., *Travels through Germany, Hungary, Bohemia, Switzerland, Italy and Lorrain*, trans. from 2nd German ed., 4 vols, London 1758.

Labat, P., *Voyages en Espagne et en Italie*, 8 vols, Paris 1730.

Lacroix, P., *The Eighteenth Century: Its Institutions, Customs and Costumes; France 1700–1789*, London 1876.

La Motraye, A. de, *Voyages . . . en Diverses Provinces et Places de la Prusse Ducale et Royale, de la Russie, de la Pologne, etc.*, The Hague, 1732.

Langlade, E., *La Marchande de Modes de Marie Antoinette, Rose Bertin*, Paris 1911.

La Tour du Pin, marquise de, *Journal d'une Femme de 50 ans, 1778–1815*, Paris 1951.

Le Camus, A., *Abdeker, or The Art of preserving Beauty*, London 1754.

Leinster, Duchess of, *Correspondence*, ed. B. Fitzgerald, 3 vols, Dublin 1949.

Lemire, B., *Fashion's Favourite: The Cotton Trade and the Consumer in Britain 1600–1800*, Oxford 1991.

Lennox, Lady S., *Life and Letters of Lady Sarah Lennox*, ed. Countess of Ilchester & Lord Stavordale, 2 vols, London 1901.

Leroy, A., *The Portraits of Madame de Pompadour, in Connoisseur*, June 1939.

Levron, J., *Daily Life at Versailles in the Seventeenth and Eighteenth Centuries*, trans, C. E. Engel, London 1968.

Lowe, A., La Serenissima: *The Last Flowering of the Venetian Republic*, London 1974.

Macartney, George, First Earl, *An Account of Russia, 1767*, London 1768.

Maeder, E. (ed.), *An Elegant Art: Fashion and Fantasy in the Eighteenth Century*, Los Angeles County Museum of Art, 1983.

Malcolm, J. P., *Anecdotes of the Manners and Customs of London during the Eighteenth Century*, London 1808.

Marshall, J., *Travels through Holland, Flanders, Germany, Denmark, Sweden, Lapland, Russia, The Ukraine and Poland, in the Years 1768, 1769 and 1770*, 4 vols, London 1772–6.

McClellan, E., *A History of American Costume, 1607–1870*, New York 1904, reprinted 1969.

Melville, L., *Lady Suffolk and her Circle*, London 1924.

Mercier, L. S., *Tableau de Paris*, 8 vols, Amsterdam 1782–8. Trans. and abridged by H. Simpson as *The Waiting City: Paris, 1782–1788*, London 1933.

Miège, G., *The Present State of Great-Britain and Ireland*, London 1715.

Mingay, G. E., *English Landed Society in the 18th Century*, London 1963.

Molmenti, P., *Venice: Its Individual Growth from the Earliest Beginnings to the Fall of the Republic*, trans. H. F. Brown, Part III: *The Decadence*, 2 vols, London 1908.

Montagu, E., *Elizabeth Montagu: Correspondence, 1720–61*, ed. E. J. Climenson, 2 vols, London 1906.

—— *Mrs Montagu, 'Queen of the Blues': Her Letters and Friendships from 1762–1800*, ed. R. Blunt, 2 vols, London 1923.

Montagu, Lady M. W., *Town Eclogues*, London 1747 (originally published, in an unauthorized edition, as Court Poems, 1715).

—— *The Complete Letters of Lady Mary Wortley Montagu*, ed. R. Halsband, 3 vols, Oxford 1965–7.

Montgomery, F. M., *Printed Textiles: English and American Cottons and Linens, 1700–1800*, New York 1970.

Moore, J., *A View of Society and Manners in France, Switzerland and Germany*, 2 vols, London 1779.

—— *A View of Society and Manners in Italy*, 2 vols, London 1781.

Moritz, C. P., *Travels of Carl Philipp Moritz in England in 1782*, intr. P. E. Matheson, London 1924.

Musée Carnavalet, *Costume Français du XVIIIᵉ siècle, 1715–1789*, Musée Carnavalet, Paris 1954–5.

—— *Elégances du XVIIIᵉ siècle: Costumes Français, 1730–1794*, Musée Carnavalet, Paris 1963–4.

Neville, S., *The Diary of Sylas Neville, 1767–1788*, ed. B. CozensHardy, London 1950.

Nisbet Bain, R., *Gustavus III and his Contemporaries, 1746–92*, 2 vols, London 1894.

—— *The Pupils of Peter the Great: A History of the Russian Court and Empire from 1697 to 1740*, London 1897.

—— *The Last King of Poland and his Contemporaries*, London 1909.

Nivelon, F., *The Rudiments of Genteel Behavior*, London 1737.

Northumberland, Duchess of, *Diaries of a Duchess: Extracts from the Diaries of the first Duchess of Northumberland, 1716–1776*, ed. J. Greig, London 1926.

Nugent, T., *Travels through Germany*, 2 vols, London 1768.

—— *The Grand Tour, or, A Journey through the Netherlands, Germany, Italy and France*, 4 vols, 3rd ed. London 1778. This is a compendium of contemporary information on the life and customs of these countries, taken from various sources such as Pöllnitz (*q.v.*) and Keysler (*q.v.*).

Oberkirch, Baroness d', *Memoirs of the Baroness d'Oberkirch*, ed. Count de Montbrison, 3 vols, London 1852.

Orléans, duchesse d', *Letters from Liselotte, Elizabeth Charlotte, Princess Palatine Duchess of Orléans, 'Madame', 1652–1722* and, trans. and ed. M. Kroll, London 1970.

Papendiek, C. L. H., *Court and Private Life in the Time of Queen Charlotte, being the Journals of Mrs Papendiek, Assistant Keeper of the Wardrobe and Reader to Her Majesty*, ed. V. D. Broughton, 2 vols, London 1887.

Paston, G., *Side-Lights on the Georgian Period*, London 1902.

—— *Social Caricature in the Eighteenth Century*, London 1905.

Perry, J., *The State of Russia under the Present Czar*, London 1716.

Pilon, E., and F. Saisset, *Les Fêtes en Europe au XVIIIᵉ Siècle*, Saint-Gratien 1943.

Piozzi, H. L., *Observations and Reflections made in the course of a Journey through France, Italy and Germany*, 2 vols, London 1789.

Place, F., *Place Collections*, British Museum, Add. MS 27827.

—— *The Autobiography of Francis Place*, ed. and intr. M. Thale, Cambridge 1972.

Pöllnitz, Baron von, *Travels from Prussia thro' Germany, Italy, France, Flanders, Holland, England, etc.*, 5 vols, 3rd ed. London 1745. This is a 'kind of glorified Baedeker for the Grand Tour'; Pöllnitz worked up the book from his notes, and did not, in fact, make the journeys as described either in time or sequence. See E. Cuthell, *A Vagabond Courtier*, 2 vols, London 1913.

Powys, Mrs P. L., *Passages from the Diaries of Mrs Philip Lybbe Powys, 1756–1808*, ed. E. J. Climenson, London 1899.

Prussia, Princess Royal of, *Memoirs of Frederica Sophia Wilhelmina, Princess Royal of Prussia, Margravine of Bareith*, Written by Herself, 2 vols, London 1812.

Purefoy, H., *The Purefoy Letters, 1735–1753*, ed. G. Eland, 2 vols, London 1931.

Pyne, W. H. ('Ephraim Hardcastle'), *Wine and Walnuts*, 2 vols, London 1823.

Rangström, L., *Kläder för tid och evighet Gustav III sedd genom sina drakter*, Livrustkammaren, Stockholm 1997.

Retif de la Bretonne, *Tableaux de la Bonne Compagnie*, 2 vols, Paris 1787.

Ribeiro, A., *A Visual History of Costume: The Eighteenth Century*, London 1983.

Richardson, S., *Pamela; or Virtue Rewarded*, 4 vols, London 1740.

—— *Clarissa Harlowe*, 8 vols, London 1748, 2nd edn 1768.

—— *Sir Charles Grandison*, 7 vols, London 1753–4.

Roche, D., *The Culture of Clothing: Dress and Fashion in the Ancien Régime*, Cambridge 1994.

—— *France in the Enlightenment*, Cambridge, Mass., 1998.

Roche, S. von la, *Sophie in London, 1786, being the Diary of Sophie von la Roche*, trans. C. Williams, London 1933.

Rochefoucauld, F. de la, *A Frenchman in England, 1784, Being the Mélanges sur l'Angleterre of François de la Rochefoucauld*, ed. and intr. J. Marchand, Cambridge 1933.

Roland de la Platière, J.-M., *Encyclopédie Méthodique*, Paris 1785.

Rothstein, N., *Silk Designs of the Eighteenth Century in the Collection of the Victoria and Albert Museum*, London 1990.

—— (ed.), *Barbara Johnson's Album of Fashions and Fabrics*, London 1987.

Rudé, G., *Hanoverian London, 1714–1808*, London 1971.

—— *Europe in the Eighteenth Century*, London 1972.

Russel, J., *Letters from a Young Painter abroad to his Friends in England*, 2 vols, London 1750.

Saint-Simon, duc de, *Historical Memoirs of the Duc de Saint-Simon*, ed. and trans. L. Norton, London 1967–72.

Saussure, C. de, *A Foreign View of England in the Reigns of George I and George II*, trans. and ed. M. van Muyden, London 1902.

Ségur, J. A. de, *Les Femmes, leur condition et leur influence dans l'ordre social*, 3 vols, Paris 1803.

—— *Memoirs and Recollections*, 3 vols, London 1825–7.

Shennan, J. H., *Philippe, Duke of Orléans, Regent of France, 1715–1723*, London 1979.

Sheridan, R. B., *The Rivals*, London 1775.

—— *School for Scandal*, Dublin 1777.

Smith, J. T., *Nollekens and his Times*, 2 vols, London 1829.

Smollett, T., *Roderick Random*, 2 vols, London 1748.

—— *Peregrine Pickle*, 4 vols, London 1751.

—— *Ferdinand, Count Fathom*, 2 vols, London 1753.

—— *Travels through France and Italy*, 2 vols, London 1766.

—— *Humphry Clinker*, 3 vols, London 1771.

Snodin, M (ed.), *Rococo: Art and Design in Hogarth's England*, Victoria and Albert Museum, London 1984.

Sobry, J. F., *Le Mode François: Discours sur les Principaux Usages de la Nation Françoise*, Paris 1786.

Spink, J. S., *Woman and Society in Eighteenth-Century France: Essays in Honour of John Stephenson Spink*, ed. E. Jacobs, W. H. Barber, J. H. Bloch, F. W. Leakey, and E. Le Breton, London 1979.

Stirling, A. M. W., *Annals of a Yorkshire House, from the papers of a Macaroni and his Kindred*, 2 vols, London 1911.

Stuart, Lady L., *Gleanings from an old Portfolio, containing some Correspondence between Lady Louisa Stuart and her sister Caroline, Countess of Portarlington, and other friends and relations*, ed. Mrs Godfrey Clark, 3 vols, Edinburgh 1895.

—— *Letters of Lady Louisa Stuart*, ed. R. Brimley Johnson, London 1926.

Swinburne, H., *Travels through Spain in the Year 1775 and 1776*, London 1779.

Swinton, A., *Travels into Norway, Denmark and Russia in the Years 1788, 1789, 1790 and 1791*, London 1792.

Talbot Rice, T., *Elizabeth, Empress of Russia*, London 1940.

Thornton, P., *Baroque and Rococo silks*, London 1965.

Topham, E., *Letters from Edinburgh, Written in the years 1774 and 1775: Containing some Observations on the Diversions, Customs, Manners and Laws, of the Scotch Nation*, London 1776.

Toth, K., *Woman and Rococo in France*, trans. R. Abingdon, London 1931.

Townsend, J., *A Journey through Spain in the Years 1786 and 1787*, 3 vols, London 1791.

Turberville, A. S. (ed.), *Johnson's England*, 2 vols, London 1933.

Twiss, R., *Travels through Portugal and Spain in 1772 and 1773*, London 1775.

Vaussard, M., *Daily Life in Eighteenth-Century Italy*, London 1962. (Originally published as *La Vie Quotidienne en Italie au XVIIIᵉ siècle*, Paris 1959.)

Vehse, E., *Memoirs of the Court and Aristocracy of Austria*, trans. F. Demmler, 2 vols, London 1856.

Vigée-Lebrun, E. L., *The Memoirs of Mme Elizabeth Louise Vigée-Lebrun, 1755–1789*, trans. G. Shelley, London 1926.

Wakefield, D., *French Eighteenth-century Painting*, London 1984.

Walpole, H., *Letters*, ed. Paget Toynbee, 16 vols, Oxford 1903–15, and suppl. vol. 1918.

Wansey, H., *Journal of an Excursion to the United States of America*, Salisbury 1796.

Ward, Mrs, *Letters from a Lady who resided some Years in Russia, to her Friend in England*, 2nd ed. London 1775.

Warwick, E., *Early American Dress*, New York 1965.

Waugh, N., *The Cut of Men's Clothes, 1600–1900*, London 1964.

—— *The Cut of Women's Clothes, 1600–1930*, London 1968.

Weatherill, L., *Consumer Behaviour and Material Culture in Britain 1660–1760*, London 1988.

Weber, F. C., *The Present State of Russia*, 2 vols, London 1723.

Weigert, R.-A., *Textiles en Europe sous Louis XV: Les Plus Beaux Spécimens de la Collection Richelieu*, Fribourg 1964.

White, C. (ed.), *The Courts of Europe at the Close of the Last Century*, 2 vols, London 1841 and 2nd edn 1895.

Winslow, A. G., *The Diary of Anna Green Winslow, 1771–3*, ed. A. M. Earle, Boston 1894.

Woodforde, J., *The Diary of a Country Parson, The Reverend James Woodforde, 1758–1802*, ed. J. Beresford, 5 vols, London 1924–31.

Wraxall, N. W., *A Tour through some of the Northern Parts of Europe*, London 1776.

—— *Memoirs of the Courts of Berlin, Dresden, Warsaw and Vienna in the Years 1777, 1778 and 1779*, 2 vols, London 1799.

—— *Historical Memoirs of His Own Time*, revised ed., 4 vols, London 1836.

Young, A., *Travels during the Years 1787, 1788 and 1789, to which is added, the register of a Tour into Spain*, 2 vols, London 1793.

Illustrations

89 A. Roslin, *Anastasia Ivanovna, Countess of Hessen-Homburg, Princess Trubetskoij*, c.1758, oil on canvas. National Gallery of Victoria, Melbourne, Everard Studley Miller Bequest, 1970.

90 F. Hayman, *A Scene from Samuel Richardson's Novel* Clarissa Harlowe: *Robert Lovelace prepares to abduct Clarissa*, c.1753–4, oil on canvas. Southampton City Art Gallery. Photograph: Bridgeman Art Library.

91 Detail of pl. 90.

92 Detail of pl. 93.

93 F.-H. Drouais, *The Marquise d'Aigurandes*, 1759, oil on canvas. Cleveland Museum of Art.

94 T. Gainsborough, study of a woman seen from behind, early 1760s, chalk. Ashmolean Museum, Oxford.

95 F.-H. Drouais, *Madame de Pompadour*, 1763–4, oil on canvas. National Gallery, London.

96 J. G. Grooth, *An Unknown Woman*, 1760s, oil on canvas. The Metropolitan Museum of Art, New York, Gift of Eduouard Jonas, 1992.

97 Detail of pl. 37a.

98 Detail of pl. 95.

99 L.-G. de Carmontelle, *The Craymoyel Family*, 1760, watercolour over red chalk. Parke-Bernet, New York, 21 October 1970, lot 24. Photograph: Courtesy of Sotheby's.

100 P. Batoni, *Lady Mary Fox, later Baroness Holland*, 1767, oil on canvas. Lady Theresa Agnew.

101 Detail of pl. 113.

102 Detail of pl. 123.

103 Detail of pl. 123.

104 M.-Q. La Tour, *Marie-Madeleine Mazade, Madame Grimod de la Reynière*, 1751, pasted on paper. Private collection. Photograph: Royal Academy of Arts, London.

105 Detail of pl. 93.

106 Detail of pl. 127.

107 Detail of pl. 157.

108 Trade card for Higgons's Warehouse, late eighteenth century. British Museum, London, Heal Collection. Photograph: English Heritage.

109 Detail of pl. 159.

110 Detail of pl. 113.

111 Detail of pl. 123.

112 'Une Boutique de fourrure', 1765, from Diderot's *Encyclopédie*. Goldsmith's Library of Economic Literature, University of London Library.

113 C.-A. Coypel, *Charlotte Philippine de Châtre de Cangé, Marquise de Lamure*, c.1745, pastel on paper. Worcester Art Museum, Worcester, Massachusetts, Bequest of Theodore T. Ellis.

114 Anon., *Pug Dog with Mule*, c.1730, oil on canvas. Sotheby's, London, 16 November 1988. Photograph: Courtesy of Sotheby's.

115 Detail of pl. 133.

116 German School, caricature of a northern European, 1790s, pen and brown ink and watercolour. Sotheby's, London, 24 February 1972, lot 104. Photograph: Courtesy of Sotheby's.

117 W. Hogarth, *Before*, 1736. British Museum, London. Photograph: Witt Library, Courtauld Institute of Art, London.

118 S. F. Patton after L.-P. Boitard, *Taste A-La-Mode*, 1745. Courtesy of the Museum of London.

119 Attributed to T. Hudson, *An Unknown Gentleman*, c.1745, oil on canvas. Sotheby's, London, 28 November 1973, lot 18. Photograph: Courtesy of Sotheby's.

120 T. Gainsborough, *The Mall in St James's Park*, 1783, oil on canvas. The Frick Collection, New York.

121 J.-B. Pillement, *Les Jardins de Benfica*, 1785, oil on canvas. Musée des Arts décoratifs, Paris. Photograph: Laurent-Sully Jaulmes.

122 After P. Longhi, *Le Lever*, mid-eighteenth century, oil on canvas. Agnew's, London.

123 F. Boucher, *La Toilette*, 1742, oil on canvas. Museo Thyssen-Bornemisza, Madrid.

124 After J.-M. Moreau, 'La petite toilette', 1789, from *Monument du Costume Physique et Moral de la fin du dix-huitième siècle*. By permission of the British Library, London. Photo-

graph: Witt Library, Courtauld Institute of Art, London.

125 N. Dupin, 'Le Seigneur et la Dame de Cour', 1776, from Le Père's *Les Costumes François Representans Les differents Etats du Royaume, avec les Habillemens*. By permission of the British Library, London.

126 Detail of pl. 133.

127 L. Tocqué, *Queen Maria Lesczynska*, 1740, oil on canvas. Musée du Louvre, Paris. Photograph: © RMN–G. Blot/C. Jean.

128 J. Gillray, *Temperance enjoying a Frugal Meal*, 1792. By courtesy of the National Portrait Gallery, London.

129 Noble, 'View of the Court at St James's with the Ceremony of introducing a Lady to Her Majesty', late 1770s–early 1780s. Court Dress Collection, Kensington Palace, London. Photograph: Crown copyright, Historic Royal Palaces.

130 M. S. Maella, *Infanta Carlota Joaquina, Queen of Portugal*, 1785, oil on canvas. Museo nacional del Prado, Madrid.

131 A. Roslin, *Gustavus III in Coronation Costume*, 1777, oil on canvas. Nationalmuseum, Stockholm.

132 After M. van Meytens, *The Empress Maria Theresa and her Family*, gouache on vellum. Whereabouts unknown.

133 J.-M. Nattier, *A Nobleman in the Costume of the Order of the Saint-Esprit*, 1732, oil on canvas. Fundação Calouste Gulbenkian, Lisbon, Museum.

134 J. Gillberg after J. E. Rehn, *Swedish National Costume*, 1778. Nationalmuseum, Stockholm.

135 P. Hilleström, *A Conversation at Drottningholm*, 1779, oil on canvas. Nationalmuseum, Stockholm.

136 Detail of pl. 135.

137 Detail of pl. 135.

138 T. Gainsborough, *Maria Walpole, Lady Waldegrave*, c.1764, oil on canvas. Los Angeles County Museum of Art, Gift of Mr. and Mrs. Alfred Hart. Photograph: © 2001 Museum Associates/LACMA.

139 Detail of pl. 145.

140 After C.-L. Desrais, 'Jeune Officier en Habit de Zèbre', 1787, from *Gallerie des Modes et Costumes Français*. Victoria and Albert Museum, London. Photograph: Witt Library, Courtauld Institute of Art.

141 A. von Maron, *Unknown Gentleman*, late 1760s, oil on canvas. Birmingham Museums and Art Gallery.

142 P. Dawe, *The Pantheon Macaroni*, 1773. British Museum, London. Photograph: Witt Library, Courtauld Institute of Art, London.

143 After P.-T. Le Clère, 'Fraque à la Polonaise', 1779, from *Gallerie des Modes et Costumes Français*. Victoria and Albert Museum, London. Photograph: Witt Library, Courtauld Institute of Art, London.

144 J. Wright, *Sir Brooke Boothby*, 1781, oil on canvas. Tate, London.

145 J. Wright, *Mr and Mrs Thomas Coltman*, *c.*1769, oil on canvas. National Gallery, London.

146 J. H. W. Tischbein, *Goethe in the Roman Campagna*, 1786, oil on canvas. Städelsches Kunstinstitut, Frankfurt.

147 F. Bayeu, *An Unknown Man*, *c.*1785, oil on canvas. National Gallery of Canada, Ottowa, Purchased 1914.

148 Vogsard after P.-T. Le Clère, 'Redingotte à trois colets', 1781, from *Gallerie des Modes et Costumes Français*. Victoria and Albert Museum, London. Photograph: Witt Library, Courtauld Institute of Art, London.

149 Attributed to J. M. Moreau, *The Hairdresser*, early 1770s, pen and brown ink, black chalk and wash. Private collection. Photograph: Witt Library, Courtauld Institute of Art, London.

150 A. Labille-Guiard, *Madame Adélaïde de France, Daughter of Louis XV*, *c.*1787, oil on canvas. Phoenix Art Museum, Phoenix, Arizona, Museum purchase with funds provided by an anonymous New York foundation.

151 R. Ducreux, *Self-Portrait with a Harp*, *c.*1790, oil on canvas. The Metropolitan Museum of Art, New York, Bequest of Susan Dwight Bliss, 1967. (67.55.1). Photograph: © 1983 The Metropolitan Museum of Art.

152 Detail of pl. 120.

153 Detail of pl. 120.

154 C. J. Vernet, *A Sea Shore* (detail), 1776, oil on copper. National Gallery, London.

155 Detail of pl. 120.

156 After E.-L. Vigée-Lebrun, *Queen Marie Antoinette*, *c.*1783, oil on canvas. National Gallery of Art, Washington, Timken Collection. Photograph: © 2001 Board of Trustees, National Gallery of Art, Washington.

157 A. Kauffmann, *Lady Elizabeth Foster*, 1786, oil on canvas. National Trust, Ickworth. Photograph: National Trust Photographic Library/Angelo Hornak.

158 'Woman in a Redingote', fashion plate from *Cabinet des Modes*, 1786. By permission of the British Library, London.

159 J. Juel, *Princess Louise Augusta*, 1787, oil on canvas. Frederiksborg Castle, Hillerød.

160 Detail of pl. 161.

161 J. Zick, *The Remy Family*, 1776, oil on canvas. Germanisches Nationalmuseum, Nuremberg.

162 'Caraco et jupon de mousseline rayé', fashion plate from the *Cabinet des Modes*, 1786. By permission of the British Library, London.

163 J.-L. David, *Anne-Marie-Louise Thélusson, Comtesse de Sorcy*, 1790, oil on canvas. Neue Pinakothek, Munich. Photograph: Joachim Blauel/ARTOTHEK.

164 'A la Zodiaque', 1777, from the *Lady's Magazine*.

165 H. Kingsbury, *A Side Box at the Opera*, 1792. British Museum, London. Photograph: Witt Library, Courtauld Institute of Art, London.

166 Sir T. Lawrence, *Mrs Papendiek with her Son Frederick*, 1789, red and black chalk on paper. The Metropolitan Museum of Art, New York, Bequest of George D. Pratt, 1935. (48.149.19).

167 S. Slaughter, *Sir Edward Walpole's Children*, 1747, oil on canvas. Minneapolis Institute of Arts, Gift of Mrs. Eugene J. Carpenter and Olivia Carpenter Coan in Memory of Mr. Eugene J. Carpenter.

168 J.-E. Liotard, *Unknown Girl with Doll*, *c.*1760, pastel. Schloss Schönbrunn, Vienna. Photograph: Kunsthistorisches Museum, Vienna.

169 F. de Goya, *Don Manuel Osorio de Zuñiga*, 1784, oil on canvas. The Metropolitan Museum of Art, New York, The Jules Bache Collection, 1949. (49.7.41). Photograph: © 1994 The Metropolitan Museum of Art.

170 Detail of pl. 197.

171 L. Carlevarijs, studies of carnival costume, early eighteenth century, pencil and ink on paper. Victoria and Albert Museum, London.

172 G. Zompini, 'The Return from the Ridotto', from *Le Arte che vanno per via nella Citta di Venezia*, 1753. By permission of the British Library, London. Photograph: Witt Library, Courtauld Institute of Art, London.

173 D. Allan, *The Carnival in Rome*, 1775. The Royal Collection © 2001 Her Majesty Queen Elizabeth II.

174 A. Watteau, *Fêtes vénitiennes*, *c.*1718, oil on canvas. National Gallery of Scotland, Edinburgh.

175 After C.-N. Cochin the Elder, 'Décoration du Bal Masqué Donné par le Roy . . .', 1745. Victoria and Albert Museum, London. Photograph: Witt Library, Courtauld Institute of Art, London.

176 Detail of pl. 175.

177 After A. Canaletto, 'A View of the Canal, Chinese Building, Rotundo &c, in Ranelagh Gardens, with the Masquerade', *c.*1750. Guildhall Library, Corporation of London.

178 A. R. Mengs, *Isabel Parreno, Marquesa de Llano*, *c.*1773, oil on canvas. Museo de la Real Academia de Bellas Artes de San Fernando, Madrid.

179 Detail of pl. 182.

180 L.-J. Le Lorrain, *Before the Masked Ball*, late 1750s, oil on canvas. National Gallery of Art, Washington, Samuel H. Kress Collection. Photograph: © 2001 Board of Trustees, National Gallery of Art, Washington.

181 Detail of pl. 180.

182 P. Hilleström, *A Tournament*, 1778, oil on canvas. Drottningholms Teatermuseum, Stockholm. Photograph: Nationalmuseum, Stockholm; Rikard Karlsson Erik Cornelius.

183 Detail of pl. 154.

184 Detail of pl. 180.

185 J. B. Vanmour, *Lady Mary Wortley Montagu and her Son Edward* (detail), *c.*1717, oil on canvas. National Portrait Gallery, London.

186 J.-E. Liotard, *Mary Gunning, Countess of Coventry*, *c.*1753–4, pastel on parchment mounted on canvas. Rijksmuseum, Amsterdam.

187 E. Aubry, *Mlle Rosalie Duthé*, 1779.

188 A. Kauffmann, *Morning Amusement*, *c.*1773, oil on canvas. Private collection.

189 Sir J. Reynolds, *Philippa Rooper, Lady Sunderlin*, 1788, oil on canvas. Government Art Collection, Department for Culture, Media and Sport, London.

190 J. W. Tischbein, *Lady Charlotte Campbell*, *c.*1789–90, oil on canvas. Scottish National Portrait Gallery, Edinburgh.

191 C.-L. Desrais, design for a ball dress, *c.*1779. Staatliche Museen zu Berlin, Kunstbibliothek.

192 P. P. Rubens, *Helena Fourment*, early 1630s, oil on canvas. Fundação Calouste Gulbenkian, Lisbon, Museum.

193 T. Gainsborough, *The Hon. Mrs Graham*, 1777, oil on canvas, National Gallery of Scotland, Edinburgh.

194 J.-H. Fragonard, *L'Etude*, 1769, oil on canvas. Musée du Louvre, Paris. Photograph: © RMN–Daniel Araudet.

195 P. Batoni, *Thomas William Coke, later first Earl of Leicester*, 1774, oil on canvas. By kind permission of the Earl of Leicester and Trustees of the Holkham Estate.

196 R. Cosway, *William, third Viscount Courtenay*, 1791, oil on canvas. Viscount Courtenay.

197 H. Morland, *The Fair Nun Unmasked*, 1769, oil on canvas. Leeds Museums and Art Galleries (Temple Newsam House). Photograph: Bridgeman Art Library.

Index